# THE GOURMET JEWISH COOK

# THE GOURMET

# JEWISH COOK

## JUDY ZEIDLER

ILLUSTRATED BY PETER SHIRE

WILLIAM MORROW AND COMPANY, INC. NEW YORK

Library of Congress Cataloging-in-Publication Data

Zeidler, Judy.
  The gourmet Jewish cook.

  Includes index.
  1. Cookery, Jewish.  I. Title.  II. Title:
The gourmet Jewish cook.
TX724.Z45   1988             641.5′676             88-5238
ISBN 0-688-06981-9

Printed in the United States of America


    4 5 6 7 8 9 10

BOOK DESIGN BY HELENE BERINSKY

TO MY HUSBAND

Marvin, super-chef in his own right, for his encouragement and inspiration and a lifetime of cooking together.

TO MY CHILDREN

Susan and Leo, Marc and Judy, Kathy, Paul and Amber, and Zeke, my earliest tasters and testers. And to my grandchildren, Aaron, Normandie, and Giamaica Day.

# ACKNOWLEDGMENTS

*Special thanks* to Sara J. Mitchell, my editor, Ann Bramson, and to my agent, Fred Hill, for their support and encouragement. *Thanks to* Betsy Balsley for giving me my start in the wonderful world of food-writing. *Thanks to* Joan Bram for her untiring efforts and creativity in testing my recipes; and my other testers: Carol Brandin, Judy Freedman, Lora Gerson, Francine Bartfield, Joanne Goldberg, Margery Katz, Ann Mitnick, Terri Sola. And to those who helped me along the way—Florine Sikking, Jerry Floreman, Carolyn See, and Leo Frishberg, the computer expert.

*Special thanks to* Michel Richard for his friendship and culinary expertise.

A special note of thanks for the inspiration derived from our friends in Italy: Nadia and Antonio Santini and Itala and Carluccio Brovelli.

# CONTENTS

# PREFACE

I love to cook, eat, entertain, and travel—collecting fabulous recipes while doing all these things. And I love to teach people how to cook. They pick up my enthusiasm and enjoy the triumph of creating food that seems so complicated when it is encountered in chic restaurants or at catered dinners.

All the comments and compliments on my recipes always include these words—"I never would have guessed it was kosher!"

That's because the old ideas about Jewish cooking are wrong. It isn't all brisket and latkes (although they are delicious, too). It can be low in fats and calories—light and fresh—beautiful to look at and delightful to taste, and still follow all the Jewish dietary laws.

Jewish/kosher cooking has come a long way in the past few years. In my research and travels, I have found there is almost no recipe that can't be translated into kosher—without any loss of flavor or appearance.

My serious cooking career started when I was raising five children in Topanga, California, in the Santa Monica Mountains. A neighbor introduced me to the wonders of yeast, and baking breads, coffee cakes, and desserts became a favorite pastime. I loved the wonderful aroma of homemade baked goods and the delight on our children's faces when they peeked at delicious surprises in the oven.

My food hobby became a profession when I was asked to bake strudel for a local restaurant. Later, women traveled to the canyon where I taught kosher cooking classes in my kitchen.

Because of the large Jewish population in Los Angeles and my contemporary approach to the preparation of Jewish holiday foods, I was asked to write a series of articles for the *Los Angeles Times* and later was offered my own television program on Jewish Television Network. Interested readers and viewers wrote and telephoned for more information—the response was terrific. They wanted advice on everything from menu planning to researching old family recipes, where to purchase a special kosher ingredient or how to adapt a recipe to kosher cuisine.

The recipes in this cookbook draw from all my experience in cooking, teaching, and traveling, plus a lively curiosity. They are the result of thirty-five years of devotion to good food and sharing it with others. That's what entertaining is all about—loving people and food and bringing them together.

# THE GOURMET JEWISH COOK

# HOW I
# ENTERTAIN

Early in our marriage, my husband and I, fearless creative cooks, decided it was important to carry on the tradition of the Jewish dietary laws. Kosher ("proper" in Hebrew) refers to foods that are permitted to be eaten, as well as the method of acquiring and preparing them. The laws include prohibitions against pork and shellfish in the diet, and the cooking or eating of meat and dairy products at the same time. Although many people believe that kosher cooking is complicated, time-consuming, and not very interesting, we were determined to prove that this was not so—that Jewish cooking could be delicious, healthful, and presented in a sophisticated contemporary manner. Creating new recipes and updating traditional ones became our way of celebrating the Jewish holidays and entertaining our family and friends.

Entertaining, and feeding friends and family, is a simple, basic part of my life-style. My mother was a good cook and my Aunt Betty a superb one; I still bake her famous orange juice cake with its tangy glaze.

Any occasion calls for inviting people to share it—not just birthdays and the Jewish holidays, but a promotion, an engagement, new friends.

Over the years my husband and I have depended on a few house rules that make entertaining easier. Organization is the secret, and here for the first time I have written down everything I've learned about how to give a perfect party for any large or small reason. I'm sharing my how-to's with you, along with my best wishes for your success.

# A Step-by-Step Plan

Just follow these few suggestions and see how fast your fear of giving parties—or even inviting a few people over for dinner—will disappear.

BUILD YOUR MENU AROUND A HOLIDAY OR SPECIAL THEME. The holidays all have their traditional foods, so menu planning is easy. But don't overlook the beautiful symbolic artifacts that are used in these celebrations as well. We have been collecting them since the early days of our marriage and our children have their own collection. Here are some examples that may inspire you:

*Hanukkah:* Hanukkiahs, the holders for candles, come in an array of designs and materials, both antique and contemporary.

Many shops now have "Happy Hanukkah" streamers and blue and white paper plates and napkins and gift wrappings, so decorating for this holiday can be fun for the whole family.

*Purim:* We now have thirty Purim groghers, or noisemakers, both old and new, in wood and silver. Each has its own history, and we use them as part of our table decoration each Purim.

*Passover:* Matzo cutters go back to ancient days when each family made their own matzo and imprinted it with the family name to identify it when they took it to the bakery to be baked. We collect these and also some beautiful brocade, linen, and embroidered matzo covers.

*Shabbat:* Special linen challah covers are a family treasure, as are silver kiddush cups. Many families have treasured cut-glass decanters for the Sabbath wine. (See "Making the Sabbath Special," page 195.)

Special holidays, like Thanksgiving, have special foods and decorations connected with them—but if the occasion is a birthday party or open house, your imagination can run wild.

Sometimes we plan a party around a color scheme or ethnic themes—Chinese, Mexican, French, etc. Or sometimes the food itself suggests the theme, as in our Pizza Party or our really unusual Pumpkin Harvest Dinner, where the courses all contain pumpkin in some form.

Of course, the season also affects the menu. In summer, chilled soups, salads, cool marinated vegetables, and a cold fish terrine will be appealing. On a cold winter night, mugs of hot soup, steaming casseroles, hearty meat dishes, and hot-from-the-oven rolls and breads are irresistible.

With my menu and table decorations in mind, I consult with my live-in wine mavin my husband. He then disappears into his wine cellar to select the wines. Later we choose the proper wineglasses and I make sure they are sparkling clean.

PLAN THE MENU CAREFULLY AND BEWARE OF UNTRIED RECIPES. My security blanket is a complete file of tested recipes. Many are original; others are inspired by books, newspapers, and magazines, while still others are from friends and students. Many of my most treasured recipes are kosher versions of recipes shared by famous chefs we have met in our travels in this country and abroad.

Experiment with your family, not your guests. If a recipe sounds strange, it will probably taste even worse!

Be sure that the colors and flavors of your foods offer an interesting variety and texture. You don't want to serve a menu that is all creamy—or all crunchy.

Don't plan too many complicated recipes in one menu; consider how much time you will have for preparation and be realistic. Entertaining is a great time for showing off—but be sure you know what you're doing.

The menus in this book are meant as suggestions to inspire you to create your own menus. Combine some of my recipes with your own personal favorites—or select an entrée from one menu, a dessert from another, and so on. When you are stuck, you'll find further inspiration in the sections of Bonus Recipes throughout the book.

INVITE A GOOD MIX OF GUESTS, AND NOT TOO MANY. Think in terms of compatible guests. We try to match people from different fields whom we think will enjoy each other's company. The most successful dinner party is one where the conversation is buzzing along at a high noise level and we feel that if we slipped out the door, we would never be missed.

Small dinner parties—no more than a dozen people; eight is ideal—are best. Conversation can flow easily around the table.

For these small groups, I arrange the plates in the kitchen and pass them to the seated guests. The plates are always garnished artistically, and the portions are not so big that they look sloppy—or so skimpy that the plates look empty.

When there are more than twelve, I usually plan two or three courses and let guests help themselves to each course from our big kitchen counter. I do the same when we have informal get-togethers and serve casual foods like pizza, salads, or big pots of pasta and chili.

I try to notify people at least a week ahead. Sometimes we act on the spur of the moment and give them only three or four days' notice, but our friends don't seem to mind when there's the promise of good food and pleasant company.

PLAN IN ADVANCE. First make a schedule of the exact dates on which everything should be done. This includes shopping, checking the freezer, cleaning the house. Assign a day to polish silver, select table linens, and plan a centerpiece.

Check on serving pieces—platters, trays, tureens, and glasses. I always set my table the night before, adding perishable things like flowers and edible centerpieces (fruits, vegetables, a giant challah) at the last minute.

Except for pouring champagne, it is almost never too early to complete some party chore. And it certainly pays off, with the most relaxed feeling and utter peace of mind on the day of your party.

TREAT YOUR FREEZER LIKE YOUR BEST FRIEND. In many of my recipes, I tell you what prepared foods can be frozen. When you are planning your party menu, it's always a good idea to see what you already have in your freezer that you might like to serve. I keep basic stocks and sauces, all kinds of pastas, boned and skinned chickens, and frozen fruits and berries that can be used for a quick dessert sauce.

Breads, rolls, and coffee cakes freeze well, and when heated in the oven they taste as good as freshly baked. Cookie dough can be frozen and ready to be sliced or rolled and baked. Ice cream, sorbets, and gelati, sealed securely, will keep for two to three weeks.

Then there's unsalted butter, frozen peas (the only frozen vegetable I like), and a large variety of nuts, which may be kept in the freezer for several months. Walnuts, pecans, cashews, peanuts, and filberts are ready to be toasted and eaten as a snack or added to recipes. Dried fruits, especially raisins, freeze well, too.

MAKE UP A COMPLETE SHOPPING LIST. Everything from caviar to dishwashing detergent will be on this master list.

Fruits, vegetables, salad greens, poultry, and fish that are not to be frozen must be as fresh as possible. Herbs, spices, flour, dried fruits, and less perishable items can be bought ahead. Frozen foods, of course, may be bought in advance, too.

Sometimes I visit the produce section of my local market to see what is available before I plan my menu. When I see the beautiful array of fresh vegetables and fruits I am really inspired, and it makes planning easier.

In general, buy fruits and vegetables in season. They will be less expensive when they are more plentiful, and often the flavor will be better. If you have a garden, nothing beats home-grown.

Be sure to place a special order to get the choicest meats, fish, and poultry. Don't just wander into your market and expect to find eight perfect steaks, ten tender veal chops, or twelve firm, coral-colored salmon fillets. It's not that easy. I usually call first and discuss my needs with my butcher or fish market. It doesn't cost any more and ensures a really choice entrée for my dinner.

ARRANGE FOR SERVING AND CLEAN-UP HELP. Don't overlook your own family. If you have a partner helping you in the kitchen, decide what each of you will do. It is important for one of you to be with your guests at all times, so planning will help.

HAVE FUN AT YOUR OWN PARTY. You know by now the things that will frazzle your nerves, so avoid them. Here are some dos and don'ts:

Do:
• Have part-time help for serving and cleaning up
• Pick a night that allows a free day afterward to relax or clean up
• Get plenty of rest the night before
• Choose what you will wear in advance—something simple and comfortable

Don't:
• Invite too many people
• Invite people who have nothing in common
• Try too many new recipes
• Attempt too many elaborate dishes
• Leave too many things to the last minute
• Fracture your budget with exotic foods
• Overreact if wine spills or the soufflé falls

I usually do not dress up very much; as a working hands-on cook, I am too busy to worry about spills or smudges and jewelry getting in the way. Sometimes it puts guests off when the hosts are dressed too formally. We may have printed menus, flowers, and six wineglasses at each place, but we usually ask our guests to dress casually and we do, too.

Greet your guests when they arrive—have a drink with them—circulate—talk to everybody. Sit with them during each course and make sure no one is left out of the conversation. Remember to eat or people may feel you don't like your own cooking.

Guests enjoy walking into my open-to-view kitchen to see what the next course will be—or to serve themselves a second helping of pasta. Let them wander a little. Don't be nervous if they want to watch you cook. Take your time—nobody minds waiting between courses when the company is interesting and they can anticipate new and exciting dishes.

KEEP A RECORD OF EVERYTHING. During the planning stages of any party, I note down the menu, the date, and the guest list. I also note ideas for flowers, serving pieces, linens, and table decor. This way I don't repeat table decorations, menus, or guests, serving exactly the same food to the same people in the same way every time.

Just before the guests arrive, I often take a photo of the table, completely set. And I photograph some of the food, too, before it is served. This helps me remember how things looked and how the foods were garnished. After the party, I record notes and comments—maybe even a few compliments. This is very useful in party planning, takes very little time, and makes a lovely memento of the event.

# TIPS AND TECHNIQUES

**APPETIZERS:** I don't believe that appetizers need to be so filling that they ruin the appetite for further food. Actually, guests tell me they look forward to trying new and tempting little dishes—and that it perks up their palate. It's not how many, but how good.

**AVOCADOS:** When picking avocados that are not yet ripe, store them in a brown paper bag at room temperature. They will ripen within a few days.

**BAKING:** Oven temperature is very important. Preheat the oven before baking so that cookies, cakes, and breads will bake evenly without burning. All recipes have been tested in a standard-size electric oven.

**BUTTER AND MARGARINE:** These are interchangeable in my recipes. Always use unsalted butter or margarine because it is difficult to adjust the amount of salt in a recipe when salted butter or margarine is used. Remember, too, that salted butter has a higher water content so more of it is needed to allow for shrinkage. Store butter or margarine in the freezer.

CLARIFIED BUTTER: Some recipes call for clarified butter—butter with the milk solids removed—which can be heated to a higher temperature than ordinary butter without burning (see page 368).

DECORATIVE BUTTER:To add special flair to your table setting, put flavored softened butter into cake-decorating tubes and squeeze onto a flat tray. Freeze, then transfer to a container and store in the freezer.

**CHICKEN LIVERS:** Trim fat particles and prepare according to kosher dietary laws.

**CHOCOLATE:** Unsweetened, bittersweet, semisweet, or sweet chocolate can be purchased in bulk. After prolonged storage, a white discoloration may appear on the chocolate, but it does not mean that the chocolate is stale. The cocoa butter has simply come to the surface, and it will blend when the chocolate is heated for cooking. Melt chocolate in a double boiler over simmering water. If it isn't melting smoothly, add vegetable oil (1 tablespoon of oil to 8 ounces of chocolate) and beat well. Adding liquid ingredients such as extracts, coffee, or cream to the melted chocolate can be a problem as it will thicken immediately and be difficult to work with. For best results, combine all the ingredients in the top of a double boiler before melting the chocolate.

**COOKBOOKS:** Don't be afraid to write in your cookbook. Make notes next to each recipe—any changes you made, etc. This record will help when you use the recipe again.

**COOKIE DOUGH:** Mix together large batches of cookie dough, but bake only the amount you intend to serve. Divide the remaining dough into small batches, wrap in clear plastic wrap, wax paper, or foil, and store in plastic bags. It will keep in the refrigerator for two or three days, or in the freezer for at least a month. Label clearly and date. Later, as needed, defrost the dough and bake in the usual way.

**CREAM CHEESE:** When a recipe calls for cream cheese, use gelatin and gum-free cream cheese, which blends more smoothly. It is available at kosher and other markets and health food stores.

**DEEP-FRYING:** When deep-frying any foods, such as the Crisp Caramelized Walnuts (see page 233) or Fried Zucchini Sticks (see page 298), the oil should be at 375°F, which allows the food to become crisp on the outside without becoming saturated with oil.

**EGGS:** Egg yolks do not freeze well, as they are high in fat content. Unbroken yolks can be stored in the refrigerator for two or three days, covered with water.

Egg whites, almost pure albumen, freeze well. Pour them into freezer trays; when frozen, remove and place in plastic bags. Defrost and use in any recipe calling for egg whites.

HOW TO BEAT EGG WHITES: Always beat egg whites in a clean bowl, preferably copper, stainless steel, or metal. Never use a plastic bowl as it retains a greasy film, which will stop the whites from inflating. Glass bowls are not good, as they tend to exude liquid from the egg whites. Cream of tartar or salt both help to stabilize the foam. Begin beating slowly with a wire whisk and increase speed as the whites increase in volume. Stop beating before the whites become too stiff and resemble gelatin.

HARD-BOILED EGGS: For perfect results, place uncooked, uncracked eggs in a pot with cold water to cover. Add salt, bring to a boil, cover, and simmer 2 minutes. Turn off heat and keep covered for 10 minutes. Immediately run cold water over the eggs. Eggs prepared this way will have no unattractive ring around the yolks, and will peel more easily.

**FLOUR:** Unbleached all-purpose flour should be used when flour is called for in this cookbook. It is not necessary to sift flour; just spoon into a measuring cup and level with a knife. Always use sifted cake flour for sponge cakes. For Passover, special baking instructions are given.

**FOOD PROCESSOR:** "What did we ever do without the food processor?" I ask myself this question every time I chop an onion, make gazpacho, liver pâté, pasta dough, or mix the ingredients for a loaf of bread. It is important NOT to overprocess. When a food processor is called for in my recipes, follow the manufacturer's instructions for your machine.

**FREEZING YEAST BREADS:** When fresh baked bread is completely cool, place in a plastic bag, twist end, and seal tightly; then place in another plastic bag, seal, and freeze. To use: remove from plastic bags, defrost, and heat at 350°F for 5 to 10 minutes. As delicious as the day it was baked.

**GARLIC:** When buying fresh garlic, always select firm heads with no soft spots. Garlic can be used whole, sectioned into cloves, chopped or minced. Unpeeled garlic cloves can be scattered in stews and roasts and when baked they soften to a rich-flavored purée inside the peel. I always keep a jar of minced garlic in oil in my refrigerator to add flavor to foods.

**GARNISHES:** Chefs create beautiful plates with the artistic use of such garnishes as peeled, diced tomatoes; green, red, or yellow bell peppers; diced celery; zucchini; carrots; beets; minced parsley; cilantro; chervil; chives; watercress; small croutons; and chopped hard-boiled eggs.

**HOOP CHEESE:** Also known as farmer cheese.

**HORSERADISH:** Grated horseradish can be found in the refrigerated section of markets and should be stored in white vinegar in your refrigerator. Fresh whole horseradish is sold in the produce sections of markets.

**KOSHER SALT:** Used in place of regular salt by many chefs and cooks, particularly those who observe the Jewish dietary laws. It has an uneven coarse texture, but can be used in the same quantity as table salt. For best results, when adding kosher salt to hot soups or sauces, dissolve with a spoonful of hot liquid before blending into the recipe.

**LEMON JUICE:** Fill ice cube trays with freshly squeezed lemon (or orange, lime, grapefruit, or tangerine) juice and freeze. Remove cubes from the trays and store in plastic bags, seal, and return to the freezer. This way you'll always have fresh-tasting citrus juices on hand.

**MARGARINE:** When margarine is called for in a recipe, always use unsalted non-dairy.

**MARINADES:** A marinade is a flavorful seasoned liquid containing an acid—such as lemon juice, vinegar, orange juice, or wine—in which fish, poultry, or meat is soaked before cooking. It both tenderizes and adds flavor, and also keeps food moister while it cooks—especially when used as a basting liquid.

**NUTS:** Store nuts of all kinds in plastic bags in the freezer. Toast nuts first to enhance the flavor and make them crisper. Spread a single layer of nuts on a baking sheet and bake at 350°F, turning or shaking frequently, until the nuts are evenly browned, 5 to 10 minutes. Watch carefully, as they burn easily. Substitute ground nuts for some of the flour in your favorite cake, pie crust, or bread recipe.

**OIL:** Whenever oil is called for, unless a recipe specifically mentions olive oil, I use safflower or vegetable oil.

**PEPPERS:** When selecting peppers, choose smooth and shiny ones without brown punctures or soft spots. They should be crisp and firm to the touch.

**PIE CRUST:** To prevent the crust from shrinking, avoid overbeating or overprocessing the flour. Be sure to stop beating the dough just as it comes together; then knead by hand and you will never have a problem. Use wax paper to separate when you fold the dough in half to fit it into the pie pan. This keeps halves from sticking together and makes handling easier.

**POMEGRANATE SEEDS:** Pomegranates are available in California from September to December. The seeds are decorative and delicious when used in salads or as a garnish.

**POWDERED SUGAR:** Also known as confectioners' sugar. Can be made by processing granulated sugar in the food processor until powdered. To decorate cakes and pastries, always dust with powdered sugar just before serving because of the moisture in the pastry.

**RAISINS:** To plump raisins, soak them in sweet wine or juice for 1 hour, overnight, or 1 week. Squeeze dry and use when recipe calls for plumped raisins.

**RAVIOLI:** For filling, cutting, and shaping ravioli there are many utensils available, such as ravioli trays (metal trays with shallow indentations). You can also find special rolling pins and cutting rollers, as well as round or square stamps that work like cookie cutters.

**REDUCTION OF LIQUIDS:** The secret of enriching a stew, soup, or sauce that is too thin or lacks an exciting flavor is to reduce the liquid by boiling it down slowly until it is concentrated and has a rich, full-bodied flavor.

**SAFFRON:** A pinch of saffron powder adds a rich yellow color to challah, soups, rice dishes, bouillabaisse, and curries.

**SAUCES AND STOCKS:** I never add flour or cornstarch to sauces to thicken them. Reducing sauces, soups, and stews by long simmering or fast boiling thickens and brings out the natural flavors. There are many commercial kosher chicken, beef, vegetable, and pareve stocks available. I use them as a basis for many sauces.

**SAUSAGES:** A food that can easily be made kosher by using plastic wrap instead of animal wrapping. Learn to make lots of different sausages (see chicken and fish sausage recipes, pages 346 and 372).

**SEASONINGS:** No two cooks like the same amount of salt and pepper. The desserts and bread recipes specify quantities of salt. The remaining recipes mention, "salt and pepper to taste," so it's up to you. With today's interest in reducing sodium in the diet, try substituting fresh or dried herbs and freshly ground black pepper.

**SERVING PLATES:** Serve hot foods on heated plates to keep them warmer longer. Salads, cold soups, and frozen desserts are best served on chilled plates.

**STEAMING VEGETABLES:** It takes longer to steam vegetables than boil them, but you retain a far greater amount of vitamins and minerals by doing so. If you don't own a steamer, place your vegetables in a colander over a pan of water; cover and simmer them until they are just crisply tender. Cauliflower, broccoli, string beans, and squash are good prepared this way.

**STUFFING POULTRY:** When stuffing chicken or turkey, put a slice of lightly oiled day-old bread or matzo in the opening of the body cavity. This acts as a lid, keeping stuffing in place. Stuffing can spoil if it sits inside the bird for more than 15 minutes at room temperature, so prepare the stuffing ahead and store it in a covered glass bowl in the refrigerator until the poultry is ready for the oven. And do not freeze cooked poultry with the stuffing inside. Remove and freeze separately.

**TERRINES:** A terrine is a very interesting, very French way to use meat, fish, and/or vegetables, slowly baked in a casserole set in a bath of hot water. It is served hot or cold with small pieces of bread or toast, as an appetizer or even an elegant picnic accompaniment.

**TOMATOES:** Vine-ripened tomatoes are one of the most delicious eating experiences. If tomatoes are not so great, here's a way to perk them up: Plunge them into boiling water, drain immediately, peel, and cut into chunks. Then place in a large bowl and marinate at least 30 minutes with 3 parts olive oil and 1 part balsamic vinegar. They really will taste almost as good as vine-ripened. For cherry tomatoes, just cut in half and marinate.

TOMATO PASTE: Freeze leftover tomato paste by tablespoons or in ice cube trays. When frozen, place in plastic bags and label for freezer storage. Use as needed.

DOUBLE TOMATO PASTE comes in a tube and is sold in Italian delis or food specialty stores. One tablespoon is added to many sauces to enhance their flavor.

PEELING TOMATOES: Using a sharp knife, cut a shallow X in the skin at the bottom of each tomato. Drop the tomatoes, 2 or 3 at a time, into boiling water; count to 10 and then lift them out with a slotted spoon. Cool for a few minutes and the peeling will slip right off.

# A WINE LOVER'S GUIDE

Growing up in a traditional kosher Jewish home, the only wine I knew was a sweet Concord grape wine, served with a special barucha (blessing), which explained that the wine was from the fruit of the vine. Later I discovered there were many more wines than that sweet purple ceremonial kind. I also learned that wine drinking wasn't limited to Jewish holidays.

Many people are afraid to serve wine to guests because of all the snobbery surrounding the beverage. We are never pretentious about wine, but when people are interested in it, we like to introduce new varietal wines and bottles from the best of the new small wineries that keep cropping up in California.

There really shouldn't be any big deal or mystery about wine—all the rules you've heard were made to be broken. You don't have to serve red wine with meat and white wine with fish; serve whatever tastes good to *you*. As for the bewildering variety of wines available, let your own taste buds serve as a guide. Sample before you buy in quantity.

In my home, we have a temperature-controlled wine room. To store wine, the ideal location is a cool, dark place with a year-round temperature of less than 60 degrees; a cupboard or a closet on an inside wall, away from heating ducts, will do fine. The bottles should be stored on their sides, so that the corks don't become dry and crumbly and let in the air that can spoil wine.

When serving white wine, chill it first to show off its crisp, clean character. But do not overchill—low temperatures can mask the true flavor and consistency of a white wine. Serve red wines at cool room temperature—60 to 65 degrees.

We usually serve a dry wine with dinner and like to pair up the wines with the menus, accenting some special dishes. For a special dinner, for example, we serve a sweet wine with a liver pâté or terrine, which is a tradition in France where foie gras (goose liver) is so popular.

Whenever possible, I use wine instead of water in recipes. The alcohol cooks away and you are left with the subtle flavor of the wine. The wines you use in cooking, of course, should be compatible with the flavors of the wines you are drinking with your meals. We use white wines many ways—in sauces, fish and poultry dishes, salad dressings, and even fruit mixtures.

White wines are the new favorites of the wine world. In the past few years, chic restaurants and bars have been serving more white wine than almost any other drink.

Red wines go well with beef, lamb, or veal. They also combine beautifully with many other foods. Try them with roast chicken or turkey. A light red wine is a good partner for salmon, too. Served with a hearty cheese and a few walnuts, a big red wine such as a Bordeaux, or sweet wines such as port, sauterne, or Madeira substitute for dessert.

Champagne is fun and festive for serious or frivolous celebrations—a graduation, an anniversary, a new home, or a toast to a new neighbor. It is the one wine that can be served throughout an entire dinner. It makes a sparkling accompaniment to brunches; when combined with orange juice, it becomes a cocktail known as a mimosa. You needn't serve expensive French champagne; many California wineries produce impressive sparkling wines at modest prices.

In the menus in this book I have made suggestions about the varieties of wine you might serve—but you may make your own choices, or eliminate the wine entirely, sticking to beer, mineral waters, coffee or tea with lemon. It's up to you.

Including wine in our menus rounds out the hospitality of an evening with family and friends. It slows down the pace of the dinner and encourages the flow of conversation. A predinner drink with interesting appetizers sets the stage for a special evening to follow. (In our house, we *never* serve hard liquor—just wine.) And a glass of champagne with a spectacular pastry or airy soufflé ends the dinner on a high note.

Wine lends itself to some interesting themes for entertaining. A wine-tasting party is great for an open house, a reception, or even a fund-raiser for charity.

If we invite people who know a lot about wine, or beginners who are truly interested, we often will have a "blind" or "paper bag" wine tasting with prizes for the most accurate palate. Some wine experts can tell the exact winery, variety of wine, and even the year without seeing the label. Wine-tasting games are fun; and they allow guests to focus more intently on the color, taste, aroma, and body of the wines served.

Wine and cheese are perfect table mates. A wine and cheese buffet replaces the old heavy-handed cocktail party. It is more leisurely and gracious and there are as many interesting cheeses to sample as there are wines. Attach little flag-like labels to the cheese platters; the wine labels will speak for themselves. Perhaps you will just feature the cheeses and wines of one country—France or Italy, for example.

Now back to kosher wines. They have come a long way from the old sweet red wine days. They can be found in most of the popular varieties—both white and red. Many winemakers in the United States offer interesting labels, but you are not limited to this country—kosher wines from Israel, France, Hungary, and Italy are available in a fascinating array. Experiment a little—the same way you do with your recipes. It will help perk up your life-style.

# THE JEWISH HOLIDAYS

**PART 1**

ROSH HASHANAH
Two-Day Rosh Hashanah Menu for 10
Rosh Hashanah Fish Dinner for 8
Bonus Recipes: Mandelbrot

YOM KIPPUR
Traditional Pre-Fast Dinner for 10
Break-the-Fast Repast for 10

SUKKOTH
Special Sukkoth Dinner for 8
Sukkoth Harvest Menu for 10

HANUKKAH
Hearty Brisket Dinner for 12
Nouvelle Hanukkah Dinner for 8
All-American Hanukkah Lunch for 12
Bonus Recipes: Latkes

PURIM
International Purim Dinner for 10
Purim Carnival Dinner for 10
Bonus Recipes: Purim Desserts and Confections

PASSOVER
A Haroseth Tasting
California Passover Seder for 12
Italian Passover Seder for 12
Ancient Persian Seder for 12
Passover Brunch for 6 to 8
Passover Buffet Lunch for 8
Bonus Recipes: Passover Desserts

SHAVUOTH
International Shavuoth Dinner for 10
Harvest Holiday Dinner for 8
Bonus Recipes: Cheesecakes

MAKING THE SABBATH SPECIAL
Sabbath Cholent Dinner for 8
Festive Sabbath Dinner for 8
Bonus Recipes: Cholent
Bonus Recipes: Sabbath Challahs

# ROSH HASHANAH

Rosh Hashanah is the Jewish New Year, a High Holy Day, a happy occasion for feasting and sharing good wishes for the year ahead. It falls in September or early October.

One of the most universal customs of Jewish families is the eating of sweet foods, especially honey, to symbolize "a sweet year" ahead. Apples—the traditional food of the New Year—and challah are dipped into honey, and apples, dates, and honey are used in many Rosh Hashanah desserts. By the same token, sour and bitter foods are avoided during this holiday.

Seasonal vegetables, such as carrots, beets, leeks, and squash, are served in a variety of dishes. On the second night of Rosh Hashanah, "new" fruits of the season are eaten—the most popular being grapes and pomegranates. The seeds of the latter have a special significance, since they symbolize all the good deeds to be done in the coming year.

Fish may also be served as a symbol of fertility and immortality (though some Jews do not eat fish on Rosh Hashanah, out of superstition). Whatever your own family's customs, try to include plenty of freshly baked challah and honey to celebrate a sweet and happy year.

# Two-day Rosh Hashanah Menu

## FOR 10

With a few simple additions, this Rosh Hashanah Eve veal roast becomes a beautiful cold buffet for the following day, perfect when Rosh Hashanah falls on Sabbath Eve.

A big golden challah is always part of our holiday or Sabbath celebration; currants add a touch of sweetness to the dough, signifying "a sweet year." (Bake the individual challahs at the same time you bake your round loaf.)

The Rosh Hashanah Eve dinner ends with the Fabulous Apple Charlotte. French in origin, caramelized apples are layered on a base of ladyfingers, then chilled and sliced in wedges and served with a Marsala Custard. In the other menu, pomegranates are frozen into ruby-colored ice, served with crisp Sesame-Honey Thins.

# FESTIVE HONEY CHALLAH

If you are making this challah for a dairy menu, you may use butter instead of margarine. I add a little saffron for a bright yellow bread.

MAKES 1 LARGE CHALLAH OR 30 SMALL ROLLS

1 package active dry yeast

1½ cups warm water (110 to 115°F)

Pinch of sugar

3 eggs

⅓ cup honey

¼ pound unsalted margarine, melted

⅛ teaspoon powdered saffron (optional)

2 tablespoons brandy

5 to 6 cups all-purpose flour

1 tablespoon salt

1 cup raisins, plumped (see page 25)

Cornmeal

1 egg white, lightly beaten

Sesame seeds

Dissolve the yeast in ½ cup of the warm water, with a pinch of sugar. In the bowl of an electric mixer, beat together the eggs, honey, and margarine. Add the remaining 1 cup warm water, saffron, and brandy and blend well. Blend in the yeast mixture. Add flour with salt, 1 cup at a time, blending with a beater after each addition, until the dough is thick enough to work by hand. Spoon it out onto a floured board and knead for 5 to 10 minutes, gradually incorporating the raisins and additional flour to make a smooth and elastic dough. Place the dough in a greased bowl and grease the top. Cover with a towel and let rise in a warm place until doubled in size, about 1 hour.

For a large challah: Divide the dough into 3 parts. Form each part into a long rope. Pinch together one end of each of the 3 ropes and braid the ropes, pinching the other ends together when you complete the braiding. To make a round challah, curve the braided dough around to join the two pinched ends and seal them together.

For small rolls: Break off small pieces of dough and form them into small ropes. Twist into knots or braids.

Place large challah or small rolls on a baking sheet or sheets lightly greased and generously sprinkled with cornmeal. Cover with a towel and let rise in a warm place until doubled, about 40 minutes.

Preheat the oven to 350°F. Brush the challah or rolls with egg white and sprinkle with sesame seeds. Bake for 30 to 40 minutes for the large loaf, 20 to 30 minutes for rolls, until golden brown.

# Warm Green Bean Salad

Green beans cook very quickly and are best when tender and still have a little crispness, especially for a salad, so follow the instructions and do not overcook them. Most vegetables continue to cook even after they have been removed from the heat.

1½ pounds green beans, trimmed

2 tablespoons minced shallots (about 2 medium shallots)

1 teaspoon Dijon mustard

¼ cup balsamic vinegar

¾ cup olive oil

Salt

Freshly ground black pepper

1 red bell pepper, stemmed, seeded, and thinly sliced

8 to 10 lettuce leaves (preferably Boston or butter lettuce)

1 medium red onion, thinly sliced, rings separated

Slice large beans in half diagonally; leave small beans whole. In a large pot, bring 2 to 3 quarts of lightly salted water to a rolling boil. Add the beans and cook them for 4 to 5 minutes, until tender but still crisp and green. Drain well.

In a small bowl, combine the shallots and mustard. Stir in the vinegar, then whisk in the oil. Add salt and pepper to taste.

Place the warm beans in a large bowl. Add red pepper slices and toss with enough dressing to coat the vegetables. Place a lettuce leaf on each serving plate and spoon the salad on top. Garnish with red onion rings.

# Rolled Veal Roast With Vegetables

2 tablespoons olive oil

2 medium onions, sliced

1 veal shoulder (6 to 8 pounds), rolled and tied

10 medium carrots, peeled and thickly sliced

10 small pearl onions, parboiled and peeled

10 medium mushrooms, halved

2 whole heads of garlic, separated into cloves but unpeeled

½ cup packed fresh parsley leaves

In a large shallow roasting pan, place a large sheet of heavy-duty foil long enough to enclose the veal and vegetables loosely.

Preheat the broiler.

In a medium skillet, heat the oil over moderate heat and sauté the onions until translucent but not browned, 3 to 5 minutes. Spoon the onions onto the center of the foil. Place the veal, fat side up, on top. Brown the veal under the broiler for 4 to 5 minutes to seal in the juices. Remove the pan from the broiler and surround the veal with the carrot slices, pearl onions, mushrooms, and unpeeled garlic cloves.

Preheat the oven to 350°F.

1 tablespoon dried rosemary

1 tablespoon dried thyme

2 garlic cloves, peeled

1 cup Chicken or Vegetable Stock (see pages 390 and 391)

¼ cup dry white wine

Salt

Freshly ground black pepper

6 sprigs fresh thyme (optional)

Red Pepper–Basil Sauce (recipe follows)

Mustard-Basil Sauce (recipe follows)

In a processor or blender, place the parsley, rosemary, dried thyme, and peeled garlic cloves. Process until finely chopped and sprinkle over the veal. Carefully pour the stock and wine around the sides of the veal. Sprinkle with salt and pepper to taste. Add thyme. Seal the foil securely to make an airtight package. Bake for 2 hours. Carefully open the foil and fold it back to expose the veal. Continue baking until the veal is tender, about 30 minutes more.

Slice the veal thin and serve surrounded by the vegetables, including the unpeeled garlic cloves for guests to squeeze soft-cooked garlic from their skins. Or serve cold with Red Pepper–Basil Sauce and Mustard-Basil Sauce.

## RED PEPPER–BASIL SAUCE

MAKES ABOUT 2 CUPS

6 large red bell peppers, roasted (see page 278)

1 tablespoon lemon juice

¼ cup packed fresh basil leaves

2 tablespoons Chicken Stock (see page 390)

Salt

Freshly ground black pepper

Pinch of sugar

In a processor or blender, place the peppers and lemon juice and process until smoothly puréed. Add the basil and process. Add enough stock to give a smooth consistency. Add salt, pepper, and sugar to taste. Transfer to a small bowl, cover with plastic wrap, and chill in the refrigerator. Serve with cold sliced veal.

## MUSTARD–BASIL SAUCE

MAKES ABOUT 1 CUP

3 tablespoons dark prepared mustard

1 teaspoon powdered mustard

2 tablespoons sugar

1 tablespoon white wine vinegar

⅓ cup olive oil

3 tablespoons chopped fresh basil

In a medium bowl, stir the prepared mustard, powdered mustard, sugar, and vinegar until well blended. With a wire whisk, gradually beat in the oil until the sauce has the consistency of thick mayonnaise. Stir in the fresh basil. Cover with plastic wrap and chill in the refrigerator. Before serving, beat the sauce briefly with a whisk. Serve with cold sliced veal.

# FABULOUS APPLE CHARLOTTE

1 cup golden raisins
¾ cup Marsala or Concord
  grape wine
6 medium apples, peeled and
  thinly sliced into rounds
¼ pound unsalted margarine
1½ cups sugar
24 Ladyfingers (see page 274)
Marsala Custard (recipe
  follows)

In a bowl, soak the raisins in the Marsala and water for 30 minutes; drain, reserving the Marsala mixture.

In a saucepan over medium heat, cook the apples and margarine until the margarine is melted. Add the raisins, sugar, and 2 or 3 tablespoons of the soaking liquid, reserving the remaining liquid. Simmer for 30 to 40 minutes, until the apples are completely cooked through and caramelized. Cool.

Line a charlotte pan or a deep bowl with foil. Dip the Ladyfingers in the reserved liquid and place them around the bottom and sides of the foil-lined bowl. Spoon in the apple mixture; cover with more liquid-dipped Ladyfingers and cover with plastic wrap. Cover with a plate and a weight and refrigerate for 12 hours.

Invert the pan onto a serving platter, lift off the mold, and peel away the foil. Slice and serve with Marsala Custard.

## MARSALA CUSTARD

6 egg yolks
4 tablespoons sugar
⅔ cup Marsala or Concord
  grape wine

In the top of a double boiler, put the egg yolks and sugar and beat until thick and pale yellow in color. Gradually add the Marsala, beating constantly.

Place the top of the double boiler over simmering water in the bottom and continue to beat vigorously until the mixture foams and thickens, being careful not to overcook.

Serve hot or cover with plastic wrap and chill in the refrigerator.

# MARINATED VEGETABLE PLATTER

1 pound string beans, trimmed
  and sliced diagonally

Steam the beans, cauliflower, broccoli, potatoes, and onions separately just until tender but still crisp; do not

1 medium cauliflower, cut into florets

3 to 4 small broccoli stalks, cut into florets and thickly sliced

6 small red potatoes, quartered

1 medium red onion, thinly sliced

Lettuce leaves

Mustard Vinaigrette Dressing (recipe follows)

overcook (see page 25). Cool, cover with plastic wrap, and chill in the refrigerator.

Arrange the vegetables separately on a lettuce-lined platter and spoon the dressing over them.

## MUSTARD VINAIGRETTE DRESSING

2 tablespoons minced onion

2 garlic cloves, minced

1 teaspoon prepared mustard

½ cup white wine vinegar

1 teaspoon dried basil

1 cup olive oil

Pinch of sugar

Salt

Freshly ground black pepper

In a processor, blender, or mixing bowl, combine the onion, garlic, mustard, vinegar, and basil. Add olive oil and blend well. Add sugar, salt, and pepper to taste.

# POMEGRANATE ICE

If you don't have an electric or hand-cranked ice cream freezer, you can freeze this ice in your refrigerator-freezer. The texture may be different, but the flavor is no less delicious.

MAKES ABOUT 1 PINT

2 cups unsweetened pomegranate juice

¼ cup lemon juice

1¾ cups Sugar Syrup (recipe follows)

1 tablespoon fruit liqueur, such as crème de cassis or Grand Marnier (optional)

In a large bowl, combine the pomegranate juice, lemon juice, sugar syrup, and fruit liqueur. Blend well. Freeze in an electric or hand-cranked freezer.

For refrigerator-freezer: Pour the mixture into flat-bottomed ice cube trays without their dividers or a freezer-proof glass bowl. Place in the freezer and stir with a fork every hour, scraping from the sides into the center. Continue stirring and freezing until the ice is set, 3 to 4 hours.

## SUGAR SYRUP

This sugar syrup keeps, covered with plastic wrap in the refrigerator, for several weeks. It makes it very convenient to have on hand for preparing any flavor ice you desire.

3 cups sugar
3 cups water

Place the sugar and water in a large heavy pot over medium heat. Stir until the sugar dissolves. Bring to slow rolling boil, reduce the heat, and simmer for 5 minutes. Pour into a glass bowl, cover with plastic wrap, and chill in the refrigerator.

# SESAME-HONEY THINS

I have suggested orange-flavored honey (or any light honey), since a strong honey flavor tends to overpower these delicate, paper-thin cookies.

MAKES ABOUT 4 DOZEN

¼ cup unsalted margarine, cut into pieces
1½ cups light brown sugar, firmly packed
¼ cup orange-flavored honey
1 teaspoon vanilla extract
1 egg
½ cup sesame seeds
1 cup flour
¼ teaspoon salt

In the bowl of an electric mixer, cream the margarine, brown sugar, honey, and vanilla until light and fluffy. Blend in the egg and sesame seeds. Add the flour and salt and beat until smooth. (You may cover the dough with plastic wrap and store in a plastic bag in the refrigerator or freezer for later use.)

Preheat the oven to 350°F.

Spoon small marble-size mounds of dough onto a lightly oiled, foil-lined baking sheet, 2 inches apart. Bake for 5 minutes, until the cookies begin to brown around the edges. Cool on the foil. When the cookies harden, carefully peel them off. Store in an airtight container with foil between the layers.

# ROSH HASHANAH FISH DINNER

FOR 8

Braided Round Challah

Gorgonzola-Apple Salad
with Honey-Mustard
Dressing

Three-Mushroom Soup

Whitefish with Zucchini
Sauce and Cucumber
"Pasta"

Molly's Mystery Meringue
Tarts

SUGGESTED BEVERAGES:

Dry sherry with soup and
light white wine with
whitefish

If you're in a chicken-for-the-holidays rut, this menu suggests a welcome change. It features my original method of poaching and broiling fish at the same time. Remarkably simple, it uses almost no oil or fat. The result is a flavorful, juicy fish that I serve here with an emerald zucchini sauce and a low-calorie "pasta" made of cucumbers.

Even the salad and soup are both new and different. Full-bodied Gorgonzola or other blue cheese combines with the apples and honey that are traditional for Rosh Hashanah. The taste is totally unexpected and completely delicious. The salad is accompanied by a round challah, symbolizing a well-rounded year. The soup, though rich and creamy, contains no cream; its flavor is enhanced by three kinds of mushrooms, a treat for mushroom lovers.

The perfect dessert for a menu filled with surprises is Molly's Mystery Meringue Tarts. Light, airy, and pretty, they're also simple to bake.

An interesting menu, appreciative diners, a warm and gracious holiday atmosphere—all add up to the beginning of a very happy New Year!

# BRAIDED ROUND CHALLAH

A large, round braided challah with a space in the center for a bowl of honey in which to dip the challah and apples is perfect for this holiday menu.

Festive Honey Challah dough
  (see page 33)
1 egg white, lightly beaten
2 tablespoons sesame seeds

Prepare the dough as directed. Divide the dough into 3 equal parts. Form each one into a rope about 26 inches long. Braid the ropes together and seal the ends by pinching.

Line a large heavy baking sheet with foil. Oil the foil and sprinkle it with yellow cornmeal. Remove the label and wash a 16-ounce empty can; oil its outside and place it in the center of the baking sheet, open end up. Transfer the challah to the baking sheet, forming it into a ring around the can; join and pinch together the ends of the braid. Cover the dough with a towel and let it rise in a warm place until doubled, about 40 minutes.

Preheat the oven to 350°F.

Brush the loaf with egg white and sprinkle with sesame seeds. Bake for 30 to 40 minutes until golden brown. Cool on a rack.

Serve the loaf on a circular tray and set a bowl of honey in the center and sliced apples for dipping.

# GORGONZOLA-APPLE SALAD

2 heads of romaine lettuce,
  torn into bite-size pieces
½ pound Gorgonzola or other
  blue-veined cheese, crumbled
2 Red Delicious apples, unpeeled and thinly sliced
Honey-Mustard Dressing
  (recipe follows)
1 cup toasted pecans or walnuts (see page 24), chopped

In a large salad bowl, place the lettuce, cheese, and apples. Before serving, add enough dressing to coat the lettuce. Add the pecans and toss well.

# HONEY-MUSTARD DRESSING

1 tablespoon Dijon mustard

3 tablespoons balsamic or red wine vinegar

1 tablespoon lemon juice

1 tablespoon honey

½ cup olive oil

Salt

Freshly ground black pepper

In a processor or blender, process the mustard, vinegar, lemon juice, and honey. Continue blending, gradually adding the olive oil until well blended. Season to taste with salt and pepper. Cover and chill in the refrigerator.

# THREE-MUSHROOM SOUP

Puréeing only half the mixture helps to thicken the soup and give it a creamy texture, while leaving slices of vegetables intact.

3 ounces dried shiitake or porcini mushrooms

5 cups (cold) strong Vegetable Stock (see page 391)

3 tablespoons olive oil

2 small leeks, white part only, thinly sliced (about 1 cup)

1 onion, thinly sliced

2 small potatoes, peeled and thinly sliced

2 garlic cloves, minced

1 pound fresh white cultivated mushrooms, thinly sliced

¼ cup minced parsley

Salt

Freshly ground black pepper

3 tablespoons dry sherry

Enoki mushrooms for garnish

Soak the dried mushrooms in 2 cups of the stock for about 30 minutes. Drain the mushrooms, reserving the stock. Strain the stock through cheesecloth or a fine sieve; combine it with the remaining 3 cups stock and set it aside with the mushrooms.

In a large saucepan, heat the oil; add the leeks, onion, potatoes, and garlic and sauté over medium heat until tender, 5 to 10 minutes. Add the sliced mushrooms and parsley and sauté for 5 to 10 minutes, stirring occasionally with a wooden spoon. Add the reserved dried mushrooms and the stock. Bring to a boil, partially cover, and simmer for 30 minutes over medium-low heat until the mushrooms are tender. Season to taste with salt and pepper.

Transfer half the soup to a processor and purée. Return to the saucepan and mix well. Add dry sherry and simmer until very hot. Ladle into heated soup bowls. Garnish with enoki mushrooms.

# WHITEFISH WITH ZUCCHINI SAUCE AND CUCUMBER ''PASTA''

Cooking with Michel Richard in my kitchen, I wanted to create a beautiful green sauce for our fish entrée. No problem—Michel invented this sauce on the spot, using just the peeling of zucchini.

1 cup sliced green onions (scallions)

1 cup dry white wine

1 cup Fish or Vegetable Stock (see page 392 or 391)

3 garlic cloves, minced

8 fillets of whitefish (about 6 ounces each)

Green Herb Butter (recipe follows)

Zucchini Sauce (recipe follows)

Cucumber ''Pasta'' (recipe follows)

Line a large broiler pan with heavy-duty foil. Add the green onions, wine, stock, and garlic. Place the fish fillets on top. Top each portion with 1 tablespoon herb butter. Cover and set aside until ready to cook.

Preheat the broiler to high heat. Broil the fish, basting once or twice during the first 5 minutes. Continue broiling for about 10 minutes more without turning the fish, until it is tender and begins to brown lightly on top.

Spoon the Zucchini Sauce onto heated plates. With a slotted spoon, arrange the Cucumber Pasta in a ring. Place the fish in the center, spooning more sauce on top. (Also delicious with salmon steaks.)

## GREEN HERB BUTTER

5 small spinach leaves, stems removed

2 tablespoons chopped parsley

2 teaspoons chopped fresh tarragon, or 1 teaspoon dried

¼ pound unsalted butter

2 teaspoons lemon juice

4 medium garlic cloves, peeled

Salt

Freshly ground black pepper

Drop the spinach, parsley, and tarragon into a pot of boiling water and boil for 5 minutes. Drain, dry on paper towels, and set aside.

In a processor, process the butter, lemon juice, and garlic until well blended. Add the cooked spinach mixture and process until smooth. Season to taste with salt and pepper. Mold into a cube, wrap in plastic wrap, and refrigerate or freeze. Unwrap the butter and cut into thin slices for serving.

## ZUCCHINI SAUCE

6 medium zucchini
1 cup Fish or Vegetable Stock
  (see page 392 or 391)
¼ cup cream
Salt
Freshly ground black pepper

Thinly peel the zucchini, placing the dark green peels in a saucepan of boiling salted water and reserving the white pulp for another use. Boil the peels until tender, 5 to 7 minutes. Drain well and transfer the peels to the bowl of a processor. Add 2 tablespoons of the stock and process until smoothly puréed. Transfer to a bowl, cover with plastic wrap, and set aside.

In a heavy saucepan, simmer the remaining stock until reduced by half. Just before serving, blend in the zucchini purée, the cream, and salt and pepper to taste.

## CUCUMBER ''PASTA''

6 large cucumbers, peeled
  and seeded
1 teaspoon salt
1 tablespoon unsalted butter
¼ cup Fish or Vegetable Stock
  (see page 392 or 391)
Freshly ground black pepper

With a French mandoline, a large grater, or the julienne blade of a processor, cut the cucumbers lengthwise into spaghetti-like strands. Toss them with the salt in a glass bowl and leave them for 5 to 10 minutes. Drain all the juices that form.

In a skillet, heat the butter and stock over moderate heat. Add the cucumbers and sauté, tossing gently with a wooden spoon, until heated through, about 2 minutes. Season to taste with salt and pepper.

# MOLLY'S MYSTERY MERINGUE TARTS
## SCHAUM TARTS

Rich, light, and airy, these meringue tarts were one of my mother's specialties. Though she never visited Paris, these tarts have the mysteriously fragile charm of those found in French patisseries—and mother was the only one who could remove them from the muffin tins in one piece.

Years later I figured out her secret technique and I've mastered the light touch of handling them, which I explain in the instructions that follow. The combination of crushed pineapple, sliced bananas, and whipped cream is irresistible—simple yet subtle. It's a lovely dessert for a light dairy lunch or dinner.

3 egg whites

1 cup granulated sugar

1 tablespoon vinegar

1 teaspoon vanilla extract

1 can (20 ounces) crushed pineapple, drained

4 bananas, thinly sliced and diced

2 cups cream

½ cup powdered sugar

Preheat the oven to 250°F.

In the large bowl of an electric mixer, beat the egg whites until soft peaks form. Gradually add the granulated sugar with the vinegar and vanilla, beating until firm peaks form. Spoon the meringue into generously buttered muffin tins. Bake until light golden, about 1 hour. With your fingertips, carefully lift the meringues out of the muffin cups by twisting them gently. Transfer them to a large platter to cool.

In a bowl, combine the pineapple and bananas. Beat the cream until soft peaks form. Add the powdered sugar and continue beating until stiff.

Just before serving, carefully cut off the tops of the meringues with a small sharp-pointed knife. Then use the back of a large spoon to make an indentation in the soft centers of the bottoms. Spoon a layer of the pineapple and banana mixture into each meringue, then add a layer of whipped cream. Add one more layer of fruit and another of cream. Replace the tops lightly and garnish with a teaspoon of whipped cream and fruit. Serve immediately.

BONUS RECIPES:

# MANDELBROT

Almond Biscottini

Biscochos

Classic Mandelbrot

**M**andelbrot, a crisp, almond-studded, twice-baked cookie, is a favorite of Jewish families around the world. During festivals and holidays, traditional confections such as mandelbrot play an important part.

European Jewish children literally teethe on mandelbrot, and every Jewish community on the Continent has its own version—from the Almond Biscottini served in

Italian homes to the anise-and-sesame-flavored Biscochos preferred by Sephardics in Spain.

The first baking of mandelbrot is in loaf form; then the loaf is sliced and the slices are baked again to golden-brown crispness. Stored in a tightly covered container, the cookies stay crisp for several weeks; in the freezer, they'll keep for many months. If they lose their crispness, pop them in a 375°F oven for 5 to 10 minutes on each side.

# ALMOND BISCOTTINI
## ALMOND MANDELBROT

MAKES ABOUT 4 DOZEN

¾ cup sugar
Grated zest of 1 lemon
Grated zest of 1 orange
¼ pound unsalted butter or
   margarine
3 eggs
½ teaspoon vanilla extract
3 cups flour
1 tablespoon baking powder
½ teaspoon salt
1 cup chopped almonds
1 teaspoon aniseed

Preheat the oven to 350°F.

In a processor or blender, combine the sugar and lemon and orange zest and process until blended. In a large mixing bowl, cream the butter and sugar mixture with an electric beater until light. Add the eggs and vanilla and blend thoroughly. In a large bowl, combine the flour, baking powder, and salt. Blend the flour mixture into the butter mixture. Add the almonds and aniseed and mix well. Wrap the dough in plastic wrap and chill for 1 hour.

Divide the dough into 3 portions. With lightly oiled hands, shape each portion into an oval loaf about 2 inches thick. Place the loaves 2 inches apart on greased baking sheets. Bake for 15 to 20 minutes, or until lightly browned. Remove the loaves from the oven and use a spatula to transfer them to a cutting board; cut them into ¾-inch-thick slices. Place them cut side down on the same baking sheet, turn off the heat, and return the loaves to the oven. Bake for 10 minutes on each side until crisp. Transfer to racks and cool.

# BISCOCHOS
## SPANISH MANDELBROT

MAKES ABOUT 6 DOZEN

½ cup safflower or vegetable
  oil
1 cup sugar
4 eggs
1 teaspoon anise extract
3½ cups flour
4 teaspoons baking powder
¼ teaspoon salt
1 cup sliced almonds
½ cup sesame seeds

Preheat the oven to 350°F.

In the bowl of an electric mixer, blend the oil and sugar thoroughly. Add 3 of the eggs and the anise and beat well. In a bowl, combine the flour, baking powder, and salt, and blend into the oil mixture. Add the sliced almonds and mix well. Roll the dough into 3 rolls about 6 inches long and 1 inch wide. Place them on a greased baking sheet. Beat the remaining egg and brush it over the loaves, then sprinkle with the sesame seeds. Bake for 15 to 20 minutes, or until lightly browned. Remove the rolls from the oven and use a spatula to transfer them to a cutting board; cut them into ½-inch-thick slices. Place them cut side down on the same baking sheet, turn off the heat, and return the rolls to the oven. Bake for 5 to 10 minutes on each side until crisp. Transfer to racks and cool.

# CLASSIC MANDELBROT

This is the classic recipe for Eastern European mandelbrot. Using an electric mixer makes this recipe much easier, but you can also make it in a large bowl with a wooden spoon—just the way our grandmothers did.

MAKES ABOUT 6 DOZEN

1 cup safflower or vegetable
  oil
1 cup plus 2 tablespoons
  sugar
3 eggs
1 teaspoon vanilla extract
1 teaspoon almond extract
1 tablespoon grated orange
  peel
4 cups flour
1 teaspoon salt

Preheat the oven to 325°F.

In the bowl of an electric mixer, blend together the oil and 1 cup of the sugar. Add the eggs, vanilla and almond extracts, and the orange peel. Blend thoroughly. In a large bowl, combine the flour, salt, baking powder, and 2 teaspoons of the cinnamon. Blend the flour mixture into the oil mixture. Add the almonds and mix well.

Divide the dough into 4 or 5 portions. With lightly oiled hands, shape each portion into an oval loaf, 2 inches wide and 1 inch high. Place the loaves 2 inches apart on greased baking sheets. Sprinkle with the remaining 2 ta-

1 teaspoon baking powder
2½ teaspoons cinnamon
1 cup sliced almonds

blespoons sugar and ½ teaspoon cinnamon and bake for 45 minutes. Remove the loaves from the oven and use a spatula to transfer them to a cutting board; cut into 1-inch-thick slices. Place cut side down on the same baking sheets, turn off the heat, and return them to the oven. Leave the mandelbrot in the oven for 10 minutes a side, or until crisp. Transfer to racks and cool.

# BISCOTTI
## ITALIAN ALMOND MANDELBROT

If I had to choose my favorite mandelbrot, this would be the one. Because it contains no fat or liquid, it cannot be prepared in an electric mixer; it must be made on a wooden board and kneaded just like a bread or pasta dough. My students are always surprised that there is no oil, butter, or margarine in the recipe; they are sure that it will not work. But it does, and the results are delicious and authentic. And it is very low in cholesterol.

It is the custom in Italy to dip the Biscotti in a glass of sweet wine.

MAKES ABOUT 6 DOZEN

2 cups flour
½ teaspoon baking powder
½ teaspoon baking soda
¼ teaspoon salt
Pinch of saffron (optional)
¾ cup ground almonds (approximately 3 ounces)
½ cup sliced almonds
2 eggs
½ teaspoon anise or almond extract
¼ teaspoon vanilla extract
1 cup sugar
1 egg white

Preheat the oven to 350°F.

Place the flour, baking powder, baking soda, salt, and saffron in a mound on a floured board. Surround the outside of the mound with the ground and sliced almonds. Make a well in the center. Place the eggs, anise, vanilla, and sugar in the well. Quickly beat the egg mixture with a fork, gradually incorporating the flour and almonds to make a smooth dough.

Divide the dough into 2 or 3 portions. With lightly oiled hands, shape each portion into an oval loaf. Place the loaves 2 inches apart on greased and floured baking sheets. Brush with the lightly beaten egg white and bake for 15 to 20 minutes, or until lightly browned. Remove the loaves from the oven and use a spatula to transfer them to a cutting board and cut into ½-inch-thick slices. Place them cut side down on the same baking sheet, turn off the heat, and return the loaves to the oven. Bake for 5 to 10 minutes on each side, or until golden brown. Transfer to racks and cool.

# CHOCOLATE-FILLED MANDELBROT

MAKES ABOUT 4 DOZEN

⅓ cup safflower or vegetable oil

1 cup plus 1 tablespoon sugar

3 eggs

1 teaspoon lemon juice

Grated peel of 1 lemon

¼ teaspoon almond extract

2¾ cups flour

4 teaspoons baking powder

¼ teaspoon salt

1 cup coarsely chopped almonds

2 tablespoons powdered cocoa

¼ teaspoon cinnamon

Preheat the oven to 350°F.

In the bowl of an electric mixer, blend the oil with 1 cup of the sugar. Add the eggs, lemon juice, lemon peel, and almond extract and mix well. Combine the flour, baking powder, salt, and almonds and blend thoroughly. Remove one quarter of the dough to another bowl and blend in the cocoa, the remaining 1 tablespoon of sugar, and the cinnamon.

With oiled hands, divide the chocolate dough into 3 parts, and roll each into a loaf about 1½ inches wide and ½ inch thick.

Divide the remaining dough into 3 parts. With your hands, flatten each into a rectangle as long as the chocolate loaves and wide enough to wrap around them—about 4 inches. Wrap each chocolate loaf in a sheet of plain dough and place it seam side down on a greased baking sheet. Bake for 30 to 40 minutes, or until lightly browned. Remove the loaves from the oven and use spatulas to transfer them to a cutting board. While still warm, cut them into ½-inch-thick slices. Place the slices cut side down on the same baking sheet, turn off the heat, return the slices to the oven, and bake for 10 minutes a side, or until crisp and lightly browned. Transfer to racks and cool.

# SUGAR-AND-SPICE MANDELBROT

MAKES ABOUT 5 DOZEN

1 cup safflower or vegetable oil

1 cup sugar

6 egg whites

Preheat the oven to 350°F.

In the bowl of an electric mixer, beat the oil, sugar, egg whites, vanilla and almond extracts, and citrus peel until thoroughly blended. Combine the flour, baking

½ teaspoon vanilla extract

½ teaspoon almond extract

1 tablespoon grated orange or lemon peel

3 cups flour

2 teaspoons baking powder

¼ teaspoon salt

1 cup sliced almonds

2 tablespoons sugar

½ teaspoon cinnamon

powder, salt, and almonds; add them to the oil mixture and beat until the dough is smooth.

Divide the dough into 4 portions. With lightly oiled hands, shape each portion into loaves 2 inches wide and 1 inch high. Sprinkle with sugar and cinnamon. Place the loaves 2 inches apart on greased baking sheets. Bake for 20 minutes, or until golden brown. Remove the loaves from the oven and use a spatula to transfer them to a cutting board; cut into ¾-inch-thick slices. Place them cut side down on the same baking sheets, turn off the heat, and return the loaves to the oven. Bake for 10 minutes a side, or until lightly brown. Transfer to racks and cool.

# FRUIT-FILLED MANDELBROT

These mandelbrot are a little richer then most and add a festive touch to special occasions like Hanukkah or Purim celebrations.

MAKES ABOUT 4 DOZEN

4 tablespoons unsalted butter or margarine

1 cup sugar

3 eggs

½ teaspoon anise extract

2½ cups plus 2 tablespoons flour

1½ teaspoons baking powder

¼ teaspoon salt

1 cup lightly toasted whole almonds (see page 24)

⅓ cup chopped candied cherries

⅓ cup cup chopped candied orange peel

1 egg white

Preheat the oven to 375°F.

In a large bowl, cream the butter and sugar with an electric mixer until light and fluffy. One at a time, thoroughly beat in the eggs. Beat in the anise extract.

In a bowl, combine the 2½ cups flour, the baking powder, and salt and gradually beat them into the butter mixture. With lightly oiled hands, knead the dough into a ball, wrap it in plastic wrap, and refrigerate for 1 hour.

In a bowl, combine the almonds, cherries, and orange peel. Transfer the dough to a floured board and, if it is sticky, knead in the remaining 2 tablespoons flour.

Divide the dough in half, and with lightly oiled hands, press each half into an 8 × 12-inch rectangle. Sprinkle with the fruit-and-almond mixture and, starting at a long edge, roll the dough up like a jelly roll. Crimp the seam to seal it and place each roll seam side down on a greased baking sheet. Brush the rolls with lightly beaten egg white and sprinkle with sugar. Bake for 20 to 25 minutes, or until lightly browned. Remove the loaves from the oven and use a spatula to transfer them to a cutting board; cut into ½-inch-thick slices. Place them, cut side down, on the same baking sheets, turn off the heat, and return the loaves to the oven. Bake for 5 to 10 minutes on each side, or until lightly browned. Transfer to racks and cool.

# WHOLE WHEAT CHOCOLATE CHIP MANDELBROT

I always enjoy working with whole wheat pastry flour. it is much lighter than whole wheat flour and more nutritious than white flours. I used it in My Signature Strudel (see page 185) when I supplied it to a well-known California restaurant.

MAKES 5 TO 6 DOZEN

½ pound unsalted butter or margarine

1⅓ cups sugar

6 eggs

2 teaspoons vanilla extract

4 cups whole wheat pastry flour

2 teaspoons cinnamon

2 teaspoons baking powder

1 cup chopped nuts

1⅓ cups mini-chocolate chips

Preheat the oven to 350°F.

In the bowl of an electric mixer, cream the butter and sugar. Add the eggs and vanilla and beat well. In another bowl, sift together the flour, cinnamon, and baking powder. Add the flour mixture to the butter mixture and mix well. Stir in the nuts and chocolate chips. Chill. Divide the dough, which will be soft and sticky, into 4 portions. With lightly oiled hands, shape each portion into a long narrow loaf. Place the loaves 4 inches apart on greased baking sheets and bake for 20 minutes, or until lightly browned.

Remove the loaves from the oven and use a spatula to transfer them to a cutting board; cut into ¾-inch-thick slices. Place cut side down on the same baking sheets, turn off the heat, return to the oven, and bake 20 minutes, or until golden brown. Transfer to racks and cool.

# YOM KIPPUR

Ten days after Rosh Hashanah is Yom Kippur, the Day of Atonement. On this holiest of Holy Days, we repent of our sins and seek renewal for the year ahead through prayer and twenty-four hours of fasting.

For the pre-fast dinner, Jews in many countries serve chicken, usually boiled and very bland and often accompanied by rice. It makes sense not to serve anything too salty or spicy before fasting.

After the fast, some families serve a simple sort of breakfast menu. A cousin told me that all her family ever wants is orange juice, chocolate milk, and coffee cake.

At the other extreme, there is a trend toward serving a hearty buffet. It begins with something simple like apples or challah dipped in honey. This is followed with brunch food—eggs, herring, bagels, cream cheese, and lox. Finally, the fasters are rewarded with baked delights—honey cake, schnecken, pastries, and seasonal fruits, along with tea and coffee.

Some families with hearty appetites go so far as to serve a light snack first, and later they sit down to a full-course dinner.

So it's up to you to create a Yom Kippur menu plan that you and your family are comfortable with.

# TRADITIONAL PRE-FAST DINNER

## FOR 10

We honor this holiday with a traditional menu of our favorite classic foods. Being a thoroughly modern cook, however, I can't resist adding a few up-dated touches.

It's important to serve food that's hearty enough to hold us over from the sundown-to-sundown fasting period. But it must not be too salty or spicy, so that thirst will not become a problem or taste buds become overly stimulated.

Since this meal will be served early, most of it can be prepared in advance. About one hour before dinner, the chicken and kugel can be popped into the oven. Both are baked at the same temperature.

The chicken soup, an all-time favorite, is heavy in rich chicken flavor and very light in salt. Another recipe turns this Classic Chicken Soup into a velvety vegetable soup, via the blender or food processor.

The kreplach, oldest of all the stuffed doughs, is filled with kasha (buckwheat groats) instead of the usual spicier ground meat.

The noodle and apple kugel supplies the necessary starch, and vegetables form a colorful garnish for the chicken—tiny onions, potatoes, carrots, mushrooms, and whole unpeeled garlic are roasted with the chicken with barely a pinch of salt and lots of fresh herbs for flavor.

For our dessert, an unusual honey cake is just rich enough to make up for twenty-four hours of abstinence from sweets—or from any food at all, for that matter.

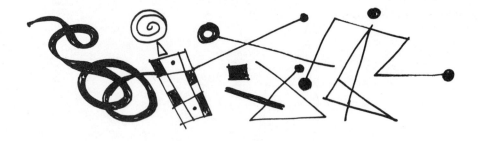

# GALA CHOPPED LIVER

This is one of the basic Jewish favorites we all remember from childhood. I used to watch my mother, sitting on the back-porch steps, chopping away at beef liver, hard-cooked eggs, and chicken schmaltz in a huge wooden bowl. It was really hard work. Now I can whip up a batch of chopped liver from scratch—enough to serve 20—in less than half an hour.

I have preserved the integrity of Mother's recipe, but enhanced it with apple, mushrooms, and a little brandy for flavor as well as for a preservative. I use a meat grinder to get an old-fashioned coarse texture, but you can also make this with a processor, resulting in a finer texture. Concord Wine Aspic adds a gala touch.

¼ cup olive oil

2 medium onions, thinly sliced

1½ pounds chicken livers (see page 21)

4 large mushrooms, thinly sliced

1 medium apple, peeled, cored, and thinly sliced

2 tablespoons brandy or cognac

2 hard-boiled eggs (see page 23), peeled

Salt

Freshly ground black pepper

Heat the oil in a large, heavy skillet and sauté the onions until lightly browned. Add the livers, mushrooms, and apple and sauté, turning the livers on both sides, until lightly browned. (Do not overcook.) Add the brandy and simmer 3 to 4 minutes.

Spoon the mixture with the eggs into a meat grinder and grind into a large bowl, making sure to add the juices from the skillet. Add salt and pepper to taste and stir well. Cover and refrigerate. Or line a mold with plastic wrap, spoon in the liver mixture, cover, and refrigerate. The plastic wrap enables you to invert and lift the molded chopped liver out of the bowl, and then it is peeled off. Serve with the Concord Wine Aspic and Homemade Wheat Thins.

# CONCORD WINE ASPIC

½ cup sugar

⅓ cup water

1½ cups Concord grape wine

¼ cup wine vinegar

1½ ounces frozen orange juice concentrate

1 tablespoon (1 package) gelatin

In a small heavy saucepan over moderate to high heat, simmer the sugar in the water, stirring until the sugar dissolves; continue simmering rapidly until the sugar reaches a caramel color. In another small saucepan, heat 1¼ cups of the wine, the vinegar, and the orange juice concentrate. Add the wine mixture to the sugar mixture and stir well. Simmer for 5 minutes.

Soften the gelatin in the remaining ¼ cup wine. Add to the hot mixture and stir until dissolved. Pour into an 8 × 8-inch baking dish and chill until set, about 2 hours. Serve with the Gala Chopped Liver.

# HOMEMADE WHEAT THINS

For as long as I can remember, packaged wheat thins were always served with chopped liver or herring. I never realized that I could make them at home until I ate some in a small restaurant where they made their own.

With the help of the food processor and a pasta machine, I was able to create a crisp, perfect wafer. Now I can serve liver pâté, chopped herring, roasted peppers, or any appetizer or salad with my own Homemade Wheat Thins.

MAKES 3 TO 4 DOZEN

1 package active dry yeast
Pinch of sugar
½ cup warm water (110 to 115°F)
1 cup whole wheat flour
1 cup rye flour
¼ teaspoon salt
Caraway seeds (optional)
Kosher salt (optional)

Dissolve the yeast and sugar in the warm water. In a processor, blend the whole wheat flour, rye flour, and salt. When the yeast foams, pour it into the processor and process just until the dough comes together.

Spoon out the dough onto a floured board and knead it into a smooth ball. Oil the top of the dough, cover it with a towel, and let it rise in a warm place for 20 minutes.

Preheat the oven to 350°F.

Divide the dough in half for easier handling. In a pasta machine or with a rolling pin, roll each half of dough as thin as possible, about ⅛ inch thick. With a knife or pastry cutter, cut the rolled dough into 2 × 3-inch rectangles or any size you wish. Sprinkle with caraway seeds and kosher salt and press lightly with a rolling pin. Place on oiled foil-lined baking sheets and bake until golden brown, 5 to 10 minutes. (They brown quickly, so watch them closely.) Transfer to racks to cool.

# CLASSIC CHICKEN SOUP

This recipe yields a truly classic version of chicken soup. For an unusual variation, or for any leftover soup, try puréeing the broth with the vegetables and serving it with Parsley Pesto Sauce (recipe follows).

1 chicken (5 pounds), cut into serving pieces, or 5 pounds chicken parts
3 medium onions, peeled and diced

In a large heavy Dutch oven or pot, place the chicken pieces, onions, and enough water to cover. Bring to a boil over high heat. Using a large spoon, skim off the scum that rises to the top. Add the carrots, celery, parsnips, and parsley. Cover, leaving the lid ajar, and sim-

3 to 4 quarts water
16 small carrots, peeled and
  cut into 1-inch pieces
5 celery ribs with tops, cut
  into 1-inch pieces
3 medium parsnips, peeled
  and cut into 1-inch pieces
8 parsley sprigs
Salt
Freshly ground black pepper
Kreplach with Kasha-Spinach
  Filling (see page 56)

mer for 1 hour. Add salt and pepper to taste. Uncover and simmer 30 minutes more.

With a slotted spoon, remove all the chicken, including any bones, from the soup. Remove the meat from the bones and return it to the soup. Let the soup cool to room temperature, then refrigerate. Remove the fat that has hardened on the top. Bring to a boil, add the kreplach, and simmer. Ladle into heated soup bowls.

## BLENDER CHICKEN SOUP WITH PARSLEY PESTO

Classic Chicken Soup (see
  preceding recipe)
Parsley Pesto Sauce (recipe
  follows)

Remove all the cut vegetables from the soup. Place them in a processor or blender with a few tablespoons of soup and purée. Pour the purée into a large pot and add enough soup liquid to give a light creamy consistency. Bring to a boil, then ladle into heated bowls. Spoon the Parsley Pesto Sauce on top.

## PARSLEY PESTO SAUCE

1 cup tightly packed parsley
  leaves without stems
½ cup tightly packed fresh
  basil leaves
2 tablespoons pine nuts or
  walnuts
2 garlic cloves, peeled
½ cup olive oil
Pinch of sugar
Salt
Freshly ground black pepper

Put the parsley, basil, pine nuts, and garlic in a processor or blender. Pulse until finely chopped. With the machine running, slowly pour in the olive oil in a thin stream. Add sugar and salt and pepper to taste. Pour into a glass bowl, cover, and refrigerate.

# KREPLACH WITH KASHA-SPINACH FILLING

Basic pasta dough (see page 288)

Kasha-Spinach Filling (recipe follows)

Prepare dough as directed. Cut the dough into 3-inch squares. Place 1 teaspoon of kasha filling in the center of each square; brush the edges with water and fold the dough into a triangle; pinch edges to seal. Place on a towel-lined baking sheet. Repeat with the remaining dough.

Drop the kreplach into lightly salted boiling water and boil for 8 to 10 minutes, until the kreplach float to the top and are tender. With a slotted spoon, transfer to the chicken soup.

## KASHA-SPINACH FILLING FOR KREPLACH

1 cup kasha (buckwheat groats)

1 egg, lightly beaten

3 tablespoons olive oil

2 cups boiling Chicken Stock (see page 390) or water

1 medium onion, finely chopped

½ cup finely chopped mushrooms

1 bunch of spinach (8 ounces), washed, blanched, drained, and chopped

Salt

Freshly ground black pepper

In a bowl, stir the kasha and egg until all the grains are coated. In a large heavy skillet, heat 1 tablespoon of the olive oil over medium heat. Add the kasha and stir constantly until the grains are separated and dry, 2 to 3 minutes. Add the stock, stir well, cover, and cook over low heat for 15 to 20 minutes, stirring occasionally, until the grains are fluffy and dry.

In a small skillet, heat the remaining 2 tablespoons oil and sauté the onion until lightly browned. Add the mushrooms and spinach and simmer until the liquid evaporates, 5 to 10 minutes. Add the kasha. Season to taste with salt and pepper. Mix well.

# ROAST CHICKEN WITH VEGETABLES AND WHOLE GARLIC CLOVES

To serve this dish, spoon the sauce onto individual heated serving plates; place the chicken pieces on top with the mushrooms and vegetables—and be sure to put an unpeeled garlic clove on top of each serving.

2 onions, thinly sliced

4 garlic cloves, minced

2 carrots, peeled and thinly sliced

5 small new potatoes, un-peeled and quartered

1 green pepper, stemmed, seeded, and thinly sliced

1 can (15 ounces) peeled to-matoes with juice

1 cup dry white wine

½ cup olive oil

2 chickens (3 pounds each), cut into pieces

12 medium mushrooms, quar-tered

¼ cup finely chopped fresh parsley

1 whole head of garlic, cloves separated, unpeeled

1 tablespoon dried rosemary or thyme

Salt

Freshly ground black pepper

Put the onions, minced garlic, carrots, potatoes, green pepper, and tomatoes in a large roasting pan. Bring to a boil over medium heat. Add the wine and simmer for 5 minutes.

Preheat the oven to 375°F.

In a large skillet, heat the oil over medium heat and quickly brown the chicken pieces on both sides to seal in the juices. Transfer the browned chicken to the roast-ing pan and baste with the onion-tomato mixture to coat the chicken. Add the mushrooms, parsley, unpeeled garlic cloves, rosemary, and salt and pepper to taste. Cover and bake for 1 hour, or until the chicken is tender.

# HOLIDAY FRUIT KUGEL

A plump, beautifully browned kugel adds a homey, old-fashioned accent to hol-iday menus. This one doesn't need a grain of sugar, because the raisins and apples add natural sweetness. Another plus is that the top of this kugel forms a crisp crust. My little secret is to use a large baking dish, because the thinner the kugel, the crisper the crust.

12 ounces flat wide egg noodles (about 7 cups)

8 cups lightly salted boiling
water

¼ pound unsalted margarine

2 apples, peeled, cored, and
diced

½ cup plumped raisins (see
page 25)

4 eggs, beaten

Salt

Freshly ground black pepper

Cinnamon sugar

Preheat the oven to 375°F.

Cook the noodles in the boiling water until tender, 5 to 10 minutes. Place the noodles, margarine, apples, and drained plumped raisins in a large bowl. Add the eggs and season to taste with salt and pepper. Mix well.

Spoon the mixture into a well-greased 9 × 13-inch baking dish. Sprinkle with cinnamon sugar and bake for 35 to 45 minutes, until the top is brown and crisp. Cut into squares. Serve hot or cold.

# COFFEE AND SPICE HONEY CAKE

This delicious, high-rise, spicy honey cake gets a light, appealing texture from beaten egg whites. Try it once, and you'll never buy another bakery honey cake.

Be sure to use strong fresh coffee and a generous measure of spices. Then prepare yourself for compliments.

16 ounces honey

1 cup sugar

1 cup strong black coffee

¼ cup safflower or vegetable
oil

4 eggs, separated

3½ cups flour

2½ teaspoons baking powder

1 teaspoon baking soda

1 teaspoon ground cinnamon

¾ teaspoon salt

½ teaspoon ground cloves

½ teaspoon ground ginger

¼ teaspoon cream of tartar

¾ cup sliced almonds

Preheat the oven to 350°F.

In the bowl of an electric mixer, blend the honey, sugar, coffee, and oil. Add the egg yolks and beat until light and smooth. In a large bowl, combine the flour, baking powder, baking soda, cinnamon, ½ teaspoon of the salt, cloves, and ginger. Gradually add the flour mixture to the batter, beating until well blended.

In a large mixing bowl, beat the egg whites with the remaining salt and cream of tartar until soft peaks form. Gently fold the beaten egg whites and the almonds into the batter. Pour the batter into an ungreased 10-inch tube pan. Bake for 1 hour, or until a toothpick inserted into the cake comes out clean. Immediately remove the pan from the oven and invert it onto a wire rack to cool. With a sharp knife, loosen the cake from the sides and from the tube. Remove the cake from the pan and transfer to a large cake platter.

# BREAK-THE-FAST REPAST

## FOR 10

Most of this menu can be prepared in advance and put on the table quickly after a long day of prayer and fasting for Yom Kippur. Nobody wants to spend too much time in the kitchen when suffering from acute hunger pangs. Be sure to meet your weary fasters with a bite of challah and honey cake when they return from the synagogue.

Our grandmothers always told us that after fasting on Yom Kippur our bodies needed a lot of salt, and the old breaking-the-fast dinners always included some herring. I'm not sure whether modern science agrees with Grandma, but to be safe I've included her very special recipe for chopped herring. It contains a little onion, a little apple, a little egg, a little challah, and lots of love.

After fasting we'll want to taste some spicy flavors, so you'll find an old-fashioned Chicken Fricassee with Turkey Meatballs, a favorite from my childhood. Corn Rye Bread is not always found in bakeries, so it's nice to bake your own. And the Oven-Browned Potato "Chips," made from tiny red new potatoes, are nothing like the commercial kind. They're fresh-tasting and contain only a fraction of the usual salt and oil.

A tangy Holiday Orange Sponge Cake, a refreshing wine-flavored ice, and Star Silhouette Cookies make nice light holiday desserts.

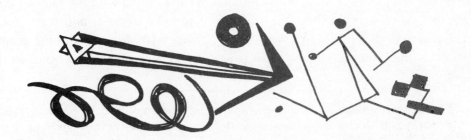

# CLASSIC HONEY CAKE

Honey cake is a holiday staple, but I keep trying to develop newer and better ones. This is truly one of the most delicious I've ever tasted. My thanks to Joan Bram, my good friend and devoted recipe tester.

1¾ cups honey
1 cup strong coffee
½ cup currants
3 tablespoons brandy
¼ cup safflower or vegetable oil
1¼ cups brown sugar, packed
4 eggs
3½ cups flour
1 tablespoon baking powder
1 teaspoon baking soda
¼ teaspoon salt
1 teaspoon cinnamon
¼ teaspoon ground cloves
½ teaspoon ginger
¼ teaspoon nutmeg
½ cup sliced almonds
1 tablespoon grated orange zest

In a saucepan, combine the honey and coffee; bring to a boil and cool. Soak the currants in the brandy.

Preheat the oven to 300°F.

In the bowl of an electric mixer, blend the oil, brown sugar, and eggs. Combine the flour, baking powder, baking soda, salt, and spices. Stir the dry ingredients alternately with the coffee into the egg mixture. Fold in the almonds, currants, and orange zest.

Oil two 9 × 5-inch loaf pans. Pour the batter in and bake for 1 hour: the top will be sticky, but a toothpick inserted into the center should come out clean.

# GRANDMA GENE'S CHOPPED HERRING

For almost every family gathering, Grandma Gene would arrive at the front door bearing a large glass dish filled with chopped herring, along with her famous corn rye bread. She always finished garnishing it when she arrived, and then would serve it very proudly. It took many years to convince her to part with the recipe. Finally, I sat there one day when she made it, measuring and taking notes as she went along.

1 pound schmaltz herring fillets, or 1 jar (1 pound) pickled herring fillets in wine sauce

If using schmaltz herring, soak in cold water overnight. Drain well. Bone and skin the herring and cut it into pieces. Soak the challah in cold water for a few minutes and squeeze out the water.

2 slices challah or egg bread

1 medium onion, cut into quarters

1 green apple, peeled, cored, and sliced

2 hard-boiled eggs (see page 23)

4 teaspoons white wine vinegar

2 or 3 tablespoons safflower or vegetable oil

Place the herring, challah, onion, and apple in a food grinder and grind. Chop the hard-boiled egg whites and combine with 3 teaspoons of the vinegar. Mix the whites into the herring mixture. Spread the chopped herring on a platter. Mash the egg yolks with the remaining 1 teaspoon vinegar and spread over the top of the chopped herring. Cover with plastic wrap and chill. Just before serving, pour 2 or 3 tablespoons of the oil over the top. Serve with thinly sliced Corn Rye Bread.

# CORN RYE BREAD

Here is a recipe that everybody likes, corn rye bread as good as the ones our generous Grandma Gene used to bring.

MAKES 2 ROUND LOAVES

1 package active dry yeast

1½ cups warm water (110 to 115°F)

Pinch of sugar

¼ cup honey or brown sugar

2 tablespoons unsalted margarine, softened

1 tablespoon salt

2 tablespoons caraway seeds

2½ cups rye flour

3 cups all-purpose flour, or more if needed

¼ cup cornmeal

1 egg white, beaten, for glaze

Dissolve the yeast with ½ cup of the warm water and a pinch of sugar and set aside until foamy.

In the large bowl of an electric mixer, combine the remaining 1 cup of water, honey, margarine, and salt. Add the yeast mixture along with 1 tablespoon of the caraway seeds and mix well. Add the two flours, 1 cup at a time, stirring well after each addition, until about 4½ cups of the flour have been added and the dough is firm enough to work by hand. Spoon the dough onto a generously floured board and knead for 5 to 10 minutes—punching, turning, and pressing down, adding more flour as needed until the dough is soft, velvety, and elastic.

Shape the dough into a ball and place it in a well-oiled bowl; oil the top of the dough. Cover with a towel and let rise in a warm place for 1½ hours. Punch down, turn out on a lightly floured board, and divide into 2 parts. Shape the dough into round or oval loaves and place them on a well-oiled, cornmeal-lined baking sheet. Cover with a towel and let rise for 45 minutes, or until doubled in bulk.

Preheat the oven to 400°F.

Use the tines of a fork to make punctures on the top

of each loaf. Or with a sharp knife cut 2 shallow slits on top. Brush the loaves with egg white and sprinkle with the remaining 1 tablespoon caraway seeds. Bake for 30 to 40 minutes, or until the loaves are golden brown and sound hollow when tapped with your knuckles. Cool thoroughly on wire racks before slicing.

# CHICKEN FRICASSEE WITH TURKEY MEATBALLS

I remember this dish from early childhood. I always loved its rich, hearty, sweet-and-sour flavor. It was always served as an appetizer in those days, but I enjoy serving it as a main course, along with noodles or potatoes so none of the delicious sauce is wasted. Although it was originally made with beef meatballs, I prefer to use lean ground turkey.

1 pound ground turkey
1 egg
1 small potato, grated
3 garlic cloves, finely chopped
3 tablespoons bread crumbs
Salt
Freshly ground black pepper
2 tablespoons safflower or
 vegetable oil
2 medium onions, thinly
 sliced
½ green bell pepper, thinly
 sliced
2 tablespoons paprika
1 can (10½ to 15 ounces) tomato sauce
1 cup dry red wine
2 to 3 tablespoons lemon
 juice
2 to 3 tablespoons brown
 sugar
1 chicken (3½ pounds) with
 giblets, cut into pieces

In a large bowl, combine the turkey, egg, potato, 1 of the garlic cloves, bread crumbs, and salt and pepper. Shape into balls the size of walnuts. Set aside.

Heat the oil in a large saucepan, then sauté the onions, pepper, and remaining 2 garlic cloves until transparent. With a wooden spoon, stir in the paprika and sauté for 2 minutes, stirring continuously. Add the tomato sauce and wine and season to taste with salt and pepper. Add the lemon juice and brown sugar to taste. Simmer for 5 to 10 minutes.

Place cut-up chicken and giblets and meatballs in the sauce mixture and simmer gently, covered, for 1 hour, or until the chicken and meatballs are done and the sauce is thick. Shake the pot every 15 minutes to avoid sticking. Serve with noodles, potatoes, or kasha.

# OVEN-BROWNED POTATO "CHIPS"

The technique of running cold water over the potatoes until the water runs clear removes a lot of the starch, prevents the potatoes from discoloring, and results in crisper chips.

20 small red potatoes, unpeeled and scrubbed
½ cup olive oil
Salt
Freshly ground black pepper

Preheat the oven to 400°F.

Cut the potatoes into ⅛- to ¼-inch-thick slices. Rinse in cold running water until the water runs clear. Place them on paper towels in a single layer and pat dry.

Spread ¼ cup of the oil on a large baking sheet with sides, making sure that the bottom is entirely coated so the potatoes don't stick. Place the potato slices on the oiled sheets in a single layer, overlapping them slightly. Sprinkle just enough oil over the potatoes to moisten them. Season to taste with salt and pepper.

Bake for 35 to 40 minutes, turning the potatoes once when they are completely brown on the bottoms, until the potatoes are cooked through, brown, and crisp. Remove with a metal spatula to heated serving plates.

# HOLIDAY ORANGE SPONGE CAKE

7 eggs, separated
¼ teaspoon salt
½ teaspoon cream of tartar
1½ cups granulated sugar
Grated zest of 1 orange
Grated zest of 1 lemon
1½ cups sifted cake flour
½ cup orange juice
Powered sugar

Preheat the oven to 325°F.

In the bowl of an electric mixer, beat the egg whites until foamy. Add the salt and cream of tartar and beat until stiff enough to cling to the side of the bowl but not yet dry. Blend in ½ cup of the sugar. Set aside.

In the bowl of an electric mixer, beat the egg yolks with the remaining 1 cup sugar and orange and lemon zests until light and fluffy. Gently fold the yolk mixture into the beaten egg whites. A little at a time, gently fold the flour alternately with the orange juice into the egg white mixture. Do not overmix.

Pour the batter into an ungreased 10-inch tube pan with a removable bottom. Bake for 50 minutes, then increase the temperature to 350°F and continue baking for 5 to 10 minutes more, until the cake springs back to the touch and a toothpick inserted into the center of the cake comes out clean.

Remove from the oven and invert immediately onto a wire rack. Cool. Loosen from the sides and center of the pan with a sharp knife and unmold to a serving platter. Just before serving sprinkle with powdered sugar.

# CONCORD GRAPE WINE ICE

¾ cup sugar
½ cup water
3 cups sweet Concord grape wine
Juice of 1 orange
Juice of 1 lemon
Mint leaves

In a large heavy saucepan, bring the sugar and water to a boil, stirring until the sugar dissolves. Simmer for 5 minutes. Cool.

In a large bowl, add the wine and the orange and lemon juices and stir well. Blend in the sugar. Pour into ice cube trays and freeze until crystals form. Break up with a fork and return to the freezer until frozen. (Ice will not freeze solid.) To serve, spoon the ice into wineglasses and garnish with fresh mint leaves.

# STAR SILHOUETTE COOKIES

The center of these cookies is cut out to form a perfect star, symbolic of the tradition that a fast does not end "until the stars come out."

MAKES ABOUT 60

¼ pound plus 6 tablespoons unsalted butter
¾ cup powdered sugar
1 egg
2¼ cups flour
Dash of salt
Apricot preserves, strained

In the bowl of an electric mixer, cream together the butter, powdered sugar, and egg. Add the flour and salt and blend until the dough is soft. Wrap in plastic wrap and chill in the refrigerator.

Preheat the oven to 375°F.

Divide the dough in quarters. On a floured board, roll out each quarter ⅛ to ¼ inch thick. Cut rounds, using a 1½-inch plain or fluted round cutter. Place on foil-lined baking sheets. With a small star cookie cutter, cut a star in the center of half of the rounds. Bake for 8 to 10 minutes, or until evenly browned around the edges. Transfer to racks to cool.

Spread a thin layer of the preserves on the plain round cookies and top with the star cutout cookies.

# SUKKOTH

Sukkoth is the Jewish equivalent of Thanksgiving—a time to offer thanks for a bountiful harvest and a time to pray for fruitful harvests to come. The holiday comes in early fall and lasts for eight days, the final day being Shemini Azeret, when special memorial services are held.

In ancient times holiday meals were served in a sukkah, a little gazebolike shed with three sides, decorated with fruits, greenery, and sheaves of grain. These little buildings were said to symbolize the huts that workers lived in during the harvest season.

Today many families build sukkahs and invite friends to join them for a meal during the eight days. If you don't have room for a full-scale sukkah, a wonderful family project is to help your children make a miniature one for a holiday centerpiece. Children also can help decorate the table with autumn fruit arrangements including apples, pears, pomegranates, grapes, and miniature pumpkins.

The foods of Sukkoth offer interesting choices. Casseroles are traditional because they could be kept hot on the trip from kitchen to sukkah. Stuffed foods, including stuffed peppers, kreplach, and strudels—fruit salads and compotes—and a vegetarian tsimmes made with fruits and vegetables are other possibilities, along with hearty cabbage borscht, goulash, and cheese-filled (stuffed) pastries.

Lemons are an important part of the Sukkoth observance. They represent the ancient ethrog, or citron, which was brought to the synagogue to be blessed during Sukkoth. After the holiday, thrifty housewives used the exotic fruit to make preserves or candy.

Nobody can complain about having two Thanksgivings in one year, so why not observe Sukkoth with special foods, holiday decorations, and a spirit of rejoicing for the beautiful bounty of the autumn harvest.

# SPECIAL SUKKOTH DINNER

FOR 8

Whether you have your own sukkah or not, this dinner will make your holiday a joyous one. Four super-special recipes add up to a dazzling display of your skills as a chef.

The first course should be served at the table to enjoy the melt-in-your mouth strudel without the annoyance of trying to balance it on your lap. Salmon packets are a self-contained entrée, complete with an array of fresh vegetables, that can be easily brought to the table or sukkah while still piping hot. It's fun to watch eyes light up as the packets are unwrapped.

The salad contains more surprises—varicolored lentils tossed with herbs, an oil and vinegar dressing, and creamy goat cheese.

And then there's dessert. Who can resist the appeal of layered vanilla and fresh strawberry cheesecake, garnished with whole fresh strawberries? It's the perfect finale for a memorable Sukkoth.

## CABBAGE STRUDEL
## WITH SOUR CREAM AND
## DILL SAUCE

It is really worth the effort that it takes to make this unusual cabbage strudel. The slightly sweet flavor of the filling, the crisp and flaky filo crust, combined with the tangy sour cream and dill are always met by exclamations of delight—and requests for the recipe.

This recipe makes several rolls of strudel and each slices into six to eight servings. Wrapped in foil before baking, it will freeze beautifully for several weeks.

It's a treasure to stash away for unexpected company or to include in a special dinner menu.

1 package filo dough
1 pound unsalted butter, melted and clarified (see page 368)
2 cups fine bread crumbs
Cabbage Filling (recipe follows)
Sour Cream and Dill Sauce (recipe follows)
Sprigs of dill

Place a damp towel on a work area and cover with wax paper. Remove 4 sheets of filo from the package. Keep the remaining sheets covered with wax paper and a damp towel to prevent drying out.

Fold the filo leaves in half like a closed book and unfold one page. Brush with clarified butter and sprinkle lightly with bread crumbs. Continue turning the pages of the filo, brushing with the butter and crumbs until you come to the center. Do not brush the butter in the center yet. Close the second half of the book over the first and work backward: Open the last leaf and continue spreading the butter and crumbs until you come back to the center. Now brush the center with the butter and sprinkle with crumbs.

Depending on how thick a strudel you want, spread 2 to 3 cups of the Cabbage Filling lengthwise on the open filo book, 2 inches from the edge closest to you and 2 inches from the sides. Cover the filling with the closest edge and fold the sides over. Brush the sides with butter and continue rolling up the filo, jelly-roll fashion.

Cover a baking sheet with foil. Brush the foil with butter. Place the strudel on the foil, seam side down, and brush it with butter. Refrigerate uncovered until the butter hardens, 15 to 20 minutes. Repeat with remaining filo and filling. (The strudel can be frozen at this point.)

Preheat the oven to 350°F. Bake the strudel for 45 minutes, or until golden brown. Slice immediately and serve hot with Sour Cream Dill Sauce and garnish with sprigs of dill.

## CABBAGE FILLING

¼ pound unsalted butter or margarine
¼ cup flour
2 tablespoons paprika
3 cups finely chopped onions
2 medium heads of cabbage shredded (4 quarts)

Melt the butter in a large heavy saucepan over medium heat. Add the flour and stir until dissolved. Add the paprika and mix well. Add the onions and continue cooking for 15 minutes, stirring occasionally to avoid sticking.

Add the cabbage, brown sugar, and salt and pepper to taste. Simmer, partially covered, for 1 hour, or until golden brown. Stir occasionally. Remove from the heat

½ cup dark brown sugar, firmly packed
Salt
Freshly ground black pepper

and cool. This mixture can be made a day ahead and stored, covered, in the refrigerator.

## SOUR CREAM AND DILL SAUCE

2 cups sour cream or non-dairy sour cream
⅛ cup snipped fresh dill

In a bowl, combine the sour cream and dill. Cover and chill.

# SALMON PACKETS IN FOIL WITH VEGETABLES

For holidays or any day, busy people will cherish this recipe. The packets can be quickly assembled in the morning, refrigerated and then baked and served to delighted diners at night.

¼ cup olive oil
3 cups chopped spinach leaves, packed
1 cup minced parsley
Salt
Freshly ground black pepper
8 thick salmon fillets (5 ounces each)
½ cup Garlic Butter (see page 383)
8 basil leaves
2 medium carrots, cut into julienne
2 medium zucchini, cut into julienne
8 lemon slices

Preheat the oven to 450°F. Line a heavy-duty baking sheet with foil and preheat it for 5 minutes.

Cut aluminum foil into 8 pieces, 11 × 12 inches each. Lightly oil the center of each piece. Combine the spinach and parsley. Spread ½ cup of the mixture evenly on the foil. Sprinkle with salt and pepper and top with a salmon fillet. Place 1 tablespoon of the Garlic Butter on the fillet and add a basil leaf. Divide the julienne carrots and zucchini into 8 equal portions and add a layer of each. Place lemon slice on top. Then carefully fold and seal each packet.

Arrange the packets on the baking sheet, seam-side down, in a single layer 1 inch apart. Bake for 5 minutes; carefully turn the packets over and continue baking for 5 minutes more. Serve immediately, either in the packets or on serving plates with the foil removed.

# Lentil and Goat Cheese Salad

I recently discovered a charming little Middle Eastern kosher market. It was an exciting experience—I felt as if I had traveled thousands of miles and was in Israel. The market was stocked with all the interesting foods we had seen in the marketplace in Jerusalem, including varicolored lentils—orange, green, and brown. This salad can be very colorful—a real conversation piece—if you use a variety of lentils.

2 cups assorted lentils
1 teaspoon salt
12 Italian parsley sprigs
12 fresh basil leaves
6 to 8 garlic cloves, unpeeled and crushed
1 carrot, peeled and finely diced
1 red onion, finely diced
1 celery stalk, finely diced
¼ cup olive oil
8 ounces goat cheese
½ cup snipped chives
¼ cup minced parsley

DRESSING

½ cup olive oil
⅓ cup red wine vinegar
Salt
Freshly ground black pepper
Sprigs of watercress for garnish
Sliced tomatoes for garnish

Pick over the lentils thoroughly and rinse them. Then place them in a medium saucepan and add water to cover and the salt. Make a bouquet garni of the parsley, basil, and 4 of the garlic cloves, wrapping and tying it in cheesecloth. Add it to the lentils and bring to a boil; reduce the heat and simmer for 10 minutes. Add the carrot, onion, and celery and simmer for 10 to 15 minutes. Continue cooking the lentils until tender, about 10 minutes more. Add hot water, ¼ cup at a time, to the pot if necessary to keep the lentils from sticking and drying.

Discard the bouquet garni. Toss the lentils with the ¼ cup olive oil and spread them out on a baking sheet to cool to room temperature.

Crumble the goat cheese into a large bowl. Add the lentils. Mince the remaining garlic and combine with the lentils, chives, and parsley. Toss well.

For the dressing, mix the olive oil with the vinegar and salt and pepper to taste. Pour this dressing into the bowl and toss gently until all the ingredients are thoroughly coated. Garnish with sprigs of watercress and sliced tomatoes.

# Two-Tone Strawberry Cheesecake

MAKES ONE 9-INCH CHEESECAKE

3 packages (8 ounces each) cream cheese (see page 22)

1 cup sugar

4 eggs

½ teaspoon almond extract

1 teaspoon strawberry extract

3 tablespoons puréed strawberries

Prebaked Almond Crust (recipe follows)

Sour Cream Topping (recipe follows)

Preheat the oven to 350°F.

In the bowl of an electric mixer, beat the cream cheese, sugar, and eggs until smooth. Blend in the almond and strawberry extracts. Remove 1¾ cups of the cream cheese mixture to a medium bowl; blend in strawberry purée and set aside.

Pour the remaining cream cheese mixture into the baked crust and bake for 10 minutes, when the filling will begin to firm up.

Carefully pour the strawberry-cheese mixture over the partially baked mixture; continue baking for 30 to 40 minutes, until the center is firm. Remove the cheesecake from the oven and spread with the Sour Cream Topping. Bake for 5 minutes more, then cool to room temperature. Cover the cheesecake and refrigerate until chilled.

## ALMOND CRUST

1½ cups sliced almonds

2 tablespoons sugar

2 tablespoons unsalted butter

1 teaspoon almond extract

Preheat the oven to 375°F.

In a processor or blender, process the almonds and sugar until the almonds are coarsely chopped. Add the butter and almond extract and process just until the mixture begins to come together. Press the almond mixture evenly into the bottom and 1 inch up the sides of a 9-inch springform pan. Bake for 5 to 10 minutes, until the crust is golden brown. Cool.

## SOUR CREAM TOPPING

2 cups sour cream

2 tablespoons sugar

1 teaspoon strawberry extract

In a medium bowl, combine the sour cream, sugar, and strawberry extract and blend well. Cover and chill.

# SUKKOTH HARVEST MENU

FOR 10

▼▲▼▲▼▲▼▲▼▲▼▲▼▲▼▲▼

Cornmeal Harvest Rolls

Leek and Rice Salad

Vegetable "Noodles"

Stuffed Cabbage Rolls

Tart Lemon Tart

Tea with Lemon

SUGGESTED BEVERAGE:

California or Israeli Cabernet Sauvignon wine

Holiday meals should include several kinds of grain and a variety of seasonal fresh fruits and vegetables. This inspires a light and nutritious menu, a tribute to the fall harvest.

One of the Sukkoth traditions in Russia and Eastern Europe is the serving of meat wrapped in cabbage, chard, or grape leaves, so I have included a recipe for Stuffed Cabbage Rolls. Vegetable "Noodles" accompany them.

Other special Sukkoth foods are golden harvest rolls, enriched with yellow cornmeal and studded with sesame seeds. A Leek and Rice Salad adds another grain to the menu.

The refreshing dessert is a Tart Lemon Tart, with a tangy filling, glazed lemon slices for garnish, and a sweet flaky pastry. The lemons have a special meaning, symbolizing the ceremonial ethrog, fruit of the citrus tree, which plays an important part in the Sukkoth ritual.

## CORNMEAL HARVEST ROLLS

This easy delicious recipe is perfect for someone with little or no bread-baking experience.

MAKES ABOUT 2 DOZEN

1 package active dry yeast

1½ cups warm water (110 to 115°F)

Pinch of sugar

¼ cup olive oil

3 eggs

1 cup yellow cornmeal

In a small bowl, dissolve the yeast with ½ cup of the warm water and a pinch of sugar until foamy.

In the bowl of an electric mixer, combine the remaining cup of water, olive oil, and 2 of the eggs and beat well. Blend in the yeast mixture, the cornmeal, salt, and flour, 1 cup at a time, until the mixture forms a soft dough. Place on a floured board and knead, adding ad-

1 tablespoon salt
4 to 5 cups all-purpose flour
Sesame seeds

ditional flour as necessary, for 5 to 10 minutes, until the dough is smooth and elastic.

Place the dough in an oiled bowl, oil the top of the dough, cover with a towel, and let rise in a warm place until doubled in bulk, about 1 hour.

Punch the dough down. If it is sticky, knead in additional flour. Pinch off handful-size pieces of the dough and shape them into round or oval rolls. Place them on a foil-lined and greased baking sheet that has been sprinkled with cornmeal. Cover with a towel and let rise in a warm place for 30 to 40 minutes.

Preheat the oven to 350°F. Brush the rolls with the remaining lightly beaten egg and sprinkle with sesame seeds. Bake for 20 to 30 minutes, or until the rolls are lightly browned and sound hollow when tapped. Cool on racks.

## LEEK AND RICE SALAD

6 medium leeks
1 cup water
2 tablespoons olive oil
3 tablespoons uncooked rice
½ teaspoon salt
¼ cup fresh or frozen peas
2 tablespoons chopped parsley
Juice of 1 lemon
Salt
Freshly ground black pepper
Paprika
Fresh cilantro leaves or parsley
Lemon wedges for garnish

Cut off and discard the roots and upper third of the green part of the leeks. Cut each leek lengthwise and hold under running water to remove all traces of sand. Cut the leeks into 1-inch pieces.

Place the leeks in a large saucepan and add the water, oil, rice, and salt. Bring to a boil, then cover and simmer over low heat for 20 minutes, or until the leeks and rice are just done. Stir occasionally to avoid burning.

With a slotted spoon, transfer the leek mixture to a serving bowl; add the peas, parsley, and lemon juice and gently toss to combine. Season to taste with salt and pepper. Sprinkle with paprika and garnish with cilantro or parsley and lemon wedges. Cover with plastic wrap and chill for at least 1 hour.

## VEGETABLE "NOODLES"

Low in calories and carbohydrates, these colorful "noodles" are spiced with a garlicky sauce and make an interesting pasta substitute.

This is a great dish for unexpected company or just when you are tired of meat and potatoes. Prepare the Garlic-Margarine Sauce before boiling the vegetables and then drop the vegetables in the hot sauce, toss, and serve. Try adding or substituting other vegetables, such as parsnips, turnips, mushrooms.

6 large zucchini, unpeeled, cut into julienne
8 large carrots, peeled, and cut into julienne
Garlic-Margarine Sauce (recipe follows)

Bring a large pot of lightly salted water to a boil. Add the zucchini and carrots and cook for 2 to 3 minutes, until tender-crisp. Drain well and add the vegetables to the sauce in the skillet; toss to coat them evenly. Serve on heated plates.

## GARLIC-MARGARINE SAUCE

4 tablespoons unsalted margarine
3 garlic cloves, minced
1 cup Chicken Stock (see page 390)
6 to 8 fresh basil leaves, chopped
Salt
Freshly ground black pepper

In a large skillet, melt the margarine over moderate heat. Add the garlic and sauté until browned and crisp. Add the stock and the basil leaves. Bring to a boil and simmer until the sauce begins to thicken, 2 to 3 minutes. Season to taste with salt and pepper. Set aside.

# STUFFED CABBAGE ROLLS

When you have to cook for a large family during the holidays, lunch and dinner come around very quickly, especially if you are in the synagogue. It is always nice to have a big pot of cabbage rolls to heat and serve the moment you come home. In fact, they are even better made a day ahead and reheated.

2 heads of cabbage

FILLING

2 pounds ground veal, beef, turkey, or chicken
¼ cup grated onion
3 tablespoons minced garlic cloves
1 potato, peeled and grated
¼ cup rice

Cut away the core of each cabbage. In a large saucepan, steam the cabbage over simmering water until soft enough to separate the leaves and fold them without tearing or breaking.

In a large bowl, combine the meat, grated onion, garlic, potato, rice, and eggs and blend well. Season to taste with salt and pepper and set aside.

In a large ovenproof pot, heat the oil and sauté the chopped onions, garlic, celery, and green pepper until tender. Add the tomatoes, tomato sauce, red wine, brown

2 eggs
Salt
Freshly ground black pepper

TOMATO SAUCE

¼ cup safflower or vegetable
    oil
2 onions, chopped
3 tablespoons minced garlic
1 celery stalk, chopped
½ green pepper, chopped
1 can (28 ounces) whole to-
    matoes, coarsely chopped
1 can (8 ounces) tomato sauce
1 cup dry red wine
½ cup brown sugar, packed
Juice of 2 lemons
Salt
Freshly ground black pepper

sugar, and lemon juice. Season to taste with salt, pepper, additional brown sugar, and lemon juice. Bring to a boil and simmer while preparing the cabbage rolls.

Place a cabbage leaf on a flat surface, shape the meat mixture into a ball, place it on the root end of the cabbage leaf, and roll it up to enclose the filling, envelope-style. Place the rolls of cabbage close together submerged in the pot of tomato sauce. Cover the pot, bring to a boil, then reduce the heat and simmer for 1 hour.

Meanwhile, preheat the oven to 350°F. Bake the cabbage rolls for 30 minutes, until flavors blend.

# TART LEMON TART

MAKES ONE 10-INCH TART

¾ cup sugar
1½ teaspoons cornstarch
¼ cup lemon juice
Grated zest of 1 lemon
4 egg yolks
Prebaked Sweet Pastry Tart
    Shell (see page 205)
Sugar-Glazed Lemon Slices
    (recipe follows)

Preheat the oven to 400°F.

In a small bowl, combine the sugar and cornstarch.

In the bowl of an electric mixer, beat the lemon juice, zest, egg yolks, and the sugar-cornstarch mixture until light and foamy, about 5 minutes. Pour this lemon mixture into a prebaked tart shell. Arrange the glazed lemon slices on top in a circular pattern.

Bake until the lemon filling is set, 25 to 30 minutes. If the filling browns too quickly, cover loosely with a piece of foil. Remove from the oven and cool on a rack.

## SUGAR-GLAZED LEMON SLICES

½ cup sugar
⅓ cup water
2 lemons, thinly sliced

In a saucepan, bring the sugar and water to a boil, mixing until the sugar dissolves. Reduce the heat to low, add the lemon slices, and simmer for 5 minutes. With a slotted spoon, transfer to a rack over wax paper to cool.

# HANUKKAH

Hanukkah is a wonderful holiday for children—delicious food, eight days (in December) of gift giving and candle lighting, with one more candle added each night, until all eight are lit.

The candles symbolize the rededication of the ancient temple of Jerusalem, when its menorah miraculously burned for eight days and nights, fueled only by a tiny vial of oil. Thus, foods fried in oil are symbolic of this event. The most popular of the fried delicacies is potato latkes, for which I include my favorite recipes, along with some other more unusual latkes.

Other traditions are dairy foods and candies made of sesame seeds, fruits, and nuts. Eastern European Jewish families use kasha, a form of buckwheat, in many forms during Hanukkah, including blintzes, kreplach, and kasha varnishkes, a dish that combines noodles, onions, and chicken fat with buckwheat groats.

Cookies cut into shapes of stars and dreidels (spinning tops) are also appropriate, and look pretty when decorated with blue and white icing, the Hanukkah colors. Specialty shops carry these cookie cutters, as well as attractive blue and white gift wrapping and decorations.

Then, of course, there is "Hanukkah Gelt," the tradition of giving gifts of money, or candy and cookies wrapped in silver or gold foil to look like money. It's easy to wrap homemade bittersweet chocolate rounds to look like the real thing. Kids love them.

But remember, Hanukkah is not just for children. So plan a latke party for the whole family and celebrate with special foods and decorations for all the eight days.

# HEARTY BRISKET DINNER

FOR 12

This hearty traditional menu will immediately put everybody in a gala mood for Hanukkah. Brisket and latkes are both closely associated with the holiday. And since we generally tend to eat meat less often these days, the succulent, tender brisket comes as a welcome treat. The dried fruit adds just the right holiday touch. So does the Beaujolais Nouveau wine, which is released at this time of the year.

Romanian Noodle Latkes are really different from the usual potato variety. Another unusual treat is the Chopped Chocolate "Ice Cream," made with chunky semisweet chocolate and no dairy ingredients; it literally melts in your mouth. This festive menu ends with an ancient Hanukkah custom—Hot Russian-Style Tea, accompanied by cubes of brandy-soaked sugar that are ignited and dropped into the glass. It's an appropriate conclusion to a meal celebrating the Festival of Lights.

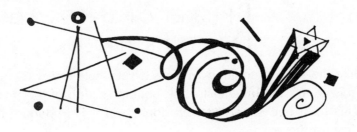

## MARINATED ZUCCHINI SALAD

It is important not to overcook the zucchini. They should be barely tender, still crisp to the bite. When marinating, a few hours in the dressing is enough for the vegetable to absorb the flavor; any more tends to make it soggy.

10 medium zucchini, trimmed
1 red bell pepper, diced
1 green bell pepper, diced
½ cup chopped green onions
  (scallions)
2 tablespoons minced fresh
  parsley
1 tablespoon chopped fresh
  dill
Salt
Freshly ground black pepper
Marinade (recipe follows)

Cut each zucchini lengthwise into 8 slices; cut each slice crosswise in half. Bring a large pot of lightly salted water to a boil. Drop in the zucchini and cook just until tender, 2 to 3 minutes. Drain the zucchini well and place in a large bowl. Add the peppers (reserving 3 tablespoons of each), the green onions, parsley, and dill, and gently toss. Season to taste with salt and pepper. Pour the marinade over the vegetables to moisten. (Save any leftover marinade for future salad-making.) Cover with plastic wrap and chill in the refrigerator for at least 1 hour. Garnish with the reserved diced red and green bell peppers.

## MARINADE

¼ cup white wine vinegar
¼ cup dry sherry or white
  wine
½ cup olive oil
1 garlic clove, minced
½ teaspoon dried tarragon,
  crushed
Pinch of paprika

In a small bowl, combine all the ingredients and blend well.

# BRISKET OF BEEF WITH DRIED FRUIT

If you don't like the idea of cooking with beer, substitute red wine, apple juice, or water. Be sure to ask the butcher for the bottom section of the brisket, which has less fat. This roast is best served well done, and it is important to slice the cooked meat against the grain.

2 tablespoons olive oil
3 garlic cloves, minced
4 medium onions, sliced
1 lean brisket of beef (8
  pounds)
2 cans (12 ounces each) beer
2 tablespoons onion soup mix
2 tablespoons canned tomato
  paste (or 1 tablespoon dou-

Preheat the oven to 500°F.

In a large skillet, heat the oil over medium heat. Add the garlic and onions and sauté until soft, about 5 minutes.

Transfer the garlic and onions to a large roasting pot and place the meat on top, fat side up. Pour in 1 can of beer, cover, and bake for 30 minutes.

In a mixing bowl, stir together the onion soup mix, tomato paste, brown sugar, and hot water to make a paste. Spoon this mixture over the brisket. Surround the meat

ble tomato paste from a
tube)
2 tablespoons brown sugar
4 tablespoons hot water
5 medium carrots, peeled and
thickly sliced
2 parsnips, peeled and thickly
sliced
¼ cup chopped fresh parsley
¼ pound dried pitted prunes
¼ pound dried apricots

with the carrots, parsnips, parsley, and remaining 1 can beer.

Reduce the heat to 325°F, cover, and bake until tender, 2 to 3 hours more; add the prunes and apricots for the last 30 minutes of baking.

# ROMANIAN NOODLE LATKES

These latkes, which are based on egg noodles, are delicious served with Glazed Apple Slices. If you wish, you can also bake the mixture kugel-style, adding 1 or 2 additional eggs and 2 or 3 tablespoons of raisins. Spoon into a greased baking dish or muffin pan. Bake at 375°F for 20 to 30 minutes, or until crusty.

MAKES ABOUT 30

8 ounces fine egg noodles
2 tablespoons unsalted margarine
Vegetable oil
1 small onion, finely chopped
2 eggs
Salt
Freshly ground black pepper

Cook the noodles according to the package directions and drain well. Transfer to a large bowl, add the margarine, and blend well. Set aside.

In a small skillet, heat 2 tablespoons of the oil over medium heat and sauté the onion until tender, about 5 minutes. Add the onion to the noodles. Blend in the eggs and salt and pepper to taste.

In a large heavy skillet, heat ¼ inch of the oil over medium heat. Drop the noodle mixture by tablespoons into the hot oil, flattening each spoonful with the back of the spoon to form a thin latke. Fry on both sides until golden brown and crisp, about 5 minutes a side. (Do not turn the latkes until the first side is golden and the top is firmly set.)

# GLAZED APPLE SLICES

This is a versatile recipe, simple to make and beautiful to look at—an elegant change from old-fashioned applesauce. It makes a great light dessert for informal meals, or a special treat for family breakfasts. The translucent slices can be used as a pie filling, or in open-face tarts. Or just drain the slices, add nuts and raisins, and you have instant strudel filling!

½ cup sugar
½ cup orange marmalade
½ cup orange juice
6 large Golden Delicious apples, peeled, cored, and thinly sliced
Juice and grated zest of 1 lemon

In a large heavy skillet, combine the sugar, marmalade, and orange juice. Cook over medium heat, stirring until the sugar and marmalade dissolve. Bring the syrup to a boil, then reduce the heat and simmer 3 to 4 minutes, just until it begins to thicken.

Place the apple slices in a large bowl and toss with lemon juice to prevent them from discoloring. Add the apples, lemon zest, and lemon juice to the syrup in the skillet and toss to coat the apples. Simmer, covered, for 10 to 15 minutes, until the apples are soft. Transfer to a glass bowl and cool to room temperature. Cover with plastic wrap and chill in the refrigerator. Serve with Romanian Noodle Latkes.

# CHOPPED CHOCOLATE ''ICE CREAM''

Nobody will believe that this dessert contains no forbidden ingredients to prevent it from accompanying a kosher meat dinner. Instead of mixing chocolate chips or grated chocolate into this frozen dessert, I pour melted hot chocolate into the cold mixture; it breaks up into very thin pieces, which melt on your tongue like good chocolate chips should.

MAKES ABOUT 1 QUART

4 egg whites
¼ teaspoon cream of tartar
¼ teaspoon salt
¼ cup powdered sugar
2 cups nondairy topping mix

In a large bowl, beat the egg whites until foamy. Add the cream of tartar and salt and beat until soft peaks form. Gradually add the sugar, beating just until the peaks are stiff and shiny. Do not overbeat or this meringue will become too stiff to fold.

½ cup unsweetened cocoa powder

1 tablespoon instant coffee

1 tablespoon vanilla extract

2 tablespoons coffee liqueur (optional)

8 ounces semisweet chocolate, broken into small pieces (1 cup)

Beat the nondairy topping until thick. Add the cocoa powder, instant coffee, vanilla, and liqueur and beat just until stiff; again, do not overbeat. Fold the meringue into the cocoa mixture and place in a freezer-proof bowl. Cover and leave in the freezer just until ice crystals form, 30 to 40 minutes.

Melt the chocolate in a double boiler over simmering water. Carefully pour and fold the hot melted chocolate into the ice mixture; small chunks of chocolate will form. Cover the bowl and return it to the freezer. Freeze the dessert 3 to 4 hours.

# LORI'S CHOCOLATE HAZELNUT COOKIES

Imagine a delicious blend of hazelnuts, currant jam, and chocolate in a brownie-like cookie. This recipe comes from Lori Gross, a longtime friend and brilliant cook, who learned to make the cookies in her native Germany.

They are very thin, with a dense chocolate flavor and chewy texture, the result of folding meringue into the batter. They are so rich that butter is not missed in the ingredients, and are certainly festive enough for a gala Hanukkah party.

MAKES ABOUT 60

5 ounces unsalted margarine

½ cup sugar

4 eggs, separated

8 ounces semisweet chocolate, grated

1½ cups hazelnuts (filberts), roasted (see page 24) and ground

1 cup flour

1½ cups currant jelly

¼ cup chocolate sprinkles

Preheat the oven to 350°F.

In a large mixing bowl, cream the margarine, sugar, and egg yolks until well blended. Add the grated chocolate and hazelnuts and mix well. Add the flour and stir until well blended. Beat the egg whites until stiff peaks form and carefully fold them into the batter.

Lightly grease two 9 × 13-inch jelly roll baking sheets. Spread the batter out in a thin layer on each baking sheet. Bake for 20 minutes. Do not overbake—the cookies should be moist inside. Remove the pans from the oven and spread the currant jelly over the entire surface. Then cover the jelly evenly with the chocolate sprinkles. Cut into 2-inch squares and cool on wire racks.

# HOT RUSSIAN-STYLE TEA

According to ancient Russian custom, songs were sung after the Hanukkah meal and guests were served glasses of hot tea. Then brandy-soaked sugar cubes were passed to each guest in individual teaspoons. A lighted candle was handed from person to person to ignite the cubes, which were then dropped into the glasses of tea.

Russians like their tea with lemon and served so hot that they often wrap a napkin around the glass to keep their fingers from burning.

**HOW TO BREW A GOOD POT OF TEA**

Rinse a 1-quart teapot made of glass, china, or earthenware. Pour 1 cup of boiling water into the pot, swirl it around to heat the pot, then pour it out. Add the tea, allowing 1 teaspoon of loose tea or 1 tea bag for each cup of water, plus 1 for the pot. Pour boiling water onto the tea leaves. Steep for 5 minutes. Pour out a little tea into a glass, look at it, and taste it: If it is not strong enough, let it steep a little longer; if too strong, add more boiling water.

# NOUVELLE HANUKKAH DINNER

FOR 8

Potato latkes and other foods fried in oil are symbolic of the miracle of the one-day supply of oil that burned for eight days in the ancient temple of Jerusalem. This dinner includes three fried foods—but why not? We can indulge once a year in the name of Jewish custom.

The potato pancake triangles are a change from the conventional latkes. I discovered them at the Domaine Chandon Winery in northern California, where they were served with a spectacular grilled fresh tuna by the talented French chef, Philippe Jeanty. The plate was garnished with a tomato rose and a cold horseradish and sour cream sauce, topped with chopped cilantro.

Begin this festive meal with a crisp green salad, garnished with deep-fried parsnip chips, followed by bowls of steaming Corn and Cheese Soup, an old family Hanukkah tradition. For dessert, enjoy a creamy and pungent Ginger Ice Cream and four holiday cookies that you can bake with the help of children and grandchildren—for the whole family to enjoy and share during the entire eight days of Hanukkah.

## LETTUCE BOUQUET SALAD WITH FRIED PARSNIP CHIPS

My favorite simple green salad combines three kinds of lettuce—Bibb, romaine, and red-leaf. Tossed with a light, tangy Lemon Vinaigrette Dressing, it complements a fish dinner perfectly.

1 head of Bibb lettuce

1 head of romaine lettuce

1 head of red-leaf lettuce

Lemon Vinaigrette Dressing
(recipe follows)

Deep-Fried Parsnip Chips
(recipe follows)

Tear the leaves from the lettuces, wash and wrap in damp paper towels, and store in plastic bags in the refrigerator until ready to assemble the salad.

In a large salad bowl, toss the lettuces together. Pour enough Lemon Vinaigrette Dressing over the lettuces to coat evenly. Spoon onto individual chilled salad plates and sprinkle generously with Deep-Fried Parsnip Chips.

## LEMON VINAIGRETTE DRESSING

¼ cup lemon juice

2 garlic cloves, peeled

½ teaspoon powdered mustard

½ teaspoon paprika

½ teaspoon sugar

¾ teaspoon ground cumin

1 tablespoons grated lemon peel

2 tablespoons chopped fresh parsley

1 cup olive oil

Salt

Freshly ground black pepper

In the bowl of a processor or blender, place the lemon juice, garlic, mustard, paprika, sugar, and ground cumin. Blend for 30 seconds. Add the lemon peel and parsley and, with the motor running, gradually add the oil in a steady stream. Season to taste with salt and pepper. Transfer to a glass mixing bowl, cover with plastic wrap, and chill in the refrigerator.

## DEEP-FRIED PARSNIP CHIPS

Though these crisp sweet chips are used here as a salad garnish, almost like croutons, they are also delicious served alone as a snack with white wine or champagne when guests arrive.

3 large parsnips, peeled and very thinly sliced

Vegetable oil for deep-frying

In a deep-fryer or a deep heavy pot, heat 3 inches of oil to a temperature of 375°F. In small batches, drop the sliced parsnips into the hot oil and fry until crisp and golden brown, 2 to 3 minutes. Drain well on paper towels.

# CORN AND CHEESE SOUP

2 tablespoons unsalted butter
½ cup minced onion
1 can (17 ounces) corn kernels, or 2 cups fresh corn removed from the cob
1 red bell pepper, finely diced
1 can (17 ounces) cream-style corn
3 cups milk
Salt
Freshly ground black pepper
½ pound jack cheese, diced
Fresh cilantro

In a saucepan, heat the butter and sauté the onion briefly. Add the corn and cook slowly over low heat for 10 minutes. Add the red bell pepper and cook another 5 minutes. Add the cream-style corn and milk and simmer over low heat for 15 minutes. Season to taste with salt and pepper. Sprinkle the diced cheese on the bottom of heated soup bowls and ladle soup over cheese. Garnish with cilantro.

# PHILIPPE JEANTY'S POTATO PANCAKES WITH GRILLED FRESH TUNA

### POTATO PANCAKES

2 large potatoes, scrubbed and finely grated
1 large onion, finely chopped
2 tablespoons minced chives
Salt
Freshly ground black pepper
4 eggs
Olive oil for frying

### SOUR CREAM SAUCE

2 cups sour cream
⅓ cup Japanese horseradish purée

### GRILLED FRESH TUNA

4 pounds tuna fillets
½ cup olive oil
Chopped cilantro

Combine the potatoes and onion with the chives and salt and pepper to taste. Squeeze excess liquid from the mixture until it feels fairly dry. Stir in the eggs.

Heat 2 tablespoons of oil in a 6-inch skillet over moderate to high heat. Spoon in enough potato mixture to fill the skillet about ½ inch deep; press with the back of a spoon to spread it evenly. Cook until the bottom is completely brown and crisp, 3 to 5 minutes, then with a spatula turn the pancake and cook the other side. Drain well on paper towels. Cut the pancake into 3 equal triangles and place them on a baking sheet. Repeat with the remaining potato mixture to make 3 more pancakes. Set aside until just before serving.

For the sauce, blend the sour cream and horseradish purée in a small glass bowl. Cover with plastic wrap and chill until ready to serve.

Preheat the oven to 450 or 500°F for the potato pancakes.

You can cook the tuna on a grill or in a heavy ridged

grill pan or cast-iron skillet. Preheat the grill until very hot, or heat 2 to 3 tablespoons of olive oil in the skillet over moderate to high heat.

Cut the tuna fillets into pieces 3 inches long and 1½ inches wide and thick. Coat them with oil.

Just before serving, bake the pancakes 4 to 5 minutes, until hot and crisp.

Grill or sauté the tuna on both sides just until seared golden, 1 to 2 minutes a side; the insides should remain pink and fairly cool. (If you prefer your tuna cooked through, you may grill it a minute or two longer, but do not let it dry out.) Slice the tuna into ¼-inch-thick rectangles.

Place the slices of tuna on each plate, cut sides up, in 3 rows radiating like spokes from the center. Space 3 hot potato triangles between the rows of tuna, pointing toward the center. Garnish the potatoes with the sour cream sauce and cilantro.

# GINGER ICE CREAM

MAKES ABOUT 1 QUART

2 cups milk
2 cups cream
1 cup sugar
1 teaspoon ground ginger
8 egg yolks
1 jar (12 ounces) ginger marmalade
½ teaspoon vanilla extract
Crystallized ginger, for garnish

In a large heavy pot, combine the milk, cream, ½ cup of the sugar, and the ground ginger. Bring to a boil over medium heat, stirring until the sugar has dissolved.

In the bowl of an electric mixer, beat the egg yolks, gradually adding the remaining ½ cup sugar, until light-colored and thick. Pour a little of the milk mixture into the egg mixture to warm it; then pour the egg mixture through a sieve or strainer and return it to the pot with the milk mixture. Simmer over medium heat, stirring frequently with a wooden spoon, until the mixture is thick enough to coat the spoon.

Transfer the custard to a large heatproof bowl set inside a larger bowl of ice cubes, mixing until cool. Blend in the ginger marmalade and vanilla. Cover with plastic wrap and chill in the refrigerator. Pour into the canister of an ice cream maker and freeze according to manufacturer's directions. Or place in the freezer and freeze until firm, 3 to 6 hours, stirring occasionally with a fork to break up ice crystals. Garnish with crystallized ginger.

# Hanukkah Cutout Cookies

Our family tradition has always included baking lots of Hanukkah cookies. We had a special set of cookie cutters that formed perfect stars, dreidels, and Hanukkiahs. Sometimes we just made round cookies and frosted them with Blue and White Icing.

MAKES 5 TO 6 DOZEN

½ cup vegetable shortening
1 cup sugar
2 eggs
1 teaspoon vanilla extract
1 tablespoon orange juice
2 cups flour
2 teaspoons baking powder
½ teaspoon salt
Colored sugars (optional)
Blue and White Icing (recipe follows)

In the large bowl of an electric mixer, cream the shortening and sugar. Beat in the eggs. Add the vanilla and orange juice and mix well. Combine the flour, baking powder, and salt and blend into the batter until smooth.

Preheat the oven to 400°F.

Divide the dough into 2 or 3 portions. On a generously floured board, roll out each portion ¼ inch thick. Cut out with flour-dipped cookie cutters, place the cookies on ungreased baking sheets, and if you like, sprinkle with yellow- or orange-colored sugar. Bake for 5 to 7 minutes, or until the edges are lightly browned. Cool. Outline edges with Blue and White Icing, if you wish.

## BLUE AND WHITE ICING

MAKES 2 CUPS

1 tablespoon lemon juice
1 tablespoon cream or milk
2 cups powdered sugar
2 or 3 drops of blue food coloring

In a bowl, blend the lemon juice, cream, and sugar until creamy. Add additional cream if needed to thin icing. Divide the icing in half. Add food coloring to half of the icing and mix until completely blended. Place each icing in a pastry bag (with star tip) and pipe onto cooled cookies.

# HANUKKAH SHORTBREAD

MAKES ABOUT 4 DOZEN

2½ cups flour
¾ cup sugar
½ pound unsalted butter or
   margarine, cut into pieces
1 teaspoon almond extract
1 cup finely chopped almonds

In the bowl of an electric mixer, blend the flour and sugar until crumbly. Add the butter and almond extract and blend until the dough begins to come together.

Preheat the oven to 300°F.

Divide the dough into 3 portions; knead and shape each into a sausagelike roll about 1½ inches in diameter. Spread the almonds on a work surface and coat the rolls of dough in them, pressing firmly until completely covered with almonds. Slice each roll into ¼-inch cookies and arrange them about ½ inch apart on oiled foil-lined baking sheets. Bake for 15 to 20 minutes, or until lightly browned. Cool on racks.

# RUSSIAN TEA COOKIES

MAKES ABOUT 5 DOZEN

½ pound unsalted butter or
   margarine
½ cup powdered sugar
1 teaspoon vanilla extract
2½ cups flour
½ teaspoon salt
1 cup walnuts, chopped
Powdered sugar for coating

Preheat the oven to 400°F.

In the large bowl of an electric mixer, blend the butter and ½ cup of the powdered sugar until fluffy. Mix in the vanilla. Add the flour and salt and blend thoroughly. Mix in the walnuts. Work the dough with your hands into a smooth ball.

Pinch off and roll the dough with your hands into 1-inch balls. Place them about 1 inch apart on ungreased baking sheets and bake for 15 minutes, or until the bottoms are golden brown. Cool slightly, then roll in sifted powdered sugar. Let them cool and roll them in sugar again.

# Chocolate-Almond Macaroons

I met Lori Tannenbaum when she was the pastry chef at Michael's Restaurant, in Santa Monica, when I asked about these sensational cookies. I spent the morning with her and she shared her expertise. I have translated them for a home kitchen and am confident that once you have made and mastered this recipe it will be one of your favorites. They are light, airy, chewy, chocolaty, what more can I say . . .

MAKES ABOUT 30

11 egg whites
3 cups granulated sugar
¾ cup cocoa powder
¾ cup powdered sugar
2 tablespoons apricot jam
2 teaspoons vanilla extract
4 cups (1 pound) toasted sliced almonds (see page 24)

In a large mixing bowl, over medium-high heat, beat the egg whites and sugar with a whisk until thick, about 5 minutes.

Transfer to the bowl of an electric mixer and beat with a whisk attachment until the mixture is the consistency of marshmallow sauce, about 5 minutes.

Preheat the oven to 250°F.

Sift together the cocoa and powdered sugar onto wax paper. When the sugar and egg white mixture is very thick, add the apricot jam and vanilla. Then add the cocoa mixture and blend thoroughly. Fold in the toasted almonds.

Dip an ice cream scoop in water and scoop batter onto brown-paper-lined baking sheets, 2 inches apart. Bake for 45 minutes, or until the cookies are dry on the outside and a toothpick inserted into the center comes out with sticky chocolate around it.

# ALL-AMERICAN HANUKKAH LUNCH

FOR 12

Carnival Ribbon Rolls
(see page 110)

Down-Home Glazed
Meat Loaf

Fresh Tomato Chili Sauce

Mini-Potato Latkes

Apple-Cranberry Slices

3-Cs Coleslaw

Carnival Ribbon Rolls
(see page 110)

Old-Fashioned Jelly
Cookies

Chocolate Nut Brownies

Chocolate Hanukkah Gelt

Frozen Chocolate Banana
on a Stick

SUGGESTED BEVERAGES:

Bordeaux or Burgundy
wine and apple cider

This party was planned for my children, grandchildren, and some friends. The menu accents the new trend for "diner" food, a return to all-American favorites like chili, meat loaf, pies, Jello, and shakes. Naturally, children of all ages enjoy this kind of food.

My meat loaf is moist and spicy, wonderful hot or cold. It combines beef and veal with some crisp vegetables and an interesting glaze. Served with this are lots of potato latkes, speedily prepared with a food processor, along with bowls of Perfect Pink Applesauce and homemade chili sauce, made from scratch with fresh tomatoes. Coleslaw, another diner favorite, adds a crunchy medley of fresh vegetables.

Desserts include chewy Chocolate Nut Brownies, Old-Fashioned Jelly Cookies, and foil-wrapped Chocolate Hanukkah Gelt. Everybody gets some cookies to take home, wrapped in blue and white Hanukkah paper.

## DOWN-HOME GLAZED MEAT LOAF

MAKES 1 LARGE OR 2 SMALL LOAVES

2 pounds ground veal
2 pounds ground beef
3 eggs
1 medium onion, grated
1 medium potato, grated

In a large bowl, combine the veal, beef, eggs, grated onion, potato, zucchini, and 6 minced garlic cloves; mix well. Add 2 tablespoons of the red wine, the rice, cumin, oregano, basil, salt, and pepper.

Preheat the oven to 350°F.

1 medium zucchini, un-
   peeled, grated
8 garlic cloves, minced
1 cup dry red wine
3 tablespoons uncooked rice
1½ teaspoons ground cumin
1½ teaspoons dried oregano,
   crushed
1½ teaspoons dried basil,
   crushed
1 tablespoon salt
1 teaspoon freshly ground
   black pepper
2 tablespoons safflower or
   vegetable oil
2 large onions, sliced
4 hard-boiled eggs (see page
   23), peeled
¾ cup catsup

Heat the oil in a skillet and sauté the remaining 2 minced garlic cloves and the sliced onions until soft; transfer them to a large roaster. Shape half the meat mixture into a flat loaf, 5 × 12 inches, on top of the onions in the roaster. Place hard-boiled eggs lengthwise along the center of the molded meat loaf. Mold the remaining meat mixture on top of the eggs, pressing to make a firm loaf. Blend the remaining wine with 2 tablespoons of the catsup. Pour the wine mixture around the meat loaf. Spread the remaining catsup on top of the meat loaf, as if you were frosting a cake. Cover and bake for 1½ to 2 hours, until baked through.

# Fresh Tomato Chili Sauce

MAKES ABOUT 2 CUPS

6 large ripe tomatoes, peeled
   and coarsely chopped
1 large red bell pepper,
   stemmed, seeded, and
   coarsely chopped
1 large green bell pepper,
   stemmed, seeded, and
   coarsely chopped
1 serrano chili, stemmed,
   seeded, and minced
1 large onion, finely chopped
1 garlic clove, minced
½ cup cider vinegar
¼ cup sugar
1 tablespoon tomato paste
½ teaspoon ground ginger
¼ teaspoon ground cloves
¼ teaspoon ground cinnamon
Salt
Freshly ground black pepper

In a large heavy pot, put the tomatoes, peppers, chili, onion, garlic, vinegar, sugar, and tomato paste. Mix well. Bring to a boil and simmer, partially covered, for 30 minutes, stirring occasionally. Blend in the ginger, cloves, and cinnamon and season to taste with salt and pepper. Simmer for 30 minutes more, or until the sauce thickens.

Cool and pour into a glass bowl or jar. Cover with plastic wrap or a lid and chill. This keeps for at least 1 week in the refrigerator. It can be stored in the freezer.

# MINI-POTATO LATKES

For thinner, crispier latkes, add one or two additional eggs. (See "Latke Hints," page 97.)

MAKES ABOUT 6 DOZEN

4 large potatoes, grated
1 onion, grated
3 eggs
Vegetable oil
⅓ cup flour
1 teaspoon baking powder
Salt
Freshly ground black pepper

In a large bowl, combine the potatoes, onion, eggs, and 1 tablespoon oil. Add the flour and baking powder and season to taste with salt and pepper.

In a large heavy skillet, heat ¼ inch of oil. With a teaspoon, spoon the batter into the hot oil and flatten each spoonful with the back of the spoon to make small, thin latkes. Cook for about 2 minutes a side, turning only once, until golden brown. Drain well on paper towels.

# APPLE-CRANBERRY SLICES

½ cup cranberry juice
½ cup raspberry jelly
⅓ cup sugar
6 large tart pippin or Granny Smith apples, peeled, cored, and thinly sliced
Juice and zest of 2 lemons

In a large heavy saucepan, combine the cranberry juice, jelly, and sugar. Cook over moderate heat, stirring until the jelly and sugar have dissolved. Bring the syrup to a boil and simmer for 2 to 3 minutes.

Put the apple slices in a large bowl and toss them with the lemon juice and zest. Add them to the jelly mixture and toss to coat evenly. Simmer until the apples are tender, stirring occasionally. Let them cool.

Transfer the glazed apples with their sauce to a large bowl, cover with plastic wrap, and refrigerate until ready to serve.

# 3-Cs Coleslaw

4 cups shredded cabbage (1
    small head)
1 cup shredded carrots (3 or 4
    medium)
3 celery stalks, thinly sliced
¾ cup mayonnaise
2 tablespoons honey
2 tablespoons lemon juice
½ teaspoon celery seed
½ teaspoon mustard seed
Salt
Freshly ground black pepper

In a large salad bowl, toss together the cabbage, carrots,
and celery.

In a mixing bowl, stir together the mayonnaise, honey,
lemon juice, celery seed, and mustard seed.

Just before serving, toss the cabbage mixture with the
dressing. Season to taste with salt and pepper.

# Old-Fashioned Jelly Cookies

MAKES ABOUT 3½ DOZEN

1 cup vegetable shortening
1 cup dark brown sugar,
    packed
2 eggs, separated
1 teaspoon vanilla extract
2 cups flour
½ teaspoon salt
2 cups coarsely chopped wal-
    nuts
Assorted preserves: straw-
    berry, red raspberry, and
    apricot

Preheat the oven to 350°F.

In a large bowl, cream the shortening and brown sugar
until light and fluffy. Add the egg yolks and vanilla and
blend until smooth. Add the flour and salt and blend until smooth. (At this stage, you can wrap the dough in
plastic wrap and a plastic bag and store it in the refrigerator or freezer.)

Pull off small pieces of dough, shaping each into a
¾-inch ball; dip each ball in lightly beaten egg whites
and roll it in chopped nuts. Place the balls on foil-lined
greased baking sheets and gently press an indentation in
the center of each ball with your finger or a thimble.
Bake for 10 minutes. Carefully press down each indentation again and continue baking for 5 minutes more, or
until golden brown. Cool on racks.

Fill the center of each cookie with a dollop of preserves.

# Chocolate Nut Brownies

MAKES 16 BROWNIES

¼ pound unsalted margarine
1 cup sugar
2 eggs
1 teaspoon vanilla extract
1 cup flour
1 teaspoon baking soda
Pinch of salt
4 ounces semisweet chocolate, melted (see page 21)
1 tablespoon strong coffee
¼ cup coarsely chopped pecans
3 ounces pecans, finely ground
16 pecan halves

Preheat the oven to 350°F.

In the large mixing bowl of an electric mixer, beat the margarine and sugar until well blended. Add the eggs and vanilla and beat well.

Combine the flour, baking soda, and salt. Combine the chocolate and coffee and add to the margarine mixture alternately with the flour mixture. Fold in the coarsely chopped pecans.

Grease an 8-inch-square ovenproof baking dish and sprinkle evenly with the finely ground pecans. Spoon in the batter and spread it evenly. Place the pecan halves evenly spaced, 2 inches apart, on top of the batter. Bake for 30 minutes, until a toothpick inserted into the center comes out dry and the cake begins to come away from the sides of the pan. Cool on a wire rack and cut into 2-inch squares.

# Chocolate Hanukkah Gelt

16 ounces semisweet chocolate, melted (see page 21)

Using a teaspoon, spoon coin-size dollops of melted chocolate onto wax-paper-lined baking sheets. Refrigerate until set. Wrap in silver or gold foil and store in the refrigerator.

# Frozen Chocolate Banana on a Stick

When we lived on our ranch in Topanga and the kids were young, I kept a constant supply of wax-paper-wrapped bananas on sticks, with or without chocolate coating. They could just open the freezer to find a ready-made dessert.

Wooden sticks are available at the butcher department of most supermarkets—
or you can substitute the thinner wooden skewers that are used for shish kebabs.

8 bananas, peeled and cut in
half crosswise

2 pounds semisweet choco-
late, melted (see page 21)

Chopped nuts, candy sprinkles, or chocolate sprinkles
for garnish

Push each wooden skewer through the center of the cut
end of the banana, about halfway into its length. Do not
push too far or the banana will crack. Wrap in wax paper like a bon bon, crimping and twisting the paper around
both ends. Freeze for at least 6 hours or overnight.

Unwrap bananas, and using a spatula or flat knife,
coat each frozen banana with the warm melted chocolate. If you like, dip the chocolate-coated bananas in nuts,
sprinkles, or other garnishes. Rewrap the bananas in the
wax paper and return to the freezer for at least 1 hour.

BONUS RECIPES:

# LATKES

Apple Dessert Latkes

Cheese Latkes with Port
Wine Sauce

Classic Potato Latkes

Food Processor Latkes

Mini-Potato Latkes (see
page 92)

Raised Potato Latkes

Romanian Noodle Latkes
(see page 79)

Salmon Latkes

Sesame-Potato Latkes

Sweet Potato Dessert
Latkes

Zucchini and Cheese
Latkes

Here are some old latke recipes and some new ones
to try, and some handy hints. There is no need
to stop with potato latkes, because Jewish people all over
the world have other unusual and exotic recipes. This
collection of recipes allows more than one kind of latke
for each of the eight nights of Hanukkah.

# APPLE DESSERT LATKES

Lighter and sweeter than most latkes, these dessert confections are more like fritters. They make a lovely addition to a Hanukkah lunch or brunch. And they're just as welcome for a warm winter dessert at any time.

MAKES 2 DOZEN

2 eggs, separated
½ cup milk or water
1 cup flour
1 tablespoon sugar
¼ teaspoon salt
1 tablespoon unsalted butter or margarine, melted
1 tablespoon lemon juice
Vegetable oil
3 or 4 medium apples, peeled, cored, and thinly sliced
Powdered sugar

Beat the egg yolks until light. Blend in the milk. Stir in the flour, sugar, and salt. Add the butter and lemon juice and beat until smooth. Beat the egg whites until stiff peaks form and fold them into the egg yolk mixture.

In a large heavy skillet, heat ¼ inch of oil. Dip each apple slice into the batter. Lift out with a fork and fry in the hot oil until browned on both sides. Drain on paper towels. Just before serving, sprinkle with powdered sugar and your favorite preserves.

# CHEESE LATKES WITH PORT WINE SAUCE

MAKES ABOUT 2 DOZEN

1 cup hoop cheese, farmer cheese, or small curd cottage cheese
3 eggs
1 cup flour
1 tablespoon sugar
¾ cup milk
½ teaspoon salt
Vegetable oil
Port Wine Sauce (recipe follows)

In the large bowl of an electric mixer or processor, beat the hoop cheese until smooth. Add the eggs, flour, sugar, milk, and salt. Blend well.

In a large heavy skillet, heat ¼ inch of oil. With a tablespoon, spoon the cheese mixture into the hot oil and fry each latke until golden brown on both sides. Drain on paper towels. Serve with Port Wine Sauce.

# PORT WINE SAUCE

MAKES 2 CUPS

1½ cups port or Concord grape wine
½ cup sugar
1 tablespoon grated orange zest

In a heavy saucepan, bring the wine and sugar to a boil, stirring until the sugar dissolves. Add the zest and simmer until the sauce is reduced by a third. Serve hot or cold, pouring from a pitcher.

---

**LATKE HINTS:**

Latkes are best fried in a Teflon pan as close to serving time as possible. Keep the first batches warm in a low oven (200°F) while cooking the remaining batter. They can also be frozen with good results.

1. For potato latkes: Before grating the potatoes, grate the onions and have everything ready to go, so the potatoes don't stand around any longer than necessary. Add a pinch of baking soda to the potato and onion mixture to help keep the potatoes white.

2. When refrigerating batter for later use: Sprinkle the entire surface with flour. When ready to begin frying the latkes, remove the flour with a large spoon and discard.

3. For crisper latkes: Fry them in very hot oil, turning only once. Latkes absorb oil that is only moderately hot, and they get soggy when they're turned too often.

4. To freeze latkes: Fry them on each side until only slightly browned. Drain on paper towels. Place them in single layers on baking sheets lined with cloth kitchen towels and freeze. Remove them from the baking sheets and place in plastic bags. Store in the freezer. To serve the latkes, place them still frozen on foil-lined baking sheets and bake at 400 to 450°F for 5 to 10 minutes, until crisp.

# CLASSIC POTATO LATKES

Florine Sikking, a longtime friend, invites friends over and has a dinner for twenty-four every night of Hanukkah. Her mother fries the thinnest, crispest, best latkes in the world. Her rule is one egg for every potato. And every night they have a contest to see who eats the most latkes. This is her recipe.

MAKES 3 DOZEN

4 potatoes, peeled
1 large onion, grated
1 tablespoon lemon juice
4 eggs
3 tablespoons flour
1 teaspoon salt
Freshly ground black pepper
Vegetable oil

Grate the potatoes, using a processor or a fine shredder. Immediately transfer them to a large bowl and add the onion, lemon juice, eggs, flour, and salt and pepper to taste. Mix well.

In a large heavy skillet, heat ⅛ inch of oil. With a tablespoon, spoon the batter into the hot oil and flatten the latkes with the back of the spoon. Cook for 3 to 5 minutes a side, turning only once, until golden brown. Drain on paper towels and then serve immediately, with applesauce, sour cream, sugar, or preserves.

# FOOD PROCESSOR LATKES

MAKES ABOUT 3 DOZEN

4 potatoes
1 onion, quartered
2 eggs
⅓ cup flour
1 teaspoon baking powder
Salt
Freshly ground black pepper
Vegetable oil

Cut the potatoes to fit the feed tube of a processor. Grate them, using very light pressure. Place the potatoes in a colander and rinse under cold water to remove the starch and to keep them from turning dark. Grate the onion in the processor. Leaving the onion in the bowl, insert the steel blade in the processor. Add the grated potatoes, eggs, flour, and baking powder. Pulse the machine briefly, a few times, just until mixed. Season to taste with salt and pepper.

In a large heavy skillet, heat ¼ inch of oil. With a tablespoon, spoon the potato mixture into the hot oil and flatten the latkes with the back of the spoon for thinner latkes. Brown well on both sides. Drain on paper towels. Serve immediately.

# RAISED POTATO LATKES

MAKES ABOUT 3 DOZEN SMALL LATKES

3 pounds potatoes, peeled
and grated
1 large apple, peeled, cored,
and grated
3 eggs, separated
1 cup flour
½ teaspoon salt
Vegetable oil

In a large bowl, combine the potatoes, apple, and egg yolks. Add the flour and blend well.

Beat the egg whites until stiff peaks form and fold them into the potato mixture. Add salt.

In a large heavy skillet, heat ¼ inch of oil. With a tablespoon, spoon the potato mixture into the hot oil and fry on both sides until golden brown. Drain on paper towels. Serve with sour cream and sugar.

# SALMON LATKES

Both my mother and mother-in-law served Salmon Latkes all year for a simple dairy lunch or dinner. Although canned salmon is much more expensive than it was in the old days, this is still an inexpensive recipe, ideal for a Hanukkah lunch.

MAKES ABOUT 2 DOZEN

1 can (15½ ounces) red or
pink salmon, skin and
bones removed, juices re-
served
2 eggs
⅔ cup finely chopped onion
½ cup bread crumbs, or
matzo meal
1 tablespoon fresh minced dill
(optional)
Salt
Freshly grated black pepper
Vegetable oil

In a large bowl, combine the salmon with its juices, the eggs, onion, bread crumbs, and dill. Season to taste with salt and pepper and mix well. Set aside for 15 minutes. With wet hands, shape the mixture into latkes.

In a large heavy skillet, heat ⅛ inch of oil. Fry the latkes until golden brown on both sides. Drain on paper towels. Serve hot or cold.

# Sesame-Potato Latkes

MAKES 2 TO 3 DOZEN

2 large potatoes (1½ pounds),
  boiled in their skins
1 garlic clove, minced
Vegetable oil
2 tablespoons bread crumbs
  or matzo meal
Salt
Freshly ground black pepper
Sesame seeds

Peel the potatoes and mash until smooth. Add the garlic, 1 tablespoon of the oil, and the bread crumbs. Season to taste with salt and pepper. Blend well. Shape into thin latkes. Pour the sesame seeds into a flat plate and press both sides of the latkes into the seeds to coat them.

In a large heavy skillet, heat ¼ inch of oil. Place the latkes in the hot oil and fry on both sides until golden brown. Drain on paper towels. Serve immediately.

# Sweet Potato Dessert Latkes

MAKES 3 DOZEN

4 large sweet potatoes
2 eggs
½ teaspoon salt
2 tablespoons matzo meal or
  flour
1 teaspoon sugar
2 tablespoons raisins,
  plumped (see page 25)
2 tablespoons chopped dates
¼ cup chopped walnuts
Vegetable oil

Peel and wash the potatoes. Place them in cold water until ready to grate to keep from discoloring.

Grate the potatoes and drain well. Transfer them to a large bowl. Add the eggs, salt, matzo meal, and sugar and blend thoroughly. Fold in the raisins, dates, and walnuts.

Heat ¼ inch of oil in a large skillet and spoon in the potato mixture. Cook about 5 minutes a side, until brown. Drain on paper towels. Serve hot with powdered sugar, sour cream, or whipped cream.

# Zucchini and Cheese Latkes

6 medium zucchini, grated

3 eggs

5 green onions (scallions), thinly sliced

½ cup chopped parsley, no stems

2 tablespoons chopped fresh mint leaves

1 cup shredded mozzarella, Gruyère, or Swiss cheese

Vegetable oil

1 to 1¼ cups flour

Salt

Freshly ground black pepper

In a large bowl, combine the zucchini, eggs, green onions, parsley, mint, cheese, and 1 tablespoon oil. Add the flour, a small amount at a time, mixing thoroughly after each addition. Use just enough flour to give the batter body, but not enough to make it thick. Season to taste with salt and pepper.

In a large heavy skillet, heat ¼ inch of oil. With a tablespoon, spoon the zucchini mixture into the hot oil and flatten with the back of a wet spoon. Cook on both sides until golden brown. Drain on paper towels.

# PURIM

Purim is the Jewish variation of the Mardi Gras—a time for joyous feasting, boisterous drinking, and masquerades. The happy holiday, which falls in early spring, celebrates an ancient event—the thwarting of the villainous Haman's plot to put the Persian Jews to death.

The Book of Esther, which is always read on Purim, tells how the charming queen, herself a Jew, was able to convince the king to spare her people. In relating this story, an important part of the Purim tradition, every time Haman's name is mentioned, it is greeted with jeers, boos, and the noisy rattling of noisemakers, known as groghers.

The foods associated with this holiday vary from country to country. Baking begins weeks in advance, because sharing delicious baked goods with less fortunate people is an ancient custom. More than thirty different foods for celebrating the holiday are mentioned in medieval writings. The most popular of these are, of course, hamantaschen, with poppy seed or other fillings. I've included some of my family's favorites in this section, along with other special Purim desserts.

Queen Esther and the wicked Haman are represented in these symbolic Purim delicacies. Braided challahs represent the ropes with which Haman was hanged; hamantaschen represent his ears, nose, or hat, depending on which version your family accepts. In the Middle East, cookies are shaped like Queen Esther's bracelets.

# INTERNATIONAL PURIM DINNER

FOR 10

Queen Esther, the Purim heroine, was a vegetarian and we are told she loved fruits and seeds and vegetables. So poppy seeds, the symbolic accent, are abundant in this holiday's menus.

This menu features a selection of foods from Italy, Russia, and Germany. Most of the recipes are quite simple and filled with exciting holiday flavors. Bake your challah and prepare the Piroshkis ahead of time. The rest of the meal can be easily assembled while the borscht is bubbling.

## POPPY SEED–ONION CHALLAH

1 package active dry yeast
¼ cup plus a pinch of sugar
1¼ cups warm water (110 to 115°F)
2 eggs
2 teaspoons salt
¼ pound unsalted margarine, melted
4½ to 5 cups flour
Poppy Seed–Onion Filling (recipe follows)

Dissolve the yeast with a pinch of sugar in ½ cup of the warm water.

In the bowl of an electric mixer, blend 1 of the eggs, the ¼ cup sugar, salt, margarine, and remaining ¾ cup water. Blend in the yeast mixture. Add the flour, 1 cup at a time, mixing until the dough comes together. Pour onto a floured board and knead, adding additional flour, a little at a time, until the dough has a smooth and elastic consistency, 5 to 10 minutes.

Place the dough in an oiled bowl, oil the top of the dough, cover with a towel, and let it rise in a warm place until doubled, about 1 hour.

Punch down the dough. Divide it in half. Roll each half out to a 20×4-inch rectangle. Spread each rectangle with the filling (reserving ¼ cup for the top) to within ½ inch of the edges. Roll each rectangle lengthwise, jelly-roll fashion, to enclose the filling, forming a long rope. Twist the two ropes together. Form dough into a ring. Pinch ends to seal and place on an oiled baking sheet. Cover and let rise in a warm place until doubled, about 45 minutes.

Preheat the oven to 350°F.

Lightly beat the remaining egg and brush it over the challah. Sprinkle the challah with the reserved filling. Bake for 40 minutes, or until the loaf is golden and sounds hollow when tapped. Transfer to a rack to cool.

## POPPY SEED–ONION FILLING

1½ cups finely chopped onion
½ cup poppy seeds
½ teaspoon salt
5⅓ tablespoons unsalted margarine or butter, melted

Combine all the ingredients in a bowl. Set aside.

# ITALIAN FRUIT SALAD WITH POPPY SEED DRESSING

Inspired by exotic Italian fruits in a mustard sauce, this fruit salad can be served as a salad or as a dessert with cookies or mandelbrot. The poppy seeds add the right Purim touch.

2 cups each of peeled and diced fresh pineapple, pears, apples, bananas, and oranges
Juice of 1 lemon
Poppy Seed Dressing (recipe follows)
1 pint strawberries, stemmed and sliced
2 kiwi, peeled and thinly sliced
Sprigs of fresh mint

Arrange the diced fruit in a large serving bowl. Toss with the lemon juice, cover with plastic wrap, and refrigerate.

Spoon the dressing, about ¼ cup for each quart of fruit, over the fruit. Toss thoroughly. Garnish with strawberries, kiwi, and fresh mint.

# POPPY SEED DRESSING

½ cup sugar
1 teaspoon powdered mustard
1 teaspoon salt
½ cup raspberry vinegar
1 cup vegetable oil
3 teaspoons poppy seeds

In a processor or blender, combine the sugar, mustard, and salt and blend a few seconds. Add the vinegar and blend again. With the machine on, slowly add the oil in a continuous stream until well blended and thick. Transfer to a glass bowl and fold in the poppy seeds.

# CABBAGE BORSCHT WITH SHORT RIBS

This has always been one of my favorite dishes. I remember my great-aunt serving it whenever we were invited to dinner, and I always looked forward to the pungent sweet and sour flavors.

Serve the borscht as a main course with the short ribs, or as a soup with the marrow bones, reserving the ribs as a main course with potatoes. And don't forget to pass a platter of crisp hot Piroshkis.

1 pound marrow bones, sliced (ask your butcher to do this)
4 pounds short ribs, sliced between the bone
3 onions, chopped
3 garlic cloves, minced
½ cup chopped parsley
1 bay leaf, crushed
1 head of cabbage, shredded
4 beets, uncooked, peeled and julienned
1 can (1 pound, 12 ounces) tomatoes, or 6 fresh tomatoes, peeled and chopped
1 tablespoon chopped fresh basil, or 1 teaspoon dried, crushed
½ teaspoon paprika
⅓ cup brown sugar, packed
Juice of 4 to 5 lemons (about ⅔ cup)
Salt
Freshly ground black pepper
Nondairy sour cream (optional)

In a large pot, combine the bones, short ribs, onions, garlic, parsley, and bay leaf. Cover with water, bring to a boil, and skim off the foam from the top. Lower the heat and simmer, covered, for 2 hours. Chill and remove layer of fat that forms.

Add the cabbage, beets, tomatoes, basil, paprika, sugar, and lemon juice and continue cooking for 1 to 2 hours. Season to taste with salt and pepper; add additional sugar and lemon juice, if needed.

Ladle into hot soup bowls and top with nondairy sour cream, if you like it.

# PIROSHKIS

MAKES ABOUT 30

1½ cups flour
¼ teaspoon baking powder
½ teaspoon salt
¼ pound unsalted margarine,
  cut into pieces
⅛ cup cold water
1 egg
Chicken Liver Filling (recipe
  follows)
Meat Filling (recipe follows)
Melted unsalted margarine or
  beaten egg yolk

In the bowl of an electric mixer or processor, combine the flour, baking powder, and salt. Add the pieces of margarine and blend or process until crumbly. Combine the water and egg and pour it into the flour mixture and blend until the dough forms a ball. Do not overmix. Wrap in wax paper and chill for 10 minutes for easier handling.

On a floured board, roll out the dough ⅛ inch thick; with a floured 3-inch-round cookie cutter, cut the dough into circles.

Place 1 tablespoon of either filling in the center of each circle. Fold it over and pinch the edges to seal. Place the piroshkis on an oiled baking sheet. Brush them with melted margarine or egg yolks.

(If you want to store the piroshskis in the freezer, place on baking sheets lined with floured towels, then cover with another towel and place in the freezer. When the piroshkis are frozen, peel them off the towels and place in a plastic bag; return to the freezer.)

Preheat the oven to 375°F. Bake the piroshkis for 20 minutes, or until golden brown and crisp.

## CHICKEN LIVER FILLING

2 tablespoons chicken fat or
  unsalted margarine
1 onion, finely chopped
1 garlic clove, minced
1 pound chicken livers,
  chopped (see page 21)
2 slices egg bread, crusts
  trimmed and discarded,
  soaked in water and
  drained
Salt
Freshly ground black pepper

In a medium skillet, melt the chicken fat and sauté the onion and garlic until soft. Add the chicken livers and bread and sauté, mixing well. Season to taste with salt and pepper. Cool to room temperature.

## MEAT FILLING

2 tablespoons unsalted margarine or oil
1 onion, minced
1 garlic clove, minced
½ cup minced mushrooms
1 teaspoon dried marjoram
1 pound ground veal, beef, or chicken
2 hard-boiled eggs (see page 23), finely chopped
1 tablespoon minced parsley
Salt
Freshly ground black pepper

In a skillet, heat the margarine and sauté the onion, garlic, and mushrooms until soft. Add the marjoram and ground meat and sauté until the meat loses its pink color, stirring with a fork to break up the meat. Add the eggs and parsley. Season to taste with salt and pepper. Stir well. Cool to room temperature.

# OLD-WORLD APPLE STRUDEL

Many old recipes should not be forgotten. This is one of them. Judy Freedman, a longtime friend who has taken many of my classes, shared her recipe for making apple strudel from scratch and also some techniques that guarantee success, such as actually pounding the dough one hundred times!

Since I am including this recipe in a meat menu, margarine is specified, but when including it in a dairy menu, by all means use butter.

2½ cups sifted, unbleached flour
1 egg, lightly beaten
¼ teaspoon salt
3 tablespoons vegetable oil
⅔ cup warm water
½ pound unsalted margarine, melted
1 cup ground nuts, bread or cake crumbs
Apple Filling (recipe follows)
Powdered sugar

Place the flour on a wooden board and make a well in the center. Break the egg into the well and add the salt, olive oil, and water. With a fork, beat the egg mixture and add the flour from the edge of the well, combining them to form a soft ball of dough.

Work the dough vigorously, picking it up and pounding it on the table 100 times. Form it into a ball, brush it with oil, and place it in a warm bowl; cover with a kitchen towel and let it rest for 30 minutes.

Preheat the oven to 375°F.

Divide the dough into 3 parts. Working with one part at a time, pat the dough into a rectangle and roll it out to about 12 inches long and 8 inches wide. Flour your hands. Lift up the dough and carefully pull and stretch it out as thin as possible (taking care not to make any holes), until the sheet of dough is about 18 inches long and 14 inches wide. Brush the thin sheet of dough with melted margarine and sprinkle it with ground nuts.

Beginning 2 inches from the wide edge, carefully arrange a 2-inch-wide row of Apple Filling. Fold the 2-inch border over the filling and continue rolling up the dough, jelly-roll fashion. Pinch the ends together to seal. Line a baking sheet with foil and brush with margarine. Place 1 roll, seam side down, on the prepared baking sheet. Repeat the entire process with the remaining dough. Brush the strudel with melted margarine and bake for 45 to 50 minutes, until golden brown. Slice while hot and sprinkle with powdered sugar just before serving.

*NOTE FOR FREEZING: It is not necessary to bake all the strudel at one time. Place strudel on foil and refrigerate until the margarine hardens. Seal the strudel with the foil and freeze.

## APPLE FILLING

6 Golden Delicious apples, peeled, cored, and thinly sliced
1 cup sugar
1 teaspoon cinnamon
1 cup raisins
1 cup walnuts or almonds, coarsely chopped

Place the apple slices in a large bowl and toss with the sugar, cinnamon, raisins, and walnuts. Cover and set aside for 10 minutes.

# Purim Carnival Dinner

FOR 10

▼▲▼▲▼▲▼▲▼▲▼▲▼▲▼▲▼

Homemade Wheat Thins
(see page 54)

Carnival Ribbon Rolls

Country Terrine with Red
Pepper Jelly

Veal and Vegetable Stew

Poppy Seed Noodles

Orange-Chocolate Tart

Maria's Korjas (see page
122)

Classic Hamantaschen (see
page 116)


SUGGESTED BEVERAGES:

Sauterne with the terrine

Light red wine with the
stew

Champagne or sparkling
wine with dessert

Add a happy note to a festive holiday with this color-ful carnival menu. The children dress in costumes, the adults drink lots of wine, and everybody enjoys an upbeat dinner.

The traditional Purim poppy seeds perk up both the noodles and the dessert. Twists of red and white dough form the colorful ribbon rolls. Red Pepper Jelly adds a brilliantly spicy accent to an authentic French country terrine—a subtle, smooth blend of chicken livers, chicken breasts, and veal.

A hearty veal stew is enhanced with crisp vegetables and served on top of Poppy Seed Noodles. (By the way, make plenty of rolls, so guests can sop up the rich juices of the stew.)

Chocolate and orange blend unexpected flavors in a rich tart. And since it's Purim, the only holiday that en-courages drinking, champagne accompanies dessert and we serve two wines with the dinner.

Good news for the cook: Much of this dinner can be prepared in advance. The stew improves with reheating; the terrine should be done in advance to age properly; the tart shell an be prebaked, awaiting the tangy orange-chocolate filling. I am also suggesting other Purim deli-cacies to add for a festive dessert table. Queen Esther never had it so good!

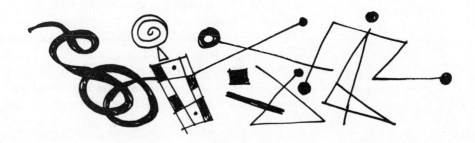

# CARNIVAL RIBBON ROLLS

Twists of red and white dough give a colorful effect.

MAKES ABOUT 24

## WHITE RIBBON DOUGH

1 package active dry yeast

¼ cup sugar

¾ cup warm water (110 to 115°F)

1 egg, lightly beaten

¼ pound unsalted margarine, melted

2 teaspoons kosher salt

4 to 5 cups flour

Vegetable oil

## RED RIBBON DOUGH

1 package active dry yeast

¼ cup sugar

½ cup warm water (110 to 115°F)

1 cup tomato sauce, warmed

1 egg, lightly beaten

¼ pound unsalted margarine, melted

2 teaspoons kosher salt

4 to 5 cups flour

## FOR BAKING

Cornmeal

1 egg, lightly beaten

Poppy seeds

For the white ribbon dough, dissolve the yeast with a pinch of sugar in ½ cup of the water.

In the bowl of an electric mixer, blend the egg, the remaining sugar, margarine, the remaining ¼ cup water, and salt. Blend in the yeast mixture. Add 4 cups of the flour, 1 cup at a time, mixing until the dough comes together. Pour onto a floured board and knead, adding additional flour a little at a time, until the dough has a smooth and elastic consistency, 5 to 10 minutes.

Place the dough in an oiled bowl, oil the top of the dough, cover with a towel, and let it rise in a warm place until doubled, about 1 hour. Punch down the dough, turn it over, and let it rise for 20 minutes more.

For the red ribbon dough, dissolve the yeast with a pinch of sugar in the ½ cup warm water.

In the bowl of an electric mixer, blend the tomato sauce, egg, margarine, and salt. Blend in the yeast mixture. Add 4 cups of the flour, 1 cup at a time, mixing until the dough comes together. Pour onto a floured board and knead, adding additional flour a little at a time, until the dough has a smooth and elastic consistency, about 5 minutes. Let the red dough rise in the same way as the white dough.

To make the ribbon rolls, pull off golf-ball-size pieces of each dough. Roll each piece into a 10 × 8-inch strip. Twist the white and red dough strips together into a rope, resembling a candy cane, then tie the rope into a knot. Repeat with the remaining dough.

Lightly oil a baking sheet, sprinkle it with cornmeal, and place the rolls on it, about 2 inches apart. Cover and let rise in a warm place until doubled, about 45 minutes.

Preheat the oven to 350°F.

Brush the lightly beaten egg over the rolls. Sprinkle the rolls with poppy seeds. Bake the rolls for about 30 minutes, until golden brown. Transfer to racks to cool.

# COUNTRY TERRINE WITH RED PEPPER JELLY

This classic country-style terrine is complemented by the sweet-spicy flavor of Red Pepper Jelly. The terrine looks pretty thinly sliced, served on your best china. It may be made a day or two in advance and refrigerated. In fact, it really tastes better the next day.

½ pound chicken fat

½ pound skinned and boned chicken breasts

½ pound ground veal

1 pound chicken livers (see page 21)

2 garlic cloves, peeled

2 eggs

¼ cup dry white wine

2 tablespoons brandy or cognac

¼ teaspoon allspice

¼ teaspoon dried thyme

2 teaspoons salt

1 teaspoon freshly ground black pepper

½ pound cooked tongue, diced

¼ pound cured breakfast beef (optional)

Red Pepper Jelly (recipe follows)

Put the chicken fat, chicken breasts, and ground veal in a processor and pulse the machine until they are finely chopped. Transfer the mixture to a large bowl.

Put ½ pound of the chicken livers, the garlic, eggs, wine, brandy, allspice, and thyme in the processor and purée. Season with salt and pepper. Set aside.

Add the purée and the diced tongue to the bowl with the chicken mixture. Mix them thoroughly.

Preheat the oven to 350°F.

Line a 1½-quart terrine or ovenproof baking dish with half the slices of breakfast beef, sliced crosswise. Fill the terrine with half the ground mixture. Arrange the remaining ½ pound of chicken livers on top. Cover with the remaining mixture. Arrange the remaining slices of breakfast beef on top. Cover tightly with 2 layers of foil, securely sealing them around the rim.

Set the baking dish in a larger baking dish filled halfway with hot water. Bake about 1½ hours, until the mixture comes away from the sides of the baking dish. Remove from the oven, leaving the baking dish inside the larger dish of water.

Place heavy weights (such as cans of food or bricks) on top of the foil. Let the terrine cool to room temperature. The excess fat will overflow as the terrine cools and firms. Cover the terrine with additional foil and refrigerate. Slice it thin and remove the slices with a metal spatula. Serve as an appetizer or a first course on a lettuce leaf with the Red Pepper Jelly.

# RED PEPPER JELLY

This jelly is especially good when used as a garnish for cold meat or poultry platters. For a dairy menu, it adds an interesting accent to cream cheese or goat cheese.

MAKES SIX TO EIGHT 8-OUNCE JARS

1½ pounds (about 4 large) sweet red bell peppers

1 cup cider vinegar

1 teaspoon salt

1 teaspoon chili powder (optional)

Pinch of crushed dried red pepper flakes

5 cups sugar

⅓ cup freshly squeezed lemon juice

1 package (6 ounces) liquid fruit pectin

Wash and cut up the peppers, discarding the seeds and stems. Process them a few at a time in a processor or blender until finely chopped.

In a large pot, combine the chopped peppers, vinegar, salt, chili powder, and crushed red pepper. Bring the pepper mixture to a boil over high heat and boil for 10 minutes. Remove from the heat and add the sugar and lemon juice, mixing well. Stir in the pectin and return to the heat. Slowly bring it to a boil, stirring constantly for 1 to 2 minutes. Remove the pot from the stove and skim off the foam with a metal spoon.

Ladle into sterilized jars and seal immediately.

# VEAL AND VEGETABLE STEW

This stew can be prepared a day ahead and tastes even better after the flavors have a chance to meld. It can be stretched for a large family gathering, and the wine is a traditional touch for this joyous holiday.

4 pounds veal shank or shoulder, boned and cut into 2-inch cubes

Salt

Freshly ground black pepper

⅓ cup olive oil

1 onion, diced

2 garlic cloves, minced

2 carrots, peeled and sliced

2 celery stalks, sliced

Preheat the oven to 350°F.

Season the veal on both sides with salt and pepper. In a large heavy pot or casserole, heat the oil and sauté the veal on all sides until brown. Add the onion and minced garlic and sauté until soft, about 5 minutes. Add the carrots and celery and sauté for 5 minutes. Add the wine and simmer for 2 minutes. Add the stock, tomato, tomato paste, paprika, potatoes, mushrooms, and unpeeled garlic cloves and bring to a boil. Combine the bay leaves, peppercorns, parsley, and fresh and dried herbs

1 cup dry white wine

3 cups Veal or Chicken Stock
(see page 390 )

1 large tomato, chopped

1 tablespoon double tomato
paste

1 teaspoon paprika

2 large potatoes, peeled and
diced

8 mushrooms, quartered

1 whole head of garlic, unpeeled and separated

2 bay leaves

10 whole black peppercorns

4 fresh parsley sprigs

8 fresh thyme, tarragon, or
oregano sprigs

4 long fresh marjoram sprigs,
or 1 teaspoon dried

1 tablespoon dried thyme,
tarragon, or oregano

12 pearl onions, parboiled for
5 minutes and peeled

in a piece of cheesecloth; tie with a string and add to
the pot. Cover and simmer for 2½ hours, or until veal is
tender. Toss in the pearl onions. Remove the cheesecloth
bag. Serve in heated soup bowls.

# POPPY SEED NOODLES

4 tablespoons unsalted margarine, melted

1 tablespoon poppy seeds

½ cup toasted sliced almonds
(see page 24)

8 ounces wide egg noodles,
cooked and drained

Salt

Freshly ground black pepper

In a saucepan, melt the margarine. Add the poppy seeds
and almonds and mix well. Add the drained noodles and
toss lightly. Season to taste with salt and pepper.

# ORANGE-CHOCOLATE TART

The tart crust can be prepared and stored in the freezer days in advance. Bake it when you're ready, then brush it with chocolate, fill it with a thin layer of orange custard, and garnish with orange sections. Voilà! A crisp-crusted pastry with just enough creamy filling to blend with the chocolate. Irresistible!

MAKES ONE 11-INCH TART

8 ounces semisweet choco-
late, melted (see page 21)
Prebaked Sweet Pastry Tart
Shell (see page 205)
4 egg yolks
¾ cup sugar
½ cup orange juice
1 tablespoon lemon juice
4 tablespoons unsalted margarine
2 tablespoons diced orange
segments, membrane re-
moved
2 oranges, cut into sections,
for garnish

Brush a thin layer of the melted chocolate over the cooled tart shell. Set it aside.

In the top of a double boiler over simmering water, beat the egg yolks until smooth and warm. Add the sugar in a slow stream, beating continuously, until smooth and light in color. Slowly add the orange and lemon juices, beating until the mixture begins to thicken, about 5 minutes. Add the margarine in pieces, beating to blend. Continue beating; the mixture will thicken in 5 to 10 minutes, so be patient. Pour it into a heatproof bowl, add diced orange sections, and let cool to room temperature.

Pour the orange mixture into the chocolate-lined tart shell, starting in the center and allowing the mixture to spread to the sides. Then smooth it with a spatula.

Just before serving, arrange the orange sections in a petal pattern on top of the filling.

BONUS RECIPES:

# PURIM DESSERTS AND CONFECTIONS

In honor of Queen Esther, we enjoy many nuts and seeds—especially poppy seeds—in baked delicacies during Purim. Remember that poppy seeds have many other uses, too. Their rich nutty flavor and texture add interest to vegetables, stews, breads, rolls, and salad dressings. The best seeds are blue-black in color and imported from Holland. If you buy poppy seeds in quantity, store them in the refrigerator or freezer.

I have been collecting Purim dessert recipes for years and have included many of the more unusual ones here— Maria's Korjas, the thinnest and crispest cookies ever; a perfect yeast ring, which does double duty as hamantaschen; some super Purim Pinwheels for chocolate lovers; and even Poppy Seed and Nut Candy.

Purim is a holiday for sharing with family and friends. So carry on this lovely tradition by lining baskets with some lace paper doilies and delivering a selection of sweets to your favorite people.

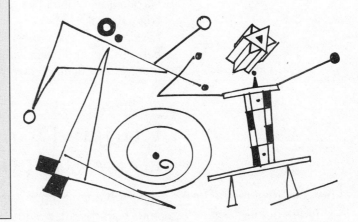

# CLASSIC HAMANTASCHEN

There are two things to remember when preparing these hamantaschen. The first is that the dough can be made in advance, wrapped in plastic wrap and then with foil or in plastic bags, and refrigerated or frozen. The dough is then defrosted, rolled out, filled, and baked just before serving. The second is that they can be prepared up to the time of filling and shaping, brushed with egg white, and refrigerated or frozen. Then defrost, bake, and serve hot from the oven.

MAKES ABOUT 5 DOZEN

3 cups flour
½ cup finely ground almonds
1½ teaspoons baking powder
¼ teaspoon salt
½ cup sugar
Zest of 1 lemon
½ pound unsalted butter or margarine
1 egg
2 tablespoons cold water
1 tablespoon lemon juice
Hamantaschen Fillings (recipes follow)
1 egg white, lightly beaten

Preheat the oven to 350°F.

In the large bowl of an electric mixer, combine the flour, almonds, baking powder, salt, sugar, and lemon zest. Blend or cut in the butter until the mixture resembles very fine crumbs.

In a small bowl, beat the egg, water, and lemon juice until well blended. Add to the flour mixture and beat until completely blended and the mixture begins to form a dough. Do not overmix.

Transfer to a floured board and knead the dough into a ball. Divide the ball into 6 or 7 equal portions for easier handling. Flatten each portion with the palms of your hands and roll it out ¼ inch thick. With a scalloped cookie cutter, cut into 3½-inch rounds. Place 1 heaping teaspoon of filling in the center of each round. Fold the edges of the dough toward the center to form a triangle, leaving a bit of the filling visible in the center. Pinch the edges to seal them.

Place the hamantaschen on a lightly greased foil-lined baking sheet and brush with egg white. Bake for 20 minutes, or until lightly browned. Transfer to racks to cool.

# COOKIE-DOUGH HAMANTASCHEN

This is the first recipe I ever used for hamantaschen, and it is still one of the best. A simple cookie dough is cut into rounds, filled with colorful fillings, and transformed into three-cornered pastries. I usually double or triple the recipe, line a basket with a cloth napkin, and fill the basket with hamantaschen to take to a friend's home for Shalach Manoth or a Purim party.

¼ pound unsalted butter or margarine, softened

½ cup sugar

3 eggs

Grated zest of 1 orange

2 cups flour

1½ teaspoons baking powder

¼ teaspoon salt

Hamantaschen Fillings (recipes follow)

Preheat the oven to 375°F.

In the bowl of an electric mixer, beat the butter and sugar until well blended. Beat in 2 of the eggs and the orange zest, blending thoroughly. Add the flour, baking powder, and salt and blend until the dough is smooth.

Transfer to a floured board and divide the dough into 3 or 4 portions for easier handling. Flatten each portion with the palm of your hand and roll it out ¼ inch thick. With a scalloped or plain cookie cutter, cut into 2½-inch rounds. Place 1 heaping teaspoon of filling in the center of each round. Fold the edges of the dough toward the center to form a triangle, leaving a bit of the filling visible in the center. Pinch the edges to seal them.

Place the hamantaschen ½ inch apart on a lightly greased foil-lined baking sheet and brush with the remaining egg, lightly beaten. Bake for 10 minutes or until golden brown. Transfer to racks to cool.

# FILO HAMANTASCHEN

Add an exotic touch to your Purim baking by making hamantaschen with filo sheets. This is inspired by ancient Moroccan pastries, crisp and flaky, with the added crunch of almonds.

½ pound unsalted butter, clarified (see page 368) or margarine

¼ cup safflower or vegetable oil

1 package (1 pound) filo sheets

1 pound almonds, ground (2 cups)

Hamantaschen Fillings (recipes follow)

Honey-Sugar Syrup (recipe follows)

Preheat the oven to 350°F.

In a medium saucepan over low heat, combine the butter and oil. Place a damp towel on a work area and cover it with wax paper. Work with 1 sheet of filo at a time, keeping the remaining filo covered at all times with wax paper and a damp towel. Cut the standard sheets of filo evenly into 2-inch strips. Work with each strip on top of a large sheet of wax paper placed on top of a damp kitchen towel. Brush them with the butter mixture and sprinkle with ground nuts. Place a teaspoon of filling 1 inch from the short edge of each strip. Fold one corner over the filling. Fold up the filo, flag fashion, in a triangle along its length to make a neat triangular package. Repeat with the remaining strips and filo.

Place the hamantaschen ½ inch apart on buttered baking sheets and brush them with the melted butter mixture. Bake for 15 to 20 minutes, until golden brown and crisp. Remove from the oven and spoon the syrup over each triangle. Cool on racks.

## HONEY-SUGAR SYRUP

1 cup sugar
½ cup water
1 tablespoon lemon juice
1 tablespoon honey

In a heavy saucepan, bring the sugar, water, and lemon juice to a boil, stirring with a wooden spoon until the sugar dissolves. Boil briskly for 5 minutes. Stir in the honey. Pour into a heatproof pitcher.

# LOW-CHOLESTEROL HAMANTASCHEN

MAKES ABOUT 5 DOZEN

7 egg whites
1 cup sugar
¾ cup safflower or vegetable oil
1 teaspoon vanilla extract
Zest of 1 lemon
4⅓ cups flour
1 tablespoon baking powder
½ teaspoon salt
¼ cup poppy seeds
Hamantaschen Fillings (recipes follow)

Preheat the oven to 350°F.

In the bowl of an electric mixer, beat 6 of the egg whites, the sugar, oil, vanilla, and lemon zest until well blended. In another bowl, combine the flour, baking powder, salt, and poppy seeds and blend into the egg mixture. Mix well.

Roll out portions of the dough on a floured board (⅛ to ¼ inch thick) and cut into 2- or 3-inch circles with a scalloped or plain cookie cutter. Place a teaspoon of filling in the center of each circle of dough. Fold the edges of the dough toward the center to form a triangle, leaving a bit of the filling visible in the center. Pinch the edges to seal.

Place the hamantaschen on lightly greased foil-lined baking sheets and brush with the remaining egg white, lightly beaten. Bake for 20 minutes, or until golden brown. Transfer to racks and cool.

# HAMANTASCHEN FILLINGS

Everyone in our family has his or her favorite hamantaschen filling and I have developed many interesting variations. If I don't have the time to prepare the filling from scratch, I often use ready-made fillings—apricot, prune, poppy seed, and almond—that can be found in supermarkets.

## APPLE FILLING

MAKES ABOUT 2 CUPS

1 cup applesauce, preferably homemade (recipe follows)
½ cup raisins, plumped and drained (see page 25)
½ cup toasted chopped walnuts (see page 24)
⅛ teaspoon cinnamon

Combine all the ingredients in a bowl and blend well. Cover with plastic wrap and refrigerate.

## APPLESAUCE

MAKES ABOUT 4 CUPS

6 Golden or Red Delicious apples, peeled, cored, and cut into chunks
Juice of 1 lemon
2 to 3 tablespoons sugar
1 piece (½ inch) cinnamon stick, or a pinch of ground cinnamon

In a large saucepan, toss the apples and lemon juice. Add sugar and cinnamon. Cover and cook slowly until tender, 15 to 20 minutes. Remove the cinnamon stick and mash or purée the mixture. Transfer to a bowl, cover with plastic wrap, and chill.

## APRICOT-COCONUT FILLING

MAKES ABOUT 3 CUPS

2 cups apricot preserves
½ cup shredded coconut
½ cup toasted chopped walnuts (see page 24)
Grated zest of 1 lemon

Combine all the ingredients in a bowl and mix well. Cover with plastic wrap and refrigerate.

## CARAMEL-PECAN FILLING

MAKES ABOUT 3 CUPS

¾ cup sugar
¼ cup water
2 cups toasted chopped pecans (see page 24)
7 tablespoons unsalted butter or margarine
½ cup warm milk
¼ cup honey

In a heavy saucepan, bring the sugar and water to a boil, mixing with a wooden spoon until the sugar dissolves. Remove from the heat and add the pecans, butter, and milk. Return to the heat, stirring constantly, and simmer for 10 minutes, or until thick. Remove from the heat and stir in the honey.

Transfer to an ovenproof glass bowl, cover with plastic wrap, and refrigerate until set. This will keep for at least 1 week.


## CHOCOLATE FILLING

MAKES ABOUT 2½ CUPS

½ cup cocoa
½ cup sugar
¼ cup milk, cream, or coffee
1 cup toasted chopped walnuts (see page 24)

Combine all the ingredients in a bowl and blend thoroughly.


## POPPY SEED FILLING
MOHN

MAKES ABOUT 1½ CUPS

4 ounces poppy seeds
½ cup milk
1 tablespoon unsalted butter or margarine
¼ cup seedless raisins, plumped (see page 25)
¼ cup toasted walnuts, pecans, or almonds (see page 24)
1 tablespoon honey
½ teaspoon vanilla extract

In a medium saucepan, combine the poppy seeds, milk, butter, raisins, walnuts, and honey. Bring to a boil and stir over medium heat until the milk is absorbed and the mixture thickens. Cool; stir in the vanilla.

## PRUNE FILLING

MAKES ABOUT 3 CUPS

1¼ cups pitted prunes
½ cup raisins
Sweet wine or water
½ cup sugar
Juice and zest of 1 lemon
Zest of 1 orange
½ cup toasted chopped walnuts (see page 24)

In a large bowl, soak the prunes and raisins in enough wine to cover for 3 hours or overnight. Drain well. Chop or mince the prunes and raisins. Add the sugar, lemon juice and zests, and walnuts and mix well. Cover with plastic wrap and refrigerate.

## QUICK PRUNE FILLING

MAKES ABOUT 1½ CUPS

1 jar (15 ounces) cooked pitted prunes, drained, or 2
   cups pitted stewed prunes
¼ cup sugar
½ cup toasted chopped walnuts or pecans (see page
   24)
1 teaspoon orange juice
1 teaspoon lemon juice

Combine all the ingredients in a large bowl and mix well. Cover with plastic wrap and refrigerate.

## WALNUT-HONEY FILLING

MAKES ABOUT 2 CUPS

1 cup toasted chopped walnuts (see page 24)
¾ cup honey
⅓ cup bread crumbs
Zest of 1 orange

In a saucepan, cook the walnuts, honey, and crumbs over low heat, stirring constantly until thick, about 5 minutes. Remove from the heat, stir in the orange zest, and cool to room temperature. Cover with plastic wrap and refrigerate.

# MARIA'S KORJAS
## CRISP POPPY SEED THINS

This recipe makes hundreds of cookies, about the texture of potato chips. I never cut the recipe in half, since the dough stores well in the refrigerator or freezer, ready to bake at any time. Simply wrap the dough tightly in plastic wrap; store it in a plastic bag and refrigerate for 3 to 4 days or freeze for 3 to 4 weeks.

MAKES ABOUT 200

1 cup safflower or vegetable oil
2 cups sugar
2 eggs
6 cups flour
3 teaspoons baking powder
¼ teaspoon salt
1½ cups milk
2 ounces poppy seeds
1 teaspoon cinnamon

Preheat the oven to 350°F.

In the bowl of an electric mixer, blend together the oil and 1½ cups of the sugar until fluffy. Beat in the eggs until smooth. Sift together the flour, baking powder, and salt. Gradually add the milk alternately with the sifted dry ingredients to the oil mixture, beating after each addition. Blend in the poppy seeds.

A heaping tablespoon at a time, roll out the dough as thin as possible on a generously floured board or on wax paper. A single spoonful should roll out to a rectangle about 8 × 11 inches. With a sharp knife, cut the dough into diamond shapes and with a metal spatula carefully transfer them to lightly oiled foil-lined baking sheets. Mix together the remaining ½ cup sugar and cinnamon and sprinkle over the cookies. Bake for 8 to 10 minutes, until golden brown. Transfer the cookies to racks to cool.

# POPPY SEED MANDELBROT

Tradition calls for a glass of sweet wine to dip these pastries in.

MAKES ABOUT 9 DOZEN

1 cup plus 2 tablespoons sugar
Zest of 1 lemon or orange
1 cup safflower or vegetable oil
3 eggs
1 teaspoon vanilla extract

Preheat the oven to 325°F.

Process 1 cup of the sugar and lemon zest in a processor or blender.

In the bowl of an electric mixer, blend together the oil and sugar mixture. Add the eggs, vanilla extract, and poppy seeds and blend thoroughly. In a large bowl, combine the flour, salt, baking powder, and 1 teaspoon

2 ounces poppy seeds
4 cups flour
1 teaspoon salt
1 teaspoon baking powder
1½ teaspoons cinnamon

of the cinnamon. Blend the flour mixture into the oil mixture.

Divide the dough into 4 portions. With lightly oiled hands, shape each portion into a 1½- or 2-inch oval loaf. Place on greased baking sheets. Combine the remaining 2 tablespoons sugar and ½ teaspoon cinnamon and sprinkle on top of the loaves.

Bake for 35 to 45 minutes, until golden brown. Remove the loaves from the oven and use a spatula to transfer them to a cutting board. Cut the loaves into ½-inch-thick slices. Place the slices cut side down on the same baking sheets, turn off the heat, and return them to the oven for 10 minutes a side, until crisp. Transfer to racks to cool.

# POPPY SEED "NEWTONS"

If your kids love old-fashioned Fig Newtons, they'll love you for making these Poppy Seed Newtons for Purim. The cookie dough is a copycat version of the famous old-fashioned confections.

MAKES 7 OR 8 DOZEN

1 cup sugar
¼ pound unsalted butter, margarine, or shortening
1 egg
½ cup milk or water
½ teaspoon vanilla extract
3½ cups flour
4 teaspoons cream of tartar
2 teaspoons baking soda
¼ teaspoon salt
2 cans (8 ounces each) poppy seed filling

Preheat the oven to 350°F.

In the bowl of an electric mixer, cream the sugar and butter until light. Blend in the egg. Add the milk and vanilla and beat until smooth. Sift together the flour, cream of tartar, baking soda, and salt. Add the flour mixture to the shortening mixture, blending until the dough is stiff and adding additional flour if needed. On a well-floured board, roll out pieces of dough to 4 inches wide, 12 inches long, and about ¼ inch thick.

Fit a pastry bag with a ½-inch tube and fill it with the poppy seed filling. Pipe the poppy seed filling lengthwise ½ inch from the long edge of the pastry. (If you prefer, just spoon the filling in.) Loosen the pastry from the floured board with a spatula and fold it lengthwise over the filling. Trim along the length of the pastry, leaving a ½-inch border, and press to seal. Cut the pastry into 2-inch bars. Place them on greased foil-lined baking sheets and bake for about 10 minutes, until lightly browned. Cool on racks.

# PURIM PINWHEELS

MAKES ABOUT 6 DOZEN

¼ pound unsalted butter or
  margarine
¾ cup sugar
1 egg
½ teaspoon vanilla extract
¼ teaspoon almond extract
1¾ cups flour
½ teaspoon baking powder
¼ teaspoon salt
1 ounce unsweetened chocolate, melted (see page 21)
2 tablespoons poppy seeds

In the large bowl of an electric mixer, cream together the butter and sugar until light. Add the egg and the vanilla and almond extracts and blend well. Combine the flour, baking powder, and salt. Add the flour mixture to the butter mixture and blend thoroughly. Divide the dough in half.

Beat the melted chocolate into one half of the dough, and the poppy seeds into the remaining half. Wrap each half with plastic wrap and refrigerate until firm.

On floured wax paper, roll out each half of dough to a 9x14-inch rectangle. Invert the white poppy seed dough onto the chocolate dough and peel off the wax paper from the white dough. Tightly roll up the dough, jelly-roll fashion, peeling off the wax paper as you roll. Wrap the roll with plastic wrap and refrigerate at least 1 hour, or freeze until needed.

Preheat the oven to 350°F.

Carefully cut the roll into ¼-inch-thick slices. Place the slices on ungreased foil-lined baking sheets and bake for 5 to 7 minutes, or until lightly browned. Transfer to racks to cool.

# POPPY SEED POUNDCAKE WITH LEMON ICING

Zest of 3 lemons
2 cups sugar
½ pound unsalted butter or
  margarine
½ teaspoon mace
4 eggs
1 teaspoon vanilla extract
1 teaspoon lemon extract, or
  1 tablespoon lemon juice
1 tablespoon poppy seeds
2½ cups flour

Preheat the oven to 350°F.

Blend the lemon zest and sugar in a processor or blender.

In the bowl of an electric mixer, beat the butter, sugar mixture, and mace until light and fluffy. One at a time, add the eggs, beating well after each addition. Blend in the vanilla extract, lemon extract, and poppy seeds.

Sift together the flour, baking powder, baking soda, and salt. Add the flour mixture, alternately with the buttermilk, to the butter mixture, blending thoroughly, but not overbeating.

1 teaspoon baking powder
½ teaspoon baking soda
½ teaspoon salt
¾ cup buttermilk
Lemon Icing (recipe follows)

Spoon the batter into a well-buttered and floured bundt pan. Bake for 50 to 60 minutes, until a wooden toothpick inserted into the center comes out dry. Cool on a rack for 10 minutes. Cover with the rack and invert. Spoon the Lemon Icing over the cake.

## LEMON ICING

1 pound (3½ cups) powdered
    sugar, sifted
½ teaspoon cream of tartar
3 egg whites, unbeaten
½ teaspoon vanilla extract
1 tablespoon lemon juice

In the bowl of an electric mixer, combine the powdered sugar, cream of tartar, egg whites, vanilla, and lemon juice. Beat at low speed until the sugar is dissolved, then beat at high speed until the mixture is light and fluffy. Keep covered with a damp towel.

# POPPY SEED YEAST RING

This is a delicious coffee cake that doubles as a hamantaschen dough. The dough is covered with a towel and refrigerated overnight, then rolled, filled, and served hot for breakfast. Or you can make the dough in the afternoon, refrigerate it for several hours, and serve the ring hot after dinner with tea or coffee.

MAKES 2 COFFEE CAKES OR 24 TO 30 HAMANTASCHEN

2 packages active dry yeast
¾ cup warm milk (110 to
    115°F)
¼ pound unsalted butter
¼ pound unsalted margarine
½ cup plus 2 tablespoons
    sugar
3 eggs, separated
2½ cups flour
Pinch of nutmeg
¼ teaspoon salt
1½ cups canned poppy seed
    filling
1 tablespoon poppy seeds

Dissolve the yeast in ½ cup of the milk. In the bowl of an electric mixer, cream the butter and margarine with 2 tablespoons sugar until light and fluffy. Add the egg yolks and beat well. Combine the flour, nutmeg, and salt. Add the yeast mixture alternately with the flour. With the back of a wooden spoon, smooth the top of the dough and brush with oil. Cover with a towel and refrigerate for several hours or overnight.

*For Yeast Ring:* Preheat the oven to 350°F.

Divide the dough into 2 portions. Roll out each portion on floured wax paper into a 16x20-inch rectangle. Beat the egg whites until stiff. Blend in the remaining ½ cup sugar and poppy seed filling.

Spread half the beaten egg white mixture over each dough half, leaving a 1-inch margin around the edges. Starting from a long edge, roll up each one, jelly-roll fashion. Bring the ends together to form a ring.

Place each ring in a 10-inch pie pan, sealing the ends together. Brush top with remaining milk and sprinkle with poppy seeds. (If you like, you can hold the rings in the refrigerator, covered, for 1 hour.) Bake for 30 minutes, or until golden brown. Serve hot.

*For Hamantaschen:* Preheat the oven to 350°F. Roll out the dough and cut it into 3-inch rounds with a cookie cutter. Place a teaspoon of poppy seed filling in the center of each circle of dough. Fold the edges of the dough toward the center to form a triangle, leaving a bit of the filling visible in the center. Pinch the edges to seal. Place the hamantaschen on oiled foil-lined baking sheets and bake for 10 minutes; pinch edges again to reseal and bake 10 minutes longer, or until golden brown. Transfer to racks and cool.

# CARAWAY BUNDT CAKE

The caraway seeds make this a perfect Purim selection. It is a wonderful accompaniment to the wines that are such an important part of the celebration.

MAKES ONE 10-INCH CAKE

½ pound butter or margarine, softened
1⅔ cups sugar
1 teaspoon vanilla extract
¼ teaspoon mace
2⅔ cups sifted cake flour
8 egg whites (1 cup)
¼ teaspoon salt
½ teaspoon cream of tartar
3 tablespoons caraway seeds
Powdered sugar

In a large bowl of an electric mixer, beat the butter, gradually adding ⅔ cup of the sugar until creamy. Add the vanilla and mace and continue beating. Gradually beat in 1⅔ cups of the flour. Set aside.

Preheat the oven to 350°F.

In another bowl, beat the egg whites with the salt and cream of tartar until foamy. Gradually add the remaining 1 cup sugar and beat until stiff. Add one quarter of the egg white mixture to the butter mixture, mixing thoroughly with a wooden spoon or spatula. Fold the butter mixture over the remaining egg whites and sprinkle with the remaining 1 cup flour. Gently fold together. Fold in the seeds, being careful not to overmix.

Generously butter and flour a 10-inch tube or bundt pan and pour in the batter.

Bake for 45 minutes, or until a toothpick inserted in the center of the cake comes out dry. Cool in the pan for 15 minutes and then carefully turn the cake out on a rack. Just before serving, sprinkle with powdered sugar.

# POPPY SEED AND NUT CANDY

MAKES ABOUT 2 DOZEN

½ cup honey
¼ cup sugar
¾ cup poppy seeds
½ cup chopped walnuts
⅓ cup slivered or sliced almonds

In a heavy saucepan, combine the honey and sugar. Bring to a boil over low heat, mixing until the sugar dissolves. Add the poppy seeds and blend thoroughly. Continue cooking until thick (250°F on a candy thermometer), about 10 minutes, stirring occasionally. Add the walnuts and cook 5 minutes longer, or until the candy returns to 250°F.

Pour the mixture into a well-greased 8-inch-square glass baking dish. Sprinkle with the almonds. Dip a knife into hot water and cut the candy into 1½-inch squares. Remove the squares to a platter while still warm.

# PEANUT BUTTER TRUFFLES

Fill a pretty box for a hostess gift or make some for Purim gift-giving and have the kids help.

MAKES ABOUT 100

½ pound unsalted butter or margarine, softened
2 cups finely crushed graham crackers
1 teaspoon vanilla extract
1 cup finely grated coconut
1 pound powdered sugar
1 cup chunk-style peanut butter
1½ pounds semisweet chocolate, melted (see page 21)

In the large bowl of an electric mixer, beat the butter until creamy. Add the cracker crumbs, vanilla, coconut, and sugar and mix thoroughly. Blend in the peanut butter. Shape into 1-inch balls and chill.

Using fingertips or a fork, dip the balls in the melted chocolate and swirl. Place in ruffled paper cups or on baking sheets lined with wax paper and chill. Store in the refrigerator.

# KOSHER TURTLES

Sometimes I think I am invited to dinner parties just because I'm known to bring a pretty box of my special crunchy, chewy, caramely signature sweets. You may have sampled them before, but never like this. They're easy to make, but you must have a candy thermometer.

MAKES 36

2 cups sugar

1 cup light corn syrup

¼ pound butter, cut into small pieces

1½ cups cream, warmed

2 teaspoons vanilla extract

108 toasted pecans halves (see page 24)

1½ pounds semisweet chocolate

In a heavy skillet, combine the sugar and corn syrup. Cook slowly, stirring constantly, until the sugar is dissolved and comes to a boil. Then boil the syrup, without stirring, over medium-high heat until a candy thermometer reaches 300°F.

Remove the pan from the heat and add a few pieces of butter. Return the pan to the heat and blend in the remaining pieces of butter. The mixture will bubble up. Add the warm cream slowly, never allowing the caramel mixture to stop boiling. Boil until the thermometer reaches 240 to 250°F, stirring constantly. This should take 15 to 20 minutes. Remove the pan from the heat and let it cool for 5 minutes. Blend in the vanilla. Cool. Pour into an ovenproof bowl.

Using 3 pecan halves for each turtle, place them in small clusters on a large baking sheet lined with wax paper. Spoon the cooled caramel into the center of each cluster. Chill until set. (Use as much caramel as needed. Cover the bowl containing the unused caramel with plastic wrap and store in the refrigerator for up to several weeks. Soften in simmering water or in the microwave before using again.)

Melt the chocolate in a double boiler over simmering water. Remove the pan from the water and beat until smooth and chocolate begins to thicken. Spoon a dollop of chocolate over the caramel on each turtle. Chill. Remove from refrigerator 5 minutes before serving.

# PASSOVER

Passover is celebrated in April or May to commemorate the deliverance from slavery in Egypt. It is also known as the Festival of Unleavened Bread; in their flight into exile, the Hebrews had time to prepare only unleavened bread (matzo) to take with them.

Every trace of flour, grains, leavening agents (baking powder, yeast, and baking soda), and legumes (peas, beans, and lentils) must be used up or discarded before the holiday begins. The searching out of crumbs of *chometz* (leavened foods) with a feather and a wooden spoon is an ancient ritual that ensures the kitchen is clean for this holiday. Many families even use special china, cooking utensils, and cutlery that are reserved just for Passover.

Most commercial canned, frozen, and packaged foods are also forbidden. But there are some commercially prepared foods marked "Kosher for Passover" that are allowed and found in a wide variety in most large markets, as well as in Jewish food stores. There are even Passover versions of many favorite soft drinks.

Although the Passover pantry sounds very complicated at first, it really isn't much of a hardship. There are no restrictions on fresh fruits or most vegetables, and all kosher fish, meats, and poultry are permitted. Matzo meal, matzo cake meal, and potato starch are good substitutes for flour, as you will find in the large selection of Passover dessert recipes that begins on page 162.

The holiday also gives us a chance to try some different foods—old and new Passover favorites. And it also offers a bonus for your health and weight, eliminating many junk foods and substituting low-sodium and lower-fat natural foods.

# A HAROSETH TASTING

In the center of the table at every Passover Seder is a plate arranged with foods symbolic of the holiday. Of these, the only one that requires a recipe is haroseth.

A mixture of fruits, nuts, and spices, haroseth represents the mortar the Jewish people made while laboring as slaves in Egypt. Depending on the fruits, nuts, and spices available, it is prepared differently in Jewish communities all over the world.

Most people are familiar with the Central European version, which consists of apples, walnuts, raisins, cinnamon, and wine. Israeli Haroseth may include peanuts, bananas, apples, dates, wine, and a little matzo meal. The Yemenite Haroseth is made with dates and dried figs and is spiced with coriander and chili peppers.

You may want to serve several of the different haroseth recipes that follow—or the others in the menus in this chapter—and offer a sampling of haroseths from all over the world. They can be made ahead, arranged on plates, covered with plastic wrap, and refrigerated until ready to serve.

## CENTRAL EUROPEAN HAROSETH

MAKES ABOUT 2½ CUPS, OR 20 BALLS

2 apples, unpeeled, cored, and finely chopped
1 cup finely chopped walnuts
2 tablespoons honey
1 teaspoon cinnamon
¼ cup sweet Passover wine

Combine the apples, walnuts, honey, and cinnamon in a bowl and mix well. Add enough wine to bind the mixture. Serve in a bowl or roll into 1-inch balls and arrange on a serving plate.

# GREEK HAROSETH

MAKES 2½ TO 3 CUPS

2 cups pitted dates, chopped
½ cup raisins, chopped
½ cup sweet Passover wine
4 ounces walnuts, ground (¼ cup)
½ teaspoon ground ginger

Place the dates and raisins in a bowl and blend with the wine. Add the walnuts and ginger and blend well. Shape into a pyramid. Cover with plastic wrap and chill.

# ISRAELI HAROSETH

MAKES 3½ CUPS

2 apples, peeled, cored, and chopped
2 bananas, chopped
Juice and peel of ½ lemon, grated
Juice and peel of ½ orange, grated
15 dates, pitted and chopped
½ cup ground peanuts or pistachio nuts
1 teaspoon cinnamon
¼ cup sweet Passover wine
5 tablespoons matzo meal

In a large bowl, combine the apples, bananas, lemon and orange juice and peels, dates, and peanuts and mix well. Add the cinnamon, wine, and matzo meal and blend thoroughly.

# SEPHARDIC HAROSETH
## ISLAND OF RHODES

MAKES ABOUT 2½ CUPS

½ cup dates, pitted
2 cups apples peeled, cored, and thinly sliced
½ cup dried apricots
½ cup chopped walnuts

In a medium saucepan, combine the dates, apples, and dried apricots. Add water to cover. Over high heat, bring the mixture to a boil, lower the heat, and simmer until the mixture is tender enough to mash with a fork. Place the mixture in a processor and process, turning on and off until the mixture is blended. Do not purée. Just before serving, fold in the walnuts.

# TURKISH HAROSETH

MAKES ABOUT 2 CUPS, OR 24 BALLS

½ cup pitted dates
½ cup dried apricots
2 cups peeled, cored, and
   sliced apples
Juice of 1 lemon
1 cup chopped walnuts

In a small saucepan, combine the dates, apricots, apples, lemon juice, and water to cover. Cook until tender, 10 to 15 minutes. Drain and mash with a fork, blending thoroughly. Mix in the walnuts. Spoon into a serving bowl or roll into balls.

# YEMENITE HAROSETH

MAKES ABOUT 1½ CUPS, OR 12 BALLS

1 cup pitted, chopped dates
½ cup chopped dried figs
⅓ cup sweet Passover wine
3 tablespoons sesame seeds
1 teaspoon ground ginger
Pinch of coriander
1 small red chili pepper,
   seeded and minced, or a
   pinch of cayenne
2 tablespoons matzo meal

In a large bowl, combine the dates, figs, and wine. Add the sesame seeds, ginger, coriander, chili pepper, and matzo meal and blend thoroughly. Roll into 1-inch balls or serve in a bowl.

# CALIFORNIA PASSOVER SEDER

FOR 12

Our family goes all out to celebrate Passover. Three generations take part in our Seders and usually twenty-five to thirty of us sit down together to read from the Hagadah and discuss the ancient lore and mysteries surrounding Passover. Did the Red Sea really part? How can we explain the plagues?

One recent Seder is typical of the way we celebrate. Twenty-three of us, ranging from six months to sixty years, participated in reading, singing, and listening to my husband's vivid Passover tales that have become a part of the family tradition. And we enjoyed some very special food with a California flair.

Of course the table was set with all the familiar ceremonial foods, including the eggs and bitter herbs and haroseths from all over the world. We tasted and compared eight different varieties.

We began with a new version of gefilte fish. Rather than forming the ground fish mixture into balls, it is spooned into a baking dish lined with thin fillets of sole and studded with chunks of fresh salmon, which gives the resulting terrine the look of a beautiful mosaic. Homemade mayonnaise, accented with freshly grated horseradish, plus sliced cucumbers and jicama, accompanied the first course, served on a crisp bed of greens.

The main course was hearty veal shanks, garnished with California dried fruits. It was served with slim stalks of tender new asparagus and rosy new potatoes with parsley.

Desserts were served as a kitchen buffet—just help yourself. Our family and friends had trouble choosing between these strictly-for-Passover sponge cakes: Banana-Nut, Citrus Chiffon, and Honey-Spice. Each had risen to lovely heights with the help of potato starch, matzo meal, and egg whites.

To add to the bounty, I also made Farfel-Nut Thins, crunchy with almonds, and I melted some Passover bittersweet chocolate to cover fresh strawberries, plump dried apricots, and toasted pecans. I made plenty of everything, so that gift packages could be wrapped to take home.

During dinner and with our desserts, we sampled a variety of the new Passover kosher wines—dry and sweet, white and red—from California wine makers. In all, we had read the Hagadah, talked, sang, and prayed for about two hours, and then eaten for another two—a fair division, we all agreed. Even the youngest grandchild had no trouble staying awake.

## SALTY EGG SOUP

This cold hard-boiled egg soup is a part of our family Passover ritual, combining two symbolic ingredients—eggs and salt. The eggs are a symbol of new life in the spring season and the salt represents the tears of the Jewish people when they were slaves in Egypt. Some families prefer to serve each person at the seder a whole hard-boiled egg to be dipped in salt.

12 eggs, hard-boiled and peeled (see page 23)
1 to 1½ quarts cold water
2 to 4 tablespoons kosher salt

In a large bowl, mash the eggs roughly with a potato masher. Add 1 quart of the water and 2 tablespoons of the salt. Add additional water and salt to taste. Cover and refrigerate until serving time. Ladle into soup bowls.

## CALIFORNIA HAROSETH

My husband and I decided to create a special California-style haroseth to hand down to our children as a family tradition, so they can include it in their Seders in years to come. Our recipe uses the avocados, lemons, almonds, oranges, and dried fruits for which California is famous.

1 large avocado, peeled and diced

Juice of ½ lemon

½ cup sliced almonds

⅓ cup raisins

4 seedless dates

2 figs or prunes

1 whole orange, peel and sections

2 tablespoons apple juice

2 tablespoons matzo meal

Toss the avocado and lemon juice in a bowl. Set aside. In a processor or blender, place the almonds, raisins, dates, and figs. Process until coarsely chopped. Add the orange peel and orange sections and process briefly to combine. Add the avocado and process just 1 or 2 seconds more. Transfer the mixture to a glass bowl and gently fold in the apple juice and matzo meal. Cover with plastic wrap and store in the refrigerator.

# Gefilte Fish Terrine

4 sole fillets, skinned and cut in halves

Vegetable oil

2 medium onions, cut into eighths

4 small carrots, peeled and sliced

1 celery rib, sliced

1 pound ling cod or other white-fleshed fish fillet, cut into 1-inch cubes

1 pound halibut or other white-fleshed fish fillets, cut into 1-inch cubes

3 eggs

½ cup cold water

Salt

Freshly ground black pepper

1 pound salmon fillet, cut into ½-inch chunks

Lettuce leaves

Horseradish-Tomato Mayonnaise (recipe follows)

Soak the sole fillets in cold water for 15 minutes. Drain and pat dry. Place them between sheets of wax paper and flatten lightly with a mallet or the side of a knife. With a sharp knife, make several slashes on the skin side of each fillet.

Lightly oil a 2-quart glass baking dish and line it with wax paper. Oil the paper. Line the entire baking dish with the sole fillets, placing them skin side down and slightly overlapping. Cover with plastic wrap and chill in the refrigerator for 30 minutes.

Place the onions, carrots, and celery in a processor or grinder. Process or grind until finely minced. Add the cod and halibut and process until well blended. Add the eggs, 1 at a time, alternating with the water. Blend well. Season to taste with salt and pepper.

Transfer the ground mixture to a large bowl. Gently fold in the salmon chunks. Spoon the fish mixture over the sole fillets in the prepared baking dish. Cover with oiled wax paper and a double layer of foil.

Preheat the oven to 350°F. Place the terrine in a large baking pan and pour in hot water to come halfway up the sides. Bake for 50 minutes, or until a knife inserted in the center comes out clean. Cool on a rack 10 minutes. Loosen foil and pour out excess liquid. Refrigerate for at least 1 hour.

To serve, invert the terrine on a platter and slice. Serve on lettuce leaves on individual serving plates with the Horseradish-Tomato Mayonnaise.

## HORSERADISH-TOMATO MAYONNAISE

MAKES ABOUT 2 CUPS

4 egg yolks
Juice of 1 lemon
½ teaspoon salt
1 cup oil
2 tomatoes, peeled, seeded, and chopped
2 tablespoons grated fresh horseradish

In a processor or blender, place the egg yolks, lemon juice, and salt and process until well blended. Add the oil, 1 tablespoon at a time, processing until the mixture thickens. Transfer to a large bowl and fold in the chopped tomatoes and horseradish. Cover with plastic wrap and chill in the refrigerator.

# VEGETABLE SOUP WITH MINI-MATZO BALLS

This soup contains a dozen fresh vegetables blended into a delicious medley of flavors. It makes a refreshing change from the predictable chicken soup. The tiny matzo balls were inspired by an Italian technique for making the small flour-and-potato dumplings known as gnocchi. The dumpling mixture is spooned into a pastry bag and piped right into the boiling soup or other cooking liquid.

¼ cup safflower or vegetable oil
6 green onions (scallions), thinly sliced with greens
2 shallots, minced
1 medium onion, thinly sliced
1 large potato, peeled and thinly sliced

In a large heavy pot, heat the oil over medium heat. Add the green onions, shallots, onion, and potato and sauté until soft, about 5 minutes. Add the carrots, broccoli, celery, and parsnip and sauté for 5 minutes longer. Add the zucchini, squash, and mushrooms and sauté for 2 to 3 minutes. Simmer very slowly until the vegetables are soft and the juices accumulate, 5 to 10 minutes. Add the tomatoes and stock and simmer, partially covered, for 45

4 carrots, peeled and thinly
   sliced
4 small broccoli stalks, thinly
   sliced
1 celery rib, thinly sliced
1 parsnip, peeled and thinly
   sliced
2 medium zucchini, thinly
   sliced
1 yellow crookneck squash,
   thinly sliced
8 medium mushrooms, thinly
   sliced
2 large tomatoes, peeled (see
   page 26) and diced
4 to 6 cups Vegetable Stock
   (see page 391)
Salt
Freshly ground black pepper
Mini-Matzo Balls (recipe follows)

minutes. Season to taste with salt and pepper. Bring to a boil over high heat. Add the Mini-Matzo Balls, cover, reduce heat, and simmer gently for 10 minutes.

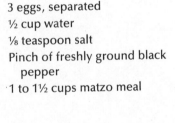

## MINI-MATZO BALLS
KNAIDLACH

3 eggs, separated
½ cup water
⅛ teaspoon salt
Pinch of freshly ground black
   pepper
1 to 1½ cups matzo meal

Put the egg yolks, water, salt, and pepper in a small bowl and beat with a fork. Set aside.

In a large mixing bowl, beat the egg whites until they form stiff peaks: do not overbeat. With a rubber spatula, gently fold the yolk mixture alternately with the matzo meal into the egg whites until well blended. Use only enough matzo meal to make a light, firm dough.

Spoon this mixture into a pastry bag with a ½-inch round tube opening. Hold the bag over the simmering soup and squeeze out the dough in 1-inch lengths, cutting them off at the tip of the tube with a sharp knife. Cover and simmer for 10 minutes; do not uncover during this cooking time. Ladle into hot soup bowls.

# VEAL SHANKS WITH PRUNES AND APRICOTS

Have the butcher cut the veal shanks into 2-inch-thick pieces. They freeze well, so have him wrap some extra ones in small packages for your freezer. If you have leftovers, the sauce, vegetables, and even the dried fruit are delicious when reheated the next day.

12 pieces veal shank, cut 2 inches thick

Salt

Freshly ground black pepper

½ cup safflower or vegetable oil

6 garlic cloves, minced (optional)

2 large onions, finely chopped

8 medium carrots, finely chopped

6 celery ribs, finely chopped

1½ cups dry white wine

6 large tomatoes, peeled (see page 26) and chopped

6 fresh thyme or rosemary sprigs

¼ cup chopped fresh parsley

6 ounces dried prunes, plumped in sweet Passover wine to cover

6 ounces dried apricots, plumped in sweet Passover wine to cover

Parsley for garnish

Wash and dry the veal shanks and lightly sprinkle with salt and pepper.

Heat the oil in a large heavy skillet over medium heat. Brown the shanks on all sides, about 5 minutes, and remove to a platter. To the same skillet, add the garlic, onions, carrots, and celery and sauté until lightly browned. Place the veal shanks on top of the onion mixture; add the wine and cook until reduced by half, 3 to 4 minutes. Add the tomatoes, thyme, and chopped parsley. Cover and simmer for 1 hour.

Add the drained prunes and apricots. Continue cooking for 30 minutes to 1 hour more, until the meat is tender enough to fall away from the bones. Serve garnished with parsley.

# STEAMED ASPARAGUS WITH GARLIC SAUCE

6 dozen asparagus spears

Garlic Sauce (recipe follows)

Minced parsley and lemon slices for garnish

Cut or break off the tough lower portion of each asparagus stalk. Place the asparagus in a steamer and steam for 10 minutes. Or tie the asparagus in bunches and place upright in a deep saucepan. Add ½ cup boiling water and cook, covered, for 12 minutes, or until tender-crisp. Drain the asparagus carefully. Arrange on serving plates and spoon Garlic Sauce on top. Sprinkle the parsley on top of the asparagus and garnish with the lemon slices.

### GARLIC SAUCE

¼ pound unsalted margarine
6 large garlic cloves, minced
1 tablespoon lemon juice
Salt
Freshly ground black pepper

Melt the margarine in a small skillet over low heat. Add the garlic and lemon juice. Simmer until the garlic is lightly browned. Season to taste with salt and pepper.

# PARSLEYED NEW POTATOES

During our Passover Seder it has become a tradition to serve steamed red new potatoes dipped in salt as one of the Seder foods, just after the egg soup. For us this symbolizes the arrival of spring, and these little new potatoes look so colorful on the dinner plate.

3 dozen small red potatoes, unpeeled and quartered
Salt
Freshly ground black pepper
1 cup minced fresh parsley

Scrub the outside of the potatoes. Place them in a steamer over simmering water and steam for 10 to 15 minutes, or until tender. Transfer to a large bowl; season to taste with salt and pepper and garnish with minced parsley.

# BANANA-NUT SPONGE CAKE

7 eggs, separated
1 cup sugar
¾ cup matzo cake meal
¼ cup potato starch
1 teaspoon salt
1 cup mashed bananas
½ cup chopped walnuts or pecans

Preheat the oven to 325°F.

In a large mixing bowl, beat the egg yolks and sugar until light in color and texture. Combine the matzo cake meal, potato starch, and salt. Add this a little at a time to the egg yolk mixture, alternately with the bananas, beating until smooth.

In a large mixing bowl, beat the egg whites until soft peaks form. Gently fold the beaten egg whites and the nuts into the egg yolk mixture.

Pour the batter into an ungreased 10-inch tube pan. Bake for 45 minutes, until a toothpick inserted into the cake comes out dry and the cake is springy to the touch. Invert the pan onto a wire rack and cool. With a sharp knife loosen the cake from the sides and center of the pan and unmold onto a cake plate.

# CITRUS CHIFFON SPONGE CAKE

9 eggs, separated
1½ cups sugar
1⅓ cups potato starch
3 tablespoons ground almonds
3 tablespoons lemon juice
2 tablespoons orange marmalade
Grated zest of 3 lemons
Five-Minute Lemon Frosting (recipe follows)
Candied Lemon Peel, for garnish (recipe follows)

Preheat the oven to 350°F.

In the bowl of an electric mixer, beat the egg whites until soft peaks form. Add ¾ cup of the sugar and continue beating until stiff but not dry. Set aside.

In another large mixing bowl, beat the egg yolks with the remaining ¾ cup sugar, potato starch and almonds until light in color and texture. Blend in the lemon juice and orange marmalade. Gently fold the egg white mixture and lemon zest into the egg yolk mixture.

Pour the batter into an ungreased 10-inch tube pan. Bake for 55 minutes, or until a toothpick inserted into the cake comes out dry and the cake is springy to the touch. Remove from the oven and invert the pan onto a wire rack to cool. With a sharp knife, carefully loosen the cake from the pan and then unmold onto a cake plate. Frost or drizzle the Five-Minute Lemon Frosting over the cake. Garnish with the Candied Lemon Peel.

## FIVE-MINUTE LEMON FROSTING

3½ cups pulverized or sifted powdered Passover sugar
3 egg whites, unbeaten
1 teaspoon lemon juice
½ teaspoon vanilla extract

In a bowl of an electric mixer, combine the sugar, egg whites, lemon juice, and vanilla. Beat at low speed until the sugar is dissolved. Then beat at high speed until the mixture is light and fluffy. Cover with a damp towel until ready to use.

# CANDIED LEMON OR ORANGE PEEL

Lemon or orange peels can be prepared in the same way to make a delicious confection. For a very special touch, dip the strips of peel halfway into melted chocolate, place them on wax paper, and refrigerate until the chocolate is solid.

Peels of 6 lemons or oranges, thinly sliced
2½ cups sugar

Use a potato peeler to shave off strips of the peel 2 to 3 inches long and about ½ inch wide. In a large heavy pot over high heat, bring about 2 quarts of water to a boil. Drop in the fruit peels, boil for 3 minutes, and then drain. Repeat this step two more times, draining and using fresh water each time. This eliminates the bitterness.

In a large pot, combine 2 more cups of water and the sugar. Bring to a boil over high heat, stirring until the sugar dissolves. Add the drained peels and mix well. Lower the heat, simmering gently until the peels are tender and glazed with a thick syrup, about 1 hour. Remove from the syrup with a slotted spoon and dry on a wire rack. (The remaining syrup may be stored in the refrigerator and used again for another batch.)

# HONEY-SPICE SPONGE CAKE

8 eggs, separated
1 cup sugar
16 ounces honey
¼ cup strong black coffee
1½ cups matzo cake meal
½ cup potato starch
1 teaspoon cinnamon
½ teaspoon ground cloves
¼ teaspoon salt
½ cup chopped walnuts or sliced almonds

Preheat the oven to 325°F.

In the bowl of an electric mixer, beat the egg yolks with the sugar until light in color and texture. Add the honey and coffee and beat well. Mix together the matzo cake meal, potato starch, cinnamon, cloves, and salt. Blend this mixture into the egg yolk mixture.

In a large mixing bowl, beat the egg whites until stiff peaks form (do not overbeat). Gently but thoroughly, fold the beaten egg whites into the batter. Fold in the nuts.

Pour this batter into an ungreased 10-inch tube pan. Bake for 1¼ hours, until a toothpick inserted into the cake comes out dry and the cake is springy to the touch. Remove from the oven and invert the pan onto a wire rack to cool. With a sharp knife, loosen the cake from the pan and unmold onto a cake plate.

# FARFEL-NUT THINS

One really nice thing about this recipe is that you can mix up the batter and keep it in a covered bowl in the refrigerator throughout Passover. Whenever you want some cookies, just spoon the batter onto a foil-lined pan and bake.

MAKES ABOUT 8 DOZEN

1 cup matzo farfel
1 tablespoon matzo cake meal
1 cup sugar
¼ teaspoon salt
¼ pound unsalted margarine,
  melted
1 egg
1 teaspoon vanilla extract, or
  1 tablespoon orange juice
½ cup ground almonds

Preheat the oven to 325°F.

In a large mixing bowl, combine the matzo farfel, matzo cake meal, sugar, and salt and mix well. Pour the margarine over the farfel mixture and blend until the sugar dissolves. Add the egg and vanilla or orange juice and blend. Mix in the almonds. Chill for 15 minutes.

Line a baking sheet with foil and drop the farfel mixture by teaspoons onto the foil, about 2 inches apart. Bake for 8 to 10 minutes, or until golden brown. Cool completely before lifting from the foil.

# CHOCOLATE-COVERED FRUITS

These are so easy to prepare, and they add a touch of glamour to the dessert table or when passed around on a plate. I serve them all year and often fill a little gift box with these and other chocolate treats to take as a gift when invited out to dinner.

3 pounds Passover semisweet
  chocolate, broken into
  small pieces
12 ounces dried apricots
12 ounces dried figs
2 pints fresh strawberries

In the top of a double boiler, melt the chocolate over simmering water, stirring as it softens, until smooth.

Select 2 or 3 baking sheets that will fit in the refrigerator and line them with wax paper. One at a time, dip the apricots, figs, and strawberries into the melted chocolate, generously coating the bottom half of each piece of fruit.

Place each dipped fruit on the prepared baking sheets. Refrigerate until the chocolate hardens, then cover lightly with wax paper and refrigerate until ready to serve. Peel the chocolate-covered fruit off the wax paper and transfer to a serving platter.

# ITALIAN PASSOVER SEDER

FOR 12

Italian Haroseth

Sogliola con Funghi

Passatelli
and
Bollito Misto with Salsa
Verde

Matzo Noodles

Agnello Arrosto

Carciofi alla Marinara

Pan di Spagna

Zabaglione

SUGGESTED BEVERAGES:

Passover Italian white and
red wines

My love affair with Italian foods inspired me one Passover to create an Italian Seder with the help of my friend Anna Maura, a charming Jewish-American-Italian ballerina. She spent a lot of time on the telephone checking on all the recipes with her grandmother in New York City. All the ingredients and measurements turned out to be perfect when I tested them, so I guess her big telephone bill was worth it.

These recipes originated in Bologna, but are also typical of those served at Seders in Florence and Rome—where some of the first Jewish settlements in Europe were founded. The Passover fish and lamb dishes have been handed down for generations. The soup is garnished with an unusual pasta made from matzo meal. The soup's broth comes from the poaching liquid used to prepare an authentic Bollito Misto—boiled meats—served with Salsa Verde. There is even an Italian-style haroseth.

Use this old-fashioned Italian menu to give your Passover Seder an entirely new flair.

# ITALIAN HAROSETH

MAKES ABOUT 2½ CUPS, OR 20 BALLS

2 apples, unpeeled, cored, and coarsely chopped
6 dates, finely chopped
1 hard-boiled egg (see page 23), finely chopped
½ cup finely chopped almonds
¼ cup finely chopped walnuts
¼ cup raisins, finely chopped
Juice of 1 lemon
1 to 2 tablespoons matzo meal

In a large bowl, combine the apples, dates, egg, almonds, walnuts, and raisins and blend thoroughly. Add the lemon juice and enough matzo meal to bind the mixture. Mound the haroseth in a bowl or roll it into 1-inch balls and arrange on a plate.

# SOGLIOLA CON FUNGHI
## SOLE WITH MUSHROOMS

When ordering your Seder fish, make sure the fish man saves the skin and bones for you when he cuts the fillets; ask him for extra bones to make up 1 pound.

1 pound fish bones
2 garlic cloves, minced
1 celery rib
2 carrots, peeled and sliced
2 sprigs parsley
1 cup water
1 cup white wine
1 teaspoon salt
½ teaspoon freshly ground black pepper
4 pounds fillet of Rex or Dover sole, cut into 2-inch-wide pieces
2 tablespoons safflower or vegetable oil
1 tablespoon capers, drained (optional)
½ pound mushrooms, thinly sliced (3 cups)
12 boiled tiny red potatoes

In a large deep pot or poacher, put the fish bones, garlic, celery, carrots, parsley, water, wine, salt, and pepper. Bring to a boil and simmer, partially covered, for 30 to 40 minutes. Strain the broth and return it to the poacher.

Place the fish pieces in the broth. Add the oil, capers, and mushrooms. Cover and simmer gently for 10 minutes, or until the fish is flaky. With a slotted spoon, remove the fish from the broth and keep it warm on a covered heated platter. Boil the broth at high heat until it reduces by half, 5 minutes. Spoon the liquid over the fish and serve with boiled tiny red potatoes.

# Passatelli and Bollito Misto with Salsa Verde

## Broth with Matzo Noodles; Boiled Meats and Green Sauce

This is a two-in-one recipe. The soup is served clear with noodles and the assorted boiled meats are served as a separate course.

This is a great favorite in family-style restaurants throughout northern Italy. A cart is wheeled from table to table with all sorts of delicious boiled meats, such as tongue, chicken, veal or beef roasts, and sausages; bowls of the green sauce and candied fruit are passed around.

1 chicken (3½ pounds), cut up
1 beef brisket (4 pounds)
1 turkey neck
2 beef marrow bones, each bone sliced in thirds (ask your butcher to do this)
1 large onion, sliced
2 carrots, peeled and sliced
2 celery ribs with tops, sliced
6 artichoke leaves
1 artichoke stem
Salt
Freshly ground black pepper
Matzo Noodles (recipe follows)
Salsa Verde (recipe follows)

Place the chicken, brisket, turkey neck, beef marrow bones, onion, carrots, celery, and artichoke leaves and stems in a large pot. Add enough water to cover. Add salt and pepper to taste. Bring to a boil and simmer gently, partially covered, for at least 4 hours. Cool.

Strain the soup and reserve the chicken, brisket, turkey neck, and beef bones for the Bollito Misto with Salsa Verde. Bring soup to a boil and add Matzo Noodles.

# Matzo Noodles

These Matzo Noodles, or pasta, are great served in the broth from Bollito Misto. For a variation, you can drain the leftover noodles and serve them with a Garlic-Parsley Sauce (recipe follows) as a pasta course. This is a benefit during Passover, since the use of flour is forbidden, and so this dish offers a rare opportunity to eat pasta during this holiday.

When I prepare a pasta dish, as you will see in my Italian recipes, I always make the sauce in a large skillet, boil my pasta, and drop it into the hot sauce. Then I coat the pasta generously with the sauce by gently tossing the two together. This keeps everything piping hot, firm, and delicious.

2 cups matzo meal

1 tablespoon safflower or vegetable oil

Pinch of nutmeg

4 eggs

Salt

Freshly ground black pepper

In a large mixing bowl, mix together matzo meal, oil, nutmeg, and eggs just until well blended. Do not overmix. Season to taste with salt and pepper. Divide dough into quarters and push each quarter of dough through a potato ricer into boiling soup. Simmer, uncovered, for 15 minutes.

## GARLIC-PARSLEY SAUCE

¼ pound unsalted margarine

4 garlic cloves, minced

¼ cup minced parsley

Salt

Freshly ground black pepper

In a large skillet, melt the margarine. Add the garlic and sauté until soft. Add the parsley and simmer until soft. Add salt and pepper to taste. Add strained cooked Matzo Noodles to the skillet and toss to coat. Serve hot.

## SALSA VERDE
### GREEN SAUCE

½ cup safflower or vegetable oil

3 garlic cloves, minced

2 carrots, peeled and minced

3 celery ribs, minced

1 green bell pepper, stemmed, seeded, and minced

1 tablespoon minced parsley

1 tablespoon white vinegar

1 teaspoon tomato paste

½ cup hot water

Salt

Freshly ground black pepper

Heat the oil and sauté the garlic, carrots, and celery until soft. Add the green bell pepper and parsley and cook until tender. Add the vinegar and simmer until it cooks out. Combine tomato paste with the hot water. Add to the garlic mixture. Season to taste with salt and pepper and simmer until sauce is thick. Serve hot with Bollito Misto.

# AGNELLO ARROSTO
## ROASTED SPRING LAMB

2 cups white vinegar

4 cups water

1 whole head of garlic, 4 peeled cloves reserved, remaining cloves minced

In a large bowl, combine the vinegar, water, minced garlic and lamb. Soak for 4 hours. Strain, discarding the liquid.

Preheat the oven to 450°F.

Combine the rosemary and the reserved garlic cloves

6 to 8 pounds lamb shoulder, cut into 2-inch chunks

3 fresh rosemary sprigs or 1 teaspoon dried rosemary

Salt

Freshly ground black pepper

1 red bell pepper, stemmed, seeded, and thinly sliced

1 green bell pepper, stemmed, seeded, and thinly sliced

2 potatoes, peeled and sliced lengthwise

½ cup olive or vegetable oil

and coarsely chop. Add salt and pepper to taste. Toss with the lamb to coat evenly. Add the red and green peppers and potatoes and toss well. Place in a large roasting pan. Pour the oil over the meat mixture. Bake, uncovered, for 10 minutes. Reduce the heat to 350°F and bake for 1 to 1½ hours, until tender.

# CARCIOFI ALLA MARINARA
## ARTICHOKES IN TOMATO SAUCE

This dish was served to us many years ago by a good friend, Lora Gerson, and it has been a favorite ever since. The catsup and dry red wine add a rich flavor to the artichokes. After you prepare this dish the first time, you might want to add sliced mushrooms, whole garlic cloves, or perhaps even raisins.

6 whole artichokes

2 tablespoons olive oil

2 onions, chopped

2 garlic cloves, minced

½ green bell pepper, chopped

1 celery stalk, chopped

¼ cup minced parsley

1 teaspoon dried oregano, crushed

1 bay leaf, crushed

6 fresh basil leaves

½ cup catsup

½ cup red wine

2 tablespoons red wine vinegar

2 cups water

Salt

Freshly ground black pepper

Prepare each artichoke by cutitng off the stem on the bottom; snip off the needle edges of each outer leaf and cut 1-inch off the top. Place each artichoke under hot water, then invert and drain. Set aside.

In a 6- to 8-quart Dutch oven, heat the oil and sauté the onions, garlic, green pepper, and celery until soft. Add the parsley, oregano, bay leaf, basil, catsup, wine, vinegar, and 2 cups water. Mix well and simmer for 10 minutes, stirring occasionally.

Place the prepared artichokes, stem side down, in the sauce and spoon the sauce over each artichoke. Cover and cook over medium heat for 2 hours, basting frequently and adding wine or water when sauce reduces too quickly and becomes too thick. The artichokes are done when a leaf pulls off easily or a sharp knife goes through the center easily. Serve hot, spooning the sauce over each artichoke.

# PAN DI SPAGNA
## ITALIAN WINE CAKE

Athough this cake is very moist and flavorful on its own, I've added a special festive topping of Zabaglione and melted chocolate. Then the cake is garnished with fresh strawberries, which are plentiful during the Passover holiday.

6 eggs, separated
1½ cups sugar
½ cup potato starch
½ cup matzo cake meal
¼ cup orange juice
¼ cup sweet Passover wine
Juice and grated peel of 1 lemon
Pinch of salt
Zabaglione (recipe follows)
8 ounces Passover chocolate, melted (see page 21)
1 pint fresh strawberries, washed and sliced

Preheat the oven to 350°F.

In a large bowl, beat the egg yolks, adding sugar in a slow stream. Continue beating until light and fluffy.

Combine the potato starch and matzo cake meal and set aside. Combine the orange juice, wine, and lemon juice and peel. Add the potato starch mixture to the egg yolk mixture alternately with the orange juice mixture, blending thoroughly.

Beat the egg whites with salt until soft peaks form. Gently fold the whites into the egg yolk mixture. Pour this batter into an ungreased 10-inch tube pan. Bake for 40 minutes, or until a toothpick inserted in the cake comes out dry. Remove the cake from the oven; immediately invert the pan and let it cool. Loosen the sides and center of the cake with a sharp knife and unmold onto a cake plate. While the cake cools, prepare the Zabaglione and melt the chocolate. Serve slices of Pan di Spagna with Zabaglione. Drizzle with melted chocolate and garnish with sliced strawberries.

## ZABAGLIONE

6 egg yolks
¼ cup sugar
⅔ cup sweet Passover wine

Using a wire whisk, beat the egg yolks and sugar until light and fluffy. Gradually add the wine, beating constantly. Place in the top of a double boiler over simmering water and continue beating vigorously until the mixture foams and begins to thicken: be careful not to overcook. Serve hot or cold.

# ANCIENT PERSIAN SEDER

FOR 12

Symbolic Hard-Boiled
Eggs, Sephardic Style

Persian Haroseth

Steamed Green Onions
with Egg-Lemon Sauce

Chicken with Dried Fruit
and Almond Stuffing

Persian-Style Lamb Shank
Stew

Apricot Sponge Cake

Passover Almond Cookies

Bowls of pistachio nuts,
raisins, dates, figs

Bowls of fresh fruit

SUGGESTED BEVERAGES:

French or Israeli Passover
white and red wines

In recent years, many Iranian Jews have settled in southern California. Iranian students in my cooking classes often showed me handwritten books of ancient Persian family recipes and they shared these cooking secrets with me.

In adapting their recipes for modern kitchens, I created this Passover menu, which even includes a Persian Haroseth—an intriguing mixture of typically Persian spices, fruits, and nuts. The entire menu makes a delicious change from the usual Passover fare. If you want to be truly authentic, serve tea as a beverage along with wine, and decorate your dessert table with bowls of nuts and fresh and dried fruits.

## SYMBOLIC HARD-BOILED EGGS, SEPHARDIC STYLE

The unusual way these eggs are cooked and served were shared with me by Regina Terika. Her family came from the Island of Rhodes, which had a vibrant, Sephardic Jewish community.

The eggs are hard-boiled for at least 2 hours, completely enclosed in a nest of brown onion skins. (They are often baked for an additional 2 hours.) The shell takes on an even deeper reddish bronze color than the onion skins themselves. These eggs symbolize the roasted eggs that were brought to the Holy Temple as an offering during Passover, and also for other holidays. The egg also symbolizes mourning, and when eggs are served at the Seder, each person is served an egg and removes the shell. If someone is in mourning, he eats the egg whole, while others will slice theirs before eating. A soup of hard-boiled eggs in salt water, often served as a first course at Passover, signifies mourning for the lost Holy Temple.

Skins of 6 brown onions
12 eggs
¼ cup safflower or vegetable oil
1 teaspoon salt
1 teaspoon freshly ground black pepper

In a large heavy saucepan, place half the onion skins. Place the eggs on top and more onion skins on top of the eggs. Add the oil, salt, pepper, and water to cover. Bring to a boil over high heat, lower the heat, and simmer for at least 2 hours.

Remove the peels and place the eggs in a shallow bowl. Place egg on Seder plate with the other symbolic foods.

# Persian Haroseth

MAKES 5 CUPS

1 unpeeled pear, cored and finely chopped
1 unpeeled apple, cored and finely chopped
1 cup finely chopped walnuts
1 cup finely chopped almonds
1 cup finely chopped hazelnuts (filberts)
1 cup finely chopped pistachio nuts
1 cup chopped dates
1 cup chopped raisins
2 teaspoons ground ginger
2 teaspoons cinnamon
2 tablespoons apple cider vinegar
1 to 2 tablespoons sweet Passover wine

In a large bowl, combine the pear, apple, walnuts, almonds, hazelnuts, pistachio nuts, dates, and raisins. Mix well. Add the ginger, cinnamon, vinegar, and enough wine to bind the mixture. Transfer to a platter and shape into a pyramid. Cover with plastic wrap and chill well.

# STEAMED GREEN ONIONS WITH EGG-LEMON SAUCE

During the Seder service, it is the Persian custom to use green onions to represent the bitter herbs, a symbol of our people's struggles. Be sure to have sharp knives available when you serve this onion recipe with your Seder dinner. The cooked green onions are hard to cut.

5 parsley sprigs
¼ cup cider vinegar
6 whole cloves
¼ teaspoon whole coriander seeds
¼ teaspoon dried thyme
8 bunches (about 42) green onions (scallions)
Egg-Lemon Sauce (recipe follows)

In the bottom of a steamer pot, put the parsley, cider vinegar, cloves, coriander seeds, and thyme. Add just enough water to touch the bottom of the steamer basket or colander. Place the green onions in the steamer, cover, bring the water to a boil, and steam for 5 to 10 minutes, until the onions are tender. Place the green onions on serving plates and spoon Egg-Lemon Sauce over them.

## EGG-LEMON SAUCE

3 egg yolks
2 tablespoons lemon juice
¼ pound unsalted margarine
Salt
Freshly ground black pepper

In the top of a double boiler, whisk together the egg yolks and lemon juice. Divide the margarine into 3 parts. Add 1 part to the yolk mixture. Over hot—not boiling—water, stir rapidly and constantly with a wooden spoon until the margarine is melted. Then add the second piece. As the mixture thickens and the margarine melts, add the third piece, stirring constantly. Continue mixing until the sauce is thick. Remove the saucepan from the heat. Add salt and pepper to taste. Pour the sauce over the green onions. Serve immediately.

# CHICKEN WITH DRIED FRUIT AND ALMOND STUFFING

This chicken is different from any I have ever tasted. The special flavor comes from the sweet, tart taste of the dried fruit, combined with the crunchy almonds. Stuff two chickens and don't worry about leftovers—it tastes just as good cold or reheated.

1 whole chicken, about 6 pounds
5 tablespoons unsalted margarine
2 onions, coarsely chopped
½ cup coarsely chopped dried apricots
½ cup coarsely chopped prunes
½ cup whole toasted almonds (see page 24)
¼ cup golden raisins
¼ teaspoon cinnamon
1 teaspoon dried tarragon
½ teaspoon dried thyme
Salt
Freshly ground black pepper

Preheat the oven to 375°F.

Wash and dry the chicken. In a large skillet, heat 2 tablespoons of the margarine over medium heat and sauté the onions until transparent, about 5 minutes.

Sprinkle half the onions onto a foil-lined large shallow roasting pan and set it aside. To the onions in the skillet add the apricots, prunes, almonds, raisins, cinnamon, tarragon, thyme, and salt and pepper to taste. Sauté for 5 to 10 minutes, mixing well to blend all ingredients. Cool.

Stuff the chicken with the onion mixture and truss. Place the chicken, breast side down, on the onions in the broiler pan. If any stuffing is left over, sprinkle it around the chicken. Rub the chicken with the remaining 3 tablespoons margarine. Roast for 30 minutes, until the skin is a light golden brown. Turn the chicken over and continue roasting for 30 minutes more, or until well-browned and crisp. Serve immediately.

# PERSIAN-STYLE LAMB SHANK STEW

Many Persian recipes use a large amount of lemon juice, presumably because the juice acted as a preservative in the days before refrigeration. It also acts as a marvelous meat tenderizer and gives a tangy flavor that goes wonderfully well with the mint, another favorite Persian seasoning.

Have your butcher remove the bones from the lamb shanks and cut the meat into 1½-inch cubes, trimming off as much fat as possible. If you like, cook the stew a day ahead. It tastes even better reheated.

4 tablespoons safflower or vegetable oil
2 large onions, finely chopped
6 pounds lamb shanks, boned and cubed
6 garlic cloves, minced
Pinch of saffron (optional)
Salt
Freshly ground black pepper
3 cups dry red wine

In a small skillet, heat 2 tablespoons of the oil and sauté the onions until transparent, about 5 minutes. In a large bowl, toss the onions with the lamb, garlic, and saffron. Season to taste with salt and pepper. Marinate in the refrigerator for several hours.

Place the lamb and onion mixture in a large pot. Add the wine and enough water to cover. Bring to a boil and simmer for 30 minutes. In a medium skillet, heat the remaining 2 tablespoons oil and sauté the celery until tender, about 5 minutes; add the celery to the lamb mixture and

8 celery stalks, cut into 1-inch
  pieces (reserve tops)
2 bunches fresh mint, finely
  chopped
2 bunches parsley, stemmed
  and finely chopped
Juice of 4 to 5 lemons

toss well. Chop the reserved celery tops and combine with the mint and parsley. Add this mixture to the shanks and cook until tender and the sauce is thick. Fifteen minutes before serving, add the lemon juice and salt and pepper to taste. Simmer until the meat is tender.

# APRICOT SPONGE CAKE

This is a little more dense than the usual sponge cake, and the flavor of the apricots is sensational. It takes a little extra care to make this cake, but the beautiful results are worth the effort.

6 ounces dried apricots
1½ cups apple juice
2¼ cups sugar
9 eggs, separated
1⅓ cups matzo cake meal
1 cup ground almonds
1 teaspoon salt
Passover sugar

Preheat the oven to 350°F.

In a small saucepan, combine the apricots, apple juice, and ½ cup of the sugar. Bring to a boil and simmer until tender, 5 to 10 minutes. Cool. Strain ⅓ cup of the liquid and reserve. Purée the remaining apricot mixture and set aside.

In the bowl of an electric mixer, beat the egg yolks with 1¼ cups of the sugar until light in color and texture. Add 1 cup of the apricot purée and blend thoroughly. In a small bowl, combine the matzo cake meal, almonds, and salt. Add to the egg yolk mixture alternately with the reserved ⅓ cup liquid from the apricots.

In a large mixing bowl, beat the egg whites until soft peaks form. Add the remaining ½ cup sugar and beat until stiff. Fold one quarter of the meringue into the batter to loosen it. Add the remaining meringue, folding in gently until blended. Bake in a 10-inch tube pan for 55 minutes, or until the cake springs back to the touch and a toothpick inserted in the center comes out dry. Remove from the oven immediately; invert the pan and cool it. Loosen the cake from the sides and center of the pan with a sharp knife and unmold onto a cake plate. Serve plain or sprinkle with pulverized or powdered Passover sugar.

# PASSOVER ALMOND COOKIES

Everyone, old and young, loves cookies, so whenever we get together for family dinners, I usually try to include a plate of them, no matter what else I am serving for dessert. These are unusual, because they contain no flour, matzo meal, matzo cake meal, or potato starch—just ground almonds, sugar, and egg whites.

MAKES 3 DOZEN

½ pound whole almonds
¾ cup sugar
¼ teaspoon salt
3 egg whites, unbeaten
½ teaspoon almond extract

Preheat the oven to 325°F.

Place the almonds on a foil-lined baking sheet in a single layer. Bake for 5 minutes, until warmed and just slightly darkened in color. Cool the almonds to room temperature. Place them in a processor or blender and process until finely ground.

Raise the oven temperature to 400°F.

In a large mixing bowl, thoroughly blend the almonds, sugar, salt, egg whites, and almond extract. Drop the batter by teaspoons, 2 inches apart, onto parchment- or foil-lined baking sheets. Bake for 10 to 15 minutes, until golden. Immediately remove with a spatula to a wire rack to cool.

# PASSOVER BRUNCH

## FOR 6 TO 8

▼▲▼▲▼▲▼▲▼▲▼▲▼▲▼▲▼▲▼

Berries in Sweet Passover
White Wine

Passover Cheese Ring

Matzo and Mushroom
Omelet

Passover French Toast

Beet Preserves

Café au Lait

SUGGESTED BEVERAGE:

Passover rosé wine

Beautiful fresh berries in white wine are a welcome starter for this holiday menu. Then a hot-from-the-oven Passover Cheese Ring is a crisp accompaniment to a fluffy omelet. Passover French Toast, made with left-over sponge cake, is served with ruby-red Beet Preserves, fragrant with ginger. Add a creamy Café Au Lait and more of the Passover white wine or rosé and your friends and family will wonder why they never thought of serving a Passover brunch before.

# BERRIES IN SWEET PASSOVER WHITE WINE

2 pints small strawberries (or
cut large berries in half)
2 pints raspberries
2 pints blueberries
Sugar
Sweet Passover white wine
Mint leaves
Candied Lemon or Orange
Peel (see page 141)

Wash berries and remove the stems. (Discard any that are not perfect.) Sprinkle berries with sugar, cover, and chill in the refrigerator.

Just before serving, spoon the berries into large wine glasses or goblets. Pour ¼ cup of wine over each serving. Garnish with mint leaves and the candied peel.

# PASSOVER CHEESE RING

1 cup milk
4 tablespoons unsalted butter
  or margarine
1 teaspoon salt
1/8 teaspoon freshly ground
  black pepper
1/8 teaspoon nutmeg
1 cup matzo meal
4 eggs
1 cup finely shredded Gruyère or Swiss cheese
Additional cheese and milk
  for topping

Place the milk in a heavy saucepan and scald it. Add the butter, salt, pepper, and nutmeg. Bring to a rolling boil. Add the matzo meal all at once, stirring vigorously until the mixture forms a ball and leaves the sides of the pan clean.

Transfer the dough to the bowl of an electric mixer and add 1 egg at a time, blending well after each addition. Stir in the cheese. Place the dough in a pastry bag fitted with a plain #6 round tip. Pipe a ring of dough around a greased 9-inch cake pan. Repeat 1 more layer on top until all the mixture is used, leaving the center open.

Sprinkle the top of the ring with additional cheese and a few drops of milk. Cover with plastic wrap and refrigerate until ready to bake.

Preheat the oven to 400°F. Bake for 30 to 40 minutes, until well puffed and golden brown. Serve immediately.

# MATZO AND MUSHROOM OMELET

Every Jewish family has its own version of an egg-and-matzo "brei" recipe. Try this one, which is a little different.

4 matzos, broken into 2 to 3-
  inch pieces
6 eggs
Salt
Dash of nutmeg
Freshly ground black pepper
4 tablespoons unsalted butter
  or margarine
1/4 cup chopped green onions
  (scallions)
4 mushrooms, thinly sliced
Bowls of preserves and honey

Moisten the matzos in hot water. Drain well. In a large bowl, beat the eggs, salt, nutmeg, and pepper. Gently fold the matzo into the egg mixture.

Heat the butter in a large skillet and sauté the onions. Add the mushrooms and sauté until soft, 3 to 4 minutes. Pour the egg mixture into the skillet. Season to taste with salt and pepper. Brown on one side, shaking the pan to avoid sticking. Turn and brown on the other side. Serve hot, with preserves or honey.

# PASSOVER FRENCH TOAST

I always bake a few extra sponge cakes for the Passover Seders. The next morning I use them for this delicious breakfast or brunch dish.

½ cup milk
2 eggs, well beaten
1 tablespoon grated lemon or orange peel
6 to 8 slices (1 inch thick) Passover sponge cake
Unsalted butter or margarine
Cinnamon
Sugar

In a large shallow bowl, combine the milk, eggs, and lemon peel and beat well. Soak the sponge cake slices in the milk mixture. In a skillet, heat the butter. Fry the cake on both sides until brown. Sprinkle with cinnamon and sugar.

# BEET PRESERVES

A wonderful Passover gift from your kitchen to share with friends.

MAKES ABOUT 2 CUPS

1 pound beets, peeled
Water
2 cups sugar
¾ teaspoon ground ginger
Juice and zest of 1 lemon

Cut the beets into thin matchstick shapes. Place them in a large heavy pot with water to cover. Bring to a boil over high heat, then lower the heat and simmer until tender, about 20 minutes. Combine the sugar and ginger and add to the beets with the lemon juice and zest. Bring to a boil, stirring until the sugar dissolves. Simmer until thick and clear, 30 to 40 minutes. Spoon into a bowl or glass jar. Cover with plastic wrap or a lid and store in the refrigerator. Serve with Passover French Toast.

# PASSOVER BUFFET LUNCH

FOR 8

Passover food is boring only if you permit it to be. I have always felt that the holiday is a real challenge for the inventive cook. Substituting is always fun and nobody need feel deprived when great sandwiches can be made from Passover lunch rolls, great salads can be made with Passover Mayonnaise—and satisfying pastries are no problem without flour or baking powder.

Even pasta lovers will not feel cheated when they taste Ground Beef and Matzo "Lasagne." Layered with matzo, meat, tomato sauce, and mushrooms into an incredible blend of flavors and textures, it will win many compliments.

My personal favorite is the Danish Apple Cake, so simple, yet it looks and tastes like the most exotic of French pastries. One bite will convince you that it will become your favorite Passover dessert.

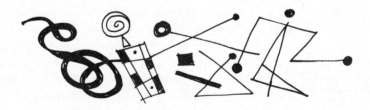

## PASSOVER LUNCH ROLLS

When our children were young, they really looked forward to Passover so they could use these rolls for their school lunches. They enjoyed filling them with gefilte fish or turkey leftovers (or chicken salad), layering them with lettuce, tomatoes, and cucumbers, and packing them into a lunch bag, with fresh fruit or some of their favorite Passover desserts.

MAKES ABOUT 24

2 cups matzo meal
1 teaspoon salt

In a large bowl, combine the matzo meal and salt. Set aside.

1 cup water
½ cup safflower or vegetable oil
4 eggs

In a medium saucepan, bring the water and oil to a boil. Pour in the matzo meal mixture and stir until blended. Transfer to a large bowl of an electric mixer. One at a time, add the eggs, beating well after each addition until completely blended. Let rest for 10 minutes.

Preheat the oven to 375°F.

With well-oiled hands, shape the dough into 3-inch balls or ovals and place 2 inches apart on a well-greased baking sheet. Bake for 40 to 50 minutes, or until golden brown. Transfer to racks and cool. Split and fill with your favorite mixture.

# MOCK GEFILTE FISH

This is an ancient and popular dish, served during Passover among the Vishnitz Hasidic Jews. It is called *falsher,* or "false fish" and is prepared the same way as gefilte fish, substituting ground turkey or chicken. It tastes much like the original, but contains no fish, because the Hasidim, who are very strict about such matters, fear that fish may contain some undigested bread and they abstain from eating it during Passover.

I serve this just like the real gefilte fish—chilled on a bed of lettuce with horseradish.

MAKES 16 TO 18 PORTIONS

2½ quarts Chicken Stock (see page 390)
2 onions, sliced
5 celery ribs, sliced
5 carrots, peeled and thinly sliced
Salt
Freshly ground black pepper
2 pounds ground chicken or turkey
2 eggs
½ cup matzo meal or potato starch
Lettuce leaves
Red horseradish sauce

In a large pot, combine the chicken stock, 1 onion, 3 celery ribs, and 3 carrots. Bring this to a boil over high heat, lower the heat, and simmer for 10 minutes. Season to taste with salt and pepper.

In a grinder or wooden bowl, combine the chicken and remaining onion, celery, and carrots. Grind or chop the mixture until well blended. Transfer to a glass bowl. Add the eggs, matzo meal, and ½ cup chicken stock from the pot. Season to taste with salt and pepper. Blend well. The mixture should be soft and light to the touch.

Wet your hands with cold water and shape the mixture into 2-inch ovals. Place them in the chicken stock. Bring to a boil, cover partially, and simmer for 30 minutes, or until done. Transfer to a large bowl with the broth. Cool, cover with plastic wrap and refrigerate. Serve on a bed of lettuce with red horseradish sauce.

# PASSOVER MAYONNAISE

MAKES ABOUT 1 CUP

1 egg
2 tablespoons lemon juice
½ teaspoon salt
Pinch of white pepper
¾ to 1 cup safflower or vegetable oil

In a processor, blender, or bowl, blend the egg, lemon juice, salt, and pepper. Continue blending, adding oil in a thin steady stream until the mixture is thick. Serve with Dad's Favorite Potato Salad (see page 353).

# PICKLED BEET SALAD

5 medium beets
1 cup cider vinegar
½ teaspoon salt
1 cup sugar
1½ teaspoons mustard seed
½ teaspoon whole allspice
½ teaspoon whole cloves
1 piece (1 inch) cinnamon stick

Cut the leaves off of the beets, leaving a 1-inch stem. Wash the beets and place them in a large pot with water to cover. Bring to a boil and cook, covered, for 1 hour, or until tender. Remove the beets with a slotted spoon, cool, and peel. Reserve 1 cup of the cooking liquid.

In a large pot, combine the reserved cooking liquid, vinegar, salt, and sugar. Place the mustard seed, allspice, cloves, and cinnamon in a cheesecloth bag and tie with string. Add these spices to the vinegar mixture. Bring to a boil and simmer for 5 minutes. Pour the vinegar mixture over the drained beets. Cool and refrigerate until ready to use. Slice the beets and serve as a salad with thinly sliced onions, on a bed of greens.

# GROUND BEEF AND MATZO "LASAGNE"

When you spoon the tomato and mushroom sauce on heated plates and place a portion of the lasagne on top, be sure to garnish with some sliced mushrooms. Serve hot. This is a delicious Passover dish.

½ cup safflower or vegetable oil

In a large skillet, heat 2 tablespoons of the oil over medium heat and brown two thirds of the onion and the

3 onions, chopped

1 pound ground beef

½ cup minced parsley

Salt

Freshly ground black pepper

1 egg

½ pound mushrooms, chopped

2 garlic cloves, minced

4 tomatoes, peeled and chopped

5 matzos

1 cup Chicken Stock (see page 390)

Tomato and Mushroom Sauce (recipe follows)

Sliced, sautéed mushrooms for garnish

ground beef, stirring until the meat is crumbly. Add parsley and season to taste with salt and pepper. Remove from the heat and cool. Stir in the egg and set aside.

In a small skillet, heat 1 tablespoon of the oil and sauté the chopped mushrooms until tender. Transfer to a bowl and set aside.

In the same skillet, heat 1 tablespoon of the oil and sauté the garlic and the remaining onion until soft. Add the tomatoes and simmer 10 minutes. Set aside.

Preheat the oven to 350°F.

Dip the matzos in the stock to soften. Place 1 matzo in an oiled 8-inch square baking dish. Layer the meat mixture, mushroom mixture, and tomato mixture alternately with the matzo, ending with a layer of matzo on top. Pour the remaining stock over the matzo. Bake for 30 to 40 minutes, or until brown, adding additional stock as necessary to keep the lasagne moist.

Spoon the Tomato and Mushroom Sauce on heated plates and place a slice of lasagne on top. Garnish with sliced, sautéed mushrooms.

## TOMATO AND MUSHROOM SAUCE

1 tablespoon oil

1 onion, minced

2 garlic cloves, minced (optional)

1 can (11 to 14 ounces) tomato and mushroom sauce

1 tablespoon dry red wine

8 large mushrooms, quartered

In a saucepan, heat the oil. Add the onion and garlic and sauté until soft. Add the tomato sauce and wine, bring to a boil, and simmer for 5 to 10 minutes. Add the mushrooms to the sauce, turn off the heat, cover, and let them soften.

# DANISH APPLE CAKE

Who would guess that this meltingly rich blend of apples, preserves, macaroons, and almonds—resembling a marzipan confection in flavor—is really a simple Passover invention that I discovered by experimenting? It's much too special to save for Passover.

1 can (1 pound) almond-flavored Passover macaroons, or homemade Hazelnut Meringues (see page 170)

1 cup toasted ground almonds (see page 24)

¼ pound unsalted margarine, melted

8 tart apples

¾ cup sugar

2 tablespoons lemon juice

½ cup golden raisins, plumped in sweet Passover wine or apple juice (see page 25)

2 jars (12 ounces each) Passover preserves (cherry, raspberry, or strawberry)

Toasted sliced almonds, for garnish (see page 24)

Fresh berries for garnish (optional)

Preheat the oven to 350°F.

Break up the macaroons into small pieces. Place them on a baking sheet and bake for 15 to 20 minutes, until lightly browned. Transfer toasted macaroons to a processor or blender and process until fine crumbs. Add almonds and margarine and blend until mixture comes together well. Generously oil an 8-inch springform pan. Remove 2 cups of the macaroon mixture and press into the bottom of the pan.

Peel, core, and slice the apples and place them in a saucepan with the sugar and lemon juice. Mix well. Cook over low heat until the juices appear and the apples soften, 15 to 20 minutes. Drain thoroughly. In a processor, chop the apples fine, but do not purée. Add the raisins and toss. Set aside.

Place half of the apple mixture on top of the crumb mixture. Spoon the preserves into a bowl and mix well. Spread half the preserves over the apple mixture. Add the remaining apple mixture and the remaining preserves. Sprinkle with the remaining macaroon mixture.

Bake for 45 to 55 minutes. Cool on a wire rack, then cover and refrigerate at least 6 hours, or overnight. Just before serving, remove the cake from the pan, place it on a platter, and garnish with toasted almonds, dollops of preserves, and fresh berries.

BONUS RECIPES:

# PASSOVER DESSERTS

Does the idea of baking beautiful, high-rising cakes, cookies and pastries without a speck of flour, grains, baking powder, baking soda, or cornstarch scare you?

Don't let it! We still have matzo meal, matzo cake meal, potato starch, and wonderful, versatile egg whites to bake all of those old favorites—and lots of new ones, too.

These quick and easy Passover baked delights and rich confections will be a welcome addition to your Seder and to other family meals during the eight days of the celebration. "Brown bag" lunches will really benefit from some sweet treats to help avoid the temptation of forbidden foods.

You'll want to share some of these recipes with timid friends to show them the terrific results that can be obtained when we lose our fears of Passover baking.

# BROWNIES FOR PASSOVER

During our first family Seders, my children were small and my store of Passover recipes even smaller. So I was pleased when a friend gave me this delectable brownie recipe. I have since added a few personal touches—the strong coffee, separating the eggs, and dusting the baking pan with ground nuts—all of which makes the brownies even better.

MAKES 16

¾ cup safflower or vegetable oil

2 cups sugar

4 eggs, separated

½ cup powdered cocoa

1 cup matzo cake meal

2 tablespoons potato starch

½ cup strong black coffee

1 cup chopped walnuts or pecans

¼ cup ground walnuts or pecans

Preheat the oven to 350°F.

In the bowl of an electric mixer, blend the oil and sugar. One at a time add the egg yolks, beating well after each addition. Combine the cocoa, matzo cake meal, and potato starch. Beat this into the oil mixture, alternately with the coffee.

Beat the egg whites until stiff enough to hold a peak. Mix one quarter of the beaten egg whites into the chocolate mixture to lighten it. Fold the remaining whites gently but thoroughly into the batter with the chopped walnuts.

Lightly oil an 8-inch square baking pan and dust with the ground nuts. Pour in the batter. Bake for 1 hour, or until a toothpick inserted in the center comes out dry. Serve plain or with Chocolate Frosting (see page 168).

# CARROT-APPLESAUCE SPONGE CAKE

9 eggs, separated

1½ cups sugar

1 cup grated carrots

1 cup applesauce (see page 119)

¼ cup lemon juice

1 tablespoon grated lemon zest

½ cup sliced almonds

¾ cup matzo cake meal

⅔ cup potato starch

1 teaspoon salt

1 teaspoon cinnamon

Preheat the oven to 325°F.

In the bowl of an electric mixer, beat the egg yolks and 1 cup of the sugar until light in color and texture. Add the carrots, applesauce, lemon juice, and zest and blend well. Combine the almonds, matzo cake meal, potato starch, salt, and cinnamon and blend into the egg yolk mixture.

Beat the egg whites until soft peaks form. Add the remaining ½ cup sugar and beat until stiff enough to hold a peak. Fold one quarter of the whites into the batter. Add the remaining whites and fold in gently until well blended.

Pour the batter into an ungreased 10-inch tube pan and bake for 1 hour and 20 minutes, or until the cake springs back to the touch and a toothpick inserted in the center comes out dry. Remove the cake from the oven; immediately invert the pan and let it cool. Loosen the sides and center of the cake with a sharp knife and unmold it onto a cake plate.

# CHOCOLATE MARBLE CAKE WITH CHOCOLATE GLAZE

The contrasting colors plus the rich flavors of the Passover cocoa, strong coffee, and the smooth Chocolate Glaze make this cake extra-special.

1 cup sugar
½ teaspoon salt
¼ cup safflower or vegetable oil
6 eggs, separated
½ cup matzo cake meal
½ cup potato starch
½ cup apple juice, wine, or water
¼ cup powdered cocoa
¼ cup strong hot coffee
Chocolate Glaze (recipe follows)

Preheat the oven to 325°F.

In the bowl of an electric mixer, blend ¾ cup of the sugar with the salt and oil. Add the egg yolks, 1 at a time, beating after each addition. Sift the matzo cake meal and potato starch together. Add them to the egg yolk mixture alternately with the apple juice.

In a large bowl, beat the egg whites until stiff enough to hold a peak. Fold the beaten egg whites into the egg yolk mixture. Pour half of the batter into another bowl and reserve.

In a small bowl, mix together the remaining ¼ cup sugar, cocoa, and coffee and fold this mixture into the reserved batter. Pour the two batters alternately (about 1 cup at a time) into a 10-inch tube pan. Bake for 45 to 55 minutes, or until the cake springs back to the touch and a toothpick inserted in it comes out dry. Remove the cake from the oven; immediately invert the pan and let it cool. Loosen the sides and center of the cake with a sharp knife and unmold it onto a cake plate. Drizzle the Chocolate Glaze over the cake.

## CHOCOLATE GLAZE

8 ounces semisweet chocolate
1 tablespoon safflower or vegetable oil
¼ pound unsalted butter or margarine, cut into small pieces

Melt the chocolate in the top of a double boiler over simmering water. Add the oil and margarine, blending until melted.

Note: This glaze recipe can be doubled.

# LOW-CHOLESTEROL STRAWBERRY SPONGE CAKE

This delicious cake contains no butter or oil and uses only egg whites, so it is low in calories as well as cholesterol.

¾ cup matzo cake meal

1⅓ cups sugar

12 egg whites (1½ cups)

1 teaspoon Passover potato starch

¼ teaspoon salt

2 tablespoons orange juice

2 tablespoons grated orange zest

Strawberries

Strawberry Sauce (recipe follows)

Preheat the oven to 350°F.

Sift the matzo cake meal together with ½ cup of the sugar. In the bowl of an electric mixer, beat the egg whites, Passover potato starch and salt until soft, moist peaks form. Gradually add the remaining sugar alternately with the orange juice and zest, beating until soft peaks form. Add the matzo cake meal mixture into the egg white mixture, a little at a time; folding in with a large balloon wire whisk.

Pour this batter into an ungreased 10-inch tube pan *and place on an oven-proof baking pan.* Bake for 50 minutes to 1 hour, until the cake springs back to the touch and a toothpick inserted into it comes out dry. Remove the cake from the oven; immediately invert the pan and let it cool. Loosen the sides and center of the cake with a sharp knife and unmold it onto a serving plate. Just before serving, slice the cake into wedges and garnish with sliced strawberries and Strawberry Sauce.

## STRAWBERRY SAUCE

2 pints fresh strawberries, washed and hulled

¼ cup sugar

2 tablespoons Passover Concord grape wine

Place the strawberries and sugar in a processor and process until puréed. Strain to remove the seeds. Add the wine, cover with plastic wrap, and chill in the refrigerator.

# RASPBERRY JELLY ROLL

6 eggs, separated

¾ cup sugar

1 tablespoon lemon juice

1 tablespoon grated lemon zest

Preheat the oven to 350°F.

In the bowl of an electric mixer, beat the egg yolks, sugar, lemon juice, and zest until light in color and texture. Gradually add the matzo cake meal, blending thoroughly. Beat the egg whites and salt until stiff enough to

¾ cup matzo cake meal

¼ teaspoon salt

1 jar (16 ounces) raspberry preserves

Chocolate Glaze (optional; see page 165)

hold a peak. Mix one quarter of the beaten egg whites into the yolk mixture to lighten the batter. Fold the remaining whites gently but thoroughly into the batter.

Line a 10 × 15-inch jelly-roll pan with foil and brush with oil. Spread the batter on the foil and bake for 20 minutes, or until golden brown. Turn out onto a sugar-sprinkled towel and then spread with raspberry preserves. Roll up from the narrow side and place on a platter. Frost with Chocolate Glaze, if desired. Slice into ¾-inch-thick portions.

# SPICY ALMOND SPONGE CAKE WITH CHOCOLATE FROSTING

Many Jewish households don't use matzo meal or matzo cake meal for cooking or baking during Passover. I have developed this recipe using potato starch in answer to the many requests for a Passover sponge cake without matzo products.

9 eggs, separated

1⅔ cups sugar

¼ cup orange or lemon juice

1 tablespoon grated lemon zest

1 cup sifted potato starch

½ cup ground almonds

¼ teaspoon ground ginger

¼ teaspoon nutmeg

¼ teaspoon cinnamon

¼ teaspoon salt

Chocolate Frosting (recipe follows)

Preheat the oven to 350°F.

In the bowl of an electric mixer, beat the egg yolks and sugar until light in color and texture. Blend in the orange juice and lemon zest. Combine the potato starch, almonds, ginger, nutmeg, cinnamon, and salt. Thoroughly blend this into the egg yolk mixture.

Beat the egg whites until stiff enough to hold a peak. Fold one quarter of the whites into the egg yolk mixture to lighten the batter. Add the remaining whites and fold in gently but thoroughly until well blended.

Pour the batter into an ungreased 10-inch tube pan. Bake for 45 minutes, or until the cake springs back to the touch and a toothpick inserted in the center comes out dry. Remove the cake from the oven; immediately invert the pan and let it cool. Loosen the sides and center of the cake with a sharp knife and unmold it onto a cake plate. Drizzle the Chocolate Frosting over the cake, or serve plain or sprinkled with Passover powdered or pulverized sugar and cocoa.

## CHOCOLATE FROSTING

MAKES ABOUT 1 CUP

2 tablespoons unsalted butter, margarine, or oil
3 tablespoons honey
¼ cup strong coffee or orange juice
6 ounces semisweet Passover chocolate

In a small saucepan, combine the butter, honey, and coffee. Bring to a boil, remove from the heat, and add the chocolate. Beat until stiff enough to spread or drizzle over the cake.

# CHOCOLATE BIT TORTE

10 eggs, separated
1 cup sugar
¼ cup honey
¼ cup orange juice
1 tablespoon grated orange zest
½ cup Passover Concord grape wine
8 ounces semisweet Passover chocolate, finely ground (1 cup)
4 ounces almonds, finely ground (1 cup)
1 cup matzo cake meal
¼ cup potato starch
1 teaspoon cinnamon
1 teaspoon salt
Chocolate Glaze (optional; see page 165)
½ cup sliced almonds

Preheat the oven to 350°F.

In the bowl of an electric mixer, beat the egg yolks and sugar until light in color and texture. Beat in the honey, orange juice, zest, and wine. Mix together the chocolate and almonds and blend them into the egg yolk mixture. Combine the matzo cake meal, potato starch, cinnamon, and salt and blend into the egg yolk mixture.

In a large bowl, beat the egg whites until stiff enough to hold a peak. Fold one quarter of the whites into the batter to lighten it. Gently fold in the remaining whites until thoroughly blended.

Pour the batter into an ungreased 10-inch tube pan and bake for 45 minutes to 1 hour, until a toothpick inserted near the center of the cake comes out dry. Remove the cake from the oven; immediately invert the pan and let it cool. Loosen the sides and center of the torte with a sharp knife and unmold it from the pan onto a cake plate. Sprinkle with pulverized sugar or Chocolate Glaze and garnish with sliced almonds.

# PASSOVER WALNUT TORTE

7 eggs, separated

1⅓ cups sugar

¼ cup orange juice

3 tablespoons lemon juice

1 tablespoon grated lemon zest

1 tablespoon grated orange zest

½ cup matzo cake meal

½ cup potato starch

4 ounces toasted walnuts (see page 24), ground (1 cup)

¼ teaspoon salt

Preheat the oven to 325°F.

In a large mixing bowl, beat the egg yolks and sugar until light in color and texture. Add the orange juice, lemon juice, and grated lemon and orange zest and blend well. Gradually blend in the matzo cake meal, potato starch, and walnuts. Beat the egg whites and salt until stiff enough to hold a peak. Gently fold them into the yolk mixture.

Pour the batter into an ungreased 10-inch tube pan. Bake for 1 hour and 15 minutes, or until the cake springs back to the touch and a toothpick inserted in the cake comes out dry. Remove the cake from the oven; immediately invert the pan and let it cool. Loosen the sides and center of the cake with a sharp knife and unmold it onto a cake plate.

# CHOPPED CHOCOLATE PASSOVER COOKIES

MAKES ABOUT 3 DOZEN

¼ pound unsalted butter or margarine

1 cup plus 2 tablespoons sugar

2 eggs

2 cups matzo meal

¼ teaspoon salt

1 teaspoon cinnamon

8 ounces semisweet Passover chocolate, chopped (1 cup)

¾ cup chopped walnuts

¼ cup orange juice

1 tablespoon orange zest

Preheat the oven to 375°F.

In the bowl of an electric mixer, beat the butter and sugar until fluffy. Add the eggs and blend thoroughly. Combine the matzo meal, salt, cinnamon, chopped chocolate, and walnuts. Add the matzo meal mixture to the butter mixture alternately with the orange juice and zest.

Drop the batter by teaspoons, 2 inches apart, onto a foil-lined and oiled baking sheet. Bake for 8 to 10 minutes, or until golden brown. Cool on a rack.

# Hazelnut Meringues

MAKES ABOUT 4 DOZEN

⅓ cup matzo cake meal
⅔ cup sugar
4 egg whites
⅛ teaspoon salt
4 ounces hazelnuts (filberts),
  finely ground (⅔ cup)
½ teaspoon vanilla extract
3 tablespoons unsalted butter
  or margarine, melted

Preheat the oven to 325°F.

Sift the matzo cake meal with ⅓ cup of the sugar. Beat the egg whites with the salt just until frothy. Gradually add the remaining ⅓ cup sugar, beating until stiff enough to hold a peak. Fold in the cake meal mixture, then the hazelnuts, vanilla, and butter. Drop the mixture by teaspoons, 2 inches apart, onto foil-lined baking sheets.

Bake for 10 to 15 minutes, or until the edges are light brown and the centers golden. Cool the meringues on the foil and then peel them off and transfer them to wire racks.

# Hazelnut-Almond Cookies

MAKES ABOUT 2 DOZEN

6 ounces hazelnuts (filberts),
  finely ground (1¼ cups)
6 ounces almonds, finely
  ground (1½ cups)
3 egg whites
½ cup sugar
¾ cup matzo cake meal
Chocolate Glaze (see page
  165)
Raspberry, strawberry, or
  apricot jam

Preheat the oven to 325°F.

In a bowl, combine the hazelnuts and almonds and set them aside. In a large mixing bowl, beat the egg whites and sugar until foamy. Blend in the nuts and fold in the matzo cake meal. Spoon the batter into a pastry bag fitted with a #6 tip. Grease a baking sheet and press out 3-inch-long strips of dough.

Bake for 15 to 20 minutes, until golden brown. Let them cool on the baking sheet. Dip one end of each cookie into the Chocolate Glaze and refrigerate until set. Spread the bottom of one cookie with jam. Top with a second cookie so that chocolate ends are on opposite sides. Keep refrigerated.

# PASSOVER MANDELBROT

Mandelbrot is a family favorite, so I developed this recipe to serve during Passover. As with traditional mandelbrot, the Passover version is baked twice: first in loaf form, then sliced and browned again. It will stay crisp for weeks if kept in a tightly covered container, or for months if frozen. If it loses its crispness, just reheat for 5 to 10 minutes on each side.

These Passover desserts take so little time to prepare, and one recipe makes a large quantity.

MAKES ABOUT 4 DOZEN

¾ cup safflower or vegetable oil

¾ cup plus 2 tablespoons sugar

3 eggs

¾ cup matzo cake meal

¼ cup matzo meal

2 tablespoons potato starch

½ teaspoon salt

2 teaspoons cinnamon

Juice and zest of ½ lemon

1 cup sliced almonds

In the bowl of an electric mixer, blend the oil and ¾ cup sugar until light. Add the eggs and blend thoroughly. In a bowl, combine the matzo cake meal, matzo meal, potato starch, salt, and 1½ teaspoons of the cinnamon and blend into the oil mixture alternately with the lemon juice and zest. Fold in the almonds. Cover and refrigerate for 1 hour for easier handling.

Preheat the oven to 350°F.

Divide the dough into 3 or 4 portions. With lightly oiled hands, shape each portion into an oval loaf, 2 inches wide and 1 inch high. Place the loaves 2 inches apart on greased baking sheets. Bake for 30 minutes, or until golden brown.

In a small bowl, combine the remaining 2 tablespoons sugar and the remaining ½ teaspoon cinnamon. Remove the loaves from the oven and use a spatula to transfer them to a cutting board; cut into ½-inch-thick slices. Place the slices, cut side up, on the same baking sheets and sprinkle with the sugar mixture. Turn off the heat and return the slices to the oven. Leave the mandelbrot in the oven for 10 minutes a side, or until lightly browned and crisp. Transfer to racks and cool.

# CHOCOLATE FARFEL-NUT CLUSTERS

I absolutely love to prepare these clusters. Knowing how easy they are to make and knowing the pleasure they bring to everyone when I serve them just makes me happy! The chocolate is melted and poured into a bowl, then tossed with toasted farfel and toasted pecans. (If you like, add some diced Passover marshmallows to make Rocky Road Bonbons.) Toasting the farfel and pecans is the important part of this recipe (see page 24).

MAKES 30 TO 40

16 ounces Passover semisweet chocolate
1½ cups toasted matzo farfel
1 cup toasted chopped pecans

In the top of a double boiler over simmering water, melt the chocolate. Pour the melted chocolate into a large bowl. Add the matzo farfel and pecans and mix thoroughly. Spoon this chocolate mixture onto a baking sheet lined with wax paper or into ruffled paper candy cups. Refrigerate until set. To serve; peel the clusters off the wax paper and place on a platter or serve in candy cups, along with Passover sponge cakes and cookies.

# FRIED MATZO PASTRIES

MAKES ABOUT 6 DOZEN

6 matzos, each 6 inches square
Vegetable oil
Pulverized or powdered Passover sugar

In a large bowl, soak the matzo in cold water for 1 minute, just to moisten. Cut the matzo into 2-inch squares.

Pour oil into a skillet to a depth of 2½ to 3 inches. Heat the oil. Test the oil by dropping in a bit of matzo; if it sizzles and turns golden right away, the oil is hot enough for frying. Fry the prepared matzos, without crowding, turning them once to brown on both sides. Drain on paper towels. Place on a serving plate and sprinkle with the sugar.

# LEMON MERINGUE PIE

Baked Passover Nut Crust (recipe follows)
3 eggs, separated
1 cup plus 6 tablespoons sugar
¼ cup potato starch
¼ teaspoon salt

Bake the crust and let cool.

In a large saucepan over medium heat, put the egg yolks, 1 cup of the sugar, the potato starch, salt, lemon zest, and lemon juice. Beat well and cook over medium heat until thick, 4 to 5 minutes. Add the water, blending thoroughly, and continue cooking until clear and thick, 5 to 10 minutes. Cool.

Grated zest of 1 lemon
½ cup lemon juice
1½ cups warm water

In the bowl of an electric mixer, beat the egg whites until foamy. Add the remaining 6 tablespoons of sugar and beat until stiff peaks form. Spoon the meringue into a pastry bag fitted with a star tip.

Preheat the broiler.

Spoon the lemon filling into the cooled pie crust. Pipe the meringue on top and place the pie under the broiler briefly to brown.

## PASSOVER NUT CRUST

2 cups walnuts or pecans
3 tablespoons sugar
3 tablespoons unsalted butter
  or margarine
⅓ cup matzo cake meal

Preheat the oven to 400°F.

Place the walnuts in a processor and process until finely ground. Add the sugar, butter, and matzo cake meal and blend until the mixture comes together. Place in a shallow 10-inch baking dish, pressing the mixture evenly on the bottom and up the sides to form a thin crust. Bake for 8 to 10 minutes, or until lightly browned. Cool.

*NOTE: Any leftover nut crust can be used to make tartlets.

# PEARS WITH STRAWBERRIES AND MERINGUE

MAKES 8 SERVINGS

4 pears, about 1½ pounds
5 tablespoons lemon juice
1¾ cups sugar
1 vanilla bean, or 1 teaspoon
  vanilla extract
3 cups whole red, ripe strawberries, cut in half
3 tablespoons orange juice
2 egg whites
Mint leaves for garnish

Peel the pears using a vegetable peeler. As each pear is peeled, place it in a large bowl containing 4 tablespoons of the lemon juice and enough water to cover.

Cut the pears in half lengthwise and, with a teaspoon, scoop out the cores to form a generous cavity.

Combine 1½ cups of water, 1½ cups sugar, and vanilla bean. Bring to a boil and add the pear halves and remaining 1 tablespoon lemon juice. When the mixture returns to a boil, reduce the heat and simmer for 10 to 15 minutes, or until the pears are tender when pierced with a fork. Remove the pears and reserve 1 cup of the cooking liquid. Let the pears cool.

Put half the berries in a processor and process, while

gradually adding the reserved pear liquid and orange juice. (This mixture is good, but it is even better if you strain it through a fine sieve or cheesecloth to remove the seeds.) There should be about 1½ cups sauce.

Fill the cavity of each pear with the remaining sliced berries, reserving a few berries to garnish each serving. Place each pear half, cut side down, onto an individual ovenproof serving dish.

Preheat the broiler.

Beat the egg whites until soft peaks form, then gradually beat in the remaining ¼ cup sugar. Continue beating until stiff. Spoon the meringue into a pastry bag fitted with a star tip. Squeeze out the meringue in a decorative pattern over the tops of the pears. Pour the sauce around the pears. Place the dishes on a baking sheet and broil them 4 inches from the heat, just until lightly browned, 1 to 2 minutes. Garnish with the reserved strawberries and mint leaves.

# SHAVUOTH

Shavuoth is notable for two reasons. It marks the receiving of the Ten Commandments on Mount Sinai, and it is the time in spring for gathering the wheat harvest and the season's first fruits. In ancient times, the harvests included not only wheat, but barley, grapes, figs, honey, and olives. To this day we include these foods in our traditional holiday menus.

It is also customary to serve dishes that feature dairy foods—milk, eggs, cheese, sour cream, and yogurt. After all, in ancient times Israel was known as "The Land of Milk and Honey." Many of these dairy foods are encased in dough, in the form of blintzes, kreplach, and knishes.

Eastern European Jews enjoy cold vegetable soups such as borscht and spinach or sorrel soups, served with sour cream. Rice dishes are also popular.

Cheese is especially important and used in many fillings for stuffed dough recipes. That's because farmers all made their cheeses at the time of the spring harvest.

Shavuoth offers a field day for vegetarians and the growing number of people who do not eat red meat. Wholesome grains, fresh fruits, and vegetables, plus an abundance of dairy foods, offer a lot of variety and a well-balanced diet.

Shavuoth desserts are very tempting. They feature the first fruits of the season and an array of dairy foods. And, of course, there's cheesecake, everybody's favorite dessert. You'll find a whole section devoted to this delicacy in the following pages.

Cookies and cakes are shaped like the Ten Commandments. Honey cakes and other confections made with honey are popular. Shavuoth is also known as The Feast of Roses, and Sephardic Jews use rose petals and rosewater in their fragrant holiday baking.

When planning your Shavuoth menu, why not decorate your table with a centerpiece of fresh seasonal fruits and perhaps a little nosegay of roses, then choose your favorite cheesecake for dessert.

# INTERNATIONAL SHAVUOTH DINNER

FOR 10

▼▲▼▲▼▲▼▲▼▲▼▲▼▲▼▲

Cheese and Green
Onion Tart

Cold Spinach Borscht

Henry's Caraway-Salt Rye
Baguettes

Cold Salmon with
Cucumber-Dill Sauce

Asparagus with Cherry
Tomato Vinaigrette

Very Strawberry Dessert
Blintzes

SUGGESTED BEVERAGE:

Riesling wine

Our first Shavuoth menu also features the traditional and symbolic foods—first fruits, grains, and dairy dishes containing milk, eggs, and cheese. They are used in unusual ways and the recipes came to me from a variety of chefs and circumstances.

## CHEESE AND GREEN ONION TART

4 tablespoons unsalted butter
  or margarine
2 bunches green onions (scallions), thinkly sliced (1 cup)
1 pound farmer or hoop
  cheese

Preheat the oven to 350°F.

In a small skillet, melt the butter and sauté the scallions until soft. Set them aside.

In a large bowl, blend the farmer's, Munster, and Jack cheeses. Beat in the eggs and mix well. Mix in the scallions. Season to taste with salt and pepper. Spoon the

4 ounces shredded Munster
cheese
4 ounces shredded Monterey
Jack cheese
3 eggs
Salt
Freshly ground black pepper
Baked Classic Pie Crust (recipe follows)

cheese mixture into the baked pie crust, spreading evenly.
Bake for 45 minutes, or until set. Serve hot.

## CLASSIC PIE CRUST

MAKES ONE 10- OR 11-INCH TART SHELL

1¼ cups flour
¼ teaspoon salt
6 tablespoons unsalted butter
or margarine
2 tablespoons vegetable
shortening
2 tablespoons ice water

In the bowl of an electric mixer, combine the flour and
salt. Cut in the butter and shortening until the mixture is
crumbly. Blend in the water until the dough begins to
come together. Do not overmix.

Knead the dough into a ball, wrap it in wax paper,
and chill it for at least 10 minutes in the refrigerator.

Roll the pastry out on 2 large sheets of floured wax
paper, to a round large enough to cover and overlap a
10- or 11-inch tart pan with a removable bottom. Cover
the pastry with another sheet of wax paper and fold the
pastry in half. (The wax paper in the center prevents the
pastry from sticking together when folded.)

Lift the pastry from the bottom wax paper and place
it on half of the tart pan. Unfold the pastry and remove
the wax paper that covers it. (At this point the pastry can
be covered with plastic wrap and foil and stored in the
freezer for several days.)

Preheat the oven to 375°F.

Bring the pastry to room temperature. Butter a sheet
of wax paper and place it, buttered side down, inside the
pastry and overlapping around the outside. Cover with
another piece of wax paper with the cut ends in the opposite directions. Fill the center of lined pie shell with
uncooked rice or baker's jewels. Bake for 15 to 20 minutes, until the sides of the pastry begin to brown. Carefully remove the wax paper with the rice and continue
baking until the bottom of the pastry is lightly browned.
Remove from the oven and fill with desired fillings.

# COLD SPINACH BORSCHT

When the children were young and I was too busy to cook, I used to serve commercially made beet or spinach borscht. Then I realized how easy it was to make them myself and how much better they tasted. Henry's Caraway-Salt Rye Baguettes are a perfect accompaniment, spread with fresh unsalted butter.

1½ pounds spinach
1 large onion, finely chopped
1½ quarts cold water
Salt
½ cup lemon juice
Sour cream
Green onions (scallions),
　thinly sliced
Cucumbers, peeled and thinly
　sliced

Wash the spinach leaves well and rinse in cold water several times. Drain and coarsely chop the leaves.

In a large pot, put the spinach, onion, water, and 2 teaspoons salt. Bring to a boil over high heat, then reduce to low and simmer for 15 minutes. Add the lemon juice and cook 10 minutes longer. Taste for additional seasoning. Cool over ice and then refrigerate. Serve with sour cream, green onions, and cucumbers.

# HENRY'S CARAWAY-SALT RYE BAGUETTES

For many years we have enjoyed this unusual salt-rye bread at the Scandia Restaurant in Los Angeles. At my request, Henry Godskesen, the pastry chef, agreed to teach me how to make these baguettes. I was so pleased to have the opportunity to work with him that I didn't mind arriving at 3 A.M., his usual bread-baking hour. This is my revised recipe, modified for home kitchens, using ingredients available in supermarkets.

MAKES 6 TO 8 BAGUETTES

2 packages active dry yeast
Pinch of sugar
1 cup warm water (110 to
　115°F)
1 cup buttermilk
3 tablespoons kosher salt
⅛ cup safflower or vegetable
　oil
5 tablespoons caraway seeds
1 cup rye flour

Dissolve the yeast and sugar in ½ cup of the water. In the bowl of an electric mixer, blend the remaining water, buttermilk, 1 tablespoon salt, oil, and 3 tablespoons of the caraway seeds. Add the yeast mixture, rye flour, and wheat flour. Blend well. Add the white flour, 1 cup at a time, mixing well after each addition, until the dough comes together. Place the dough on a floured board and knead until it is smooth and springs back to the touch. Place the dough in a greased bowl; grease the top of the dough; cover with a towel and let it rise for 30 minutes.

1 cup unbleached wheat flour
4 cups unbleached white flour
Yellow cornmeal
1 egg, well beaten

Divide the dough into 6 to 8 pieces and knead each piece into a smooth ball. Cover with a towel and let them rest for 30 minutes. Roll the balls into long thin loaves, punching down and folding them until they are 10 to 12 inches in length. Place on greased pans sprinkled with cornmeal and let them rest, covered, for 30 minutes.

Preheat the oven to 375°F.

Brush the loaves with egg. In a small bowl, combine the remaining 2 tablespoons of salt and 2 tablespoons caraway seeds. Brush the loaves with the egg again and sprinkle with the salt mixture. Bake for 30 to 40 minutes, or until golden brown.

# COLD SALMON WITH CUCUMBER-DILL SAUCE

6 to 8 salmon steaks (⅔ inch thick)
1 cup mayonnaise, preferably homemade (see page 326)
Fresh parsley sprigs
Lemon slices
Cucumber-Dill Sauce (recipe follows)

Preheat the broiler at medium heat.

Place the salmon on a foil-lined baking pan. Spread with a thin layer of mayonnaise and broil for 7 minutes, about 4 inches from the heat. Turn, spread with the remaining mayonnaise, and broil for 7 minutes. Cool. Cover with foil and chill.

Just before serving, remove the foil from the salmon steaks and place them on a serving platter. Garnish with parsley sprigs and lemon slices. Serve with Cucumber-Dill Sauce

## CUCUMBER-DILL SAUCE

MAKES ABOUT 1½ CUPS

1 large cucumber, unpeeled
½ cup plain yogurt
¼ cup mayonnaise
2 teaspoons lemon juice
2 teaspoons grated onion
1 tablespoon minced parsley
½ teaspoon dried dill, or 1 teaspoon fresh
Salt
Freshly ground black pepper

Shred the cucumber and set it aside. In a bowl, blend the yogurt, mayonnaise, lemon juice, onion, parsley, and dill. Stir in the cucumber. Season to taste with salt and pepper.

# ASPARAGUS WITH CHERRY TOMATO VINAIGRETTE

50 stalks (about 4 pounds)
fresh asparagus, peeled and
trimmed
Roasted red bell pepper strips
(see page 278)
Cherry Tomato Vinaigrette
(recipe follows)
Chopped fresh chervil or
parsley

In a vegetable steamer or on a steamer rack over simmering water, steam the asparagus, covered, until tender-crisp, 5 to 10 minutes depending on the size and freshness; test their doneness by inserting a fork into the stem.

Divide the asparagus into 10 equal bundles and "tie" each with a strip of pepper. Place on a large serving plate and spoon the vinaigrette over them, with the cherry tomatoes on one side. Sprinkle with fresh chervil or parsley.

## CHERRY TOMATO VINAIGRETTE

Juice of 2 lemons
¾ cup of olive oil
10 cherry tomatoes, stemmed
and halved
Salt
Freshly ground black pepper

In a medium bowl, beat the lemon juice and olive oil with a wire whisk. Add the cherry tomato halves. Mix well. Season to taste with salt and pepper. Cover with plastic wrap and chill in the refrigerator.

# VERY STRAWBERRY DESSERT BLINTZES

MAKES ABOUT 2 DOZEN

4 eggs
1 cup flour
¼ teaspoon salt
1¾ cups milk
Unsalted butter
Cheese Filling (recipe follows)
Strawberry Sauce (recipe follows)
Strawberries
Orange zest, cut into long
thin strips

In a large bowl, beat the eggs well. Gradually add the flour and salt, alternately with the milk, and beat until smooth. Stir in ¼ cup melted butter. Cover and chill for 30 minutes.

In a small skillet or crepe pan, melt 1 tablespoon butter over low heat. When the butter begins to bubble, pour in about ¼ cup of the batter and rotate the pan quickly to spread the batter as thin as possible, pouring off any excess. (The first blintz will be thicker than the rest.) Cook on one side only, until lightly browned around the edges, and turn it out onto a towel to cool. Repeat with the

Sweetened Whipped Cream
(recipe follows)

remaining batter, stacking the cooled blintzes on a platter with a square of wax paper between each one.

Spoon 1 tablespoon of the cheese filling into the center of each blintz. Fold the blintz around the filling like
an envelope, completely enclosing it. Place the blintzes
on a large platter, cover, and refrigerate until ready to
serve.

To prepare the blintzes for serving, heat 4 tablespoons butter in a large skillet and brown the blintzes
lightly, 1 to 2 minutes a side. Serve with the Strawberry
Sauce and garnish with sliced strawberries, orange zest,
and whipped cream.

## CHEESE FILLING

4 ounces cream cheese (see
page 22)
⅓ cup sugar
1 egg yolk
⅛ teaspoon salt
2 cups ricotta cheese
Grated zest of 1 orange
1 cup sliced strawberries

In a large bowl, blend the cream cheese, sugar, egg yolk,
and salt. Add the ricotta and orange zest and beat until
light and fluffy. Fold in the sliced strawberries.

## STRAWBERRY SAUCE

MAKES ABOUT 2 CUPS

2 cups sliced strawberries
½ cup strawberry preserves,
strained
1 tablespoon strawberry
liqueur

Place the strawberries in a processor or blender and purée.
Strain the purée into a bowl. Blend in the preserves and
liqueur.

## SWEETENED WHIPPED CREAM

1 cup heavy cream
2 tablespoons sugar
1 tablespoon strawberry
liqueur

In a large mixing bowl, beat the cream, sugar, and liqueur until stiff peaks form. Spoon the whipped cream
into a pastry bag fitted with a decorative tip and pipe
over the blintzes.

# HARVEST HOLIDAY DINNER

FOR 8

▼▲▼▲▼▲▼▲▼▲▼▲▼▲▼▲▼▲▼▲

Hearty Lentil Soup with
Herbed Sour Cream

Harvest Seed Loaves

Barley and Kasha Salad

Tricolor Squash Casserole
with Three Cheeses

My Signature Strudel

SUGGESTED BEVERAGE:

Chenin Blanc or Riesling
wine

This menu incorporates some traditional foods in modern versions. It is light and nutritious, accenting the "first fruits," grains and dairy foods that symbolize Shavuoth.

We begin with a hearty soup, topped with sour cream and served with crusty Harvest Seed Loaves. Then comes a spicy Barley and Kasha Salad, an interesting variation of the Middle Eastern tabbouleh. The main-course casserole combines the textures, flavors, and colors of three different kinds of squash, enriched by the addition of three different cheeses. For dessert, there's a rich walnut and coconut strudel.

# HEARTY LENTIL SOUP WITH HERBED SOUR CREAM

1½ cups dried lentils
2 bay leaves, crushed
4 tablespoons unsalted butter
  or margarine
1 tablespoon olive oil
3 garlic cloves, minced
4 medium carrots, peeled and
  finely chopped
1 medium parsnip, peeled
  and finely chopped
1 large onion, finely chopped

Soak the lentils in 4 cups of water for 6 hours or overnight. Drain the lentils and place them in a large pot with 2½ quarts of warm water and the bay leaves. Over high heat, bring the water to a boil, reduce the heat, partially cover, and simmer for 15 to 20 minutes, or until the lentils are tender.

In a large skillet, heat the butter and olive oil. Add the garlic, carrots, parsnip, onion, celery, and parsley. Sauté this mixture for 10 to 15 minutes, or until the vegetables are tender. Add the rosemary and tomatoes and simmer for 10 minutes.

2 celery stalks, thinly sliced

½ cup minced fresh parsley

1 tablespoon fresh rosemary, or 1 teaspoon dried

4 large tomatoes, peeled and finely chopped

Salt

Freshly ground black pepper

Herbed Sour Cream (recipe follows)

Grated Parmesan cheese (optional)

Remove 2 cups of the cooked lentils and ½ cup of the liquid and purée in a processor blender. Return the purée and the sautéed vegetable mixture to the soup pot. Mix well. Season to taste with salt and pepper. Over medium heat, bring to a boil, cover, reduce the heat, and simmer, covered, until the soup thickens, 30 to 40 minutes.

Ladle the soup into warm bowls and garnish with Herbed Sour Cream and a sprinkle of Parmesan cheese, if you wish.

## HERBED SOUR CREAM

2 cups sour cream

1 tablespoon minced parsley

1 tablespoon minced green onions (scallions)

1 tablespoon minced fresh basil, or 1 teaspoon dried

In a small bowl, beat the sour cream, parsley, green onions, and basil until well blended. Cover and chill.

# HARVEST SEED LOAVES

MAKES 6 SMALL LOAVES

2 packages active dry yeast

Pinch of sugar

1 cup warm water (110 to 115°F)

1½ cups warm milk (110 to 115°)

4 tablespoons unsalted butter or margarine, melted

¼ cup honey

4 eggs

6 to 7 cups unbleached flour

2 cups whole wheat flour

1 tablespoon salt

½ cup sunflower seeds

¼ cup sesame seeds

¼ cup poppy seeds

2 tablespoons celery seed

¼ cup yellow cornmeal

In a small bowl or measuring cup, dissolve the yeast and the sugar in the water. In the bowl of an electric mixer, beat together the milk, butter, and honey. Add 3 of the eggs, 1 at a time, beating well after each addition. Blend in the yeast mixture, 1 cup of each of the flours, and the salt. Beat until well blended. Add the remaining 1 cup whole wheat flour and 1 cup at a time of the remaining unbleached flour, beating until the dough is thick enough to work by hand.

In a small bowl, combine the sunflower, sesame, poppy, and celery seeds. Reserve ¼ cup of this seed mixture for the top of the loaves. Turn the dough out onto a floured board and knead for 5 to 10 minutes, gradually adding the remaining seed mixture and enough flour to make a smooth and elastic dough. Place the dough in an oiled bowl and oil the top of the dough. Cover with a towel and let rest in a warm place until doubled in bulk and the dough springs back to the touch, about 1½ hours.

Divide the dough into 6 equal pieces. Shape each part into a loaf and place them in six 3 × 7-inch loaf pans that have been oiled and sprinkled with yellow cornmeal. Cover with towels and let rest in a warm place until doubled, about 1 hour.

Preheat the oven to 375°F. Brush the loaves with the remaining egg and sprinkle with the reserved seed mixture. Bake them for 20 to 30 minutes, or until brown. Unmold from the loaf pans while still hot and cool on wire racks.

# BARLEY AND KASHA SALAD

1 cup barley
1 cup kasha (roasted buckwheat kernels)
1 cup minced fresh parsley
½ cup finely diced celery
1 large red bell pepper, finely diced
1 cup thinly sliced green onions (scallions)
Lemon-Tahini Dressing (recipe follows)
Lettuce leaves
Black olives
1 red bell pepper, stemmed, seeded, and thinly sliced

In a large heavy pot, bring 2 quarts of lightly salted water to a boil. Stir in the barley and simmer for 20 to 30 minutes, until tender; drain well, transfer to a medium bowl, and cool. Cover with plastic wrap and refrigerate.

In a large heavy pot, bring 2 quarts of lightly salted water to a boil. Stir in the kasha and simmer 5 to 10 minutes, until tender; drain well, transfer to a medium bowl, and cool. Cover with plastic wrap and refrigerate.

In a small bowl, combine the parsley, celery, diced pepper, and green onions. Set aside.

To assemble the salad, gently toss the barley, kasha, and parsley mixture in a large bowl until well blended. Pour the Lemon-Tahini Dressing into the barley mixture and toss again. Place lettuce leaves on individual salad plates and spoon the Barley and Kasha Salad on top. Garnish with black olives and red pepper slices.

## LEMON-TAHINI DRESSING

¼ cup lemon juice
2 tablespoons tahini (sesame seed paste)
½ cup olive oil
¼ teaspoon ground cumin
Salt
Freshly ground black pepper

In a small bowl, beat the lemon juice, tahini, olive oil, and cumin until well blended. Season to taste with salt and pepper.

# Tricolor Squash Casserole with Three Cheeses

4 large zucchini, sliced cross-
    wise ⅛ inch thick
Tomato Sauce (see page 271)
1 cup grated Parmesan cheese
2 cups shredded mozzarella
    cheese
4 large pattypan squash,
    sliced ⅛ inch thick
2 cups shredded Monterey
    Jack cheese
4 large crookneck squash,
    sliced crosswise ⅛ inch
    thick
Salt
Freshly ground black pepper

Preheat the oven to 375°F.

Lightly oil a 9 × 13-inch ovenproof baking pan. Cover the bottom with all of the zucchini slices. Spoon a generous amount of the Tomato Sauce over the zucchini and sprinkle with one third of the Parmesan and half the mozzarella.

Arrange the pattypan squash over the cheeses and spoon half the remaining Tomato Sauce on top. Sprinkle with half the remaining Parmesan and half the Jack cheese. Arrange the crookneck squash on top and cover with the remaining Parmesan, mozzarella, and Jack cheeses. Season to taste with salt and pepper. Bake for 30 to 40 minutes, or until the squashes are tender and the cheeses have melted.

# My Signature Strudel

This strudel got me started in serious cooking. After making it for my friends, a famous restaurant, the Discovery Inn, asked me to bake it for them—and I was in business!

½ pound unsalted butter or
    margarine
2 cups whole wheat pastry or
    unbleached flour
1 cup sour cream
6 tablespoons vegetable
    shortening
1 jar (2 pounds) apricot-pine-
    apple preserves
1 package (1 pound) shredded
    coconut
3 to 4 cups toasted chopped
    walnuts (see page 24)
Powdered sugar

In the large bowl of an electric mixer, blend the butter and flour until crumbly. Add the sour cream and beat until the mixture comes away from the sides of the bowl. Do not overbeat.

Turn the dough out onto a pastry board lined with generously floured wax paper. Toss the dough around on top of the floured wax paper to coat it lightly with the flour. Flatten it with the palm of your hand, shaping it roughly into a rectangle. Then use a well-floured rolling pin to roll it out into a rectangle about 6 by 10 inches.

Drop 6 small pieces (½ teaspoon) of the shortening equally spaced on top of the pastry; with your finger, smear them down, then fold the pastry into thirds. Turn the pastry 90 degrees with the ends facing you. Roll it out again, dot with the shortening, and fold into thirds again. Turn and repeat this procedure 2 more times. Wrap the pastry in wax paper and store in a plastic bag in the refrigerator for at least 2 hours.

Cut the dough into 4 equal pieces. Roll out each piece on floured wax paper into a rectangle about 6 by 10 inches and as thin as possible. Spread generously with the preserves; sprinkle with the coconut and walnuts. Lifting the pastry with the wax paper as a guide, roll up the strudel jelly-roll fashion.

Preheat the oven to 375°F.

Place the strudel on a foil-lined baking sheet. Bake for 30 to 40 minutes, until golden brown. Lift the edges of the foil to transfer the strudel to a wooden board; loosen the strudel with a knife, if necessary, and carefully roll it off the foil so it rests on the board seam side down. Cut it while still hot into 1-inch slices and transfer them to a cake plate or platter. Just before serving, sprinkle with powdered sugar.

∗NOTE: If you wish to store the strudel before baking, follow these steps: Place the strudel, seam side down, on a sheet of foil large enough to enclose it completely. Seal the foil securely around the strudel. It will keep for up to 3 weeks in the freezer. The strudel does not need to be defrosted before baking. Just open the foil, place the strudel on a baking sheet, and bake as directed.

# CHEESECAKES

Smooth and creamy, dense or light and airy, with a variety of crusts and fillings, or even with no crust at all, cheesecakes are one of the easiest desserts to prepare and serve.

Cheesecake keeps well in the refrigerator, too, and can be made in many sizes and shapes. I often like to make them in small muffin tins, which produce bite-size cheesecakes that add charm to a sweet table. Most recipes can be frozen.

Imagine the possibilities. Flavorings can include citrus, spices, coffee, chocolate, nuts, and vanilla and rum extracts. Toppings can be chosen from sour cream, whipped cream, fruit glazes, and a whole array of whole or puréed berries and fresh fruits. Then there are the crusts: cookie crumbs, cracker crumbs, bread crumbs, crushed nuts, dry cereals, or even a simple pie or cookie dough crust.

I like to use a gelatin-free, gum-free cream cheese, without a trace of additives. You'll find it at kosher markets and health food stores. This pure cream cheese is not only kosher, but it blends more easily, especially with eggs, resulting in a smoother cake.

Here's a group of my never-fail cheesecake favorites.

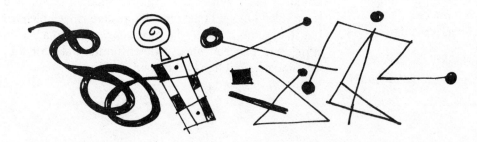

# CARROT-SPICE CHEESECAKE

The taste is truly addictive! The secret: two kinds of ginger, spices, and a smooth carrot purée atop a crisp, nutty crust.

MAKES ONE 9-INCH CHEESECAKE

Vanilla-Pecan crust, baked (recipe follows)

¾ pound carrots, boiled and puréed

½ cup (packed) light brown sugar

3 tablespoons ginger preserves

2 tablespoons candied ginger

1 tablespoon fresh lemon juice

1 teaspoon orange zest

¼ teaspoon ground cinnamon

¼ teaspoon ground mace

¼ teaspoon ground allspice

2 packages (8 ounces each) cream cheese

4 eggs

¼ cup chopped pecans

Prepare the Vanilla-Pecan Crust.

In the bowl of an electric mixer, beat the carrot purée, brown sugar, preserves, candied ginger, lemon juice, orange zest, cinnamon, mace, and allspice until well blended. Add the cream cheese and blend.

Beat in the eggs, 1 at a time, until smooth. Pour into the prepared crust and sprinkle with pecans. Bake for about 50 minutes, until the center is firm and a toothpick inserted comes out clean. Cool. Cover and refrigerate for at least 1 hour before serving.

## VANILLA-PECAN CRUST

⅔ cup finely ground vanilla wafers (4 ounces)

⅔ cup finely ground ginger snaps (4 ounces)

⅔ cup finely ground pecans (4 ounces)

⅓ cup sugar

4 tablespoons unsalted butter

Preheat the oven to 375°F.

In the large bowl of an electric mixer or blender, combine the vanilla wafers, ginger snaps, pecans, and sugar. Blend in the butter until the mixture is well blended but still crumbly. Spoon the mixture evenly into a 9-inch springform pan and press it down firmly. Bake for 5 to 10 minutes, until lightly browned. Cool.

# ITALIAN RICOTTA CHEESECAKE

This unusual recipe features a sweet lattice-topped pastry crust using wine, ricotta instead of cream cheese, and candied fruit peels.

MAKES ONE 9-INCH CHEESECAKE

Marsala Pastry Crust, partially baked (recipe follows)

5 cups (2½ pounds) ricotta cheese

½ cup sugar

4 egg yolks

1 teaspoon vanilla extract

1 tablespoon orange zest

1 tablespoon flour

½ teaspoon salt

1 tablespoon golden raisins, plumped and drained (see page 25)

1 tablespoon diced candied orange peel

1 tablespoon diced candied lemon peel

3 tablespoons toasted pine nuts (see page 24)

1 egg white, lightly beaten with 1 tablespoon water

Prepare and partially bake the Marsala Pastry Crust.

Preheat the oven to 350°F.

In the bowl of an electric mixer, beat the ricotta cheese, sugar, egg yolks, vanilla, orange zest, flour, and salt until thoroughly blended. Stir in the raisins and candied orange and lemon peel. Spoon the filling into the partially baked pastry, spreading evenly with a rubber spatula. Sprinkle the top with the pine nuts. Weave or crisscross the remaining strips of pastry across the cake to make a lattice design. Brush the strips with the egg white mixture. Bake for 1 to 1¼ hours, or until the crust is golden and the filling is firm.

Remove the cake from the oven and slide off the outside rim. Cool on a wire cake rack.

## MARSALA PASTRY CRUST

2 cups flour

¼ cup sugar

½ teaspoon salt

¼ pound plus 4 tablespoons unsalted butter or margarine

3 egg yolks

3 tablespoons dry Marsala

1 teaspoon lemon zest

In the bowl of an electric mixer, combine the flour, sugar, and salt. Blend in the butter until the dough has the consistency of coarse cornmeal. Add the egg yolks, Marsala, and lemon zest and mix just until the dough holds together. Form into a ball, wrap with plastic wrap, and chill. (The dough can be rolled out at once, but if it seems at all oily, refrigerate for about 1 hour, or until firm but not hard.)

Preheat the oven to 350°F.

Break off one quarter of the dough and set it aside in the refrigerator. Roll out the remaining dough to the desired thickness and carefully place it in a 9-inch springform or false-bottom cake pan, allowing pastry to hang over sides about 2 inches. Line with buttered wax paper or parchment, fill with baker's jewels or beans, and bake for 15 minutes. Carefully remove the wax paper and baker's jewels and continue baking until golden brown, about 20 minutes longer. Cool and trim off overhanging pastry.

Roll the remaining pastry out about 12 inches long and 9 inches wide. With a pastry wheel or a sharp knife, cut it lengthwise into ½-inch-wide strips. Reserve them to make a lattice top on the finished cheesecake.

# CLASSIC CHEESECAKE

MAKES ONE 9-INCH CHEESECAKE

Classic Graham Cracker Crust
(recipe follows)
1 pint sour cream
1 cup plus 1 tablespoon sugar
2 teaspoons vanilla extract
½ teaspoon almond extract
3 packages (8 ounces each)
cream cheese, softened
4 eggs

Prepare and refrigerate the Classic Graham Cracker Crust.

In a small bowl, beat the sour cream and 1 tablespoon of the sugar, 1 teaspoon of the vanilla, and ¼ teaspoon of the almond extract until well blended. Cover with plastic wrap and refrigerate.

Preheat the oven to 350°F.

In the bowl of an electric mixer, beat the cream cheese with the remaining 1 cup sugar until light and fluffy. Add the eggs, 1 at a time, mixing well after each addition. Blend in the remaining vanilla and almond extracts. Pour this filling into the prepared crust.

Bake for 50 minutes, or until the center is set and the top is golden. Remove the cake from the oven. Spread the prepared sour cream mixture on top and return to the oven for 5 minutes. Cool. Remove from the springform pan and serve cold.

## CLASSIC GRAHAM CRACKER CRUST

1¼ cups graham cracker
crumbs
1 tablespoon sugar (optional)
4 tablespoons unsalted butter
or margarine

In a large mixing bowl, thoroughly blend the crumbs, sugar, and butter. Spoon the mixture evenly into a 9-inch springform pan and press it down firmly. Refrigerate at least 15 minutes.

# LIGHT-AND-LEMONY CHEESECAKE

Low-fat farmer cheese and evaporated skim milk save lots of calories in this chiffonlike cake.

MAKES ONE 9-INCH CHEESECAKE

1 pound farmer cheese

1 cup sugar

4 eggs, separated

1 can (13 ounces) evaporated milk (or evaporated skim milk)

2 tablespoons lemon juice

1 tablespoon lemon zest

2 teaspoons vanilla extract

2 tablespoons flour

½ teaspoon salt

Zwieback Crumb Crust (recipe follows)

Preheat the oven to 350°F.

Blend farmer cheese in a processor or blender until creamy. Transfer to the large bowl of an electric mixer, beat the farmer cheese and sugar until fluffy. Beat in the egg yolks, 1 at a time. Gradually add the milk, lemon juice, lemon zest, vanilla, flour, and salt; mix thoroughly. Beat the egg whites until soft peaks form. Fold the egg whites into the cheese mixture.

Pour the batter into the crust. Bake for 45 minutes to 1 hour, or until firm. Allow the cake to cool in the oven with the door open for 20 minutes. The cake will drop a little. Remove it from the oven. Cool and chill in the refrigerator.

## ZWIEBACK CRUMB CRUST

3½ tablespoons unsalted butter, melted

1⅓ cups finely ground zwieback

1 teaspoon vanilla or almond extract

Preheat the oven to 350°F.

Brush a 9-inch springform pan with 1½ tablespoons of the butter. In a large mixing bowl, blend the zwieback crumbs with the remaining butter and vanilla until evenly mixed. Spoon the mixture evenly into the bottom of the buttered pan and press it down firmly. Bake for 5 minutes. Cool to room temperature before filling.

# NO-BAKE CHOCOLATE CHEESECAKE

MAKES ONE 9-INCH CHEESECAKE

Chocolate Wafer Crust (recipe follows)

2 packages (8 ounces each) cream cheese

½ cup sugar

1 teaspoon vanilla extract

2 eggs, separated

6 ounces semisweet chocolate, melted (see page 21)

1 cup cream, whipped

¾ cup toasted chopped pecans (see page 24)

Whipped cream for garnish

½ cup toasted pecan halves

½ cup semisweet chocolate shavings

Prepare the Chocolate Wafer Crust and refrigerate.

In the bowl of an electric mixer, blend the cream cheese, ¼ cup of the sugar, and vanilla. Add the egg yolks and melted chocolate, beating until smooth. Fold in the whipped cream.

Beat the egg whites until soft peaks form. Gradually beat in the remaining ¼ cup sugar. Fold the meringue into the chocolate mixture. Fold in the chopped pecans. Pour into the prepared pan. Cover and freeze. Just before serving, remove from the freezer and garnish with dollops of whipped cream, pecan halves, and chocolate shavings.

## CHOCOLATE WAFER CRUST

1¼ cups chocolate wafer crumbs

⅛ teaspoon cinnamon

1 teaspoon instant coffee powder

5⅓ tablespoons unsalted butter

In a large mixing bowl, thoroughly blend the crumbs, cinnamon, coffee, and butter. Spoon the mixture evenly into a 9-inch springform pan and press it down firmly. Refrigerate at least 15 minutes.

# SLOW-BAKE CHEESECAKE WITH RASPBERRY SAUCE

Instead of the usual sour cream topping, Raspberry Sauce adds color and tangy flavor.

MAKES ONE 9-INCH CHEESECAKE

Graham-Nut Crust (recipe follows)

Prepare and refrigerate the Graham-Nut Crust.
Preheat the oven to 325°F.

1 pound cottage cheese, at room temperature

2 packages (8 ounces each) cream cheese, at room temperature

1½ cups sugar

4 eggs

2 teaspoons vanilla extract

3 tablespoons flour

4 tablespoons cornstarch

¼ pound unsalted butter, melted

1 pint sour cream

Zest of 1 lemon

Raspberry Sauce (recipe follows)

Press the cottage cheese and cream cheese through a sieve into the bowl of an electric mixer. Stir in the sugar. Add the eggs and vanilla and mix well. Sift the flour and cornstarch together and gradually stir into the cheese mixture until well blended. Add the butter, sour cream, and lemon zest and mix well.

Pour the batter into the prepared crust. Bake for 2 hours, until well browned and firm in the center. Turn off the heat and open the oven door, allowing the cake to cool and set for 2 hours. Chill. Remove the cake from the springform; transfer to a cake plate and serve with Raspberry Sauce.

## GRAHAM-NUT CRUST

1 cup graham cracker crumbs

1 cup ground walnuts or pecans (4 ounces)

1 tablespoon sugar

4 tablespoons unsalted butter or margarine

In the large bowl of an electric mixer or in a processor, combine the crumbs, walnuts, sugar, and butter and blend well. Spoon the mixture evenly into a 9-inch springform pan and press it down firmly. Refrigerate at least 15 minutes.

## RASPBERRY SAUCE

MAKES ABOUT 1 CUP

1 cup fresh or frozen raspberries

¼ cup Sugar Syrup (see page 39)

1 tablespoon strawberry or raspberry liqueur or sweet red wine

In a processor or blender, purée the raspberries until smooth. Strain through a sieve to remove all the seeds. Stir in the simple syrup and liqueur and blend well. Transfer to a bowl, cover with plastic wrap, and chill.

# Mini-Cheesecake Pouches

Enclosed in a delicate pastry pouch, these bite-size cheesecakes are perfect for buffets. They're small and dainty and may be picked up with the fingers.

MAKES 4 DOZEN

2 cups flour
½ teaspoon salt
¼ pound unsalted butter or margarine
2 packages (8 ounces each) cream cheese, softened
½ cup sugar
1 egg
1 teaspoon vanilla extract
Powdered sugar

In the large bowl of an electric mixer, place the flour and salt. Add the butter and 1 package of the cream cheese; blend until the mixture comes together. Transfer the dough to a board and knead it until smooth. Roll the dough out into a rectangle. Fold it in thirds, wrap in wax paper, and refrigerate for 2 hours.

In another mixing bowl, blend the remaining 8 ounces of cream cheese until very creamy. Blend in the sugar, egg, and vanilla. Set aside.

Preheat the oven to 375°F.

Divide the dough into 3 parts for easier handling. Roll out one part on a floured board into a rectangle ⅛ inch thick. Cut the dough into 3-inch squares. Fit the pastry squares into ungreased mini-muffin pan cups, easing it in lightly without pressing. Drop 1 teaspoonful of the cheese filling into each pastry square. Bring opposite corners of the squares to the center and pinch them together lightly to seal in the filling. (At this point, the cheesecakes can be covered with foil and stored in the freezer for several days.)

Bake for 15 to 20 minutes, or until lightly browned. Remove from the pans immediately and cool on racks. Just before serving, sprinkle with powdered sugar.

# MAKING
# THE SABBATH
# SPECIAL

**W**hen modern women talk about "having it all," it would be nice to include reviving the old traditions centered on Shabbat. Didn't your mother and your grandmother prepare a festive dinner and light candles and have a gleaming house? And shouldn't we be doing that for our kids, so they can have an example to pass on to their children? Maybe you can even get them to dress up a little. With our five children growing up on a ranch, life was casual, and it was hard to enforce a dress code, but my kids all knew that you'd better "neaten up" for Shabbat—or else.

It doesn't take much extra work to have the Shabbat dinner an occasion to look forward to each week. Fresh flowers or a tiny plant or—particularly appropriate—a freshly baked challah in a pretty basket, wrapped in a white napkin, can decorate your table. This is a time to serve traditional foods—chopped liver, chicken soup, gefilte fish, and challah.

I think what my kids liked most, when they got home from school and opened the door to the kitchen, was the wonderful smell of bread baking in the oven.

One of the most important responsibilities we have as parents is to offer religion, with all its traditions, festivals, and rituals, to our children and let them take it from there. At least they won't grow up wondering what they missed.

# SABBATH CHOLENT DINNER

FOR 8

▼▲▼▲▼▲▼▲▼▲▼▲▼▲▼▲▼▲▼▲▼

**Potato Challah**

**Romaine and Mushroom Salad with Parsley-Anchovy Dressing**

**Classic Eastern European Cholent**

**Kasha with Mushrooms**

**Herbed Green Beans**

**Macadamia Nut Tart**

**Hot Russian-Style Tea (see page 82)**

SUGGESTED BEVERAGE:

**Israeli Cabernet Sauvignon**

This is a traditional menu that may be prepared largely in advance, following the custom of not cooking on the Sabbath. The cholent is the classic recipe European Jews have served for centuries, made with brisket and dried lima beans. Kasha and crisp green beans, along with an unusual challah, add up to a hearty menu.

If you've never made cholent, here's a chance to introduce your family to a food steeped in history. They'll enjoy this historical version and you'll want to try some of the others included in this chapter.

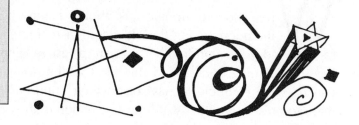

# POTATO CHALLAH

Potato Challah originated in Eastern Europe, and was the traditional Sabbath bread. Unlike the usual sweet challah, this potato challah is crusty and has a robust sourdough taste. The heavy texture makes the bread more moist and so it keeps fresh longer.

Challah is the ideal bread to serve with a hearty cholent, using it to sop up the wonderful thick sauce.

MAKES 1 LARGE CHALLAH

3 large red or white potatoes, unpeeled

Boil the potatoes in water to cover until tender. Drain, reserving ¾ cup of the water. Peel and mash the pota-

4 tablespoons unsalted margarine, melted

2 tablespoons sugar

2 teaspoons kosher salt

2 packages active dry yeast

⅓ cup warm water (110 to 115°F)

4 eggs

5 cups flour

Yellow cornmeal

Poppy seeds or sesame seeds

toes. Combine them with the reserved water. In the bowl of an electric mixer, add the margarine, sugar, and salt and mix well.

Dissolve the yeast in the warm water with a pinch of sugar. Add to the potato mixture and blend well. Blend in 3 of the eggs. Add flour, 1 cup at a time, blending to make a soft dough. Place the dough on a floured board and knead until smooth, 5 to 10 minutes. Place the dough in an oiled bowl, oil top of the dough, cover with a towel, and let rise in a warm place until doubled in size, about 1½ hours. Roll dough between your palms into a long rope about 1½ inches thick. Brush a baking sheet with oil and sprinkle it with cornmeal. Place a rope of dough on the cornmeal. Starting from the outer circle, coil the rope like a snail, working inward and tucking in all loose ends. Cover with a towel and let rise in a warm place until doubled in size, about 1 hour.

Preheat the oven to 400°F.

Beat the remaining egg and brush it on the top of the challah. Sprinkle with poppy seeds. Bake for 10 minutes. Reduce the heat to 325°F and bake an additional 20 to 30 minutes, or until golden brown. Pierce loaf several times with a large needle to allow any air to escape. Cool on a rack.

# ROMAINE AND MUSHROOM SALAD WITH PARSLEY-ANCHOVY DRESSING

The simplest salads are often the best, especially when the dressing is on the exotic side. The firm-textured romaine holds up well under the rich anchovy dressing, and the mushrooms add interest.

2 to 3 heads of romaine lettuce, tender center leaves only

1 pound mushrooms, sliced

Parsley-Anchovy Dressing (recipe follows)

Wash the lettuce and dry, wrap in damp paper towels, and store in plastic bags in the refrigerator until ready to use.

In a large salad bowl, combine the lettuce, torn into bite-size pieces, with the mushrooms and toss. Pour enough of the salad dressing over the mixture to moisten completely. Serve immediately.

## PARSLEY-ANCHOVY DRESSING

MAKES 1½ CUPS

1 large bunch parsley, stems removed

1 cup olive oil

3 tablespoons balsamic vinegar

¼ cup diced onion

1 can (2 ounces) flat anchovy fillets with oil

Wash and dry parsley and set aside. In a processor or blender, combine the oil, vinegar, onion, and anchovies and process until well blended. Add the parsley, little by little, until well blended and dressing is a deep green color. Transfer to a small bowl, cover with plastic wrap, and refrigerate. This salad dressing keeps about 1 week in the refrigerator. Mix well before using.

# CLASSIC EASTERN EUROPEAN CHOLENT

½ pound (1¼ cups) dried lima beans

3 tablespoons safflower or vegetable oil

2 large onions, thinly sliced

6 large potatoes, peeled and quartered

1 beef marrow bone, cut in quarters (ask your butcher to do this)

3 pounds brisket, short ribs, stew meat, or lamb shanks

1 whole head of garlic, cloves separated and unpeeled

Salt

Freshly ground black pepper

1 teaspoon paprika

2 cups dry red wine (optional)

Boiling chicken broth or water to cover

In a large bowl, soak the lima beans in cold water until soft, 5 to 6 hours.

Preheat the oven to 375°F.

In the bottom of a large heavy pot or Dutch oven with a tight-fitting lid, heat the oil and sauté the onions until soft, 2 to 3 minutes. In layers, add the drained lima beans, potatoes, marrow bone, brisket, and garlic cloves. Add salt, pepper, and paprika to taste. Add the wine and enough boiling chicken broth or water to cover. Cover tightly and bake for 30 minutes. Give the pot a shake before returning to the oven. Reduce the heat to 225°F and bake overnight.

# KASHA WITH MUSHROOMS

It is very important not to overcook kasha or it becomes very mushy. When it is prepared properly, with each grain tender but firm, it can be a delicious experience. This recipe can be prepared the day before, undercooked. The next day, add a little chicken broth, mix well, reheat, and serve.

¼ pound unsalted margarine
1 medium onion, minced
1 cup Kasha (whole, roasted buckwheat kernels)
1 egg
2 cups Chicken Stock (see page 390)
Salt
Freshly ground black pepper
6 large mushrooms, sliced

In a large skillet, heat 4 tablespoons of the margarine over medium heat and sauté the onion until soft, 3 to 4 minutes. Combine the kasha and egg and add them to onion mixture. Sauté the mixture until the kasha becomes dry and crunchy, 2 to 3 minutes. Add the stock and salt and pepper to taste, bring to a boil, and simmer for 15 minutes, until the kasha is tender and the stock has been absorbed; while the kasha is cooking, uncover and mix to prevent it from sticking to the pot.

In a small skillet, heat the remaining 4 tablespoons margarine and sauté the mushrooms until soft. Add them to the cooked kasha and gently toss until evenly distributed.

# HERBED GREEN BEANS

Green beans cook very quickly and are best when tender but still slightly crisp, so be careful; follow the instructions and do not overcook. (Most vegetables continue cooking even after they have been removed from the heat.)

1 pound green beans
Garlic-Margarine Sauce (see page 74)
Salt
Freshly ground black pepper

Pinch the ends from the green beans and blanch in plenty of lightly salted boiling water for 2 to 3 minutes, until the beans are tender but crisp and bright green. Drain. Transfer to a large skillet in which the Garlic-Margarine Sauce was cooked and mix well. Season to taste with salt and pepper.

# MACADAMIA NUT TART

The crust of this tart will stay crisp overnight, so you can bake it the day before the Sabbath. The filling can also be prepared the day before.

MAKES ONE 11-INCH TART

⅓ cup dark brown sugar, firmly packed

¼ cup granulated sugar

½ cup light corn syrup

2 eggs plus 2 egg yolks

1 tablespoon unsalted margarine

½ vanilla bean, split lengthwise down the center

1½ tablespoon Frangelico or fruit liqueur

1½ cups coarsely chopped toasted Macadamia nuts (see page 24)

Prebaked Sweet Pastry Tart Shell (see page 205)

Preheat the oven to 350°F.

In a large mixing bowl, use a wire whisk to beat the brown sugar, granulated sugar, corn syrup, eggs, and egg yolks until light and airy.

In a small skillet over medium-high heat, brown the margarine with the vanilla bean. Add the Frangelico and simmer for 30 seconds. Pour it into the brown sugar mixture and stir well. Add the nuts and stir vigorously until foamy. Pour into the prebaked pastry shell and bake for 25 to 30 minutes, until firm.

# FESTIVE SABBATH DINNER

FOR 8

This menu is perfect for any special occasion. Since the chicken is butterflied, it takes very little time to bake. The pâté and salad dressing may be prepared in advance.

## CARROT–WHOLE WHEAT CHALLAH TWISTS

Once a challah recipe has been mastered and successfully made for a period of time, it is fun to develop different textures, flavors, and shapes.

These twists are one example. By adding grated carrots and using whole wheat flour, a hearty flavor and texture are created. Serve toasted with sweet butter, homemade preserves, or honey for breakfast, as well as with your Shabbat dinner. Make into small loaves or rolls and store them in the freezer for unexpected company.

2 cups whole wheat flour

2 cups unbleached flour

1 package active dry yeast

1 teaspoon kosher salt

1 cup warm water (110 to 115°F)

¼ cup safflower or vegetable oil

2 tablespoons honey

2 eggs

1 cup peeled, grated carrots

Poppy seeds or sesame seeds

Combine the flours. Place 2 cups of the flour mixture, yeast, and salt in the bowl of an electric mixer. Heat the water, oil, and honey in a saucepan or microwave oven until very warm, 115 to 120°F. Add the water mixture to the flour mixture, beating until well blended. Beat in 1 of the eggs, carrots, and enough flour to make a soft dough. Turn dough onto a floured board and knead for 5 to 10 minutes, adding additional flour to make a smooth and elastic dough. Place dough in an oiled bowl and oil the top. Cover with a towel and let rise in a warm place until doubled in size, about 1½ hours.

Punch down the dough. Divide it into 3 parts. Form each part into a long rope. Pinch together one end of each of the 3 ropes, and after braiding the ropes, pinch the other ends together. Or break off small pieces of dough (about 30), form into long ropes, twist into knots, and place on a greased baking sheet. Cover with a towel and let rise in a warm place until doubled, about 1 hour.

Preheat the oven to 350°F. Brush the top of the challah or rolls with the remaining egg, lightly beaten. Sprinkle with poppy seeds and bake for 30 to 40 minutes for bread and 20 to 30 minutes for rolls, until golden brown.

# PICKLED TONGUE PÂTÉ

Serve this pâté in a crock on a platter garnished with parsley, tiny tomatoes, sliced red peppers, Red Pepper Jelly (see page 112), and thin slices of pumpernickel, rye bread, or Carrot–Whole Wheat Challah Twists.

My favorite lunch meat for the children when they were growing up was pickled tongue. It keeps for days and supplies an emergency meat for omelets, sandwiches, and snacks. Buy a corned or pickled tongue, and if it is very salty soak it in cold water for several hours. Then place the tongue in a large heavy pot with water to cover and boil it until completely tender when a fork is inserted in the center.

2 pounds cooked pickled tongue, skin and fat removed

Put the tongue through a meat grinder twice, then transfer it to a large bowl. In a small saucepan, melt the margarine. Add the wine, nutmeg, sage, cloves, and 1

½ pound unsalted margarine

2 tablespoons Concord grape wine

½ teaspoon grated nutmeg

⅓ teaspoon dried crushed sage

¼ teaspoon ground cloves

2 tablespoons minced parsley

Salt

Freshly ground black pepper

tablespoon of the parsley to the margarine. Simmer for 3 to 4 minutes.

Add the margarine mixture to the ground tongue. Season to taste with salt and pepper. Beat the mixture with a wooden spoon over ice until well blended and cool. Tightly pack the tongue into a crock or a deep serving bowl. Cover with plastic wrap and seal with a lid or heavy foil and chill in the refrigerator until serving time.

# APPLE-SPINACH SALAD

I call this my "telephone salad," because after serving it to guests I am always deluged with phone calls asking for the recipe for this crisp, crunchy, tart and tangy mixture. It's a versatile recipe that will fit into many menus. It works equally well for a baby shower, luncheon, deli menu for poker nights, or a complete Middle Eastern repast.

This salad is a good choice for a Sabbath dinner, since it can be prepared the day before, refrigerated, and the spinach tossed into the apple mixture just before serving.

3 apples, peeled, cored, and diced

3 green onions (scallions), thinly sliced

3 celery stalks, diced

Juice of 2 lemons

¼ cup mayonnaise

¼ cup tahini (sesame seed paste)

2 tablespoons honey

4 cups spinach leaves, torn into bite-size pieces

¼ cup toasted sesame seeds (see page 24)

In large bowl, toss the apples, green onions, and celery with the juice of 1 lemon to keep the apples from darkening. Set aside.

In a blender, processor, or a small bowl, blend together the mayonnaise, tahini, honey, and remaining lemon juice; the mixture will be very thick. Toss with the apple mixture. Cover with plastic wrap and chill. Just before serving, place spinach in a large bowl, add the apple mixture, and toss to coat the spinach thoroughly. Garnish with sesame seeds.

# ROAST CHICKEN WITH ZUCCHINI STUFFING

A small roasted whole chicken represents a real treasure to the busy cook or career woman. Roasted chickens can be served hot or cold in so many ways. And they're very useful for last-minute dinner guests, too.

When I attended a food processor class taught by Belle Rhodes, a very creative cook, I discovered a sophisticated version of our old family favorite. The stuffing is a blend of fresh vegetables and garlic that everybody seems to like. Heat at sundown because stuffed chicken is not good cold.

1 whole chicken (4 pounds) or
  2 smaller chickens

**MIREPOIX (SMALL CUBES OR SLICES OF VEGETABLES)**

1 onion, sliced and diced

2 garlic cloves, minced

4 carrots, peeled and thinly sliced

1 parsnip, peeled and thinly sliced

2 tablespoons minced parsley

**MARINADE**

⅓ cup olive oil

¼ teaspoon each dried basil, thyme, and rosemary, crushed

**STUFFING:**

3 garlic cloves, minced

2 medium onions, minced

3 tablespoons margarine or oil

8 zucchini, shredded (about 4 cups)

Salt

Freshly ground black pepper

1 egg

Bread crumbs or matzo meal

Dry white wine

1 whole head of garlic, cloves separated, unpeeled

Split the chicken along the entire length of the back, removing backbone from tail to neck. Open it out, skin side up. With a mallet (for big chickens) or heel of hand, flatten with a firm whack, fracturing the breastbone and ribcage. Turn the chicken over and take out the ribcage and cartilage with a very sharp boning knife, taking care not to break the skin.

Combine the mirepoix mixture and sprinkle on a foil-lined large roasting pan. Place the chicken on top, skin side up. Rub the top of the chicken with the marinade and marinate while preparing the stuffing.

Preheat the oven to 450°F.

In a large skillet, sauté the garlic and onion in the margarine until soft, about 5 minutes. Add the zucchini and stir with a wooden spoon to avoid sticking. Add the salt and pepper and sauté until soft and well blended. Add the egg and bread crumbs to make a firm stuffing. Cool to room temperature.

Working with your fingertips, separate the skin from the meat of the chicken, beginning at the neck end, being careful not to tear the skin. Place the stuffing under the skin, filling the drumsticks and thighs first. Force the stuffing into place; mold the skin with your hands to resemble the natural contour of the chicken.

Pour the white wine over the mirepoix and unpeeled garlic cloves. Return the chicken to the roasting pan. Bake for 10 minutes. Reduce the oven temperature to 375°F and bake for 45 minutes to 1 hour longer, depending on the size of the chicken. Baste every 20 minutes. If chicken browns too quickly, cover it loosely with foil. If the wine cooks away too quickly, add more. Remove the foil during the last 10 minutes, allowing the chicken to brown.

# CRANBERRY MERINGUE TART

The secret of making a crisp tart is to cook the filling first then cool it and spoon it into a prebaked, cooled tart shell. Then add the meringue, place under the broiler, or bake in the oven until toasted. This Cranberry Meringue Tart is a perfect example. If the crust browns too quickly, simply cut a round of foil to fit the tart with a large hole in the center to expose the filling. This keeps it from burning.

Prebaked Sweet Pastry Tart
　　Shell (recipe follows)
4 cups fresh cranberries
⅔ cup orange juice
1 tablespoon grated orange
　　peel
2 cups light brown sugar
3 egg whites
Pinch of salt
¾ cup granulated sugar

Prepare the tart shell and cool. Preheat the oven to 350°F.

In a large heavy skillet, combine the cranberries, orange juice, peel, and 1½ cups of the brown sugar. Bring to a boil, stirring until sugar dissolves, and simmer, uncovered, for 10 to 15 minutes. Stir occasionally. The cranberries will pop and become very soft. Blend in remaining ½ cup brown sugar and continue cooking 5 minutes longer. Cool. Spoon into baked tart shell.

In the bowl of an electric mixer, beat egg whites with salt until soft peaks form. Add the granulated sugar, a little at a time, beating well until stiff peaks form. Fill a pastry tube fitted with decorative tip with the meringue. Cover the cranberry filling completely with meringue rosettes, including the edge of the crust. Bake for 5 to 10 minutes, or place under the broiler until meringue is lightly toasted.

## SWEET PASTRY TART SHELL

If I had to choose one pie crust recipe for a bake-off contest, this would be the winner. It is as sweet, crisp, and crunchy as a sugar cookie and a perfect match for the tangy cranberry filling in this tart. I would not use this crust for an onion tart, nor would I choose it for a very sweet filling. For a dairy menu substitute butter for margarine and milk for the liquid.

MAKES ONE 11-INCH TART SHELL

1½ cups flour
½ teaspoon salt
⅓ cup powdered sugar
¼ pound unsalted margarine
3 tablespoons water or non-
　　dairy liquid creamer

In the bowl of an electric mixer, combine the flour, salt, and sugar. Cut in the margarine until the mixture is crumbly. Blend in the water until the dough begins to come together. Do not overmix. Knead the dough into a ball, wrap it in wax paper, and chill it for at least 10 minutes in the refrigerator.

Roll out pastry on 2 large sheets of floured wax paper to a round large enough to cover and overlap an 11-inch flan pan with a removable bottom. For easier handling, cover the pastry with another sheet of wax paper and fold pastry in half. (The wax paper protects the center of the pastry from sticking together.)

Lift the pastry from the bottom wax paper and place on half of the flan pan. Unfold the pastry and remove the wax paper that covers it. (At this point the pastry can be covered with plastic wrap and foil and stored in the refrigerator or freezer for several days.)

Preheat the oven to 375°F.

Bring the pastry to room temperature. Spread a light coating of margarine on a sheet of wax paper and place it, coated side down, inside the pastry, overlapping around the outside. Cover with another piece of wax paper with the cut ends in the opposite direction. Fill the center of the lined pie shell with uncooked rice or baker's jewels. Bake for 15 to 20 minutes, until the sides of the pastry begin to brown. Carefully remove the wax paper with the rice and continue baking until the bottom of the pastry is light brown. Remove from the oven and cool.

BONUS RECIPES:

# CHOLENT

Hungarian Cholent

Adafina (Moroccan Cholent)

Classic Eastern European Cholent (see page 198)

Low-Fat Vegetarian Cholent

Cholent, a hearty thick stew, is served on the Sabbath by Jews all over the world. It was usually served at noon in earlier days, but there is no reason you can't have a casserole of cholent waiting for a break-the-fast meal on Yom Kippur, or for an early Sabbath dinner, if you wish.

Traditionally made with meat, vegetables, beans, and barley or kasha, cholent was usually prepared in a large casserole and started on Friday afternoon in a wood-burning oven. It is the slow baking that gives Cholent its special character. And today it works just as well in an ordinary gas or electric oven. A crock-pot or electric roaster will also give good results.

The cholent recipes are adapted from various Jewish communities in Europe and Africa.

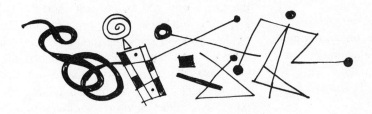

# HUNGARIAN CHOLENT

Traditionally, this cholent was cooked overnight and then eaten at noon the next day. Orthodox Jews could not open the pot on the Sabbath, so the old recipe allowed for an extra cup of water to keep it moist. It can be made in advance and cooled, with the fat skimmed off. Then it is delightful reheated—even more than once.

2 garlic cloves, finely chopped
1 medium onion, diced
⅓ cup vegetable oil
2 to 3 cups water
1 cup dry red wine
1½ cups dried small white or
 lima beans, uncooked
½ cup barley
1 beef tongue
1 tablespoon paprika
1 large tomato, quartered
2 celery stalks, sliced
1 pound brisket of beef
2 raw eggs, in their shells
1 tablespoon salt
Freshly ground black pepper
1 Stuffed Chicken Neck (recipe follows)

Preheat the oven to 250°F.

Sauté the garlic and onion in the oil. Using a heavy 6-quart casserole, combine garlic and onion, water, wine, lima beans, barley, tongue, paprika, tomato, celery, brisket, eggs, salt and pepper to taste, and stuffed chicken neck. Bring to a boil on top of the stove. Cover and bake for 4 to 6 hours. After the cholent has been baking for about 2 hours, stir and check to see if there is enough water and add some if needed. Serve in hot soup bowls, with the eggs peeled and cut into quarters and the Stuffed Chicken Neck sliced.

## STUFFED CHICKEN NECKS
HELZEL

8 chicken necks
4 tablespoons safflower or
  vegetable oil
1 onion, chopped
1 garlic clove, minced
1 celery stalk, finely chopped
3 carrots, peeled and grated
1 zucchini, grated
½ cup minced parsley
¼ cup flour
¼ cup bread crumbs
¼ cup quick-cooking oatmeal
Salt
Freshly ground black pepper

Sew up the narrow end of the chicken necks. Clean and wash thoroughly. Set aside.

In a skillet, heat 2 tablespoons of the oil and sauté the onion and garlic until soft. Add the celery, carrots, zucchini, and parsley and continue sautéing until almost tender, about 5 minutes. Blend in flour, bread crumbs, oatmeal, and remaining 2 tablespoons oil to bind the vegetables together. Season to taste with salt and pepper. Fill the necks only two thirds full, since the stuffing expands as it cooks. Sew up the other end. Add to the cholent (or add to a roast, turning Helzel so they become crisp and golden on both sides).

# ADAFINA
## MOROCCAN CHOLENT

A young French Jewish friend who lived in Morocco for several years assured me that this is the same cholent that Moroccan Jews prepared for centuries in outdoor wood or coal-burning ovens. But it can be prepared just as authentically—and much more easily—in today's modern ovens.

The Moroccans layered the ingredients in large heavy pots and simmered them for hours on a bed of hot coals or in their primitive ovens. The word "adafina" derives from the Arabic word "dafana," meaning to cover or bury. And you will pronounce it "delicious."

½ pound (1¼ cups) dried
  chick-peas
¼ cup safflower or vegetable
  oil
3 leeks, white part only,
  cleaned and diced
1 large onion, finely diced
4 garlic cloves, minced
½ cup uncooked rice

Soak the chick-peas in cold water to cover overnight. Drain and place in cheesecloth or foil and tie or seal. Set aside.

Preheat the oven to 300°F.

In a large Dutch oven or heavy pot, heat the oil and sauté the leeks, onion, garlic, and rice. Layer the lamb, chicken, marrow bone, eggs, carrots, cabbage, sausage, and mint leaves. Place the cheesecloth containing the chick-peas on top. Add the water. Place the Pelota at the

3 pounds boneless lean lamb,
   cubed
1 chicken, cut into pieces
1 marrow bone, sliced
6 raw eggs, in their shells
3 carrots, peeled and thickly
   sliced
1 small cabbage, trimmed and
   quartered
½ pound garlic sausage,
   thickly sliced (optional)
2 mint sprigs
3 to 4 cups water or chicken
   broth
Pelota (recipe follows)
1 teaspoon ground cumin
Salt
Freshly ground black pepper

very top. Add cumin and salt and pepper to taste. Cover and bake for 3 hours. Reduce the heat to 225°F and keep warm until ready to serve.

When ready to serve, carefully remove the Pelota and place them in the center of a large soup tureen or individual soup bowls. Surround the Pelota with the meat, vegetables, chick-peas (cheesecloth removed), peeled and halved eggs, and sauce.

## PELOTA
MEATBALLS

MAKES ABOUT 12 PELOTA

¾ pound ground lean beef,
   veal, or lamb
1 egg, beaten
⅛ teaspoon each nutmeg,
   ground cloves, and cumin
Salt
Freshly ground black pepper
1 cup bread crumbs or matzo
   meal

In a bowl, combine the meat, egg, nutmeg, cloves, cumin, and salt and pepper to taste. Form into meatballs and roll in bread crumbs. Brown in hot oil.

# LOW-FAT VEGETARIAN CHOLENT

This cholent was created in answer to many requests for a vegetarian version for the Sabbath. The meat is not missed at all, since the pareve chicken-flavored soup mix and herbs add a lot of flavor. Add any other hearty fresh vegetables as well: turnips, parsnips, rutabaga, and sometimes even a whole head of garlic.

3 cups (1 pound) dried large
  lima beans

2 tablespoons safflower or
  vegetable oil

4 garlic cloves, minced

3 large onions, thinly sliced

6 celery ribs, thinly sliced

4 large or 8 small potatoes,
  peeled and quartered

4 carrots, peeled and thinly
  sliced

2 bay leaves, crushed

3 tablespoons instant chicken-
  flavored soup mix (pareve)
  (see page 25)

8 cups hot water

Salt

Freshly ground black pepper

Soak the beans overnight in water to cover, then drain.

Preheat the oven to 400°F.

In a large heavy Dutch oven or pot, heat the oil and sauté the garlic, onions, and celery until tender. Add the potatoes, carrots, beans and bay leaves. Dissolve the soup mix in 1 cup of the hot water and add to the vegetables with the remaining water. Add salt and pepper to taste. Cover tightly; bring to a boil over medium heat, then bake in the oven for 30 minutes. Reduce the heat to 250°F and cook overnight.

BONUS RECIPES:

# SABBATH CHALLAHS

Apple-Filled Egg Challah

Classic Challah

Low-Cholesterol Challah

No time to bake challah? Listen to this story one of my students, a busy young mother, told me:

Every Friday morning, she mixed and kneaded her challah dough and placed it in a covered bowl in the family automobile while she went to the morning meeting at her daughter's nursery school. After an hour or so, while the dough was rising, she would return to her car and punch down the dough. When she returned home with her child, she braided the dough into challah, let it rise again, and baked it in the oven.

This energetic lady proves that a little organization and a lot of determination can add enjoyment to the Sabbath meal.

Besides the other challahs and holiday breads in this book, here are a few of my favorites:

# APPLE-FILLED EGG CHALLAH

Because of the apples and honey in this challah, it is also a delightful bread for Rosh Hashanah. And to carry on the tradition, serve it with apple slices and honey for dipping.

MAKES 1 CHALLAH

1 package active dry yeast
½ cup sugar
1 teaspoon salt
1 cup warm water (110 to 115°F)
4 to 5 cups flour
6 egg yolks
¼ cup safflower or vegetable oil
4 tablespoons unsalted butter or margarine, melted
Apple Filling (recipe follows)
1 egg yolk beaten with 1 teaspoon water
Cinnamon sugar

In the bowl of an electric mixer, blend together the yeast, sugar, salt, warm water, and 2 cups of the flour. Blend in the egg yolks and oil. Add the remaining flour, 1 cup at a time, blending after each addition, until the dough is thick enough to work by hand. Gather the dough into a ball. Place it on a floured board and knead 5 to 10 minutes, adding additional flour, until the dough is smooth and elastic. Shape the dough into a ball and place it in an oiled bowl, and oil the top. Cover with a towel and let rise in a warm place until doubled in size, about 1½ hours.

Punch down the dough and divide into 3 parts. Roll each part into a rectangle. Brush with melted butter and top with the apple filling. Roll each rectangle into a long rope. Seal the ends of the rope together and braid. Place it on an oiled baking sheet. Cover with a towel and let rise in a warm place for 45 minutes, or until doubled in size.

Preheat the oven to 350°F. Brush with egg yolk wash, then sprinkle with cinnamon sugar. Bake for 30 to 40 minutes. Cool on a rack.

## APPLE FILLING

3 apples, peeled, cored, and diced
Juice of 1 lemon
2 tablespoons honey
½ teaspoon cinnamon

In a bowl, combine the apples, lemon juice, honey, and cinnamon. Cover with plastic wrap and chill. Drain and use for the challah filling.

# CLASSIC CHALLAH

MAKES 3 SMALL OR 1 LARGE CHALLAH

2 packages active dry yeast
2 cups warm water (110 to 115°F)
¼ cup plus a pinch of sugar
¼ cup safflower or vegetable oil
2 tablespoons salt
4 eggs
8 cups flour
3 tablespoons yellow cornmeal
Sesame seeds or poppy seeds

Dissolve the yeast in ½ cup of the warm water with a pinch of sugar.

In the bowl of an electric mixer, beat together the remaining 1½ cups warm water, ¼ cup sugar, oil, salt, and the yeast mixture. Add 3 of the eggs and blend well. Add the flour, 1 cup at a time, blending after each addition, until the dough is thick enough to work by hand, 4 to 5 cups. Spoon the dough out on a floured board and knead for 5 to 10 minutes, adding additional flour to make a smooth and elastic dough. Place the dough in an oiled bowl, and oil the top of the dough. Cover with a towel and let rise in a warm place until doubled in size, about 1½ hours. Punch down the dough, turn it over, cover, and let it rise 30 minutes longer.

Divide the dough into 3 parts. Divide each part into 3 parts. This will make 3 individual challahs. Form each part into a long rope. Pinch together one end of each of the 3 ropes and braid the ropes, pinching the other ends together.

To shape for Rosh Hashanah (round challah): Using one third of the dough, form into a large rope, 12 to 15 inches long and several inches thick. Starting in the center, begin making concentric circles of the rope until a large snail-like shape is created. Seal ends.

Place the round challah in a large cake pan, oiled and generously sprinkled with cornmeal. Place the individual challahs on baking sheets or in bread pans lightly greased and generously sprinkled with cornmeal. Cover with a towel and let rise in a warm place until doubled, about 1 hour.

Preheat the oven to 375°F. Brush with the remaining egg, lightly beaten, and sprinkle with sesame seeds. Bake for 30 to 40 minutes, or until golden brown. Cool on racks.

# LOW-CHOLESTEROL CHALLAH

This recipe for a challah made with egg whites came about in answer to many requests for a low-cholesterol bread. This is the perfect challah for the family to dip in honey before the traditional Rosh Hashanah dinner. To add color, include a pinch of saffron powder when mixing the dough and a cup of raisins for holiday menus.

MAKES 1 LARGE OR 2 MEDIUM CHALLAHS

1 package active dry yeast
1½ cups warm water (110 to 115°F)
Pinch of sugar
1 tablespoon salt
3 tablespoons sugar or juice from the plumped raisins
¼ cup safflower or vegetable oil
5 egg whites
6 to 7 cups flour
1 cup golden raisins, plumped (see page 25)
Sesame seeds or poppy seeds
Yellow cornmeal

Dissolve the yeast in ½ cup of the warm water with a pinch of sugar. Set aside until foamy.

In the bowl of an electric mixer, beat together the remaining 1 cup warm water, salt, sugar, oil, and 4 of the egg whites. Blend in the yeast mixture. Add 4 cups of flour, 1 cup at a time, blending with a beater after each addition. Combine the drained raisins with 1 cup of flour and knead into the dough. Spoon the remaining 2 cups flour on a wooden board. Pour the dough onto the flour and knead for 5 to 10 minutes, incorporating enough flour to make a smooth and elastic dough. Place the dough in a greased bowl and grease the top. Cover with a towel and let rise in a warm place until doubled in size, about 1½ hours.

Punch down the dough and divide into 6 equal parts. Roll each part into ropes about 15 inches long. Braid 3 ropes into a challah. (For a round challah, bring the ends together and seal.) Repeat with remaining 3 ropes. Sprinkle with seeds.

Preheat the oven to 350°F.

Place the 2 challahs on baking sheets or two 8-inch round cake pans lightly oiled and generously sprinkled with cornmeal. Bake for 30 minutes, or until golden brown and a hollow sound is made when tapped with a finger. Cool on racks.

# BONUS RECIPE

## GRANDMA GENE'S GEFILTE FISH

MAKES ABOUT 40 FISH BALLS

Grandmothers always had the precious task of preparing gefilte fish, and no one else ever could measure up. In our family, my mother-in-law had to relinquish the task when she broke her elbow and was forced to sit and direct me. A special grinder had to be used. Special fish was purchased. The chopping had to be done in a certain direction, always smoothing the ground mixture down in a circular motion. Each year after that we made the fish together, gradually introducing electric grinders, food processors, or mixers to make the job easier. Now that Grandma Gene is gone, I am happy to have her original cherished recipe.

5 onions, thinly sliced, skins reserved

1 cup sliced celery tops

6 carrots, peeled and thinly sliced

1 pound fish bones and skin

3 pounds filleted carp

2 pounds filleted turbot

1 pound filleted ling cod or black cod

1 pound filleted sucker, rock cod or white fish

4 celery ribs, sliced

3 eggs

½ cup matzo meal

1 cup water

Kosher salt

Freshly ground black pepper

Lettuce, jícama, cucumber, pickled beets, and horse-radish sauce for garnish

In a large pot, place 3 of the onions, the onion skins, celery tops, 2 of the carrots, the fish bones and skin. Set aside.

In a grinder or food processor, grind the remaining carrots, remaining onions, celery ribs, and fish. Place the ground mixture in a large mixing bowl and blend with eggs and matzo meal. Transfer mixture to a large wooden chopping bowl and chop fish mixture, adding water gradually with 1 tablespoon Kosher salt and 2 teaspoons pepper as you chop. (Mixture should be soft and light to the touch.)

Wet your hands with cold water and shape the fish mixture into oval balls. At this point long strips of fish skin can be wrapped around fish balls, if desired. Place fish balls over onions in a pot. Add warm water to completely cover the fish balls. Add salt and pepper to taste. Cover partially and bring to a boil. Shake the pot to distribute salt and pepper. Cook over medium heat for 1 hour or until done. Cool, transfer to a glass bowl, cover with plastic wrap and foil, and refrigerate. Serve on a lettuce leaf with jícama, cucumber, and pickled beets. Top with horseradish sauce.

# PART 2  INTERNATIONAL ENTERTAINING

**MEXICAN MENUS**
South-of-the-Border Fiesta for 10
Mexican Sampler for 12

**CHINESE MENUS**
A Chinese Banquet for 12
Chinese New Year Dinner for 8

**FRENCH MENUS**
A French Chef's Dinner for 12
Bouillabaisse Menu for 8
Country French Duck Dinner for 8

**ITALIAN MENUS**
2 Primi Piatti Dinners for 8
Italian Veal Dinner for 8
Pasta Party for 8
Pizza Party for 12

**BRAZILIAN MENU**
Rio Brunch for 12 to 16

**MOROCCAN MENU**
Couscous Dinner for 8 to 10

**ISRAELI MENU**
Breakfast Buffet for 24

**SCANDINAVIAN MENU**
Three-Course Brunch for 12

# MEXICAN MENUS

# SOUTH-OF-THE-BORDER FIESTA

FOR 10

▼▲▼▲▼▲▼▲▼▲▼▲▼▲▼▲▼▲▼

Fresh Tuna Seviche *or*

Halibut Seviche Cocktail

Ensalada de Nopales

COMBINATION MEXICAN
PLATE

Taquitos

Chicken Enchiladas

Chicken Tostada "Salad"

Frijoles Negros Refritos

Mexican Fried Rice

Lime Ice with Tropical
Fresh Fruit

Sopaipillas

SUGGESTED BEVERAGE:

Ice-cold Mexican beer or
chilled Beaujolais wine

W hen my husband and I were teenagers, we loved
to visit the east side of Los Angeles, with its
many little Mexican restaurants, fragrant with the spicy
aroma of ethnic delicacies. We loved tacos and tostados
more than hot fudge sundaes. After we married, our travels through Mexico taught us more about the varied—
and often sophisticated—cuisines of that country.

Later our children became as enamored of Mexican
food as their parents. Sunday nights would find them pil-
ing beans, lettuce, tomatoes, and guacamole on the tortillas their father had fried.

Now we serve a more elaborate Mexican menu to
our friends. We tell them to dress casually, hand out
aprons, and let everybody pitch in.

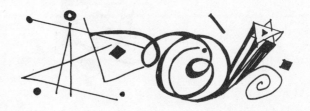

# FRESH TUNA SEVICHE
## MARINATED FISH

This seviche is made from fresh tuna fillets and is arranged attractively on small salad plates.

1 pound center cut fillet of
   fresh tuna
2 cups fresh lime juice
1 tablespoon salt
Lettuce leaves
1 large red onion, sliced into
   rings and separated
Cilantro sprigs

Slice the tuna fillet very thin (about ⅛ inch thick). Place the slices in a glass or ceramic mixing bowl with the lime juice and salt. Stir well and let the fish marinate for just a few minutes, until it turns lighter in color and opaque.

Place lettuce leaves on individual serving plates. Drain the tuna slices and place them on top of the lettuce. Garnish with onion rings and cilantro.

# HALIBUT SEVICHE COCKTAIL
## MARINATED FISH WITH SALSA

This seviche is made from halibut and tossed with a fresh tomato sauce, chilies, and chunks of avocado. Serve it in large goblets or wineglasses.

1 pound fresh halibut fillet
2 cups fresh lime juice
1 tablespoon salt
Fresh Tomato and Avocado
   Salsa (recipe follows)
Salt

Slice the halibut fillet very thin (about ⅛ inch thick). Place the slices in a glass or ceramic mixing bowl with lime juice and salt. Stir well and let the fish marinate for just a few minutes, until it turns lighter in color and opaque. Drain the halibut fillets and toss with the salsa. Season to taste with salt. Cover with plastic wrap and chill in the refrigerator.

## FRESH TOMATO AND AVOCADO SALSA

2 serrano chilies, stemmed, seeded, and finely minced

1 large tomato, diced

4 large tomatoes, peeled (see page 26), puréed, and strained

1 avocado, peeled and diced

Tabasco sauce to taste

1 medium onion, finely diced

¼ cup finely chopped cilantro

In a large bowl, combine the chilies, tomatoes, avocado, Tabasco, onion, and cilantro.

# ENSALADA DE NOPALES
## CACTUS SALAD

The flavor and texture of the prickly pear cactus are definitely an acquired taste, but if you're a fan of okra, you're well on the way to liking it. Some Mexican markets carry fresh nopales in plastic bags in the vegetable section, but they require a lot of preparation. I find the more widely available nopales in cans and jars work wonderfully.

3 jars (1 pound each) diced nopales

¾ cup chopped green onions (scallions)

2 large tomatoes, finely chopped

½ cup finely chopped cilantro leaves

1 tablespoon white wine vinegar

3 or 4 serrano chilies, stemmed, seeded, and minced

2 garlic cloves, minced

Salt

In a colander, drain the nopales, rinse thoroughly, and drain again. In a large glass bowl, combine the nopales, green onions, tomatoes, cilantro, and vinegar. Toss well. Add the chilies and garlic and toss gently until well blended. Season to taste with salt. Cover with plastic wrap and chill at least 1 hour to allow the flavors to blend.

# TAQUITOS
## ROLLED TACOS

For an authentic Mexican flavor and texture, it is important to shred the meat by hand into stringy strips.

24 corn tortillas, 6 inches in diameter
2 pounds leftover roasted meat (brisket, pot roast, or flank steak), shredded by hand
2 medium onions, finely chopped
Tomato-Chili Salsa (recipe follows)
Oil for deep-frying

Heat the tortillas until soft. Spread the meat in a wide strip across the diameter of the tortilla. Sprinkle with onion and salsa. Fold one end over the filling and tightly roll up the tortilla like a cigar, ¼ to ½ inch in diameter. Insert one half of a toothpick at each end of the tortilla seam to secure it. Wrap the taquitos, seam side down, in foil and refrigerate.

Heat ¾ inch of oil in a large heavy skillet. In separate batches, place the taquitos, seam side down, in the oil; fry, turning them as they brown, until crisp on all sides, about 5 minutes total. Remove with tongs, tilting each taquito so any oil drips back into the skillet. Drain well on paper towels. Remove the toothpicks before serving.

## TOMATO-CHILI SALSA

3 large tomatoes, coarsely chopped
3 tablespoons lime juice
1 small white onion, finely diced
2 or 3 serrano chilies, stemmed, seeded, and finely minced
1 small bunch of cilantro, finely chopped
Salt

In a bowl, combine the tomatoes, lime juice, onion, chilies, and cilantro and mix well. Add salt to taste. Cover and chill.

# CHICKEN ENCHILADAS
## CHICKEN-FILLED TORTILLAS

Though this recipe calls for chicken breasts only, buy a whole chicken and reserve the legs and thighs for the tostada recipe that follows. The chilies are very hot, so wear gloves to protect your hands.

6 skinned and boned chicken breasts

3 tablespoons safflower or vegetable oil

4 dried ancho chilies

3 cups hot Chicken Stock (see page 390)

¼ of a large onion, coarsely chopped

3 garlic cloves, minced

2 serrano chilies, stemmed, seeded, and minced

10 corn tortillas

Toasted sesame seeds for garnish

Cilantro sprigs for garnish

Heat the oil in a large skillet and brown the chicken breasts on both sides. Slice thin.

In a large heavy pot, soak the ancho chilies in stock to cover until plumped, 15 to 20 minutes. Drain, reserving the broth. Remove the seeds and stems and place the ancho chilies in a processor or blender with 2 cups of the chicken-ancho broth, onion, garlic, and the serrano chilies. Blend until the mixture becomes a smooth purée, adding more broth if needed. Return the sauce to the saucepan and keep it warm.

Heat a heavy cast-iron griddle or a large skillet over high heat. Warm the tortillas, 1 or 2 at a time, until they are pliable, about 30 seconds a side. Place the chicken breast slices in the center of each tortilla and roll up. Place on large, individual warm plates and spoon the hot ancho chili sauce over each serving. Sprinkle with toasted sesame seeds and garnish with cilantro leaves.

# CHICKEN TOSTADA "SALAD"

Tostadas are simply tortillas fried until crisp and piled high with whatever fillings you choose, to create a salad. Possible toppings include sliced tomatoes, lettuce, beans, guacamole, salsa, and chicken, veal, or whatever meat you like. Here is my version, including the sauces.

12 small corn tortillas, fried crisp

Frijoles Negros Refritos (recipe follows)

Lettuce

Sliced tomatoes

Onions, finely diced

Guacamole (see page 225)

Shredded cooked chicken or meat

Tomato-Chili Salsa (see page 220)

Cilantro sprigs for garnish

To assemble, place 1 fried tortilla on a plate and spoon on a tablespoon of beans. Spread around, then top attractively in this order with: lettuce, tomato, onion, Guacamole, and chicken or meat, then the salsa. Garnish with cilantro.

# Frijoles Negros Refritos
## REFRIED BLACK BEANS

1 pound dried black beans, sorted, rinsed, and drained

1 medium onion, finely chopped

Chicken Stock (see page 390) or water to cover

¼ cup solid vegetable shortening

Salt

Place the beans in a large saucepan with the onion. Add enough stock to cover and bring to a boil over high heat. Reduce the heat, cover, and simmer for 2 hours, adding additional liquid if needed, until the beans are soft and will mash easily when tested with a fork. Do not drain: There should be about 1½ cups of liquid left in the saucepan.

Melt the shortening in a large skillet over moderate-to-high heat. Add the beans and their liquid and cook for 15 to 20 minutes, stirring constantly and occasionally mashing the beans lightly with a potato masher, leaving some of the beans whole. When the liquid is almost totally absorbed, add salt to taste. Keep the beans warm until serving.

# Mexican Fried Rice

⅓ cup olive oil

1 large onion, finely chopped

1 large red bell pepper, finely chopped

1 large Anaheim chili pepper, finely chopped

1 cup uncooked rice

¼ cup minced parsley

2 cups Chicken Stock (see page 390)

Salt

Freshly ground black pepper

In a large heavy skillet, heat the oil and sauté the onion and peppers. Add the rice and stir until each grain of rice is coated with the oil. Add the parsley, stock, and salt and pepper to taste. Simmer, covered, for 15 to 20 minutes. Mix and continue cooking until all the liquid is absorbed.

# Lime Ice with Tropical Fresh Fruit

For a novel touch, this ice is garnished with fresh fruits: pineapple, papaya, and/or mangoes. If you like, add the dramatic contrast of a sprinkling of chili powder—as they do in Mexican restaurants.

2 cups Sugar Syrup (see page 38)
⅓ cup fresh lime juice
⅓ cup fresh lemon juice
1⅓ cups water
1 tablespoon tequila (optional)
Fresh pineapple, papaya, or mangoes
Fresh mint leaves
Chili powder

In a 1-quart glass measuring cup or mixing bowl, combine the Sugar Syrup, lime and lemon juices, water, and tequila. Mix well. Transfer to ice trays or a shallow glass bowl and freeze. Every hour, scrape the sides of the tray or bowl and mix the crystals that form. This process takes about 5 hours. Or freeze in a hand or electric ice cream maker according to the directions. Garnish with fresh fruit and mint leaves and sprinkle with chili powder.

*NOTE: For a creamier version, 10 minutes before the ice is finished, remove 2 tablespoons and place in a large mixing bowl with 1 egg white. Beat until thick and foamy; add to the Lime Ice and continue to freeze.

# SOPAIPILLAS

The first time I tasted these Mexican "doughnuts" was on a river raft trip in northern California. Nobody had ever heard of them then—but now they are a trendy favorite in Santa Fe, New Mexico, which has developed its own interesting Southwest cuisine.

Sopaipillas would be great for a Hanukkah dinner, since foods fried in oil are traditional for this holiday.

1¾ cups flour
2 teaspoons baking powder
1 teaspoon salt
2 tablespoons margarine
⅔ cup cold water
Vegetable oil for deep-frying
Powdered sugar
Honey

In a large mixing bowl, combine the flour, baking powder, and salt. Add the margarine and blend until of a coarse consistency. Add water and mix until dough comes together. Turn out on a floured board and gently knead until smooth. Cover with a towel and let rest for 5 minutes. Roll out about ⅛ inch thick.

Cut the thin pastry into 3-inch squares. Fill a deep-fryer or a large heavy pot with oil, 3 to 4 inches deep. Heat the oil to 375°F on a deep-frying thermometer. Drop 3 to 4 pastries into the hot oil, frying 2 to 3 minutes on each side and turning them 3 or 4 times, until golden brown. Sopaipillas will puff up like little pillows. Serve immediately, sprinkled with powdered sugar. Pass the honey.

# MEXICAN SAMPLER

FOR 12

Mexican food is perfect for entertaining. Most of it can be prepared in advance in large quantities. It uses inexpensive ingredients like beans and rice, and small amounts of meat and poultry go a long way. Served with chilled Mexican beer and pitchers of margaritas, it creates a warm-hearted, relaxed party spirit for family and friends. A Mexican theme adds color and excitement to Sunday brunches, informal suppers, children's parties, and all sorts of lively and informal occasions.

Don't miss the fun of sampling Mexican favorites just because they are full of lard and pork and sausages in Mexican restaurants. I have eliminated all the unkosher elements and each recipe is perfect for a kosher kitchen.

## QUICK MARGARITA COCKTAIL

MAKES 2 COCKTAILS

2 slices of lime
Salt (table salt or finely
   ground rock salt)
2 ounces white tequila
1 ounce Triple Sec
2 tablespoons fresh lime juice
1 cup crushed ice

Chill 2 large cocktail glasses and prepare them by rubbing the rims with the lime slices and then swirling them in a saucer filled with salt.

Put the tequila, Triple Sec, lime juice, and crushed ice cubes into a blender and blend until frothy. Pour the foamy mixture into the prepared glasses. Serve immediately.

# TORTILLA CHIPS

This recipe includes two methods for crisp Tortilla Chips. The first is to fry them in a deep-fryer; the second is to oven-fry, which uses no oil at all and the result is wonderful.

24 corn tortillas
Oil for deep-frying (optional)
Salt

Cut each tortilla into 6 to 8 wedges.

To deep-fry: In a large deep-fryer or a deep heavy skillet, heat the oil to 375°F on a deep-frying thermometer and fry the tortilla wedges in small batches until very crisp. (Never overcrowd, or the chips won't be as light and crisp as possible.) Drain on paper towels in a single layer. Sprinkle with salt to taste.

To oven-fry: Preheat the oven to 300°F. Place tortilla triangles in a single layer on baking sheets. Sprinkle with salt and bake for 10 to 15 minutes, or until they are dried and beginning to brown on the edges. Serve hot.

# GUACAMOLE
## AVOCADO APPETIZER

Most guacamoles are mashed so smooth that the color and texture of the rich green, velvety avocado is hidden. This recipe has a chunky texture and rich color and is a welcome addition to tacos and tostada salads—or serve as a dip with tortilla chips and crackers.

2 avocados, peeled and seed removed
Juice of 1 large lemon or 2 limes
2 serrano chilies, stemmed, seeded, and finely chopped
2 tomatoes, seeded and diced
¼ teaspoon chili powder
¼ teaspoon ground cumin
1 tablespoon chopped cilantro
Salt
Freshly ground black pepper
Lettuce leaves
Tortilla chips

Cut the avocados into ¼-inch dice and place in a large bowl. Add the lemon or lime juice, serrano chilies, and tomatoes and toss gently. Add the chili powder, ground cumin, cilantro, and salt and pepper to taste. Serve on lettuce leaves with tortilla chips.

# Green Pea and Cilantro Guacamole

Simple, smooth, and deliciously spiced, this brand-new version of guacamole can be made in minutes. When people taste it, they have a strange questioning look as if to say, "What is this?" They almost never guess the "secret ingredient," green peas. I always keep frozen peas on hand so I can whip it up for unexpected company.

2 packages (10 ounces each) frozen peas, thawed
2 tablespoons minced cilantro leaves
2 tablespoons minced parsley leaves
½ teaspoon ground cumin
½ teaspoon chili powder
2 tablespoons fresh lemon juice
Salt
Freshly ground black pepper
Tortilla Chips (see page 225)
Jicama, peeled and thinly sliced

In a processor or blender, purée the thawed peas. Press through a strainer or food mill to purée further, then return the puréed peas to the blender. Add cilantro, parsley, cumin, and chili powder and blend. Pour into a medium bowl and add lemon juice and salt and pepper to taste. Cover with plastic wrap and chill until ready to serve. Serve with tortilla chips and sliced jicama.

# Quesadillas
## CORN TORTILLAS WITH MELTED CHEESE

This is the Mexican version of our grilled cheese sandwich. Caterers are serving Quesadillas at catered Mexican dinners and cocktail parties, but they are easy to make at home.

24 corn tortillas
1 pound Monterey Jack cheese, grated
6 Roasted Anaheim Chili Peppers (recipe follows)
24 cilantro sprigs

Heat a heavy cast-iron griddle or a large skillet over high heat. Heat tortillas, 1 or 2 at a time, until they are pliable, about 30 seconds a side. Sprinkle some cheese across the width of each tortilla and place a strip of green chili and a cilantro sprig on top. Roll the tortilla tightly like a cigarette.

Cut aluminum foil into 24 squares, about 2 inches larger than the tortilla. Wrap each rolled tortilla in foil and seal the ends. Heat in the packages on the hot griddle, turning frequently, until the cheese melts inside, about 5 minutes. Transfer to a large serving platter.

# ROASTED ANAHEIM CHILI PEPPERS

My father-in-law, a produce merchant, supplied us with jars of these mild-to-hot green Anaheim peppers, which had been roasted, peeled, and seeded, then marinated with garlic, olive oil, salt, and pepper. They were so delicious that we began making them ourselves.

Anaheim, California, is the home of pungent green chilies, which may be quite mild, or so hot you can barely swallow them. In fact, whenever you handle chilies, keep your hands away from your eyes; the oils in the flesh and seeds can burn. Some people even wear gloves when working with chilies.

6 to 8 green Anaheim chili
  peppers
3 garlic cloves, minced
Olive oil
Salt

Preheat the oven to 375°F.

Turn up the sides of a sheet of foil to resemble a baking sheet and place it on the lower rack of your oven. Place the peppers on a separate rack just above the foil-lined rack. Bake them for 20 to 30 minutes, until their skins have puffed and darkened slightly on top; then carefully turn each pepper over and continue baking for 10 to 15 minutes more, or until top skin puffs up. Carefully remove the peppers from the oven to an ovenproof plate.

As soon as they're cool enough to handle, peel off the skin. Discard the seeds and remove the stems. Tear or cut the peppers into long strips. Place them in a bowl in single layers; alternate each layer with some of the garlic, olive oil, and salt. After the final layer, add enough olive oil to cover. Cover with plastic wrap and refrigerate. These will keep for several days as long as they are completely covered with oil.

# CHILES RELLENOS CON HONGOS FRESCOS
## GREEN CHILIES STUFFED WITH MUSHROOMS

This recipe was inspired by Chef John Sedlar at his restaurant Saint Estephe, in Manhattan Beach, California. John does a wonderful nouvelle version of traditional southwestern dishes. After seeing and tasting his recipe, I developed this one, and have since taught it on my televison show. Many of the steps can be done in advance.

12 fresh Anaheim chilies, straight and plump

6 tablespoons unsalted butter or margarine

¼ cup minced green onions (scallions)

1½ pounds mushrooms, finely diced

1 tablespoon Madeira or dry sherry

Salt

Freshly ground black pepper

6 ounces goat cheese

½ to 1 cup cream

Red Pepper Jelly (see page 112)

Fresh cilantro sprigs

Preheat the oven to 375°F. Roast and peel the chilies, following the method in the recipe on page 278, but do not stem them. Let them cool.

Carefully make a slit along one side of each chili and remove the seeds with a teaspoon, leaving the stem intact. Wrap each chili in plastic wrap and refrigerate. (The recipe may be done in advance to this point.)

In a large skillet, heat 4 tablespoons of the butter. Add the onions and sauté until soft, about 5 minutes. Add the mushrooms and sauté, stirring occasionally, until the moisture evaporates from the mushrooms, about 5 minutes. Add the Madeira and cook for 1 minute more, or until the liquid evaporates. Season to taste with salt and pepper. Let the mixture cool.

Unwrap the chilies and carefully stuff each one with the mushrooms, closing the chili securely around the filling. Rewrap with plastic wrap and store in the refrigerator until you are ready for the final preparation.

In a heavy skillet over medium heat, melt the remaining 2 tablespoons butter. Add the cheese and cream and simmer, mashing the cheese with a fork, until the cheese is melted and the sauce is smooth. Cover the skillet, remove it from the heat, and hold the sauce until ready to serve.

Preheat the oven to 375°F. Unwrap the chilies and place them in an ovenproof baking dish. Cover with foil and bake just until the chiles are heated through, 5 to 10 minutes. Ladle the cheese sauce onto individual heated serving plates and carefully arrange a stuffed chili on the center of each plate. Garnish with Red Pepper Jelly and sprigs of cilantro.

# SOPA SECA DE FIDEOS
## DRY NOODLE SOUP

The interesting name derives from the fact that the noodles are fried rather than boiled. This is typical of the hearty peasant cooking found in Mexican homes and that has been handed down for generations.

2 tablespoons olive oil

½ pound vermicelli noodles

1 onion, finely chopped

Heat the oil in a large heavy skillet over medium heat. Break the noodles into 2-inch pieces and fry them, stirring constantly, until lightly browned, 2 to 3 minutes.

2 garlic cloves, finely chopped

1 can (13 ounces) tomatoes, coarsely chopped, juice reserved

¼ teaspoon sugar

½ teaspoon dried oregano, crumbled

1½ cups Chicken or Vegetable stock (see page 390 or 391)

Salt

Freshly ground black pepper

Remove the noodles with a slotted spoon, leaving as much of the oil in the skillet as possible. Add the onion and garlic to the skillet and sauté until soft, 2 to 3 minutes, then add the tomatoes, sugar, and oregano.

Return the noodles to the skillet, add the stock, and stir well. Season to taste with salt and pepper. Cover the skillet and cook over very low heat for about 30 minutes, stirring occasionally, until the noodles have absorbed most of the liquid. Serve on heated plates right from the skillet.

# MEXICAN FISH STEW WITH RED PEPPER SAUCE

This savory, spicy delight is midway between a stew and a soup—a Mexican version of the French bouillabaisse. It is based on a tangy fresh tomato salsa, made right in the soup pot—so all you do is add some nice fresh fish, simmer for a few minutes, and you have a dish that tastes as though it had cooked for hours and hours. If there is any left over—which is highly unlikely—it tastes very good reheated, too.

9 large tomatoes, cut into ¼-inch cubes (about 12 cups)

½ cup thinly sliced green onions (scallions), with greens

4 serrano chilies, stemmed, seeded, and minced

2 red chilies, minced

1 cup finely chopped cilantro, tightly packed

1 tablespoon fennel seeds

Pinch of sugar

1 cup dry white wine

1 cup Fish or Vegetable Stock (see page 392 or 391)

2 to 3 teaspoons salt

Freshly ground black pepper

3 pounds assorted fish fillets, halibut, ling cod, red snapper, and sea bass

Red Pepper Sauce (recipe follows)

In a large bowl, combine tomatoes, green onions, chilies, and cilantro and mix well. (You can cover this with plastic wrap and refrigerate overnight.)

Place tomato mixture in a large heavy pot and add the fennel seeds, sugar, wine, stock, salt, and pepper. Bring to a slow boil and simmer for 10 minutes. Add the fish fillets 15 minutes before serving and simmer. Ladle into hot soup bowls. Spoon on a dollop of Red Pepper Sauce and pass an extra bowl of sauce.

## RED PEPPER SAUCE

MAKES ABOUT 1½ CUPS

8 garlic cloves
1 roasted green Anaheim chili pepper (see page 227)
1 roasted red bell pepper (see page 278)
4 corn tortillas, crumbled and softened in warm water
½ cup olive oil
2 tablespoons tomato paste
½ cup fish stew broth

In a processor or blender, place the garlic, peppers, tortillas, olive oil, tomato paste, and broth. Process to make a smooth paste. Add additional broth if mixture is too thick. This sauce can be made a day or two ahead and stored in the refrigerator.

# DESSERT TAMALES

The corn husks called for in this recipe are sold in Mexican markets. You can substitute foil and wrap or fold in the same manner.

12 dried corn husks
2 cups masa harina (finely ground cornmeal)
⅔ cup solid vegetable shortening
½ cup sugar
4 teaspoons baking powder
½ teaspoon salt
1 can (7 ounces) pineapple chunks, drained and cut into pieces

Soak the corn husks in hot water for 1 hour. Combine the masa harina and 2 cups water and soak for 1 hour.

With an electric mixer, cream the shortening with the sugar until light and fluffy. Add the soaked masa harina, baking powder, and salt and beat until a little ball of the batter will float in a glass of cold water. Fold in the pineapple.

Drain the corn husks. Place 2 heaping tablespoons of the batter in the center of each corn husk. Fold one end of the corn husk over the batter; fold in the sides, then gently roll up the tamale. Place the tamales, seams down, in the tray of a steamer. (You can improvise a steamer by placing a colander above a pot of simmering water and covering the colander with a plate or a pot lid.) Steam them over briskly simmering water for about 30 minutes, until cooked through.

# Oatmeal Tequila Cookies

Mexican desserts are usually very sweet, as was this original recipe. It called for piloncillo, which is a pure unrefined cane sugar that comes in a hard cone. Since piloncillo is hard to find, I have substituted a combination of dark brown sugar and granulated sugar. Tequila, a potent Mexican alcoholic beverage, is used very sparingly in both the cookie dough and the icing.

MAKES ABOUT 72

1½ cups flour
1 teaspoon baking soda
1 teaspoon salt
½ pound unsalted butter or margarine
1 cup firmly packed dark brown sugar
1 cup granulated sugar
2 eggs
1 teaspoon tequila
3 cups quick-cooking rolled oats
½ cup shredded sweetened coconut
1 cup toasted, chopped pecans (see page 24)
Tequila Icing (recipe follows)

In a mixing bowl, stir together the flour, baking soda, and salt. In a separate bowl, cream the butter, then gradually add the brown sugar and granulated sugar. Cream until light and fluffy. Add the eggs and tequila and beat well. Add the flour mixture and blend thoroughly. Gradually add the rolled oats, mixing well after each addition. Stir in the coconuts and pecans.

Divide the dough into 2 parts. Shape each part into a large ball of dough. (You can wrap the dough in plastic wrap and refrigerate or freeze it at this point.)

Preheat the oven to 375°F. Shape the dough into 1-inch balls and flatten slightly. Place them 1½ inches apart on a baking sheet that has been lined with foil and greased. Bake for 10 to 12 minutes, until golden brown. Transfer to a wire rack to cool. Spread or pipe Tequila Icing on each cookie and top with sprinkles.

## TEQUILA ICING

MAKES ABOUT 2 CUPS

¼ pound unsalted butter or margarine
4 cups powdered sugar
½ cup orange juice
2 tablespoons tequila

In a mixing bowl, cream the butter. Gradually add the sugar, blending after each addition. Add the orange juice and tequila and stir until the icing has a spreading consistency.

# CHINESE MENUS

## A CHINESE BANQUET

FOR 12

Marinated Quail Eggs with Cucumbers

Crisp Caramelized Walnuts

Pot Stickers with Dipping Sauce

Cold Spicy Noodles

Drunken Chicken

Stir-Fried Eggplant with Beef

Whole Steamed Fish with Ginger and Black Mushrooms

Perfect Steamed Rice

Jasmine Tea and Pear Ice

Chinese Almond Cookies

Fortune Cookies

SUGGESTED BEVERAGES:

Champagne, Gerwurztraminer, or Riesling wine, and Orange Pekoe or Jasmine tea

Do you love Chinese food but hesitate to eat it in a restaurant because you fear it is filled with forbidden ingredients? Well, you're right! Most Chinese food contains pork, shellfish, lard, and what my children call "mystery meat." Even so-called vegetable dishes, such as stir fries, chow mein, and chop suey may contain some of these things. Fried rice is another taboo. And the reason those delicious almond cookies are so rich is because they contain incredible amounts of lard.

But cheer up. It's easy to indulge in all the Chinese delicacies you crave. You can make them yourself in your own kosher kitchen. Chinese food uses virtually no cream, milk, or butter. Which means that if you control cooking oils and eliminate shellfish, pork, and lard, you not only make Chinese food kosher but also cut back on cholesterol and benefit your health. And it's easy on the budget, too.

Through careful research and consulting with some terrific Chinese chefs, I've developed these authentic versions of many of our favorite Chinese dishes—even some very sophisticated ones.

# MARINATED QUAIL EGGS WITH CUCUMBERS

Most people are not familiar with these tiny quail eggs, which add a delightful surprise to your Chinese menu. They also make a beautiful garnish.

Quail eggs are now available in the refrigerator section of some large markets, and you are sure to find them in oriental specialty markets.

2 dozen quail eggs, hard-
  boiled (see page 23)
2 tablespoons light soy sauce
2 tablespoons dark soy sauce
2 whole star anise, broken
2 tablespoons brewed tea
1 large thin cucumber, unpeeled and thinly sliced

Peel the quail eggs and set them aside. In a large bowl, combine the soy sauces, anise, and tea. Place the peeled eggs in the sauce; cover with plastic wrap and marinate for several hours. Serve surrounded by cucumber slices.

# CRISP CARAMELIZED WALNUTS

A mystery surrounds these unusual sugared walnuts, so crisp that they literally melt in your mouth. Everyone loves them but nobody knows how to make them. And if they do, they are not telling.

A famous Chinese cooking teacher flatly refused to tell her class the secret. And one friend told me she had offered one hundred dollars for the recipe, with no takers. But here at long last is the recipe, generously shared with me by a dear Chinese lady.

2 cups walnut halves
1 cup sugar
Vegetable oil for frying

In a large heavy saucepan, bring 4 cups water to a boil. Add the walnut halves. Remove the pan from the heat and let the walnuts sit for 2 minutes. Drain them into a colander or strainer and quickly transfer them to a large mixing bowl. Toss the walnuts with the sugar until they are evenly coated.

Line a baking sheet with wax paper. Spread the sugared nuts on the sheet and let them cool until the sugar coating hardens.

In a deep-fryer or a large heavy skillet, heat 3 inches of oil to 370–375°F on a deep-frying thermometer. In small batches, fry the walnuts for about 2 minutes, until they turn dark brown, stirring occasionally to keep them from sticking together. (Watch carefully: they brown quickly.) Remove them with a slotted spoon, spreading them out on a lightly oiled, foil-lined baking pan or ovenproof platter. Continue to fry the remaining walnuts. With a fork, separate the walnuts so they don't stick together as they cool.

# POT STICKERS WITH DIPPING SAUCE
## CHINESE DUMPLINGS

Be warned that the name means what it says—these tiny crisp dumplings will stick to the pot, so watch them. They are really a Chinese version of kreplach, fried instead of cooked in soup.

Don't let the unfamiliar ingredients keep you from making them. Wonton wrappers, sesame oil, fresh ginger, and tofu are available at many supermarkets, and if they're not you can secure them easily at any grocery in Chinatown or oriental neighborhoods.

1 pound lean ground beef or veal
6 ounces firm tofu, drained and finely chopped
4 green onions (scallions), minced
3 tablespoons sesame oil
1/4 teaspoon white pepper
1 tablespoon minced fresh ginger
1 tablespoon cornstarch
1 1/2 tablespoons soy sauce
Pinch of sugar
1/4 teaspoon salt
36 round wonton wrappers
Vegetable oil
1/2 cup Chicken Stock (see page 390) or water
Dipping Sauce (recipe follows)

In a bowl, combine the beef or veal, tofu, green onions, sesame oil, pepper, ginger, cornstarch, soy sauce, sugar, and salt. Mix well.

Holding a wonton wrapper on the fingers of one hand, place about 1 tablespoon of the mixture on the top half of the wrapper, just above the center. Moisten the edges of the wrapper with a little cold water. Fold the bottom half over the filling and pinch together the two edges when they meet at their central point; hold the pinched edges under your thumb. Then, starting just one side of the center, pleat the topmost edge of the wrapper over toward the center and pinch it under your thumb. (See diagram.) Pleat that side twice more, toward the center, in the same way, sealing it completely. Repeat on the other side to form a symmetrically pleated and sealed pouch. Repeat with remaining wrappers. Place on a baking sheet lined with a towel.

In a large skillet, preferably nonstick, heat 1/4 inch of the oil over medium-high heat. Reduce heat to medium.

Arrange the pot stickers in the skillet snugly, side by side, starting at the center and working outward in a spiral. Raise the heat slightly to make the dumplings sizzle. When their bottoms are browned after 3 or 4 minutes, add the stock. The liquid will sizzle loudly.

Adjust the heat to maintain a simmer and cover the skillet tightly to steam the dumplings. When the liquid has almost all been absorbed, after about 5 minutes, remove the lid. With a spatula, lift out a dumpling and cut it open to see if the filling is done. If not, cover the skillet again and cook for a few minutes more. Add 2 tablespoons more oil to glaze the bottom of the pot stickers. Cook for 1 minute more, turn off the heat, move the skillet off the burner, and loosen the bottoms of the dumplings with a spatula (not necessary with a nonstick skillet).

Invert a round serving plate, larger than the skillet, over the skillet. Holding the skillet and plate tightly together, invert them both. Lift off the skillet, leaving the pot stickers—browned sides up—on the plate. Serve with Dipping Sauce.

## DIPPING SAUCE

MAKES 1 CUP

¼ cup dark soy sauce

¼ cup well-aged Chinese black vinegar or balsamic vinegar

1 teaspoon finely minced fresh ginger

1 teaspoon sesame oil

¼ to 1 teaspoon Chinese hot chili sauce (optional)

In a small mixing bowl, stir together the soy sauce, vinegar, ginger, and sesame oil. Stir in chili sauce to taste.

# COLD SPICY NOODLES

Chinese noodles add a hearty touch to any Chinese menu and are a welcome change from the usual rice. They are easy to prepare and with interesting garnishes can be a very impressive addition to a Chinese repast.

This recipe is the most popular one I have ever prepared on my cooking show on Jewish Television Network. It brought me many letters from listeners, who commented on how good it looked on the television screen.

8 ounces fresh Chinese egg noodles, homemade or packaged

2 tablespoons sesame oil

¼ cup dark soy sauce

1 tablespoon dry sherry or white wine

3 green onions (scallions), chopped

2 green serrano chilies, seeded and minced

¼ cup safflower or vegetable oil

1 tablespoon Japanese rice vinegar or white wine vinegar

1 tablespoon sugar

Salt

Freshly ground black pepper

1 red bell pepper, stemmed, seeded, and thinly sliced

1 yellow bell pepper, stemmed, seeded, and thinly sliced

1 medium cucumber, peeled and thinly sliced lengthwise

4 ounces snow peas, trimmed but left whole

¼ cup Chinese preserved red ginger, thinly sliced (optional)

2 green onions (scallions), thinly sliced

Cilantro sprigs, for garnish

Bring a large pot of lightly salted water to a boil. Drop in the noodles and boil for 4 to 5 minutes, until tender. In your sink, prepare a large bowl of ice and cold water. Carefully pour off the boiling water from the pot, and pour the noodles into the ice water to cool them quickly. Drain the noodles well and put them into a large bowl. Toss them with the sesame oil.

In a small bowl, combine the soy sauce, sherry, chopped green onions, and chilies. Heat the oil in a small skillet over moderate heat. Pour the hot oil into the soy sauce mixture. Stir in the vinegar, sugar, and salt and pepper to taste. Pour this sauce over the noodles and gently toss until well mixed. Place the noodles on a large serving platter. Top with rows of red and yellow peppers, cucumbers, snow peas, preserved ginger, sliced green onions, and cilantro. Toss lightly at the table.

# DRUNKEN CHICKEN

This remarkable recipe—the most tender and moist chicken I have ever tasted—is the result of a delightful dinner that a Chinese friend cooked for us in our home. The oriental food was fantastic—from soup to caramelized nuts. But it was the Drunken Chicken that made the biggest impression.

After that evening, I have served this recipe again and again—and always received gratifying compliments for it. Drunken Chicken makes a perfect Purim feast, since Jewish tradition decrees that everyone should drink wine to excess on this holiday. Fortunately, this is the only Jewish festival that encourages drunkenness.

1 whole chicken (3 pounds), washed and dried
1 tablespoon kosher salt
1 quart Chicken Stock (see page 390)
6 green onions (scallions), cut into 3 pieces each
6 slices fresh ginger, about ⅛ inch thick, cut into julienne
1½ cups Chinese rice wine, vermouth, sherry, or dry white wine
Cilantro sprigs for garnish
Carrot for garnish

Rub the chicken inside and out with salt and refrigerate for 1 hour. In a large pot, bring Chicken Stock to a boil and add half the green onions and ginger. Stuff the rest of the green onions and ginger into the chicken and add the chicken to the pot. Cover and boil for 20 to 30 minutes, or until chicken is tender. Remove the pot from the heat and let the chicken cool in the liquid. Remove the chicken from the pot, reserving the broth. Cut the chicken into serving pieces (cutting each breast crosswise into 3 or 4 pieces), and place them in a large shallow bowl skin side down. Combine the rice wine and 1½ cups of the reserved broth and pour over the chicken pieces to cover.

Cover with plastic wrap and marinate in the refrigerator for 1 to 2 days. Transfer to a large serving platter. Garnish with the cilantro and carrots.

# STIR-FRIED EGGPLANT WITH BEEF

This dish is one of my favorites, and I was very happy when I discovered that I could prepare it at home, using beef instead of pork. The red peppers, garlic, and ginger, along with the soy sauce and the combination of beef and eggplant, create a very exciting hot, spicy flavor. It is a perfect accompaniment to the Drunken Chicken, which is very subtle. Be sure to include a bowl of steamed rice to soak up the sauce and counteract the spiciness.

1 large eggplant (about 1
 pound), unpeeled

4 tablespoons safflower or
 vegetable oil

2 tablespoons dark soy sauce

1 teaspoon red wine vinegar
 or balsamic vinegar

2 to 3 teaspoons chili sauce
 with garlic

2 garlic cloves, minced

1½ tablespoons minced fresh
 ginger

4 green onions (scallions),
 finely chopped

¼ pound ground beef or veal

¼ cup Chicken Stock (see
 page 390)

1 teaspoon sesame oil

Cut the eggplant diagonally into 1-inch slices and cut each slice into ½-inch-wide strips. Heat 2 tablespoons of the oil in a wok or a large skillet with sloping sides. Stir-fry the eggplant about 5 minutes, or until very tender. Transfer it to a bowl and set aside.

In a small bowl, combine the soy sauce, vinegar, and chili sauce with garlic and set aside. Heat the remaining 2 tablespoons of oil in the wok, over high heat. Stir-fry the garlic, ginger, and half the green onions until you can smell their aroma, about 30 seconds. Add the beef and stir-fry over high heat until the meat is no longer pink, 2 to 3 minutes. Add the soy sauce mixture and stir-fry 30 seconds more. Add the eggplant and stir-fry for 1 minute. Add the remaining green onions and chicken stock, stirring for 2 to 3 minutes until the liquid has evaporated and the eggplant is tender. Add the sesame oil and stir-fry briefly. Serve immediately.

# WHOLE STEAMED FISH WITH GINGER AND BLACK MUSHROOMS

Fish is a lucky food to the Chinese, symbolizing good fortune. It also symbolizes a good voyage, and when Chinese children start off to school, they are served a whole fish to give them "A good beginning and a good ending." When the Chinese are honoring somebody at a dinner, a whole fish is served with the head pointing to the special guest.

The Chinese usually include a fish course as one of the three or four dishes served in a family dinner. Steaming or frying a whole fish is the traditional method, and the ginger, green onions, and black mushrooms in the recipe give delicately steamed fish a wonderful flavor.

1 whole (2 to 3 pounds) red
 snapper, sea bass, rock
 cod, or carp

1 teaspoon kosher salt

½ teaspoon freshly ground
 black pepper

½ teaspoon sugar

4 tablespoons safflower or
 vegetable oil

Wash and dry the fish. With a large sharp knife, score it twice diagonally, ¼ inch deep, on each side.

In a small bowl, combine the salt, pepper, sugar, and 2 tablespoons of the oil. Rub the fish with this mixture inside and out. Stuff the inside of the fish with half of the green onions and ginger. Place the fish on a rack or steaming tray. Place the remaining green onions and ginger and the drained black mushrooms on top of the fish.

3 green onions (scallions),
  shredded
3 slices fresh ginger,
  shredded
4 Chinese black mushrooms,
  soaked in broth or water 30
  minutes until soft, stemmed
  and thinly sliced
⅓ cup dark soy sauce
1 tablespoon dry sherry

Bring water to a boil in a steamer. Place the rack or tray on top. Steam for 15 to 20 minutes, or until the flesh comes away from the bone easily.

In a small skillet, heat the remaining 2 tablespoons oil until it bubbles. In a separate small pan, heat the soy sauce and sherry until boiling. Transfer the fish to a serving platter. Pour the hot oil over the fish, then the soy sauce and sherry. Serve immediately with steamed rice.

# PERFECT STEAMED RICE

You will notice that there is no salt in this rice recipe. That is because it is eaten with dishes that are flavorful and have salted sauces that season the rice perfectly.

2 cups rice (long-grain white
  or jasmine)
2½ cups cold water

Put the rice in a bowl and add enough cold water to cover it completely. Stir thoroughly, then drain. In a large heavy pot, place the rice and 2½ cups cold water and bring to a boil. Cover, reduce the heat to low, and simmer for 15 minutes, until the rice is tender. Remove the lid and fluff the rice with chopsticks or a fork. Serve hot.

# JASMINE TEA AND PEAR ICE

This delicate, unusual blend of fruit and tea flavors makes the smoothest ice you've tasted—a perfect finale for an oriental banquet.

MAKES 1 QUART

4½ cups water
3 cups sugar
3 tablespoons fragrant dry jasmine tea leaves
¼ cup boiling water
4 large (2 pounds) very ripe
  pears
¼ cup lemon juice
2 tablespoons pear liqueur
  (optional)

In a heavy medium saucepan, combine the water and sugar. Bring them to a boil over high heat, stirring until the sugar dissolves. Reduce the heat to low and simmer for 5 minutes. Cool to room temperature. Cover with plastic wrap and refrigerate.

Brew the tea leaves in the boiling water for 2 to 3 minutes. Set aside.

Peel, core, and dice the pears and place them in a large bowl, tossing with the lemon juice to keep the pears from discoloring.

Place the pear mixture in a large heavy saucepan and

bring to a boil over medium heat. Reduce the heat and simmer for 6 to 8 minutes, until pears are transparent and soft. With a slotted spoon, remove the pears to a bowl and cool. Place the pears in a processor and purée. This should make 2 cups. If it does not, add some of the liquid the pears were cooked in.

In a large bowl, combine 2 cups of the sugar syrup, the brewed tea, the pear liqueur, and the pear purée and mix well.

Transfer to ice cube trays or a shallow bowl and freeze, stirring every 30 minutes with a fork until firm, but not frozen hard. This will take about 4 hours. Or freeze in a hand or electric ice cream freezer, according to manufacturer's directions.

# CHINESE ALMOND COOKIES

After experimenting with many recipes, making my own adjustments and testing them on my husband, I finally put all the right ingredients together and came up with what we think are the real thing—authentic Chinese Almond Cookies, really rich and chewy, but without a trace of lard.

MAKES ABOUT 60

¼ pound plus 4 tablespoons unsalted margarine
1 cup sugar
1 egg plus 3 egg yolks
1 teaspoon almond extract
⅓ cup ground almonds
3 cups flour
1 teaspoon baking soda
½ teaspoon salt
¾ cup safflower or vegetable oil
1 cup whole blanched almonds, toasted (see page 24)
1 tablespoon water

In the bowl of an electric mixer, cream together the margarine and sugar until light and fluffy. Blend in the whole egg and the almond extract. In another bowl, combine the ground almonds, flour, baking soda, and salt. Gradually beat the almond mixture into the margarine mixture, adding the oil gradually as you combine them. Beat the dough until smooth.

Preheat the oven to 350°F.

One tablespoon at a time, mold the dough into ½-inch-thick rounds. Place them about 2 inches apart on lightly greased foil-lined baking sheets. Press a toasted almond into the center of each cookie. Bake for 5 to 7 minutes, until cookies begin to look dry on top. Beat the 3 egg yolks with the water and brush the mixture on top of the cookies. Continue baking until the cookies are golden brown, 5 to 7 minutes more. Transfer the cookies to a wire rack and cool.

# FORTUNE COOKIES

MAKES ABOUT 3 DOZEN

3 egg whites
¾ cup sugar
Pinch of salt
¼ pound unsalted margarine, melted
¼ teaspoon vanilla extract
1 cup flour
1 teaspoon almond extract
2 tablespoons water

Write fortunes of your own devising on little slips of paper and set them aside.

In a large mixing bowl, beat the egg whites, sugar, and salt. Stir in the margarine, vanilla, flour, and almond extract and water. Cover the batter with plastic wrap and chill in the refrigerator for 15 minutes.

Place a level teaspoon of batter on a greased baking sheet and spread it around with the back of the spoon, using a circular motion, to make a very thin 3-inch circle. Bake 2 cookies at a time, for 5 minutes, or until the edges turn brown. Remove each cookie with a spatula to a nonstick surface; work quickly, because they become set in only 10 seconds as they cool. Place a fortune in the center and fold the cookie in half, so it resembles a turnover, pressing the center edge to seal. Then bend the cookie in half slightly and place over the edge of a bowl to give it the traditional fortune cookie shape. If you break one, save the crumbs to garnish ice cream.

# CHINESE NEW YEAR DINNER

FOR 8

My good friend Evelyn Jui invited us to her Chinese New Year dinner one year and introduced us to a wonderful new way of cooking—the Do-It-Yourself Hot Pot.

When I returned home, I sat up for hours, translating Evelyn's menu into kosher without losing any of the exciting flavors. Then I couldn't wait to invite friends to share the fun of cooking together with a hot pot (in this case, my electric wok, instead of the traditional Chinese contraption).

One of the nicest things about this menu is that the soup, vegetables, and meat are all self-contained in the hot pot. With a simple dessert of Chocolate-Coated Litchis and Pineapple, some crisp deep-fried wonton pastries, and some Chinese cookies and tea, the menu couldn't be easier to prepare. And, of course, your guests do a lot of the work!

Enamel or porcelain bowls and inexpensive chopsticks add charm. Eating Chinese food with a fork is a no-no; the food tastes better with chopsticks.

## SPICY FRIED WONTONS

MAKES ABOUT 36

½ pound Chinese cabbage
(Napa cabbage or bok
choy), finely chopped

Place the cabbage in a kitchen towel or cheesecloth and squeeze it to extract as much moisture as possible.

In a large bowl, combine the meat, garlic, green on-

1 pound lean ground beef, veal, or turkey

3 garlic cloves, minced

¼ cup finely chopped green onions (scallions)

1 tablespoon chopped fresh cilantro

1 tablespoon finely chopped fresh ginger

1 dried hot red pepper, seeded and minced

1 egg

1 tablespoon Chinese rice wine or pale dry sherry

1 tablespoon soy sauce

2 tablespoons sesame oil

Sugar

Salt

36 to 40 wonton wrappers

Vegetable oil for frying

Dipping Sauce (recipe follows)

ions, cilantro, ginger, red pepper, egg, wine, soy sauce, and sesame seed oil. Add the cabbage. Mix them together until thoroughly blended. Season to taste with sugar and salt.

Place 1 to 2 teaspoons of the spicy filling in the center of each wonton wrapper. Brush the edges of the wonton with a little water and wrap it around the filling, shaping into a ball and pinching the edges to seal the wrapper. Transfer each finished ball to a baking sheet lined with a lightly floured towel. Cover with another towel while you prepare the remainder.

In a heavy deep-fryer or wok, heat the oil to 375°F. In several batches, carefully drop in the balls one at a time so they do not touch each other. Fry them until golden brown, 1 to 2 minutes, turning them as necessary. Remove them with a slotted spoon and drain well on paper towels.

Serve immediately with a bowl of the Dipping Sauce.

## DIPPING SAUCE

1 tablespoon safflower or vegetable oil

1 cup Chicken Stock (see page 390)

¼ cup soy sauce

2 tablespoons white vinegar

Hot chili oil or paste (optional)

In a bowl, combine the oil, chicken stock, soy sauce, and vinegar and mix well. Add chili oil to taste.

# DO-IT-YOURSELF HOT POT

The guests cook their own meats for the first course, and after finishing that part of the meal, the cooking broth becomes a hearty soup, enhanced by the flavor of the vegetables and meat that have been cooked in it.

3 to 4 quarts Chicken or Vegetable Stock (see page 390 or 391)
8 raw eggs, in their shells
2 cups light soy sauce
Sesame oil
Chili paste with garlic
Sugar
Green onions (scallions), thinly sliced
Cilantro

ASSORTED MEATS:

1 pound rib steak, thinly sliced
1 pound chicken breasts, skinned, boned, and thinly sliced
1 pound veal shoulder, thinly sliced
1 pound lean boned lamb, thinly sliced
Platter of cabbage and spinach leaves, whole green onions, snow peas, tofu, and Chinese glass noodles

Fill an electric wok with the stock and bring it to a boil. Carefully place the wok in the center of the dining table. Place a Chinese soup bowl in front of each guest with a raw egg in its shell in each bowl. Give each guest a small long-handled wire mesh strainer.

Pass a platter containing a pitcher of soy sauce, sesame oil, a bowl of chili paste with garlic, sugar, a bowl of sliced green onions, and another of cilantro. Let each guest make his own dipping sauce, by cracking the egg, discarding the shell, and stirring in the sauces, green onions, and cilantro.

Pass platters of the sliced meats so guests may select whatever they like to fill the baskets of their long-handled mesh strainers. Each guest then lowers the strainer into the boiling chicken stock; as the meats are cooked, they are dipped into the individual bowl of sauce and eaten.

After everyone has eaten their fill of the meats, place the cabbage, spinach, green onions, snow peas, tofu, and glass noodles into the broth. Cover the wok and simmer for 5 to 10 minutes, until the vegetables are tender-crisp. Ladle the soup with the vegetables into fresh bowls for the next course. The soup is rich and delicious because of the flavors of all the foods that were cooked in it.

# CHOCOLATE-COATED LITCHIS AND PINEAPPLE

These are wonderfully festive—a perfect ending to a Chinese New Year dinner. Transfer them to a chilled platter just before serving.

MAKES ABOUT 5 dozen

1 can (20 ounces) pineapple chunks, drained
2 pounds semisweet chocolate, melted (see page 21)
1 can (20 ounces) whole peeled litchis in syrup

Place the drained pineapple chunks, in a single layer, on a tray or baking sheet lined with wax paper. Insert a toothpick into each chunk for easier handling. Cover with wax paper and freeze. When completely frozen, dip them in the warm chocolate, allowing the excess chocolate to drip off. Return to the tray or baking sheet and refrigerate until the chocolate hardens.

Drain the litchis and place them on paper towels, pitted sides down. Chill in the refrigerator for at least 20 minutes. Follow the same procedure used for pineapple chunks.

# Deep-Fried Wontons with Powdered Sugar

These sweet fried wontons are perfect for a Chinese New Year celebration and it's a practical use for the unused wonton wrappers from the appetizers.

MAKES 3 DOZEN

36 wonton wrappers
Vegetable oil for deep-frying
Powdered sugar

Cut a slit in the center of each wrapper and put one end through the slit to form a bow tie. Place on a floured baking sheet and set aside.

In a large heavy skillet or wok, heat oil to 375°F. Deep-fry the wontons, turning them occasionally, for 2 to 3 minutes, or until they are golden brown and crisp. When done, transfer them to paper towels to drain and cool. Just before serving, sprinkle the wontons with powdered sugar.

# FRENCH MENUS

## A FRENCH CHEF'S DINNER

FOR 12

My husband and I often have famous chefs from around the world as dinner guests when they visit Los Angeles. And what do they want to do on vacation? Cook, of course. What a delight it is to watch them in action in our own kitchen.

This French menu was inspired by one served to us by the talented Grégoire Sein, head chef of the famous Michel Guérard Restaurant in Eugénie-les-Bains, France. This popular dining haven is noted for its nouvelle cuisine, the lighter, less caloric version of classic French cooking.

Because Grégoire didn't know anything about kosher cooking, I took each of his recipes and painstakingly checked the ingredients to make sure they were appropriate for a kosher kitchen and didn't contain any dairy foods, since this dinner included sweetbreads and lamb.

Grégoire's charming menu will give you a quick introduction to French cooking. The ingredients are all easy to find in your neighborhood markets and the results are very elegant. Try this dinner when you want to impress someone special. It is, in fact, perfect for Hanukkah, with its potato latkes. As a matter of fact, that is exactly when Grégoire cooked it for us.

# Oven-Dried Tomatoes on Potato Pancakes

Once you've tasted these silky slices of herb-enhanced Oven-Dried Tomatoes, you'll want to add them to dozens of dishes. Grégoire Sein served them to us on puff pastry, but I like them so much with potato latkes that I always do them this way now. You can also add them to pizzas, pasta, fish, or veal, and they're incredible with bagels, lox, and cream cheese. Their color is rich and their flavor is the most intense tomato essence you can imagine. The trendy sun-dried tomatoes that are sold for incredibly high prices at gourmet food stores are not nearly as good.

24 small tomatoes
2 whole heads of garlic, each clove unpeeled but smashed with the side of a sharp knife
Salt
Freshly ground black pepper
3 tablespoons sugar
16 fresh thyme sprigs, with stems
¾ cup olive oil
Mini-Potato Latkes (see page 92)
Pistou (recipe follows)

Preheat the oven to 300°F.

Using a sharp knife, cut a shallow X in the skin at the bottom of each tomato. Drop the tomatoes, 2 or 3 at a time, into boiling water; count to 10 and then lift them out with a slotted spoon and plunge them into a bowl filled with ice and water. Peel the tomatoes, cut them in half, and gently squeeze the juice and seeds out of each half. (Reserve the juice and seeds for a sauce or soup.)

Place the tomato halves side by side, cut side down, on a well-oiled jelly-roll pan (baking sheet with sides). Scatter with the garlic cloves and sprinkle with salt, pepper, sugar, thyme, and olive oil. Bake for 3 to 4 hours, shaking the pan occasionally so the tomatoes do not stick, until all the liquid in the tomatoes has evaporated. The tomatoes will become very brown around the edges. Immediately transfer them with a spatula to a glass dish to cool in a single layer. Cover with plastic wrap and refrigerate. If keeping for more than 2 to 3 hours, cover them with olive oil.

Preheat the oven to 400°F. Brush the middle of each fried potato latke with the Pistou, top with a tomato, and brush with additional Pistou. Place on a foil-lined baking sheet and bake for 10 to 15 minutes, until heated through. Serve immediately.

## PISTOU

10 fresh basil leaves
1 garlic clove, peeled
1 tablespoon olive oil
Salt
Freshly ground black pepper

Place the basil leaves and garlic in the processor and blend. Add the olive oil and blend. Add salt and pepper to taste.

# SWEETBREADS IN HOT VINEGAR SAUCE

This is a fabulous recipe that makes preparing sweetbreads a breeze—the way Chef Grégoire does them. It took barely any time at all. The secret is the rinsing, boiling, and weighting down the sweetbreads (under a heavy object) for 1 hour. Many French cooks are familiar with this method, which prevents the sweetbreads from being tough and gritty. The vinegar sauce is another French inspiration.

6 to 8 sweetbreads
¼ cup olive oil
1 large onion, thinly sliced
6 carrots, peeled and thinly sliced
8 parsley sprigs
¼ cup tomato concentrate in a tube or tomato paste
2 cups dry white wine
1 to 2 cups Chicken Stock (see page 390)
1 celery root, peeled and cubed
24 mushrooms, quartered
24 fresh asparagus tips, steamed
24 small lettuce leaves

Place the sweetbreads in a bowl and rinse them in cold water for several minutes, then put them in a large pot with water to cover. Bring to a boil. Remove the sweetbreads and place them on a baking sheet. Place another baking sheet on top. Place a heavy pot filled with water on top to weight down the sweetbreads for 1 hour.

Heat the olive oil in a large skillet over medium heat and brown the sweetbreads evenly, 1 to 2 minutes a side. Add the onion, carrots, parsley, tomato concentrate, white wine, and enough chicken stock to cover. Simmer for 2 hours; for the last half hour, add the celery root and mushrooms.

Let the sweetbreads cool in their liquid, then refrigerate at least 1 hour. Remove the sweetbreads from the liquid. Peel off the membranes and trim the rough edges and reserve for the Vinegar Sauce. Cut or separate the sweetbreads into bite-size pieces. Strain the stock, re-

Caramelized Pearl Onions
(recipe follows)

Vinegar Sauce (recipe follows)

Italian flat-leaf parsley

½ cup thinly sliced sorrel
leaves

serving 2½ cups of the liquid for the onions and Vinegar Sauce. Serve the sweetbreads, along with the carrots, celery root, and mushrooms, on lettuce leaves. Garnish with asparagus tips, Caramelized Pearl Onions, Vinegar Sauce, Italian parsley, and sorrel.

## VINEGAR SAUCE

2 tablespoons olive oil

Trimmings reserved from the
sweetbreads

2 garlic cloves, minced

1½ cups stock reserved from
the sweetbreads

2 shallots, minced

¼ cup red wine vinegar

¼ cup walnut oil

2 tablespoons chopped
parsley

2 teaspoons minced chives

Fresh or dried tarragon

½ cup thinly sliced sorrel
leaves

In a saucepan, heat the olive oil over medium heat and brown the reserved trimmings and garlic, 3 to 4 minutes. Add the stock and simmer for 10 minutes. Strain. Return the stock to the pot and skim off the fat that forms on top. Add the shallots and 2 tablespoons of the vinegar. Simmer over low heat for 10 minutes. Just before serving, add the walnut oil, additional vinegar, parsley, chives tarragon to taste, and sorrel. Mix well.

# CARAMELIZED PEARL ONIONS

1 tablespoon sugar

1 teaspoon water

2 tablespoons unsalted margarine

24 pearl onions, blanched and
peeled

1 cup stock reserved from the
sweetbreads

In a small saucepan, place the sugar, water, and margarine. Bring to a boil, add the onions, and brown until they are caramelized. Add the stock and simmer for 10 minutes. Keep warm.

# EYE OF THE LAMB ROAST

There are a few secrets to preparing lamb the French way, so that it is always tender and moist—not like the dry, gray meat we find in American restaurants. Here are the secrets that Grégoire taught me:

• Have your butcher prepare the rack of lamb by trimming the eye of the lamb fillets and wrapping the bones and fat separately to be used for your stockpot. When storing the fillets, tie them with cord at ½-inch intervals and wrap in plastic wrap before refrigerating.

• Allow plenty of time to prepare your stock. It is best cooked 1 day before you plan to roast the lamb because it takes 6 hours to cook. It is well worth the trouble because the 2 to 3 cups of sauce that you end up with will give a rich, thick, fat-free glaze, very seldom found in a kosher kitchen.

• When browning the lamb, you must sear it quickly on both sides in a very hot, heavy skillet so all the juices are sealed in. Then it is roasted in the oven for 5 to 10 minutes more, depending on how rare you like it.

• Another hint: Grégoire arranged the spinach in perfect rounds in the center of each plate and topped it with the slices of lamb; he spooned the sauce around it to make a very artistic plate.

4 racks of lamb, separated into bones, trimmings, and fillets
2 large onions, thinly sliced
½ celery stalk, cut into chunks
2 large carrots, peeled and thickly sliced
1 medium leek, cut into chunks
1 can (28 ounces) whole tomatoes with juice
Stems from 1 bunch of parsley, tied
4 sprigs of fresh thyme, or 1 to 2 tablespoons dried
Salt
¼ cup olive oil
Sautéed Spinach and Parsley (recipe follows)
Freshly ground black pepper
Italian flat-leaf parsley for garnish

Preheat the oven to 475°F.

For the stock, place the lamb rack bones and trimmings in a large roaster or Dutch oven and brown for 30 minutes. Pour off the fat. Add the onions, celery, carrots, leek, undrained tomatoes, and parsley stems. Season with thyme and salt. Bake for 10 minutes longer, shaking the pot to avoid sticking. Remove from the oven. Add water to cover the bones completely.

Bring to a boil on top of the stove and simmer, uncovered, for 6 hours. If the water reduces too quickly, add enough additional water to keep the bones covered.

Strain the stock into a heavy pot. Bring to a boil, then simmer until the stock is reduced to 2 to 3 cups. Keep warm.

Preheat the oven to 375°F.

In a large heavy skillet, heat the olive oil and brown the lamb fillets on all sides. Transfer to a baking pan and bake for 10 minutes. Transfer to a heated platter, cover, and keep warm until ready to serve. Remove the cords and slice into ¾-inch-thick rounds.

Spoon the Sautéed Spinach and Parsley in the center of each heated plate. Then arrange the slices of lamb on top, sprinkle with pepper, and spoon the reduced stock around the lamb. Garnish with parsley and serve immediately.

# Sautéed Spinach and Parsley

1 pound spinach, trimmed and chopped (8 cups)
4 bunches parsley, tops only
Salt
Freshly ground black pepper
1 teaspoon freshly grated nutmeg
¼ cup olive oil
1 garlic clove, unpeeled and mashed

Wash the spinach and parsley in water and drain well. Bring a large pot of water to a boil and blanch the spinach and parsley for 1 minute, then drain. Combine the spinach, parsley, salt and pepper to taste, and nutmeg. Toss with olive oil and garlic. In a large skillet over medium heat, sauté the spinach mixture for 5 minutes. Remove the garlic. Keep warm.

# Pear Soufflé

Soufflés are not usually included in menus for the home kitchen, because many cooks are under the impression that they are difficult to prepare. By carefully following this recipe, however, you will get successful results with surprising ease. The timing is important, but most of the work can be done ahead and the egg whites folded in at the last minute, just before baking and serving. You can serve it in the individual soufflé ramekins, in the center of a large plate, surrounded with assorted fruits placed in an attractive pattern.

3 pears, peeled and cored
Juice of 1 lemon
1 cup sugar
2 cups water
4 eggs, separated
1 tablespoon pear brandy

Place the pears in a bowl and toss with the lemon juice. In a large saucepan, over high heat, bring ½ cup of the sugar and the water to a boil and stir until the sugar dissolves. Lower the heat and add the pears with the lemon juice. Simmer for 10 to 15 minutes, or until soft when pierced with a fork.

Put the pears in a processor or blender and purée. Add the remaining ½ cup sugar, egg yolks, and pear brandy and blend well. Transfer to a large bowl, cover with plastic wrap, and chill.

Preheat the oven to 400°F.

In a large bowl, beat the egg whites until soft peaks form. Gently but thoroughly fold them into the pear mixture. Spoon into lightly greased individual (½ cup) soufflé dishes, until three quarters full. Place on a baking sheet and bake for 10 minutes, or until the soufflés rise and turn golden.

# ARLETTES
## PUFF PASTRY COOKIES

When I explained to Grégoire that we had to use nondairy margarine for the pastry, he said, "No problem." He told me that they often use it at his restaurant and get marvelous results. So here is a simplified version of his recipe, which he cut into cookies, coated with powdered sugar, and then baked to a deep brown glaze.

This pastry takes a little time, so be prepared to do the first part the day before you want to serve the cookies. And it is worth the effort: not only are the cookies absolutely delicious, but the puff pastry can also be used for many other recipes, such as fruit or vegetable strudels and appetizers to hold the oven-dried tomatoes instead of the Mini-Potato Latkes.

MAKES 60 TO 70

Quick Puff Pastry (recipe follows)
Powdered sugar

Preheat the oven to 400°F.

Divide the Quick Puff Pastry into 4 parts. Working with 1 part at a time, wrap remaining parts with plastic wrap and refrigerate. Put the puff pastry on a floured board or cold marble slab. Roll it out to a 6x8-inch rectangle. Roll lengthwise into a tight cigar shape about 1 inch round. Chill. Slice each roll into ½-inch rounds. Sprinkle the work area generously with sifted powdered sugar. Place a round of the puff pastry, cut side up, on the sugar and sprinkle the top with sifted sugar. With a rolling pin, using a back and forth motion, form into an oval shape. Turn over and continue rolling gently until the cookie is very thin and measures about 5 inches long and 2 inches wide. Sprinkle with powdered sugar and place on a foil-lined baking sheet. Repeat with the remaining rounds. Bake for 4 to 5 minutes; watch carefully as they brown quickly. Turn over and bake on the other side for 2 to 3 minutes or until golden brown. Transfer to wire racks and cool.

# QUICK PUFF PASTRY

2 cups flour
½ teaspoon salt
¼ pound plus 6 tablespoons
  cold unsalted margarine,
  cut into small pieces
¼ to ⅓ cup ice water

In the bowl of an electric mixer, or processor, blend the flour and salt. Add the margarine and blend until the mixture resembles coarse meal. Add ice water and blend until dough begins to come together. On a floured surface, knead the dough into a ball and roll it into a 6x12-inch rectangle, cutting in a little flour if it sticks to the rolling pin.

Fold the top third of the rectangle over the center and the bottom third over the top to form a rectangle about 4 by 6 inches. Press down the top edge with the rolling pin to seal it; turn the dough seam side down and brush any excess flour from the dough. With the open (narrow) side facing you, roll the dough out again into a 12x6-inch rectangle and fold it into thirds as before. Repeat this 2 more times, always starting with the seam side down and an open end facing you. Wrap the dough in wax paper and a plastic bag and chill in the refrigerator at least 30 minutes or overnight. (The pastry can be wrapped well and frozen; it can be defrosted in the refrigerator overnight or at room temperature for several hours.)

# BOUILLABAISSE MENU

FOR 8

▼▲·▼·▲·▼·▲·▼·▲·▼·▲·▼·▲·▼·▲·▼·▲

Aïoli with Raw and Cooked
Vegetables

Tarte aux Poireaux

French Baguettes (see page
262)

Bouillabaisse with Rouille

Hearts of Lettuce with
Warm Cheese Dressing

Florentines

Lemon Mousse Slices with
Chocolate-Apricot Glaze

SUGGESTED BEVERAGES:

Burgundy or Bordeaux and
Sauterne or white dessert
wine

This is a perfect menu for a wine tasting. White or red wines go well with the Leek Tart. A French Burgundy or Bordeaux accompanies the Bouillabaisse and the Hearts of Lettuce with Warm Cheese Dressing. The crisp, chocolate-dipped Florentines and Lemon Mousse Slices are a sweet finale, and with it we serve a Sauterne or some other fruity dessert wine.

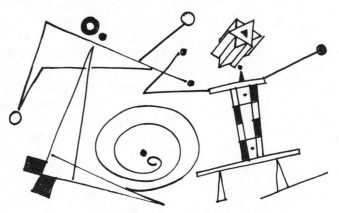

## AÏOLI

### GARLIC MAYONNAISE

This sauce is also excellent with fish. For a warm Aïoli, make it in a metal bowl over a pan of very warm water.

MAKES ABOUT 3 CUPS

1 medium baked or boiled
  potato
3 egg yolks

Mash the potato and put it through a strainer, ricer, or food mill. (Do not use a processor, which can make the potato gummy.) Beat with an electric beater or mixer un-

4 garlic cloves, minced
Juice of ½ lemon
Salt
Freshly ground white or black
   pepper
1½ cups olive oil
Raw and cooked vegetables

til very smooth. Beat in the egg yolks, 1 at a time, mixing well after each addition. Add the garlic, lemon juice, and salt and pepper to taste. Beat until the mixture is completely smooth.

Gradually add the oil, in a very thin stream, beating constantly with a wooden spatula. When all the oil is added the sauce should have the consistency of thick mayonnaise. (If the sauce becomes too thick, it may separate. You can avoid this by adding a little lukewarm water as you go along.) Serve as a dip with raw and cooked vegetables.

# TARTE AUX POIREAUX
## LEEK TART

The art of serving a perfect tart, whether it be a savory or dessert tart, is to fill a prebaked pie crust, then bake and serve it right from the oven. This savory tart is a perfect example. The leek custard can be prepared, covered with plastic wrap, and stored in the refrigerator 2 to 3 hours before serving time.

Prebaked Classic Pie Crust
   (see page 177)
2 tablespoons unsalted butter
2 large leeks, white part only,
   washed and thinly sliced
Salt
Fresh ground black pepper
4 eggs
1 cup milk
1 cup cream
Pinch of nutmeg

Prepare and prebake the pastry tart shell.

Heat the butter in a saucepan and gently sauté the leeks on low heat, stirring frequently, until soft, about 20 minutes. Season to taste with salt and pepper.

In a large bowl, beat the eggs, milk, and cream until blended. Add the leek mixture and nutmeg, plus additional salt and pepper. Cover and refrigerate until ready to bake.

Preheat the oven to 400°F.

Pour the leek mixture into the tart shell and bake for 30 minutes; then reduce the heat to 350°F and bake until set, about 10 minutes more. Cut into wedges and serve hot.

# BOUILLABAISSE WITH ROUILLE

## FISH STEW WITH GARLIC SAUCE

How can you make bouillabaisse in a kosher kitchen? It's easy. Just don't use shellfish, swordfish, or any other nonkosher seafood. And follow this recipe.

This stew is ideal for a large group. Just use a larger pot and double or triple the recipe. The Rouille—I give a choice here of a classic version and one featuring fresh basil—adds an extra piquant taste.

I remember the first time I met Julia Child and explained how I began with her bouillabaisse recipe and made the necessary changes for kosher requirements. She was delighted at the idea and speaks of it whenever we meet.

¼ cup olive oil
2 onions, diced
2 leeks, thinly sliced, with greens
3 garlic cloves, minced
4 celery stalks, sliced
2 carrots, thinly sliced
1 can (28 ounces) whole tomatoes, or 3 cups chopped fresh tomatoes
1 tablespoon tomato paste
1 teaspoon thyme
2 teaspoons fennel seeds
2 bay leaves
3 cups dry white wine
Pinch of saffron (optional)
5 cups Fish Stock (page 392)
3 to 4 pounds white firm-fleshed fish fillets (such as halibut, whitefish, or sea bass), cut into 1½-inch chunks
2 or 3 potatoes, peeled, diced, and parboiled
Salt
Freshly ground black pepper
Tabasco sauce
2 large carrots, julienned, parboiled, and drained
Rouille (recipe follows)

Heat the oil in a large saucepan and sauté the onions, leeks, and garlic until tender but not yet browned, about 5 minutes. Add the celery and carrots and simmer for 5 minutes. Add the tomatoes, tomato paste, thyme, fennel seeds, bay leaves, and wine. Bring to a boil and simmer for 20 to 30 minutes. Add the saffron and fish stock. Simmer for 1 hour.

Add the fish and potatoes. Season to taste with salt, pepper, and Tabasco. Simmer for 15 to 20 minutes, or until the fish is cooked through; do not overcook. Ladle into hot soup bowls and garnish with the julienned carrots. Let guests add Rouille to taste.

## CLASSIC ROUILLE

2 slices white bread, crusts
  trimmed

4 garlic cloves

½ roasted red bell pepper
  (see page 298)

2 tablespoons tomato paste

1 teaspoon paprika (optional)

4 to 5 drops of Tabasco sauce

½ cup olive oil

½ to 1 cup Fish Stock (see
  page 392)

Soak the bread in cold water and squeeze dry.

In a processor or blender, process the garlic, bell pepper, bread, tomato paste, paprika, Tabasco, olive oil, and ½ cup fish stock, turning the machine on and off for 5 seconds. Then continue processing 10 seconds to make a smooth paste. Add additional fish stock if needed.

## FRESH BASIL ROUILLE

6 garlic cloves

1 teaspoon salt

12 large fresh basil leaves

1 roasted red bell pepper (see
  page 278)

½ cup crumbled fresh white
  bread, lightly packed

1 egg yolk

1¼ cups olive oil

2 or 3 drops of Tabasco sauce

In a processor or blender, blend the garlic, salt, and basil. Add the bell pepper, bread, and egg yolk. Add the olive oil in a thin stream until the sauce is thick. Season to taste with Tabasco. This sauce can be prepared a day or two in advance, covered, and stored in the refrigerator. Bring to room temperature and beat with a fork before serving.

# HEARTS OF LETTUCE WITH WARM CHEESE DRESSING

2 heads each Bibb and ro-
  maine lettuce, center leaves
  only, torn into bite-size
  pieces

3 ounces Brie, diced

3 ounces blue cheese, diced

3 tablespoons balsamic or red
  wine vinegar

½ cup olive oil

Wash and dry the greens; toss them in a large salad bowl.
  Preheat the oven to 375°F.
  Just before serving, place the diced cheeses on a foil-lined baking sheet. Bake for 5 to 10 minutes, until the cheeses melt. Toss the lettuce mixture with vinegar and olive oil. Immediately spoon the melted cheese over the salad and toss again. Place on individual serving plates and serve immediately.

# FLORENTINES

The batter for these cookies can be prepared days ahead, covered, and stored in the refrigerator for up to 1 week. Then instead of dropping the batter from a spoon, shape it into round flat disks with your fingers. They bake more evenly using this technique.

MAKES ABOUT 2 DOZEN

½ cup sugar
⅓ cup cream
⅓ cup light corn syrup
2 tablespoons unsalted butter
¼ cup flour
1 cup sliced almonds
⅓ cup slivered glazed orange peel
¼ teaspoon vanilla extract
Chocolate Glaze (see page 165)

In a heavy medium saucepan, combine the sugar, cream, corn syrup, and butter. Cook over low heat until the sugar dissolves. Increase the heat and boil until the syrup registers 238°F on a candy thermometer. Transfer to a mixing bowl and beat in the flour. Stir in the almonds and peel. Remove from the heat and mix in the vanilla. Chill.

Preheat the oven to 375°F.

Shape the dough into 1-inch rounds, flatten and place 2½ inches apart on foil-lined baking sheets. Bake for 8 to 10 minutes, until golden. Cool until the cookies are firm enough to peel off of the foil; place them on racks. Serve them plain or drizzle Chocolate Glaze onto them from a pastry bag. Cool until the chocolate is set.

# LEMON MOUSSE SLICES WITH CHOCOLATE-APRICOT GLAZE

A lemon dessert is my favorite way of refreshing the taste buds after a fish dinner. The chocolate glaze is just the right accent.

8 egg yolks
2 cups sugar
2 cups lemon juice
Zest of 3 lemons
2 packages (¼ ounce each) unflavored gelatin
3 cups heavy cream, whipped
Chocolate-Apricot Glaze (recipe follows)

In the bowl of an electric mixer, beat the egg yolks and sugar until light and fluffy, about 20 minutes.

In a small saucepan over low heat, warm the lemon juice and zest; add the gelatin, stir it until dissolved and cool to room temperature.

In a mixing bowl set over a larger bowl of ice, beat together the egg yolk and lemon juice mixtures until cool, just before the gelatin sets. Fold in the whipped cream. Line a 6x10-inch loaf pan with a large sheet of plastic wrap. Spoon in the lemon mixture. Cover and freeze until serving time.

Just before serving, remove the pan from the freezer and unmold the mousse onto a chilled platter, peeling away the plastic wrap. Frost with a thin layer of the chocolate glaze. Slice and serve.

## CHOCOLATE-APRICOT GLAZE

1 cup apricot jam
6 ounces cocoa powder
3 ounces crème de cacao

In a medium saucepan, combine the jam, cocoa powder, and crème de cacao; bring the mixture to a boil, stirring continuously. Place in a processor and blend until smooth. Strain and cool to room temperature.

# COUNTRY FRENCH DUCK DINNER

FOR 8

Michel Richard is a talented chef who grew up in the French countryside and learned to cook at the age of seven. The recipes in this menu, combining the flavors of duck, turnips, and a tomato-eggplant terrine, were developed by Michel especially for his new restaurant, Citrus, in Los Angeles.

Michel has a great sense of humor, and when he was a guest cook on my TV show he worried that he didn't know "how to cook kosher." With a little coaching, there was no problem. He even invented a super-rich halvah dessert!

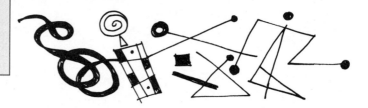

## TERRINE OF TOMATO AND EGGPLANT WITH BASIL-EGGPLANT SAUCE

Only a creative French chef could dream up an eggplant sauce to top an elegant and colorful eggplant terrine.

MAKES ONE 4x7-INCH TERRINE

1 cup olive oil
2 large eggplants, thinly sliced
 lengthwise

In a large heavy skillet, heat 2 tablespoons of the olive oil and sauté a single layer of eggplant slices until soft on both sides. Drain on paper towels. Continue in this

4 large tomatoes, peeled (see page 26)

⅓ cup beet juice (from boiled or canned beets)

1 teaspoon gelatin, softened in 1 tablespoon cold water

1 teaspoon tomato paste

Salt

Freshly ground black pepper

Basil-Eggplant Sauce (recipe follows)

manner, adding oil as needed, until all the eggplant is sautéed.

Line a terrine or loaf pan with wax paper, overlapping the sides by about 3 inches. Place a single layer of the eggplant slices on the wax paper, going up about 2 inches on each side.

With a sharp knife, cut each tomato into one long spiral slice, about 5 inches long by 3 inches wide, cutting it away from the seeds and pulp.

In a small saucepan, heat the beet juice. Mix in the gelatin, tomato paste, and salt and pepper to taste.

Dip the flattened tomato slices in the beet juice mixture and place a single layer of them on top of the eggplant in the pan. Layer with additional slices of eggplant, then more slices of tomato, ending with the eggplant. Press down firmly after each layer is added. Fold over the overlapping eggplant of the first layer and cover with the wax paper. Place a weight on top of the terrine and refrigerate for at least 2 hours.

Just before serving, invert the terrine onto a work surface; unmold it and remove the wax paper. With a sharp knife, cut the terrine into ½-inch slices. Place on individual serving plates and spoon the Basil-Eggplant Sauce on the side.

## BASIL-EGGPLANT SAUCE

1 large eggplant

½ cup plus 2 tablespoons olive oil

¼ cup fresh sweet basil leaves

Juice of 1 lemon

4 drops Tabasco sauce

Salt

Preheat the oven to 350°F.

Cut the eggplant in half lengthwise. Brush the cut sides with 2 tablespoons of the olive oil and place them cut side down on a baking sheet. Bake for 1 hour or until tender.

Scoop out the eggplant pulp with a spoon and place it in a processor or blender. Process for 30 seconds. Transfer to a large bowl.

Place the basil in the processor and process until smoothly puréed, adding the remaining ½ cup oil in a thin stream to give a creamy consistency. Add the basil purée and lemon juice to the eggplant and stir well. Season to taste with Tabasco and salt. Cover with plastic wrap and chill in the refrigerator.

# FRENCH BAGUETTES

Baguettes are the long skinny loaves of French bread that you see Parisians carrying in their arms or in their bicycle baskets.

This is one of my favorite bread recipes because it has only a few ingredients, which I always have on hand, so I can whip it up quickly. My cooking classes like it, too; it's great for beginning cooks. Baguettes freeze beautifully, and when heated in the oven, they're as crisp and fragrant as if they were just baked.*

MAKES 4 LOAVES

1 package active dry yeast
2 cups warm water (110 to 115°F)
1 tablespoon unsalted margarine
1 tablespoon sugar
2 teaspoons salt
5 cups flour
½ cup yellow cornmeal

Dissolve the yeast in ½ cup of the warm water with a pinch of sugar.

In the bowl of an electric mixer, beat together the remaining 1½ cups warm water, margarine, sugar, and salt. Blend in the yeast mixture. Add flour, 1 cup at a time, blending after each addition, until the dough is thick enough to work by hand. Spoon the dough onto a floured board and knead 5 to 10 minutes, gradually adding more flour to make a smooth, elastic dough.

Place the dough in a greased bowl and grease its top. Cover with a towel and let rise in a warm place until doubled in size, about 2 hours.

Divide the dough into 4 parts and shape into rounds; then, by pounding and shaping, form them into long baguettes. Place on oiled baking sheets that have been sprinkled generously with cornmeal; cover with a towel and let rise in a warm place until doubled, about 40 minutes.

Preheat the oven to 400°F.

With a sharp knife, cut 3 small diagonal slits on top of each baguette; brush the loaves with water. Bake for 40 to 50 minutes, until golden brown. Remove from baking sheets and cool on racks.

*See instructions for storing and freezing breads (page 23).

# DUCK WITH TURNIPS

This recipe uses the whole duck, but in several different ways. The duck is boned and the carcass and giblets are used for a stock; the legs and thighs are roasted on top of the stock as it cooks; the duck breast fillets are browned in a very hot frying pan just before serving.

The stock takes four to six hours to cook, and the results are spectacular—a rich sauce that is pure essence of duck, which you can store in the refrigerator or freezer and use for many meat dishes.

2 ducks (3 pounds each), with liver
4 carrots, unpeeled and sliced
1 celery stalk
2 onions, unpeeled and diced
1 whole head of garlic, un-peeled and cut in half
8 fresh thyme sprigs
8 medium turnips, peeled and quartered (peels reserved)
3 shallots, peeled and finely chopped
1 bay leaf, crumbled
2 tomatoes, quartered
1 teaspoon whole black pep-percorns
2 cups dry red wine
1 tablespoon sugar

Divide each duck into 3 parts: breasts, legs and thighs, and carcass.

Preheat the oven to 450°F.

Place the duck carcasses and giblets in a heavy roasting pan with the carrots, celery, onions, garlic, and thyme. Bake for 30 minutes, to brown the ingredients and melt away the duck fat.

Transfer the carcass and vegetables to a large heavy pot: add the turnip peels, shallots, bay leaf, tomatoes, peppercorns, wine, and water to cover. Bring to a boil and simmer for 4 hours, adding wine or water to keep the solids covered.

During the last hour, place the legs and thighs in the stockpot to cook until tender. Remove them and keep them warm.

Strain the liquid into a skillet; bring to a boil and simmer until thick (10 to 15 minutes). Add the turnips and cook them until tender. Transfer them with a slotted spoon to a bowl.

While the turnips are cooking, heat a large skillet. Place the duck breasts on a wooden board and sprinkle with salt and pepper. Place the breasts, skin down, in the heated skillet and sauté over high heat until brown and the skin is crisp, about 5 minutes. Then turn and sauté 5 minutes more, until medium rare. Let them rest for 5 minutes.

While the duck breasts are resting, add ½ cup of the reduced liquid and the sugar to a large skillet. Heat until the sugar dissolves and sauté the turnips until glazed. Keep warm.

To assemble the dish, slice the duck breasts diagonally, ¼ inch thick, and arrange them on each serving plate with one of the legs. Spoon the turnips onto each plate and spoon on the reduced glaze. Garnish with Fried Shoestring Beets (recipe follows). Serve immediately.

# FRIED SHOESTRING BEETS

Michel uses a Japanese vegetable slicer to cut beautiful, uniform shoestrings. If you think of beets as borscht or pickled, you will be amazed at the glamorous appearance this vegetable takes on with a little French touch.

4 large beets (about 2 pounds), peeled
Oil for deep-frying
Salt

With a French mandoline, a Japanese vegetable slicer, a large grater, or the julienne blade of a food processor, cut the beets lengthwise into spaghetti-like strands, about 2½ inches long and ⅛ inch thick.

In a large heavy skillet or deep-fryer, heat the oil to 370°F on a deep-frying thermometer.

Drop a handful of beets into the frying basket and immerse the basket in the hot oil, shaking it gently to prevent the beets from sticking together. Fry them for about 15 seconds, just until tender and pale in color. Drain on paper towels; fry and drain the remaining beets. You can hold the beets at this stage for as long as an hour.

Immediately before serving, reheat the oil until it reaches 385°F. Drop the beets into the basket and, shaking the basket, fry them until crisp, about 15 seconds. Drain on paper towels and transfer to a large platter or bowl. Sprinkle lightly with salt and serve at once.

# SALAD OF WILD GREENS AND ROASTED PEPPERS

For his Citrus restaurant, Michel Richard offers a specially mixed salad bouquet consisting of the freshest and most unusual lettuces and other greens he can get. Go to the best greengrocer in your area and make up your own special selection of greens.

8 cups (lightly packed) mixed greens, such as red leaf, Boston, and Bibb lettuces, radicchio, arugula, and mâche, torn into bite-size pieces

Citrus Restaurant Vinaigrette (recipe follows)

1 cup each diced roasted red and yellow bell peppers (see page 278)

½ cup finely chopped flat-leaf parsley

In a large salad bowl, toss together the mixed greens. Pour the vinaigrette over the greens and toss again. Place the salad on individual chilled serving plates and garnish with roasted peppers and parsley.

## CITRUS RESTAURANT VINAIGRETTE

2 tablespoons Dijon mustard

⅓ cup red wine vinegar or sherry vinegar

1 cup olive oil

¼ teaspoon salt

Freshly ground black pepper

In a bowl, beat the mustard and vinegar with a wire whisk. Slowly whisk in the olive oil until well blended. Season to taste with salt and pepper.

# HALVAH–CHOCOLATE MOUSSE NAPOLEON

Michel fell in love with halvah when he lived and worked in Athens. He likes it so much that he always adds some when he makes his own birthday cake.

He created this recipe for my kosher TV program, making a chocolate mousse without butter or cream and using it as a filling between layers of halvah. He calls it his halvah napoleon—a new twist on the classic French pastry. He serves it with a chocolate sauce, but it would be equally good with a caramel or raspberry sauce—or by itself.

12 ounces semisweet chocolate

½ pound unsalted margarine, at room temperature

Juice of ½ lemon

4 egg whites

2 tablespoons sugar

1 pound halvah, cut into ½-inch-thick slices to fit molds

Chocolate Sauce (recipe follows)

Fresh mint leaves and strawberries for garnish

Melt the chocolate in the top of a double boiler over simmering water. Then let it cool to room temperature.

In the large bowl of an electric mixer with a whisk attachment, beat the chocolate and margarine until light and fluffy. Add the lemon juice and beat it in. In another bowl, beat the egg whites until soft peaks form, add sugar, and beat until stiff but not dry. Fold into the chocolate mixture. Spoon the chocolate mixture into a pastry bag fitted with a plain round tip.

Line two 3x7-inch molds with parchment paper, allowing enough of it to hang over the edges so you can completely enclose the finished dessert. Carefully arrange slices of halvah to cover the entire bottom of each mold. Pipe a single layer of chocolate mousse about ½ inch thick over the halvah and then cover with another layer of halvah. Pipe a second layer of mousse and add another layer of halvah until you have 3 layers of halvah and 2 of mousse. Cover with the parchment paper and refrigerate for at least 2 hours.

About 30 minutes before serving, remove the dessert from the refrigerator. Invert the mold, releasing the paper-lined dessert; peel off the paper. Cut the mousse into 1-inch slices, dipping a sharp knife into hot water between slices. Place on chilled dessert plates, cover with plastic wrap, and refrigerate. Just before serving, spoon the Chocolate Sauce on one side of the mousse. Garnish with a mint leaf and fresh strawberries.

## CHOCOLATE SAUCE

MAKES ABOUT 1 CUP

8 ounces semisweet chocolate, coarsely chopped

½ cup strong hot coffee

½ cup apricot or strawberry preserves, strained

1 tablespoon fruit liqueur (optional)

In the top of a double boiler over simmering water, place the chocolate, coffee, preserves, and liqueur. With a wooden spoon, mix constantly until the mixture is melted and well blended. Transfer to a glass bowl, cover with plastic wrap, and refrigerate. Serve hot or cold.

# ITALIAN MENUS

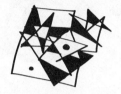

# 2 PRIMI PIATTI DINNERS

FOR 8

My collection of Italian recipes begins with two menus featuring *primi piatti,* "first plates"—meals made up entirely of first courses and appetizers. This is a wonderful way to learn about Italian cooking in depth by tasting small portions of a lot of different foods, served in separate courses.

Planning a *primi piatti* menu at home enables me to serve many of my favorite hot and cold dishes in the same meal. I might begin with a dish of eggplant in garlic and olive oil, served on a bright bed of fresh tomato coulis, or zucchini prepared in the same way, but with a sauce of red bell pepper purée instead.

Next, I serve pasta dishes—perhaps a homemade ravioli with an unusual filling, or tagliatelle, risotto, or gnocchi. Antipasti and marinated vegetables are other possible choices. Small individual pizzas are yet another enjoyable course. I end the menu with a rich dessert or two and espresso. Throughout the meal, we taste a selection of fine Italian wines, and grappa or Nocino as a "digestivo," or Rosolio, a special after-dinner wine made from rose petals, is served in tiny glasses.

Try combining any of the dishes in the two menus that follow to make your own Italian grazing party. But, as I've done, be sure to include a representative, well-balanced selection of dishes: some marinated vegetables, a pasta or two, a cheese course, home-baked breads, and a spectacular dessert as a finale.

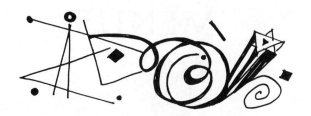

# GRISSINI
## ITALIAN BREADSTICKS

These crisp breadsticks are a great family nosh and make a special addition to a dinner party. Fill several wineglasses with breadsticks and place them at each end of the table for a festive atmosphere.

Instructions are given for hand-rolling the sticks or using a pasta machine.

Baked breadsticks can be stored in plastic bags in the freezer and heated in the oven; they taste as fresh as the day they were made.

If you like, twist or shape the dough into pretzel-like knots before baking, leaving a two-inch hole in the center. The result: an edible napkin ring or menu holder!

MAKES 3 TO 4 DOZEN

1 package active dry yeast
Pinch of sugar
1 cup warm water (110 to 115°F)
3 tablespoons olive oil
1 teaspoon salt
3 to 4 cups flour
3 egg whites
Kosher salt
Sesame seeds, caraway seeds, or poppy seeds

Dissolve the yeast and sugar in ½ cup of the water until foamy. In the large bowl of an electric mixer, combine the oil, salt, and the remaining ½ cup warm water. Blend in the yeast mixture and 1 cup of the flour and beat until smooth.

In a large mixing bowl, beat 2 of the egg whites until stiff but not dry. Fold the beaten egg whites into the yeast mixture. Add the remaining flour, 1 cup at a time, beating well after each addition, to make a soft dough. Knead the dough on a well-floured board for 5 minutes and place it in an oiled bowl; oil the top of the dough. Cover with a towel and let the dough rise for 15 minutes. Punch it down again and let it rise for 15 minutes more.

*For hand-rolled breadsticks:* Divide the dough into quarters and roll out each quarter on a floured board into rectangles ⅓ inch thick. Cut each rectangle into 2-inch squares; roll each square up tightly and then roll back and forth with the palm of your hand into a long, narrow stick, as thin as a pencil and 10 to 12 inches long.

Carefully transfer each stick to a foil-lined 10 × 15-inch greased baking pan, placing the strips ¼ to ½ inch apart. Keep the strips straight and press the ends down so they stick to the foil. Repeat until all the dough is used. Cover with a towel and repeat the procedure with a second baking pan.

Preheat the oven to 350°F.

Let the breadsticks rise in a warm place until round and puffy, about 15 minutes. Brush them with the remaining egg white, lightly beaten, and sprinkle with kosher salt and seeds. Bake for 15 to 20 minutes, until golden brown and crisp.

Carefully remove the breadsticks to racks to cool.

*For pasta machine breadsticks:* Pinch off a ball of dough 2 inches in diameter and flatten it with the palm of your hand to a ½-inch thickness. Lightly dust with flour.

Set the pasta machine rollers as far apart as possible. Guide the dough between the rollers and roll it through. Coat it with flour and feed the sheet through the wide noodle-cutting blades, cutting it into strips about ¼ inch wide and 10 to 15 inches long. Carefully place the sheet of cut strips on floured board and quickly separate each strip. Place on baking sheets and bake as described above.

# Bruschetta
## GARLIC BREAD WITH TOMATOES
## AND BASIL

We first tasted this delicious appetizer in a little restaurant in Italy and I couldn't wait to return home to try it on guests. It is a perfect last-minute accompaniment to an appetizer tray—unbelievably easy to prepare with ingredients usually on hand. For a change, replace the fresh tomato mixture with Oven-Dried Tomatoes (see page 247).

½ cup olive oil
3 tablespoons minced garlic
12 slices (½ inch thick) crusty Italian bread
5 tomatoes, diced
2 tablespoons chopped fresh basil leaves
Salt
Freshly ground black pepper
12 whole small basil leaves for garnish

In a large skillet, heat the olive oil and 1 tablespoon of the garlic over medium heat. Add the bread slices in a single layer and fry them on both sides until crisp.

Meanwhile, in a bowl, combine the tomatoes, the remaining 2 tablespoons garlic, the chopped basil leaves, and salt and pepper to taste. Place the bread slices on a large serving platter and spoon the tomato mixture onto each slice. Garnish with whole basil leaves and serve immediately.

# FAGIOLI E CAVIALE

## BEANS AND CAVIAR

This dish, a specialty of Florence, is often called "Poor Man, Rich Man"—beans, of course, are considered a poor man's dish, while caviar, being so expensive, is obviously a rich man's choice. Whatever you call it, this recipe is an unsual blend of two contrasting flavors and makes a really different appetizer or first course.

2 cups dried cannellini beans, or 2 cans (15 ounces each) cannellini beans
7 tablespoons olive oil
3 garlic cloves, peeled and minced
1 teaspoon dried rosemary
Salt
Freshly ground black pepper
3 ounces whitefish or salmon caviar

If dried beans are used: Soak the beans overnight in a bowl of cold water. The next morning drain the beans and rinse them under cold running water. Place them in a large heavy saucepan; add 4 tablespoons of the oil, the garlic, and rosemary. Pour in enough cold water to cover the beans by 1 inch. Cover and simmer for 1 to 1½ hours, stirring occasionally, until tender. Add additional water as needed. Season to taste with salt and pepper. Cool.

If canned beans are used: Place the beans and their liquid in a pot. Add 4 tablespoons of the oil, the garlic, and rosemary. Add water, if needed, to cover the beans. Cover and simmer for 5 to 10 minutes, stirring occasionally to avoid sticking. Season with salt and pepper to taste. Cool.

Spoon the cooked beans into individual dishes, drizzle them with the remaining 3 tablespoons oil, and top them with the caviar. Serve cold or at room temperature.

# Melanzane al Forno con Pomodori Salsa

BAKED EGGPLANT WITH FRESH
TOMATO SAUCE

The first time I had this dish was in a restaurant called Mustard's in California's Napa Valley. It was so outstanding that I re-created this simple recipe to enjoy at home. It has a very authentic Italian flavor.

8 to 10 Japanese eggplants
1 whole head of garlic, separated into 6 cloves and minced
1 cup olive oil
Salt
Freshly ground black pepper
Fresh Tomato Sauce (recipe follows)

Preheat the oven to 400°F.

Wash and dry the eggplants. Starting about ½ inch from the stem end, slice the eggplants into fans, cutting them lengthwise into 3 or 4 sections and taking care not to cut through the stems. In a bowl, combine the garlic with the olive oil, reserving 2 tablespoons of oil. Spoon the garlic mixture over the eggplants, pushing it between the slices.

Line a baking pan with foil and brush the foil with the remaining 2 tablespoons oil. Place the prepared eggplants on the foil, spreading them flat in a fan shape. Brush with additional olive oil and salt and pepper to taste. Bake for 20 minutes, or until tender.

Spoon the cold tomato sauce on serving plates and place the eggplant on top. Serve at once.

## FRESH TOMATO SAUCE

3 pounds ripe tomatoes
2 tablespoons fresh oregano, or 2 teaspoons dried
½ cup minced fresh basil leaves
¼ cup coarsely chopped fresh parsley
4 garlic cloves, minced
⅓ cup olive oil
Salt
Freshly ground black pepper

Peel and halve the tomatoes. Squeeze out and discard the seeds and chop the tomatoes fine. Or cut the tomatoes into large chunks and pass them through a tomato pulper. Add the oregano, basil, parsley, and garlic and blend until smooth. Add the olive oil in a thin stream and season to taste with salt and pepper. Set aside.

The sauce can be served immediately or can be left to ripen in the refrigerator for several hours or overnight. Serve cold, discarding excess liquid.

# Asparagi con Uova
## ASPARAGUS AND EGGS

When we are in Italy during the asparagus season, it is always a joy to see how many delightful ways they serve this vegetable. One of my favorites is the following recipe, where the surprise is that instead of hollandaise sauce, the asparagus is topped with a golden fried egg.

Informality is the key to enjoying this dish. Each diner picks up a spear with his fingers and dips it into the egg yolk.

Many years ago, I found a set of French asparagus plates in an antiques shop. They are beautifully decorated and each plate has a deep well for the sauce, or for holding the fried egg.

When I can find quail eggs, in Chinatown or in a local market, I use two of them for each serving. The tiny fried eggs make a stunning presentation.

48 asparagus spears, trimmed and peeled
3 tablespoons unsalted butter or margarine
1 garlic clove, minced
8 eggs (or 16 quail eggs)
Salt
Freshly ground black pepper
Grated Parmesan cheese (optional)

Tie the asparagus in a bundle with kitchen string and steam it standing up in a pot of simmering water or on a steam tray set above a large pot of boiling water. When it is tender-crisp, drain the asparagus, remove the string, and place 6 spears each on 8 heated plates.

In a large skillet, melt half the butter with half of the garlic over moderate heat and fry half the eggs sunny side up, with the yolks slightly runny. With a metal spatula, carefully transfer the eggs and place them on the plates with the asparagus. Repeat with the remaining butter, garlic, and eggs. Season to taste with salt and pepper and Parmesan cheese, if you like.

# Risotto con Funghi
## RICE WITH MUSHROOMS

This is the only way to prepare a real risotto. The rice is not boiled in water but is sautéed in broth, which is added gradually and must be watched constantly. So invite guests into the kitchen while you prepare it for their dinner. It's served as a separate course in heated shallow soup bowls—the authentic Italian way.

6 tablespoons unsalted butter
1 onion, finely chopped

In a large heavy skillet, melt 4 tablespoons of the butter until foamy. Add the onion and sauté over medium heat

2½ cups arborio rice

6 to 8 cups hot pareve chicken broth or Vegetable Stock (see page 391)

½ cup thinly sliced domestic mushrooms

½ cup sliced dried porcini mushrooms, soaked in water for 30 minutes

¼ cup minced parsley

½ to 1 cup cream

1 cup freshly grated Parmesan cheese

Salt

Freshly ground black pepper

until soft. Add the rice and mix well with a wooden spoon. Add 1 or 2 ladles of hot broth or enough to cover the rice. Cook, stirring constantly, as the broth is absorbed. Continue adding broth, a little at a time, until the rice is just tender, 10 to 15 minutes.

In a small skillet, melt 1 tablespoon of the butter and sauté the domestic mushrooms until soft.

With a slotted spoon, transfer the porcini mushrooms from their soaking liquid to a bowl. Strain the soaking liquid into a small saucepan; bring to a boil and simmer for 5 to 10 minutes, until thick and the flavor intensifies.

Add the sautéed mushrooms, the porcini, parsley, and cream to the rice mixture. Mix well and cook 3 to 4 minutes longer. Risotto should be served al dente—creamy and chewy—never mushy, so do not overcook. When the rice is tender but firm to the bite, blend in ½ cup of the Parmesan cheese and the remaining 1 tablespoon butter. Season to taste with salt and pepper. Serve immediately in heated shallow bowls. Garnish each serving with the reduced porcini liquid. Serve the remaining Parmesan in a bowl, to be passed separately.

# GORGONZOLA E MIELE
## GORGONZOLA AND HONEY

Some food combinations are so unusual and unexpectedly delicious that you simply have to try them. Words alone can't describe the exciting flavors.

The first time we were served this combination of Gorgonzola and sweet, almost crystallized, honey was in Ristorante del Pescatore in Canneto sul Oglio, Italy. What a wonderful surprise! The tart and tangy taste of the cheese with the sweetness of the honey made our taste buds tingle.

When honey sits on the kitchen shelf long enough it crystallizes by itself. If you don't have any crystallized honey, by all means use regular honey.

Served on a plate with slices of pears or apples, this cheese delight will win raves. For a light meal, no other dessert is needed.

½ pound Gorgonzola or other blue cheese

1 cup crystallized honey

Place a slice of cheese on each serving plate and spoon a dollop of honey on the side. Serve at once with toast triangles or hot crusty bread.

# TIRAMISÚ
## ITALIAN LAYERED DESSERT

This is a very special dessert found in many restaurants in northern Italy. Each one has its own version, a little different from all the others. The Biscotti alla Nevio (Ladyfingers) are dipped in coffee and layered with the custard and mascarpone, a creamy Italian cheese, or whipped cream. I have included a recipe for Ladyfingers, but you may substitute packaged ones if you don't have time to make them. My favorite Tiramisú has unsweetened cocoa sprinkled on top.

2 cups cold espresso or strong black coffee

¼ to ½ cup rum

24 Biscotti alla Nevio (recipe follows)

6 eggs, separated

6 tablespoons sugar

1 pound mascarpone, or 1 pound ricotta blended until smooth

12 ounces semisweet chocolate, chopped (1½ cups)

Unsweetened cocoa powder

Combine the coffee and rum in a shallow bowl. Dip the biscotti in the coffee mixture and place 1 layer of biscotti on the bottom of a rectangular or oval glass baking dish, 8×10×2 inches.

In a large mixing bowl, beat the egg yolks with the sugar until light. Stir the mascarpone or ricotta into the egg yolk mixture and blend until smooth.

In another large mixing bowl, beat the egg whites until stiff but not dry. Gently fold the egg whites into the yolk mixture. Spoon half the yolk mixture over the layer of biscotti. Sprinkle with the chopped chocolate. Place another layer of the coffee-dipped biscotti on top of the custard mixture. Repeat with another layer of the remaining custard. Sprinkle a generous amount of the cocoa over the entire surface. Cover with plastic wrap and foil and refrigerate for at least 1 hour.

# BISCOTTI ALLA NEVIO
## LADYFINGERS

MAKES ABOUT 24

3 eggs, separated

⅛ teaspoon salt

2 tablespoons granulated sugar

1 teaspoon vanilla extract

1 cup powdered sugar, sifted

¾ cup flour, sifted

Preheat the oven to 350°F.

In the large bowl of an electric mixer, beat the egg whites with the salt until they begin to thicken. Gradually add the granulated sugar and continue beating until they form a stiff meringue, about 1 minute. Set aside.

In a large bowl, beat the egg yolks, vanilla, and powdered sugar for 3 to 4 minutes, until thick and light in color. Gently fold the yolk mixture into the meringue. Sift small amounts of the flour on top of the meringue mixture, gently folding until completely absorbed, but do not overmix.

Line a baking sheet with foil, then oil and flour the foil. Fit a pastry bag with a plain round tip (⅝ inch in diameter). With a rubber spatula, carefully fill the bag with the meringue and pipe Ladyfingers 3 inches long and 1 inch wide on the prepared baking sheet. Bake for 6 to 8 minutes, or until evenly brown and somewhat crisp. Remove from the oven and use a metal spatula to transfer them to racks to cool. Store in an airtight container.

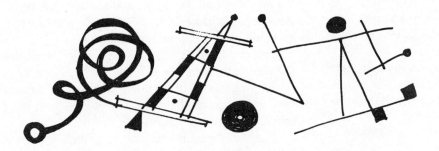

Mozzarella Marinara

Manicotti Melanzane

Peperoni Arrostiti con Acciughe

Insalata di Finocchio

Affogato

Biscotti (see page 47)

Espresso

SUGGESTED BEVERAGE:
Italian red Chianti wine

Our Italians friends have inspired me to buy the special equipment needed to make some of our favorite recipes—including a pasta maker, a gelato machine for icy desserts, and a cappuccino machine.

Some of the recipes that follow, from the small hillside towns of northern Italy, have never appeared before in a cookbook—let alone a Jewish one.

# MOZZARELLA MARINARA
## FRIED CHEESE WITH TOMATO SAUCE

This is another of those dishes that is so impressive in Italian restaurants and so easy to make at home.

The cheese cubes should be soft and melted inside, so it is important to fry them just moments before serving. Have the sauce ready to spoon onto individual serving plates, place the fried cheese on top, and serve at once.

1 pound mozzarella cheese, finely diced

6 eggs

1¼ cups bread crumbs

1 teaspoon dried oregano

2 garlic cloves, minced

½ teaspoon salt

2 tablespoons dry vermouth or brandy

2 tablespoons grated Parmesan cheese

2 parsley sprigs, stems removed

4 fresh basil leaves

1 cup flour

Oil for frying

Classic Marinara Sauce (see page 300)

Melt the mozzarella over hot water in a double boiler. Pour it into the large mixing bowl of an electric mixer and beat in 2 of the eggs. Add ¼ cup of the bread crumbs, the oregano, half the garlic, and salt and mix well. Press the cheese mixture into a 5×7-inch glass dish. Cover and chill at least 1 hour, or until firm.

In a bowl, lightly beat the remaining 4 eggs. Blend in the vermouth. Set aside.

In a processor or blender, process the remaining 1 cup bread crumbs, Parmesan cheese, parsley, basil, and remaining garlic. Set aside.

Cut the cheese mixture into 1½-inch squares (about 15 pieces). Dip each into the flour, then the egg mixture, and finally into the bread crumb mixture to coat evenly. Place on paper towels and chill 30 minutes in the refrigerator.

In a heavy skillet or deep-fryer, heat 3 inches of oil to 375°F on a deep-frying thermometer. Fry the cheese pieces, a few at a time, until evenly golden brown on both sides. Drain on paper towels. Serve at once with Classic Marinara Sauce.


# MANICOTTI MELANZANE
## ROLLED EGGPLANT WITH THREE SAUCES

This Italian eggplant casserole is baked with a Parmesan cheese sauce and served with two other sauces, resulting in the colors of the Italian flag. The contrasting colors and the herb garnish are eye-appealing as well as delicious. This is a wonderful dish to serve for a dairy menu on Shavuoth, when we want to include lots of cheeses.

2 pounds ricotta or hoop cheese

1 cup grated Parmesan cheese

3 tablespoons minced parsley

3 tablespoons minced fresh basil, or 2 teaspoons dried

4 eggs

2 large eggplants

Flour

¼ cup olive oil, or as needed

8 ounces mozzarella cheese, cut into sticks 2 inches long and ½ inch wide and thick

Creamy Parmesan Sauce (recipe follows)

Sweet Pepper Sauce (recipe follows)

Spinach Sauce (recipe follows)

Fresh basil leaves

In a large bowl, combine the ricotta, Parmesan, parsley, basil, and eggs. Blend thoroughly. Cover with plastic wrap and chill.

Slice the eggplants lengthwise, ⅛ to ¼ inch thick. Dredge the slices in flour, shaking off the excess.

In a heavy skillet over medium heat, heat the oil and sauté the eggplant slices on both sides until soft and lightly browned. Drain on paper towels. Cool.

Preheat the oven to 350°F.

Place 1 or 2 tablespoons of cheese filling (depending on the size of the slices) across the narrow portion of a slice of eggplant. Press a stick of mozzarella into the filling. Roll up the eggplant tightly around the filling. Place the eggplant rolls, seams side down, in a buttered baking dish. (You can cover them with plastic wrap and foil at this point and store in the refrigerator for 1 to 2 hours; do not freeze.)

Spoon the Creamy Parmesan Sauce over the eggplant rolls. Bake for 15 minutes, or until hot and bubbling. Spoon Sweet Pepper Sauce on one half of heated plates and the Spinach Sauce on the other half. With a slotted spoon, carefully place one or two of the eggplant rolls on top. Garnish with basil leaves. Serve immediately.

## CREAMY PARMESAN SAUCE

6 tablespoons unsalted butter

4 tablespoons flour

2½ cups hot milk

4 or 5 tablespoons grated Parmesan cheese

1 teaspoon salt

Nutmeg

In a heavy saucepan, melt the butter over medium heat. When it foams, stir in the flour all at once and cook gently for a few minutes without letting the flour brown. Take the pan off the heat and gradually pour in the hot milk, stirring constantly with a wire whisk.

Return the pan to the heat. Stir in the Parmesan cheese. Season to taste with salt and nutmeg. Cook, stirring constantly, until the sauce is moderately thick. Place a little butter on top to prevent a skin from forming and cover with foil until ready to use.

## SWEET PEPPER SAUCE

2 tablespoons olive oil
1 onion, finely chopped
1 celery stalk, finely chopped
2 red bell peppers, finely
   chopped
⅓ cup chopped fresh tomato
Salt
Freshly ground black pepper
1 tablespoon cream

In a skillet, heat the oil over moderate heat and sauté the onion, celery, and peppers until soft, about 10 minutes. Add the tomatoes. Season to taste with salt and pepper and cook over low heat for 20 minutes. Pass the sauce through a sieve or fine strainer and add the cream. Blend thoroughly with a whisk.

## SPINACH SAUCE

1 pound spinach, with stems
   removed
4 tablespoons unsalted butter
1 garlic clove, minced
1 cup cream
Salt
Freshly ground black pepper

Wash the spinach in cold water, rinse carefully several times, and drain.

Cook the spinach in boiling water until tender, about 5 minutes. Drain well, cool, and press out the excess liquid. Chop fine or process in a processor until puréed.

In a heavy saucepan, heat the butter and sauté the garlic. Add the spinach purée and continue cooking and blending. Blend in the cream and simmer, stirring constantly, until thick. Season to taste with salt and pepper. Set aside until ready to serve.

# PEPERONI ARROSTITI CON ACCIUGHE
## ROASTED PEPPERS WITH ANCHOVIES

Here is a never-fail, really easy way to roast peppers. I always try to keep a bowl of them, covered with oil and garlic, in the refrigerator for an appetizer or to garnish a salad.

When selecting peppers, choose the ones that are smooth and shiny, without brown punctures or soft spots. They should be crisp and firm to the touch.

For an easy appetizer, arrange the peppers on a large platter or shallow serving dish, garnished with anchovy fillets, olives, and parsley or watercress.

4 to 6 firm, crisp red, yellow,
   or green bell peppers

Preheat the oven to 375°F.
   Place a large sheet of foil on the lower rack of the

2 to 3 garlic cloves, minced
Olive oil
1 can (2 ounces) anchovy
  fillets
Parsley sprigs for garnish

oven. Place the peppers on the rack above, in the middle of the oven. Bake for 20 to 30 minutes, or until the skin has puffed and darkened slightly on top. Turn each pepper over and continue baking for 10 to 15 minutes longer.

Remove the peppers from the oven, and while they are still warm, very carefully peel off the skins, reserving the juices. Pull out the stems and discard the seeds. Cut the peppers into segments that follow their natural ridges. Layer the peppers in a bowl with the juices, garlic, and enough oil to cover. Cover with plastic wrap and refrigerate.

When ready to serve, arrange the peppers on a serving dish and garnish with anchovies and parsley sprigs.

# Insalata di Finocchio
## Fresh Fennel Salad

Italians serve a salad dressing, called *pinzimonio*, in which no vinegar or lemon juice is used. It is just a mixture of olive oil, coarse salt, and black pepper, which they serve as a dip for raw finocchio (fennel), celery, and sweet peppers.

This salad, which stars fennel, has a dressing inspired by *pinzimonio*, to which I like to add just a little balsamic vinegar.

3 or 4 medium fennel bulbs
1 small red onion, peeled,
  halved, and thinly sliced
½ cup olive oil
Salt
2 tablespoons balsamic
  vinegar
½ cup small black Italian olives for garnish

Trim the tops and bottoms from the fennel and cut in half lengthwise. Then cut the fennel crosswise into thin slices and place them in a bowl with the onion slices. Toss with the olive oil and salt and chill in the refrigerator.

Just before serving, spoon the salad onto chilled plates. Sprinkle each serving with balsamic vinegar and garnish with olives.

# AFFOGATO
## COFFEE–ICE CREAM DESSERT

Almost every restaurant in Italy will serve you this special dessert, but you have to ask for it.

It has many names, depending on which city you are in. Often served in a deep saucer, sundae dish, or wineglass, it is simply a scoop of gelato (Italian ice cream) with espresso poured over it and topped with Caramel-Nut Brittle.

8 large scoops Gelato alla Vaniglia (recipe follows)
2 cups freshly brewed espresso or very strong black coffee
1 cup Caramel-Nut Brittle (recipe follows)

Place a scoop of gelato in each bowl and pour ¼ cup hot espresso over it. Sprinkle with brittle and serve at once.

## GELATO ALLA VANIGLIA
### VANILLA ICE CREAM

To enjoy the rich flavor and aroma of real old-fashioned vanilla ice cream, you should use vanilla beans. They are available at most fine markets and easy to use in many recipes. If you use vanilla extract, be sure to add it to ingredients that have cooled—never to hot mixtures.

2 cups milk
1 cup sugar
1 vanilla bean, split lengthwise, (or 1 teaspoon vanilla extract)
6 egg yolks
2 cups cream

In a large heavy saucepan, heat the milk and ½ cup of the sugar until it begins to boil. Add the vanilla bean (do not add the extract, if using, until later), cover, turn off the heat, and set aside for 5 minutes.

In the bowl of an electric mixer, beat the egg yolks with the remaining ½ cup sugar until thick and pale in color, about 3 minutes. Slowly add ½ cup of the warm milk mixture to the egg yolks, blending thoroughly. Return this egg yolk mixture to the saucepan; simmer and cook until thick (about 180°F on a candy thermometer). Pour into a heatproof bowl.

Fill a larger bowl with ice cubes and cold water and place the bowl of custard inside. Add the cream (and vanilla extract, if using) and stir until the mixture is cool. Cover with plastic wrap and chill in the refrigerator.

Pour the chilled mixture into the canister of an ice cream maker, removing the vanilla bean, and freeze according to manufacturer's directions.

# CARAMEL-NUT BRITTLE

¾ cup whole or sliced almonds

1 cup sugar

¼ cup water

Preheat the oven to 325°F.

Toast the almonds on a foil-lined baking sheet until lightly browned, about 10 minutes. Cool.

In a small heavy saucepan, combine the sugar and water. Cook over medium heat, stirring until the sugar dissolves. Continue cooking, without stirring, until the syrup turns a light caramel color. Remove from the heat and stir in the almonds.

Pour the mixture onto a lightly oiled baking sheet or marble slab, spread it out with a metal spatula, and let it cool, loosening it with a metal spatula as it hardens. Break the brittle into small pieces; place them in a processor and process until coarsely chopped.

# ITALIAN VEAL DINNER

FOR 8

Crostata di Cipolle

Ossobuco

Focaccia

Tuscan Salad Bar

Sorbetto al Limone

Biscotti (see page 47)

Espresso

SUGGESTED BEVERAGE:

Barolo or Barbaresco or
any robust Italian red wine

All the recipes in this authentic menu are ever so simple to make, and the entire meal can be handled on a limited budget. The appetizer, salad bar, entrée, and dessert just *look* expensive. Try this dinner out on eight of your favorite people and then double the number of guests the next time around.

By the way, did you know that Ossobuco is kosher? It's just veal shanks with an Italian accent. The Onion Tart and Balloon Bread add a little glamour, and only pennies to the total cost. And be sure to serve a robust Italian wine.

## CROSTATA DI CIPOLLE
ONION TART

Basic Prebaked Pie Crust (recipe follows)

5 tablespoons olive oil

2 pounds (3 large) onions, thinly sliced

2 garlic cloves, minced

Salt

Freshly ground black pepper

1 can (2 ounces) anchovy fillets, drained

10 pearl onions, boiled and peeled, for garnish

Prepare the pie crust and cool. Preheat the oven to 350°F.

Heat 4 tablespoons of the olive oil in a large skillet. Add the onions and garlic. Season to taste with salt and pepper. Cover and cook on low heat for 30 minutes. Stir occasionally to avoid sticking. Do not allow onions to brown.

Place the onion mixture in the baked pastry shell. Garnish with anchovies and pearl onions in a circular pattern. Sprinkle with the remaining 1 tablespoon oil. Bake for 30 minutes, or until golden brown.

# BASIC PREBAKED PIE CRUST

I usually like to prepare this crust in advance. Cover it with plastic wrap and foil and store it in the freezer, ready to bring to room temperature and bake. A wonderful feeling to know you have this treasure in your freezer.

MAKES ONE 11-INCH PIE CRUST

2½ cups flour
½ teaspoon salt
¼ pound plus 4 tablespoons unsalted margarine
1 egg
3 to 4 tablespoons water

Preheat the oven to 350°F.

In the bowl of an electric mixer, combine the flour, salt, and margarine. Blend together until they reach the consistency of cornmeal. Add the egg and water and mix until the dough holds together. Form the dough into a ball and chill in the refrigerator.

Roll out the dough, about ¼ inch thick, onto a large sheet or 2 sheets of wax paper, forming a circle large enough to fit and overlap an 11-inch round tart pan with a removable bottom. For easier handling, cover the pastry with another sheet of wax paper and fold the pastry in half. (The wax paper prevents the halves from sticking to each other.)

Lift the folded pastry from the bottom sheet of wax paper and slip it into half the tart pan. Unfold the pastry and remove the wax paper.

Brush a sheet of wax paper with margarine and place it inside the pastry, overlapping around the sides. Cover with another piece of wax paper with the cut ends in the opposite directions.

Fill the center of the lined tart shell with uncooked rice or baker's jewels (available in kitchen specialty stores). Bake for 15 to 20 minutes, or until the sides of the pastry begin to brown. Carefully remove the wax paper with the rice and continue baking until the bottom of the pastry is lightly browned. Remove from the oven and cool.

# OSSOBUCO

## VEAL SHANKS WITH VEGETABLES

Since the veal shanks are cooked on top of the stove, it is important to use a skillet large and deep enough to hold them all. This Ossobuco tastes better than any I've ever eaten in a restaurant.

8 veal shank pieces, cut 2 inches thick
½ cup flour
Salt
Freshly ground black pepper
⅓ cup olive oil
2 large onions, chopped
4 garlic cloves, minced
3 carrots, finely chopped
3 celery stalks, finely chopped
½ cup chopped mushrooms
1 cup dry white wine
1 can (28 ounces) crushed Italian-style tomatoes
1 tablespoon tomato paste
3 tablespoons chopped parsley
8 whole mushrooms, cut in half or quarters if large
Gremolata for garnish (recipe follows)

Tie the veal shanks with kitchen string. Season the flour to taste with salt and pepper and lightly dust the shanks with the flour. Heat the oil in a large heavy skillet over medium heat. Brown the veal shanks on all sides. Transfer them to a platter. Add the onion, garlic, carrots, celery, and chopped mushrooms to the skillet and sauté until lightly browned.

Place the veal shanks on top of the onion mixture; add the wine, raise the heat, and simmer briskly until the wine reduces by half. Add the tomatoes, tomato paste, and parsley. Cover and simmer gently for 1½ to 2 hours, basting and turning veal every half hour, until the meat is tender enough to fall away from the bone; add the whole mushrooms 10 minutes before serving. Season to taste with salt and pepper.

Snip off the strings around the shanks. Spoon the vegetable sauce onto heated plates; place the shanks on top and spoon additional sauce over them. Garnish with Gremolata.

## GREMOLATA

½ cup fresh parsley leaves
2 tablespoons lemon zest
1 garlic clove, peeled

Place the parsley, lemon zest, and garlic in the bowl of a food processor and process until minced and well blended.

# FOCACCIA
## HOT ITALIAN BALLOON BREAD

While visiting a friend's restaurant in Italy, a plate of Focaccia, a hot bread made from pizza dough, was placed on our table. It was baked in a special wood-burning oven at an extremely hot temperature, until the dough expanded like a balloon. Olive oil and salt were generously sprinkled on top and it was served piping hot.

Back at home, I was determined to serve Focaccia myself in the Italian manner. Using pizza dough, I rolled out small rounds, placed them on a baking sheet in the hottest part of the oven, baked them until they puffed up, and then sprinkled them with olive oil and kosher salt. It was so easy, and great fun to serve as an appetizer or an accompaniment to a salad.

1 recipe pizza dough (see
 page 299)
Olive oil
Kosher salt

Preheat the oven to 450°F.

Prepare the pizza dough, allowing it to rise. Tear off small pieces the size of a golf ball; place them on a floured board and press them into flat circles with your palms. Using a rolling pin, roll out each piece of dough into a perfect circle about ¼ inch thick, giving the dough one-quarter turns as you roll it.

Grease a heavy-duty nonstick baking sheet or pizza brick with olive oil. Place the pieces of dough on the prepared baking sheet and put it in the oven. Do not open the oven door at all during the first 3 or 4 minutes; undisturbed, the breads should puff up like balloons. Continue baking until golden brown, about 5 minutes longer. Remove the breads from the oven, drizzle them with olive oil, and sprinkle with kosher salt.

# TUSCAN SALAD BAR

Serve this salad bar just as they do in Italy—with bowls of crisp vegetables so that guests can create their own salads, using just as much oil, vinegar, salt, and pepper as they prefer.

It is worth the effort to find the freshest vegetables. Often I must shop at three or four markets, or find a local grower, but when you have tasted vine-ripened tomatoes, cucumbers, lettuce, and red, yellow, and green bell peppers fresh from the farm, you won't regret the time spent.

Dressing a salad in Italy is done at the table, just before serving. Choose individual salad bowls large enough to give all the greens or vegetables room to be tossed. Pour the salt, oil, and vinegar directly over the greens in the bowls. Toss gently but thoroughly to distribute the dressing evenly. This is important with tender greens and soft lettuce, which can bruise easily.

LETTUCE AND VEGETABLES

Romaine, radicchio, and arugula

Red onions, thinly sliced

Cherry tomatoes, red and yellow

Tomatoes, thinly sliced

Fennel, thinly sliced

Red, yellow, or green bell peppers, thinly sliced

Grated carrots

DRESSING

Olive oil

Balsamic vinegar

Salt

Freshly ground black pepper

Wash and refresh the vegetables in ice water. Drain thoroughly and dry; place in individual bowls, cover with plastic wrap, and refrigerate for not more than 1 hour. Put out bowls of vegetables and dressing ingredients and let guests help themselves.

# SORBETTO AL LIMONE
## LEMON SHERBET

1 cup lemon juice

2 cups Sugar Syrup (see page 38)

2 tablespoons Grand Marnier (orange liqueur)

1 tablespoon lemon zest

Combine all the ingredients in a large bowl and stir well. Pour into the canister of an ice cream maker and freeze according to manufacturer's directions. Or place in the freezer and freeze until firm, 3 to 6 hours, stirring occasionally with a fork to break up ice crystals. Continue stirring and freezing until the mixture is set.

Scoop the sherbet into chilled glass bowls or goblets and garnish with sliced fresh fruit.

# Pasta Party

## FOR 8

Ever since our first trip to Italy, when I had a taste of truly fresh pasta in an amazing variety of shapes, I've loved making my own pasta.

I try to include a fresh pasta or noodle course whenever we have company, but for me the ultimate thrill is to create a pasta party. Everyone enjoys the menu, and loves to pitch in with the preparation.

The first course is often simply marinated eggplant or artichokes simmered in an aromatic sauce. But the rest of the menu usually consists of two or more pasta dishes. The sauces and pastas in this menu are all interchangeable—enough to start you on the road to improvising your own party. Mix and match them as you like. The important thing to keep in mind is to serve small portions—just enough so each guest enjoys a taste of each dish.

All the pastas can be made ahead and dried the sauces can be prepared the morning of your party. Then you just have to assemble everything before serving.

Sometimes we ask guests to come early and everyone makes the pasta together. We serve a glass of wine, pass out aprons, and have the pasta machine ready. The hosts don't have to do anything but supply the ingredients and direct traffic.

For the full Italian atmosphere, don't forget the red-checked tablecloths, breadsticks, and Bonet—a custard dessert you can make the day before—followed by espresso. And serve lots of Italian wine. It need not be the expensive kind, either.

# Marinated Eggplant

2 large eggplants
Kosher salt
Olive oil
⅓ cup balsamic or sherry
   vinegar
Freshly ground black pepper
1 cup fresh basil leaves,
   chopped
4 garlic cloves, minced

Cut the eggplants lengthwise into ½-inch slices, but do not peel. Sprinkled both sides with Kosher salt and set aside for 1 hour.

In a large heavy skillet, heat 1 inch of oil over medium heat. Pat the eggplant slices dry and fry them until golden brown, about 3 minutes a side. Remove immediately, without draining, to a 9x12-inch baking dish, arranging the eggplant slices in a single layer. Brush with the vinegar and sprinkle with pepper, basil, and garlic. Repeat the layering until all the eggplant, vinegar, basil, and garlic are used.

Cool, cover with plastic wrap, and refrigerate. Turn the eggplant from time to time and marinate overnight, if possible.

Serve as an appetizer, or as a first course with Fresh Tomato Sauce (see page 271).

# Basic Pasta Dough— Processor Method

MAKES 1 POUND

4 cups flour
½ teaspoon salt
4 eggs
2 tablespoons olive oil

Place the flour and salt on a wooden pastry board and make a well in the center. Break the eggs into the well and add the oil. With a fork, beat the eggs and oil, gradually drawing the flour from the edge of the well and incorporating it into the egg mixture to form a dough that can be gathered into a ball.

Knead the dough for 5 to 10 minutes, working in extra flour as necessary, until it is no longer sticky. Cover dough with inverted bowl until ready to roll out.

Homemade pasta is far superior to the commercial kind. But don't hesitate to buy dried pasta shapes that are hard to make by hand, and use them with the sauces in this menu. Mixing the dough is simple, but rolling it out can be very difficult. My solution is to buy a hand-cranked pasta machine; if you shop around a bit, you can find one for less than twenty-five dollars. It will pay for itself many times over. Today many of our Italian friends prefer the machine method as a time-saver to the ancient hand-rolled way.

# Basic Pasta Dough— Processor Method

The quantities and directions that follow require a large capacity food processor. If your processor has a more limited capacity, make the dough in two or more batches.

MAKES 1 POUND

3 cups flour
½ teaspoon salt
4 large eggs
2 tablespoons olive oil
2 tablespoons water

Place the flour and salt in the processor fitted with the steel blade. Turn the machine on and off once. Then, with the machine running, drop in 1 egg and, the instant it is blended in, turn off the machine. Repeat with the remaining eggs, until the dough is crumbly or resembles a coarse meal. Add the olive oil and water and process just until the dough begins to come away from the side of the bowl. (Do not overprocess.)

Remove the dough to a floured wooden board and knead just until smooth. Divide the dough into 3 or 4 parts for easier handling. When rolling out the first piece, cover the remainder with a large bowl so the dough does not dry out.

# Green Pasta Dough— Hand Method

MAKES 1 POUND

Red or orange pasta can be prepared using the same quantities and method as the green, substituting beets, tomatoes, or roasted red bell peppers for the red and carrots for the orange.

3 cups flour
Pinch of salt
2 eggs
1 tablespoon olive oil
1 to 2 tablespoons minced
    fresh basil
1 tablespoon Spinach Purée
    (recipe follows)

Place the flour and salt on a wooden pastry board and make a well in the center. Break the eggs into the well; add the oil, basil, and Spinach Purée. With a fork, beat the egg mixture well, gradually drawing the flour from the edge of the well and incorporating it into the egg mixture to form a dough that can be gathered into a ball.

Knead the dough for 5 to 10 minutes, working in extra flour as necessary, until it is no longer sticky.

## SPINACH PURÉE

1 pound fresh spinach, stems
    removed

Wash the spinach leaves thoroughly several times. Drop the leaves into salted boiling water and boil for 5 minutes. Drain, cool under cold water, and squeeze dry. Place in a processor or blender and process until puréed.

## TO ROLL OUT PASTA WITH A PASTA MACHINE

Set the rollers at the widest opening. Divide the dough into 4 parts for easier handling. Working with one part at a time, flatten the dough with the palm of your hand into a thick strip no wider than the machine. Dust it lightly with flour and crank it through the machine. Fold it in half or thirds, pressing it down with your fingertips, dust with flour, turn it 90 degrees (a quarter turn) and run it through the machine again. Repeat this process 3 or 4 more times, dusting with flour, until the dough is smooth, elastic, and no longer sticky. Now the dough is ready to stretch into a long sheet.

Set the machine to the next opening, bringing the rollers closer together, and run the dough through. This time, do not fold or turn the dough. Set the rollers another notch closer and run the dough through again. Continue rolling the dough with a smaller opening each time, stopping just before the next-to-narrowest setting. (The dough strip will become very long, so allow ample work space, or cut the dough in shorter strips.)

For stuffed pasta, follow the directions in the recipe, using the pasta sheets while they are still moist. For noodles, let the pasta dry about 15 minutes (so that the noodles don't stick together), depending on the temperature and humidity of the kitchen. If the kitchen is hot, the pasta will dry quickly.

Attachments are available for cutting the pasta into 1- to 3-inch-wide plain edge or scalloped edge. These sizes have special names, such as tagliatelle, lasagne, and angels' hair to name a few. You can even make kasha and varnishka ''bows.''

Sprinkle the cut pasta generously with flour and continue to dry on towel-lined baking sheets.

# PRIMAVERA CREAM SAUCE WITH PASTA

¼ pound unsalted butter

4 garlic cloves, minced

1 cup Vegetable Stock (see page 391) or pareve chicken broth

½ cup cream

2 medium zucchini, cut into julienne

5 medium carrots, peeled and cut into julienne

½ cup fresh or frozen peas

6 broccoli florets, blanched

1 pound fresh tagliatelle (¼ or ½ inch wide), boiled and drained

Parmesan cheese

In a heavy skillet, melt the butter and sauté the garlic until soft. Add the stock, bring to a boil, and reduce the heat into a simmer. Add the cream and mix well.

In a large saucepan, bring salted water to a boil. Add the zucchini and carrots and cook for 2 to 3 minutes. Drain and add to the sauce. Fold in the peas and broccoli. Add the pasta and toss until completely coated. Serve at once. Pass a bowl of Parmesan cheese.

# PESTO GENOVESE WITH PASTA AND POTATOES

In Italy, nobody takes food for granted; everybody is interested in what they eat, and takes pride in their regional specialties. We have often been invited to a friend's home in the small town of Thiene, not far from Venice. On one occasion, one of the guests was a cousin from a city near Genoa. He had actually hand-carried a large jar of his own homemade pesto sauce, so that the hostess could prepare it, Genovese-style, with sliced potatoes and pasta. This is his recipe.

2 cups fresh basil leaves, stemmed

2 garlic cloves

¼ cup pine nuts or walnuts

½ cup olive oil

1 teaspoon salt (or to taste)

½ cup freshly grated Parmesan cheese

2 tablespoons freshly grated Romano cheese

1 pound fresh tagliatelle, boiled and drained

3 medium potatoes, peeled, boiled, and thinly sliced

3 tablespoons unsalted butter, softened

In the bowl of a processor or blender, combine the basil, garlic, pine nuts, olive oil, and salt. Blend until the mixture is smooth and thick. If it seems too thick, blend in additional olive oil. Pour into a bowl, spoon a little olive oil over the top, cover with plastic wrap, and chill. Just before serving, mix in the cheeses.

To serve, drain the tagliatelle into a large heated bowl reserving some of the cooking liquid; add the prepared potatoes and toss with the soft butter. Add 1 or 2 tablespoons of the cooking liquid to the pesto. Pour into the pasta and potato mixture and toss to coat.

# PARSLEY PESTO SAUCE

When fresh basil is not available, this pesto sauce, using parsley, makes a fine substitute.

2 cups Italian flat-leaf parsley, stemmed and loosely packed

8 walnut halves

4 tablespoons cream

2 to 3 garlic cloves, minced

6 tablespoons freshly grated Parmesan cheese

½ cup olive oil

Salt

Freshly ground black pepper

In the bowl of a processor or blender, process the parsley, walnuts, cream, garlic, and Parmesan until smooth. With the machine running, add the olive oil in a thin stream. Season to taste with salt and pepper. Cover with plastic wrap and chill.

# SPAGHETTI ALLA PUTTANESCA

## SPAGHETTI WITH TOMATOES, CAPERS, ANCHOVIES, AND OLIVES

½ cup olive oil

6 to 8 garlic cloves, minced

¼ cup drained capers

1 can (2 ounces) flat anchovy fillets, drained

¼ cup coarsely chopped black ripe olives

¼ cup chopped fresh basil, or 1 tablespoon dried

2 cups Classic Marinara Sauce (see page 300)

½ teaspoon crushed dried red pepper

1 pound spaghetti, cooked al dente

In a large skillet, heat the oil and sauté the garlic over low heat until lightly browned. Add the capers, anchovies, olives, and basil. Process the Marinara Sauce coarsely and add to the oil mixture. Add the crushed red pepper and mix well. Simmer for 10 minutes.

To serve, drain the spaghetti and add to the sauce in the skillet; toss to coat. Serve at once.

# GNOCCHI VERDI

## SPINACH DUMPLINGS

Try rolling the gnocchi in ground nuts instead of flour; I prepare them that way for a friend whose diet restricted her from eating grains.

MAKES ABOUT 4 DOZEN

3 pounds fresh spinach

1 pound fresh ricotta cheese

5 egg yolks

3 cups grated Parmesan or Romano cheese

Salt

Freshly ground black pepper

Nutmeg

1 cup flour

½ pound unsalted butter

2 garlic cloves, minced

Rinse the spinach and remove the stems. Place in lightly salted boiling water and boil for 10 minutes. Drain, cool, and squeeze dry in cheesecloth; chop fine.

In the bowl of an electric mixer, combine the spinach, ricotta, egg yolks, and 2 cups of the cheese; mix well. Season to taste with salt, pepper, and nutmeg.

Place the flour in a large bowl. Roll the spinach mixture into 1½-inch balls; roll each ball in flour, shaking off the excess. Place on a towel-lined baking sheet and set aside.

Bring a large pot of water to a boil; reduce the heat to maintain a gentle simmer.

Melt the butter and add the garlic. Pour into heated serving dishes. Gently drop the gnocchi into the water without crowding. They should rise to the surface after 1 or 2 minutes. Remove with a slotted spoon and place in the prepared serving dishes. Sprinkle generously with Parmesan cheese. Pass additional grated cheese.

# RICOTTA RAVIOLI WITH GORGONZOLA-WALNUT SAUCE

We first enjoyed this dish at the Ristorante Gatto Bianco in Biella, a tiny town in northern Italy.

The creamy sauce is a blend of rich Gorgonzola cheese and nuts, garnished with chopped whole oranges—peel and all. The flavor is incredible, and the chopped oranges add a tang that keeps your taste buds busy to the last exciting bite. It is delicious with noodles or ravioli.

2 cups ricotta cheese
2 cups freshly grated Parmesan cheese
3 egg yolks
2 tablespoons minced parsley
1 tablespoon chopped fresh basil
Salt
Freshly ground black pepper
Basic Pasta Dough (see page 280)
Gorgonzola-Walnut Sauce (recipe follows)
1 small orange, unpeeled and chopped

In a large bowl, combine the ricotta, the Parmesan, the egg yolks, parsley, and basil. Stir until well blended. Season to taste with salt and pepper. Cover with plastic wrap and chill.

Roll out the pasta into 2 long thin sheets (see page 290). Imagine a checkerboard divided into 2-inch squares on one sheet of pasta. Using a pastry bag or a spoon, pipe out or spoon about 1 teaspoon of the cheese filling in the center of each square. Dip a pastry brush or your index finger into a bowl of water and paint vertical and horizontal lines along the checkerboard pattern between the mounds of cheese filling. Carefully place the second sheet of pasta on top of the first, pressing down firmly around each mound of filling and along the wet lines to seal the pasta sheets together.

With a ravioli cutter, pastry wheel, or small knife, cut the pasta into ravioli squares enclosing the filling. Place a kitchen towel on a baking sheet and dust it with flour. Place the ravioli on the floured towel. When they are dry on one side, turn them to allow the other side to dry. When thoroughly dry, the ravioli are easy to separate.

To cook the ravioli, drop them into lightly salted, rapidly boiling water and stir gently with a wooden spoon, to keep them from sticking together. Boil for 6 to 8 minutes, until tender.

To serve, drain the ravioli into the Gorgonzola-Walnut Sauce in the skillet and carefully spoon it over them to coat. With a large spoon, carefully transfer the ravioli and sauce evenly onto heated plates. Spoon the sauce left in the skillet on top. Spoon the chopped orange in the center of each serving.

## GORGONZOLA-WALNUT SAUCE

4 tablespoons unsalted butter
1 cup cream
6 ounces Gorgonzola or other blue cheese
¼ cup finely ground walnuts
Salt
Freshly ground black pepper
1 medium orange, unpeeled and chopped

In a heavy skillet, melt the butter over medium heat. Add the cream and stir well. Add the cheese, mashing it with a fork to blend. Stir in the walnuts. Cook over low heat, stirring constantly, until the sauce thickens. Season to taste with salt and pepper. Garnish with chopped orange.

# FUNGHI E FORMAGGIO IN INSALATA
## MUSHROOM AND PARMESAN CHEESE SALAD

10 large mushrooms, thinly sliced
Juice of 2 lemons
1 pound spinach, stems removed
½ pound Parmesan cheese
8 small fresh basil leaves
½ cup olive oil
Salt
Freshly ground black pepper

In a large bowl, toss the mushrooms with the lemon juice.

Wash the spinach and rinse several times; dry on paper towels. Place 4 large spinach leaves on each chilled salad plate. With a potato peeler, shave the Parmesan cheese into curls 1 inch wide. Add the shaved cheese, basil leaves, and ¼ cup of the olive oil to the mushrooms and toss lightly. Add remaining olive oil to taste. Season with salt and pepper. Spoon the mushroom mixture onto the center of each prepared salad plate. Serve immediately.

# BONET

## PIEDMONTE CUSTARD DESSERT

We have often seen this subtly flavored custard dessert in Italy, and were pleased to have it served to us recently in an Italian couple's home in Los Angeles. Our hostess, Daniella Pironti, said her family recipe dated to her mother's childhood. When she asked if I would like to take some home, I said, "I would rather have the recipe." She gave it to me in the original Italian version. Here is my translation:

6 tablespoons sugar

3 tablespoons cold water

8 eggs, separated

½ cup sugar

3 tablespoons cocoa powder, sifted

Zest of 1 lemon

13 small amaretti cookies, ground

2 cups milk

3 tablespoons Marsala or rum

Preheat the oven to 250°F.

In a small heavy saucepan, combine the sugar and water; cook over medium heat until caramel-colored, about 5 minutes. Quickly pour into a 5½x10½-inch glass baking dish and cool.

In the large bowl of an electric mixer, beat the egg yolks and sugar until light and fluffy, about 5 minutes. Add the cocoa, lemon zest, and cookies, then gradually, in a very thin stream, beat in the milk. Stir in the Marsala or rum.

In a separate bowl, beat the egg whites until soft peaks form. Fold this into the egg yolk mixture.

Pour the custard mixture into the prepared baking dish and cover with foil. Place in a larger baking dish filled with 2 inches of water and bake for 3 hours. Turn off the heat and cool in the oven for 15 minutes. Then cool at room temperature and refrigerate overnight. Invert onto a large platter, slice, and serve with the caramel sauce.

# Pizza Party

FOR 12

One of our favorite family get-togethers is an informal do-it-yourself pizza party. It adds to the fun of a birthday, anniversary, or any special occasion.

Prepare all the fillings in advance and simply set them out in bowls for everyone to make his or her own selections. Make the dough a half hour before everyone arrives and it will be ready to roll out and put in the oven. If you have any dough left over, place it in a plastic bag, refrigerate it, and the next day, follow my recipe for making breadsticks (see page 268). Another variation is to use this same dough to make Focaccia (see page 285).

The pizzas are the main attraction to this party menu, so the rest of the food should be fairly simple, with two festive dessert surprises. One pops like magic out of paper cups and the other combines three kinds of chocolate contained in the form of a truffle. Fried Zucchini Sticks can be nibbled while the pizzas are baking, and a tangy Italian salad accompanies them. Big red and white checked napkins add color—and if small children are present, I would advise the paper kind.

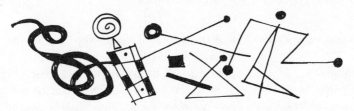

## Anchovy Aïoli
### ANCHOVY-GARLIC SAUCE

One Sunday afternoon, during our Jewish chefs' cooking get-together, Bruce Marder, an innovative chef, created this aïoli so we would have something to nibble on with an array of raw vegetables while we sipped our champagne and cooked. It is so delicious—with a distinctive flavor that anchovy lovers will enjoy.

2 cups cream

4 tablespoons unsalted butter

1 garlic clove, minced

2 cans (2 ounces each) anchovy fillets, drained and
chopped

3 tablespoons Vegetable
Stock (see page 391)

**RAW VEGETABLES**

Carrot sticks

Endive leaves

Small asparagus, trimmed

Celery sticks

Red, yellow, and green bell
peppers, stemmed, seeded,
and sliced

Zucchini sticks

Cherry tomatoes

In a heavy saucepan over medium heat, bring the cream to a boil; reduce the heat and simmer for 10 to 15 minutes, stirring occasionally, until it is thick enough to coat the back of a spoon and reduces to about 1 cup.

In a skillet, melt the butter; add the garlic, anchovies, and stock and simmer a few minutes. Add to the reduced cream and mix well. Transfer to a bowl and serve warm with raw vegetables.

# FRIED ZUCCHINI STICKS

These crisp and crunchy zucchini sticks go well with any menu. They must be fried at the last moment, however, to be at their crisp and crunchy best.

They can be served during Passover by substituting matzo meal cake flour for the flour and matzo meal for the bread crumbs.

4 medium zucchini, unpeeled

1 cup flour

1 cup bread crumbs

2 garlic cloves, peeled

6 fresh basil leaves, or 1 teaspoon dried basil

Salt

Freshly ground black pepper

2 to 3 eggs

Vegetable oil for frying

Grated Parmesan cheese

Slice the zucchini lengthwise into quarters; cut in half, crosswise, and set aside.

In a small brown paper bag, place the flour and set aside. In the bowl of a processor or blender, blend the bread crumbs, garlic, and basil. Season to taste with salt and pepper. Place this mixture in a small brown paper bag and set aside. Place the eggs in a bowl and beat well.

Drop 4 to 6 zucchini sticks into the bag containing the flour, shaking the bag to coat. Transfer to a metal strainer and shake off the excess flour. Dip the flour-coated zucchini into the beaten egg and then coat with the bread crumb mixture. Place on a baking sheet lined with paper towels. (You can hold them at this point for at least 1 hour.)

Preheat the oil in a deep-fryer or wok to 375°F.

Drop the coated zucchini sticks into the heated oil; do not crowd; fry until golden brown. Drain on paper towels. Transfer them to a napkin-covered platter; sprinkle with grated Parmesan Cheese. Serve immediately.

# DO-IT-YOURSELF PIZZA

When you order a pizza in Italy, it usually means you are going to get a pizza with tomato sauce and cheese. This is called Pizza-Margherita. But when you do it yourself, you can add any extras you want before baking.

My personal preference is lots and lots of cheese, melted to perfection when it arrives on the plate in front of me. Timing is the secret to perfect pizza.

2 packages active dry yeast
Pinch of sugar
1¼ cups warm water (110 to 115°F)
¼ cup olive oil
3½ cups flour
1 teaspoon salt
Cornmeal
Classic Marinara Sauce (recipe follows)
Mozzarella cheese
Parmesan cheese

TOPPINGS

Mushrooms, sliced
Anchovies
Onions, sliced
Pitted olives
Oven-Dried Tomatoes (see page 247)
Roasted peppers (see page 278), cut into strips

Dissolve the yeast with the sugar in ½ cup of the water and set aside until foamy.

In the bowl of an electric mixer, combine the remaining ¾ cup water, the olive oil, and yeast mixture. Mix the flour and salt and stir in, 1 cup at a time, until the dough begins to come together into a rough ball. Spoon onto a floured board and knead until smooth and elastic. Place the dough in an oiled bowl, oil its top, cover, and set in a warm place to rise for about 1 hour, until doubled in bulk.

Punch down the dough and break off golf-ball-size pieces to make 8- to 10-inch or individual pizzas. Knead each piece of dough on a floured board for 1 minute, working in additional flour to make it smooth and no longer sticky. Roll it out into a thin circle. Dust a round pizza baking pan with cornmeal and place the rolled-out dough on top.

Preheat oven to 400°F.

Spoon a thin coating of the sauce onto the pizza, spreading it with the back of a spoon to within 1 inch of the edge. Add any other toppings you desire. Sprinkle generously with mozzarella and Parmesan cheeses. Drizzle with 2 tablespoons olive oil and bake on the lowest rack of the oven for 10 minutes, or until the crust is crisp and brown and the cheese is hot and bubbling. Serve immediately.

# CLASSIC MARINARA SAUCE

3 tablespoons olive oil
3 garlic cloves, minced
2 onions, finely chopped
1 red bell pepper, chopped
2 carrots, finely chopped
2 celery stalks, finely chopped
1 can (28 ounces) whole
  peeled tomatoes with liquid
1 cup dry red wine
1 tablespoon fresh oregano,
  or 1 teaspoon dried
1 tablespoon fresh basil, or 1
  teaspoon dried
2 tablespoons minced parsley
½ teaspoon sugar
Salt
Freshly ground black pepper

In a heavy skillet, heat the oil. Add the garlic, onions, red pepper, carrots, and celery and sauté until the onions are transparent. Dice the tomatoes and add with liquid, red wine, oregano, basil, parsley, and sugar. Bring to a boil and simmer on medium heat, stirring occasionally, until thick, about 30 minutes. Season to taste with salt and pepper. Transfer to a bowl, cover with plastic wrap, and set aside.

# PEAR AND MUSHROOM SALAD

Simple ingredients create a light salad to refresh the palate before dessert.

4 pears, peeled, cored, and
  thinly sliced
2 cups thinly sliced fresh
  mushrooms with stems removed
Lemon-Parsley Dressing (recipe follows)
1 head of radicchio, leaves
  separated
1 small bunch of arugula
  leaves, separated

In a large bowl, toss the pears and mushrooms. (Reserve the stems for soups or sauce.) Pour the Lemon-Parsley Dressing over the pear mixture and toss. Serve on a bed of radicchio and arugula.

# LEMON-PARSLEY DRESSING

½ cup lemon juice
3 tablespoons water
½ cup minced parsley
1 tablespoon grated onion
Pinch of sugar
½ cup olive oil

In a small bowl, combine all the ingredients. Cover with plastic wrap and chill in the refrigerator until ready to use.

# TRIPLE CHOCOLATE TARTUFI
### TRUFFLES

These chocolate ice cream balls, studded with chocolate chips and covered with semisweet chocolate, are a very popular dessert in Italy. Some are factory made and others homemade, using the finest ingredients.

#### MAKES ABOUT 12 TRUFFLES

2 cups milk
1¼ cups sugar
1¼ cups cocoa powder
9 egg yolks
2 cups cream
2 pounds semisweet chocolate
2 tablespoons safflower oil

In a large heavy pot, combine the milk and ½ cup of the sugar. Sift in the cocoa. Bring to a boil over medium heat, stirring until the sugar and cocoa dissolve.

In the bowl of an electric mixer, beat the egg yolks, gradually adding the remaining ¾ cup sugar, until light-colored and thick. Pour a little of the milk mixture into the egg mixture to warm it; then pour the egg mixture through a sieve or strainer and return it to the pot with the rest of the milk mixture. Simmer over medium heat, stirring frequently with a wooden spoon, until the mixture forms a custard thick enough to coat the spoon, about 5 minutes.

Transfer the custard to a large heatproof bowl set inside a larger bowl of ice cubes and water. Add the cream and stir until cool. Cover with plastic wrap and chill in the refrigerator.

Melt the chocolate in a double boiler over simmering water.

Pour the custard into the canister of an ice cream maker and freeze according to manufacturer's directions. Just as the custard begins to freeze, slowly pour 1 cup of the hot melted chocolate, in a thin stream, into the custard mixture; small chunks of chocolate will form.

Or you can place the custard in a freezer-proof bowl and freeze until firm, 3 to 6 hours, stirring occasionally with a fork to break up ice crystals. (Stir in the hot melted chocolate when the mixture is almost frozen but not yet solid.)

With an ice cream scoop, shape the gelato into balls and freeze them on a foil-lined baking sheet or tray until very hard.

Melt the remaining chocolate again and add the oil in a thin stream. Dip each ball, using 2 spoons to turn and coat them all over as quickly as possible. Return to the baking sheets and refreeze. Half an hour before serving, remove from the freezer to allow them to soften slightly.

# VERSILIA
## ITALIAN GELATO DESSERT

Versilia is made in a factory in Italy, but I have developed a streamlined version, which you can make as the perfect finale for your own pizza party. It is a heavenly rich blend of cake, chocolate, wine, and gelato—all sealed in a paper cup. When the cup is cut open and inverted onto a serving plate, the syrup is released—a delightful surprise!

8 ounces semisweet chocolate, melted
12 Ladyfingers or 1 Holiday Orange Sponge Cake (see pages 274 or 63)
2 cups Marsala
1 quart Gelato alla Vaniglia (Vanilla Ice Cream) (see page 280), softened

Line a small baking sheet with wax paper and spread with a thin layer (⅛-inch) of melted chocolate. Refrigerate until set. Cut into 12 rounds to fit into 8- or 10-ounce paper cups and refrigerate.

Cut the Ladyfingers or cake into ¼-inch-thick rounds to fit on the bottom of the paper cups. Dip in Marsala and place in the bottom of each cup, reserving Marsala. Spoon about ¼ cup of gelato on top. Make a deep well in the center of the gelato and fill with Marsala. Cover with foil and freeze.

Remove the cups from the freezer and place the chocolate rounds on top of the gelato. Cover with foil and freeze until the chocolate hardens. Spoon in enough gelato to fill the cup. Cover with plastic wrap and foil and freeze. When ready to serve, bring to room temperature for a few minutes. Make a lengthwise slit in each paper cup, invert dessert on serving plates and peel away the cups.

# BRAZILIAN MENU

## RIO BRUNCH

FOR 12 TO 16

One of the nicest things about entertaining at home is that you can enjoy an ethnic menu from any country in the world without stepping outside your kitchen door. Recently, we enjoyed a fabulous family holiday in Rio de Janeiro celebrating my daughter Susan's wedding, and we were all overwhelmed by the spicy, exotic food. So on Susan's first anniversary, we decided to re-create some of the wonderful food we all remembered so fondly.

The main course is Feijoada, Brazil's national dish— a stew of black beans and smoked meats, with a blend of fascinating flavors. When I adapted the slow-cooking stew for kosher kitchens, I was struck by its similarity to the traditional cholent, which is cooked all day Friday and eaten on Saturday.

The hearty Feijoada is accompanied by palate-cleansing sliced oranges, rice, corn, stewed okra, tomato salsas, and other delicacies, spooned into individual serving bowls in the prescribed ceremonial order. Strong Brazilian coffee, rum drinks, exotic Mango Sherbet and a Brazil nut confection round out our feast.

# BATIDA PAULISTA
## BRAZILIAN RUM DRINK

A blender makes this drink easy to prepare. In Brazil the limes are often replaced with fresh fruit of the season, such as strawberries, papaya, guava, or passion fruit. The Cachaca is sometimes sold with the Ypioca label.

### MAKES TWELVE 4-OUNCE DRINKS

12 limes
1½ cups superfine sugar
3 cups Cachaca (Brazilian rum), or other light rum
20 ice cubes, chipped

With a vegetable peeler, zester, or very sharp knife, remove strips of peel from limes. Quarter the limes and place them in a blender. Add the sugar and rum and blend. Spoon a heaping teaspoon of ice chips into each chilled glass. Pour the lime and rum mixture over them and garnish with the lime strips. Serve immediately.

# FEIJOADA
## SMOKED MEAT AND BEAN STEW

The easiest way to prepare this stew is over a period of two days. The beans, tongue, and corned beef are soaked overnight, so plan ahead. Read over the recipe in advance. Have everything you'll need on hand, including two large pots.

5 cups dried black beans
2 pounds smoked tongue
2 pounds corned beef
8 chicken legs
1 pound smoked turkey
2 pounds kosher beef or veal sausages
Salt
Freshly ground black pepper
1 tablespoon vegetable shortening
2 large onions, chopped
4 garlic cloves, minced
2 large tomatoes, chopped
2 tablespoons chopped fresh parsley
1 green jalapeño pepper, stemmed and minced

Pick over the beans, rinse them, then soak in cold water overnight. Soak the tongue and corned beef in cold water overnight.

The next morning, drain the beans, cover with fresh cold water, and cook for about 2½ hours in a covered saucepan, stirring occasionally, until tender. Add additional water to keep them covered. Cool and set aside. Reserve ½ cup of the liquid for the Corn and Tomato Salsa.

Place the tongue, corned beef, and chicken in a large pot. Cover with tepid water, slowly bring to a boil, and simmer until the meats are tender, about 1½ hours.

Drain the meats and add them along with the turkey and sausages to the beans. Simmer for 30 minutes, until the meats are very tender and the beans are soft enough to mash easily. Season to taste with salt and pepper.

About 30 minutes before serving, melt the shortening in a large skillet and gently sauté the onions and garlic.

Add the tomatoes, parsley, and jalapeño pepper. Remove 3 cups of the beans with liquid and mash together with the onion mixture. Simmer until thick. Add this mixture to the pot containing the beans and meat.

Simmer for 30 minutes more, until thoroughly blended. Season to taste with salt and pepper.

To assemble the Feijoada, slice the tongue, corned beef, and turkey and arrange them with the sausages and chicken legs on a large heated platter. Ladle the beans into a large heated bowl.

# ONION AND YELLOW HOT PEPPER RELISH

3 or 4 malagueta peppers (small yellow hot peppers), stemmed but not seeded
1 fresh green jalapeño pepper, stemmed but not seeded
1 small onion, sliced
1 garlic clove
½ teaspoon salt
½ cup lemon juice
¼ cup fresh orange juice

In a blender, blend the peppers, onion, garlic, and salt until smooth. Add the lemon and orange juices and let stand for 1 hour before serving. This sauce must be used fresh, or it will ferment.

# BRAZILIAN RICE

MAKES ABOUT 8 CUPS

3 cups long-grain rice
4 tablespoons unsalted margarine or vegetable shortening
2 small onions, thinly sliced
2 tomatoes, peeled and chopped
3½ cups lightly salted boiling water, or a mixture of water and chicken broth
Salt
Freshly ground black pepper

Rinse the rice well. Melt the margarine in a large skillet over medium heat. Add the rice and onion and sauté, stirring with a wooden spoon, until the mixture begins to brown slightly, about 5 minutes.

Add the tomatoes and stir well. Add the boiling water and stir again. Bring to a boil, reduce the heat to low, cover, and cook 20 to 30 minutes, until all the water has been absorbed and the rice is tender. Add additional water if necessary to keep the rice from drying out before it is done. Remove from the heat and season with salt and pepper. Spoon into a heated serving dish.

# CORN AND TOMATO SALSA

2 firm ripe tomatoes, diced
1 small onion, minced
½ cup cooked corn kernels
2 green jalapeño peppers,
  stemmed, seeded, and
  diced
½ cup bean broth (reserved
  from Feijoada)
1 tablespoon lemon juice
1 tablespoon white wine
  vinegar
2 tablespoons minced parsley
¼ cup minced cilantro
Salt
Freshly ground black pepper

In a large bowl, combine the tomatoes, onion, corn, and peppers. Add the broth, lemon juice, and vinegar and mix well. Mix in the parsley and cilantro; season to taste with salt and pepper.

# ORANGE SLICES

Guests should be instructed as to the traditional way to assemble their plates. Four or five orange slices are placed on top of the rice, beans, and meats. An unusual and unexpectedly refreshing contrast of flavors.

16 oranges

With a very sharp knife, cut a slice from one end of each orange. Place the oranges on a work board and slice the peel and membrane away from the orange. Slice the oranges crosswise into ¼ inch-rounds. Place in a circular pattern on a large platter, cover with plastic wrap, and refrigerate until serving time.

# SAUTÉED KALE

2 pounds kale, shredded (6
  cups)
¼ cup olive oil
2 garlic cloves, minced
Salt
Freshly ground black pepper

Bring a large saucepan of lightly salted water to a boil. Plunge in the kale and boil until tender, 4 to 5 minutes. Drain well.

Heat the oil with the garlic in a large skillet over medium heat. Add the kale and sauté about 5 minutes. Season to taste with salt and pepper. Spoon into a heated serving bowl.

# Stewed Okra and Tomatoes

1 pound okra, stems trimmed, cut into ¼-inch slices
2 large tomatoes, coarsely chopped
1 small onion, finely chopped
1 garlic clove, finely chopped
1 cup water
Salt
Freshly ground black pepper

In a medium saucepan, put the okra, tomatoes, onion, garlic, and water. Season to taste with salt and pepper. Bring to a boil over medium heat, then reduce heat, cover, and simmer until the okra is tender and the flavors are blended, about 15 minutes.

# Farofa
## CEREAL TOPPING

The rice is spooned on each plate, then the beans and meats and so on in a special order, and last of all the Farofa is sprinkled on top.

3 tablespoons olive oil
1 onion, chopped
2½ cups manioc flour or cream of wheat or farina
2 bananas
1 egg

In a large skillet, heat oil and sauté onion until soft. Add manioc and stir often until golden brown, about 10 minutes.

Mash the bananas until smooth and blend in the egg. Add to the onion mixture and mix well. Serve warm.

# Mango Sherbet

2 large, very ripe mangoes
1⅓ cups Sugar Syrup (see page 38)
¼ cup fresh lime juice
1 lime, thinly sliced for garnish
Mint leaves for garnish

Peel the mangoes. Cut the pulp into chunks and put them in a processor. Process until puréed. You should have 2 cups. Press the mixture through a fine strainer or sieve set over a large bowl. Stir in the Sugar Syrup and lime juice.

Put the mixture into freezer trays in the freezer. When it begins to turn solid, spoon it into a mixer or blender and mix well. Return to the freezer and freeze completely. (Or pour the mixture into an ice cream maker and freeze according to manufacturer's directions.) Serve a scoop of sherbet garnished with lime slices and mint leaves.

# Brazil Nut Chocolate Truffles

MAKES ABOUT 36 TRUFFLES

12 ounces semisweet chocolate, melted (see page 21)
1 cup Brazil nuts, coarsely
chopped

In a large bowl, stir together the chocolate and nuts. Place ruffled paper candy cups on a baking sheet. Spoon the chocolate mixture into the cups. Refrigerate until set. Remove from the refrigerator 10 minutes before serving.

# MOROCCAN MENU

## COUSCOUS DINNER

FOR 8 TO 10

Jewish families that settled in faraway lands developed a cuisine based on native foods. The Moroccan Jews of North Africa are more at home with couscous than with chopped liver and gefilte fish. All the recipes in this menu were gathered from Jewish families with a Moroccan heritage. Couscous is the name of a dish we are serving and also the name of a grain—fine semolina, the basis of many pastas. It makes an authentic addition to the Lamb Kebabs.

The Bastilla uses filo dough to encase chicken, scrambled eggs, almonds, and spices. The pastry is sprinkled with powdered sugar and cinnamon.

A Moroccan dinner usually includes a medley of salads and a chicken or lamb dish plus couscous. Interesting pastries and fruits are served for dessert, along with Moroccan Tea, made with fresh mint, for a refreshing finale.

# CARROT-CUMIN SALAD

1 pound carrots, peeled and
  sliced diagonally
1 garlic clove, minced
1 teaspoon chili powder
1 teaspoon cumin
1 teaspoon paprika
2 tablespoons lemon juice
¼ cup minced parsley
¼ cup minced cilantro
1 tablespoon tomato paste
1 teaspoon sugar
1 tablespoon olive oil
Salt
Freshly ground black pepper

Cook the carrots in lightly salted water with the garlic until tender, about 10 minutes.

In a bowl, combine the chili powder, cumin, paprika, lemon juice, parsley, cilantro, tomato paste, sugar, oil, salt, and pepper. Gently mix into the drained carrots. Cover with plastic wrap and refrigerate.

# MOROCCAN EGGPLANT SALAD

Salt
Freshly ground black pepper
1 eggplant
1 garlic clove, minced
1 teaspoon chili powder
1 teaspoon cumin
1 teaspoon paprika
2 tablespoons lemon juice
¼ cup minced parsley
¼ cup minced cilantro
¼ cup safflower or vege-
  table oil
1 tablespoon tomato paste
1 teaspoon sugar

Preheat the oven to 400°F.

Line a baking sheet with foil and brush with oil. Sprinkle with salt and pepper. Cut the eggplant in half lengthwise and place cut side down on foil. Bake for 20 to 30 minutes, or until eggplant is tender. Peel and slice lengthwise into thin strips.

In a small bowl, combine the garlic, chili powder, cumin, paprika, lemon juice, parsley, cilantro, oil, tomato paste, sugar, and salt and pepper to taste. Gently mix sauce into the eggplant strips. Cover with plastic wrap and refrigerate.

# BASTILLA

## CHICKEN PIE

With a little organization, this recipe is fairly simple.

Prepare the three or four fillings for the Bastilla in advance and place them in shallow bowls. The fillings are then simply layered on the leaves and topped with additional margarine-brushed filo leaves. The pie can be covered and baked just before serving, and brought to the table piping hot, after the salads. If you want to be truly authentic the pie should be eaten with the fingers.

### FOR THE CHICKENS

2 chickens, 3 pounds each, with giblets
¼ cup olive oil
4 tablespoons unsalted margarine or oil
1 teaspoon ground ginger
1 cup chopped onion
1 garlic clove, crushed
½ cup chopped parsley
½ cup chopped cilantro
Salt
Freshly ground black pepper

### FOR THE FILLINGS

1 pound unsalted margarine
1½ cups sliced almonds
½ cup minced onion
3 garlic cloves, minced
9 eggs
3 tablespoons chopped parsley
1 tablespoon chopped cilantro
Salt
Freshly ground black pepper
6 tablespoons sugar
2 teaspoons cinnamon
½ teaspoon ground ginger
¼ teaspoon nutmeg

### FOR THE ASSEMBLY

1 package (1 pound) filo sheets
Powdered sugar
Cinnamon

Place the whole chickens, breast bone down, in a Dutch oven. Add the giblets, oil, margarine, ginger, onion, garlic, parsley, cilantro, salt, pepper, and 2 cups water, or enough to reach one third up the sides of the chickens.

Preheat the oven to 450°F.

Bring to a boil, turn chickens breast side up, and stir to mix spices. Place in the oven for 1 hour. Baste the chickens with the sauce. If chickens are a little pink, they will cook again inside the Bastilla. When chickens are cooked, cool, reserving the broth. Bone, separating meat into bite-size pieces, and set aside.

For the fillings, melt 3 tablespoons of the margarine in a skillet and sauté the almonds until golden brown. Set aside.

In another skillet, melt 3 tablespoons of the margarine and sauté the onion and garlic until soft. Beat the eggs in a bowl with the parsley, cilantro, and salt and pepper to taste. Set aside.

In a small bowl, combine the sugar, the 2 teaspoons of cinnamon, the ginger and nutmeg and set aside.

Melt the remaining margarine and use it to brush a large ovenproof pie pan. Place 1 sheet of filo on the bottom. Brush with margarine and continue in this manner using 8 sheets of filo. Spread the chicken in an even layer over the pastry and top with the egg mixture, spreading evenly. Combine almonds and sugar mixture and sprinkle over the eggs.

Place a sheet of filo over the filling and brush with margarine. Continue in this manner until all the filo leaves are used. Fold top layers of filo under the bottom ones. Brush under seam and top with margarine. Can hold at this point for at least 2 hours.

Preheat the oven to 350°F.

Bake for 25 to 30 minutes, or until golden brown and crisp. Just before serving, sprinkle with powdered sugar. For an attractive pattern, cover the top of the Bastilla with a paper stencil for crisscross, so the cinnamon can be sprinkled on in a heavy crisscross. Transfer to a large serving platter.

# LAMB KEBABS

4 pounds lamb, cut into 1-inch cubes
Salt
Freshly ground black pepper
2 medium onions, thinly sliced
2 garlic cloves, minced
1 teaspoon dried oregano
½ teaspoon dried rosemary
½ tablespoon dried thyme
1 bay leaf, crumbled
1 cup lemon or lime juice
3 tablespoons olive oil
2 green bell peppers, stemmed, seeded, and cut into chunks
2 large onions, peeled and cut into chunks
24 cherry tomatoes

Place the meat in a shallow bowl. Sprinkle with salt and pepper. Cover with the sliced onions, garlic, oregano, rosemary, thyme, and bay leaf; sprinkle with lemon juice and olive oil. Cover and marinate in the refrigerator for several hours or overnight, turning occasionally.

Thread the meat onto metal skewers. Thread the peppers, onion chunks, and tomatoes onto metal skewers. Place the prepared skewers on a foil-lined broiler rack, 4 inches from heat source, or on a grill over hot coals. Cook, turning frequently to brown evenly, until done as desired, 3 minutes on each side for rare meat. Serve hot.

# VEGETABLE COUSCOUS

2 tablespoons olive oil
2 garlic cloves, minced
1 onion, chopped
1 parsnip, peeled and sliced diagonally
2 carrots, peeled and sliced diagonally
1 can (8 ounces) tomatoes, drained

In a large skillet, heat the oil and sauté the garlic and onion until tender. Add the parsnips, carrots, tomatoes, raisins, salt, cumin, and 1 cup of the stock. Bring to a boil. Reduce heat to low; cover and simmer for 10 minutes, or until the vegetables are tender yet firm.

Add the zucchini and chick-peas; cook until the zucchini is just tender.

In a large saucepan, heat the remaining 1½ cups stock

½ cup plumped raisins (see page 25)

½ teaspoon salt

½ teaspoon ground cumin

2½ cups Chicken or Vegetable Stock (see page 390 or 391)

1 zucchini, sliced

1 can chick-peas (8 ounces)

4 tablespoons unsalted margarine

1 cup couscous

Garnish with cilantro

and margarine. Add the couscous. Cover and remove from the heat. Let stand for 5 minutes.

Spoon the couscous onto warm plates and top with the vegetables and some of the broth. Garnish with cilantro.

# STUFFED FIGS

⅓ cup plus 12 whole blanched almonds

1 ounce semisweet chocolate, grated

12 large dried figs

Preheat the oven to 350°F.

Place the almonds on a foil-lined baking sheet and bake for 5 minutes until lightly golden. Blend the ⅓ cup almonds until finely ground, reserving the 12 almonds. Cool. Mix with grated chocolate and set aside.

With scissors or a knife, remove the stems from the figs. With an index finger or handle of a small spoon, press or hollow out each fig. Stuff them with the chocolate mixture. Pinch each opening together firmly. Place the stuffed figs, stem side up, on a foil-lined baking sheet. Bake for 5 minutes. Turn figs and bake another 5 minutes, or until the bottoms begin to brown.

Press a whole almond into each fig and reseal.

# MOROCCAN MINT TEA

MAKES 8 SERVINGS

2 tablespoons green tea

⅔ cup sugar

12 fresh mint sprigs

6 cups boiling water

In a teapot, combine the tea, sugar, and mint; cover with the water and let steep for 3 to 4 minutes. Pour into small glasses and garnish with additional mint leaves. Serve very hot.

# ISRAELI MENU

# BREAKFAST BUFFET

FOR 24

A hearty Israeli breakfast, like this one patterned after meals served in the kibbutz, where people have worked half a day by 8 A.M., is an elaborate affair. I am duplicating the menu of one we enjoyed at the Dan Carmel Hotel in Haifa on a recent trip to Israel. You don't have to serve all the items, but the menu will give you some interesting choices. In general, the categories include fresh fruits, dried fruit compotes, and fresh juices, plus cheeses, fish, eggs, yogurt, and lots of salads. I've also added very special rolls. Most of the buffet can be prepared a day ahead and stored in the refrigerator, awaiting your early-morning guests.

Summer is the best season for your Israeli feast, when there's a colorful array of fresh fruits and vegetables. Appetites will peak after a long bicycle ride, eighteen holes of golf, or some lively tennis matches. Then transform your home into an Israeli one for a few hours with this authentic brunch.

Mini-Pecan Schnecken (see
page 384)
Coffee

SUGGESTED BEVERAGE:
Fruit punch or Israeli wine

# MARINATED FRESH FRUIT WITH YOGURT

2 large oranges, peeled and
sectioned
1 small grapefruit, peeled and
sectioned
4 cups watermelon chunks
4 cups diced fresh ripe pineapple
2 pints ripe strawberries,
stems removed
2 peaches, peeled, pitted, and
sliced
1 mango, peeled, pitted, and
sliced
2 kiwi fruit, peeled and sliced
1 tablespoon minced fresh
mint leaves
Marinade Syrup (recipe follows)
Whole mint leaves for garnish
2 cups yogurt

Arrange the fruit artistically in a large glass bowl. Sprinkle with the minced mint and strain the syrup over it.
Garnish with whole mint leaves. Spoon into large wine
goblets or shallow soup bowls. Serve with yogurt.

## MARINADE SYRUP

2 cups water
½ cup sugar
1 vanilla bean, split
1 piece (2 inches) lemon zest
4 pieces (4 inches) orange zest
3 fresh mint sprigs

In a large heavy saucepan, bring the water, sugar, vanilla
bean, lemon and orange zest, and mint to a boil. Remove from the heat and let the syrup cool. Cover with
plastic wrap and chill in the refrigerator.

# Kibbutz Lachmaniot

## ISRAELI ROLLS

A friend's son who now lives in Israel and cooks on a kibbutz shared this Israeli recipe with me. Benji uses a large wooden spoon to get started and then switches to his hands. It saves time, however, to use an electric mixer.

### MAKES ABOUT 4 DOZEN

2 packages active dry yeast
2 tablespoons sugar
8 to 9 cups plus 2 tablespoons flour
1 cup warm water (110 to 115°F)
¾ cup warm tap water
¾ cup milk
¾ cup safflower or vegetable oil
½ cup sugar
6 eggs
1 tablespoon salt
Sesame seeds or raisins

In a large bowl, combine the yeast, sugar, 2 tablespoons flour, and 1 cup warm water and blend well. Cover with a towel and place in a warm place for 15 minutes until the yeast rises—the water should not be too hot or it will kill the yeast.

In the large mixing bowl of an electric mixer, combine the tap water, milk, oil, sugar, and salt, and 4 of the eggs and blend well. Add the yeast mixture and the remaining flour, 1 cup at a time, until the dough no longer sticks to your hands or the bowl. Cover with a towel and place in a warm place to rise for 1 to 2 hours.

Preheat the oven to 350°F.

To form each roll, grab a handful of dough, stretch into a 4-inch rope, then tie in a knot. (It resembles a twisted dinner roll.)

Beat the remaining 2 eggs and brush on the rolls. Sprinkle with sesame seeds or raisins.

Bake for 45 to 55 minutes, or until golden brown. Cool on racks.

# Herring and Apple Salad

1 jar (12 ounces) herring in wine, drained and cubed
1 apple, peeled, cored, and thinly sliced
1 orange, peeled and thinly sliced
1 small red onion, thinly sliced
1 cup sour cream (or yogurt)
1 tablespoon sugar

In a large glass bowl, combine the herring, apple, orange, and onion. Toss well.

In a small bowl, mix the sour cream and sugar and pour over the herring mixture. Mix thoroughly with a wooden spoon. Cover with plastic wrap and refrigerate for at least 2 hours, or overnight. Before serving, toss to distribute the sauce.

# FRUITED BULGUR SALAD

16 ounces bulgur wheat

1 cup raisins, plumped and
drained (see page 25)

1 cup chopped, pitted dates

1 cup minced parsley

½ cup minced fresh mint

4 green onions (scallions),
thinly sliced

3 oranges, peeled and cut
into sections

Lemon-Orange Dressing (recipe follows)

Salt

Freshly ground black pepper

1 cup roasted sliced almonds
(see page 24)

1 orange, peeled and thinly
sliced in rounds for garnish

Sprigs of mint for garnish

In a large bowl, soak the bulgur in enough cold water to
cover by 1 inch for about 45 minutes, or just until tender.
Squeeze the water from the bulgur wheat by handfuls,
or by pressing it in a cheesecloth-lined strainer.

Transfer the bulgur to a large bowl. Add the drained
raisins, dates, parsley, mint, green onions, and orange
sections. Pour the dressing over the salad and toss gently.
Season to taste with salt and pepper.

Just before serving, stir in the almonds. Garnish with
the orange rounds and mint leaves.

## LEMON-ORANGE DRESSING

¾ cup olive oil

½ cup lemon juice

3 tablespoons orange juice

1 teaspoon cinnamon

1 teaspoon cumin

1 tablespoon sugar, or to taste

In a small bowl, whisk together the olive oil, lemon juice,
and orange juice. Whisk in the cinnamon, cumin, and
sugar. Cover with plastic wrap and chill.

# ISRAELI-ORIENTAL SALAD

There is no one recipe for an Israeli-Oriental Salad. The main ingredients depend
on the availability of fresh ripe vegetables in the market the day the salad is to be
made. In addition, the mood or personal preference of the cook plays an important role in the composition of the salad. Whatever the ingredients, preparation is
simple.

4 tomatoes, diced

2 cucumbers, peeled and
diced

1 green bell pepper, chopped
or small dice

1 red bell pepper, chopped or
small dice

1 small red onion, diced

10 green or black olives, pitted and chopped

½ cup olive oil

2 tablespoons lemon juice

Salt

Freshly ground black pepper

Whole green or black olives
for garnish

1 red onion, thinly sliced

In a large salad bowl, place the tomatoes, cucumbers, peppers, onion and chopped olives. Toss gently with a wooden spoon. Sprinkle with the oil and lemon juice and toss. Season to taste with salt and pepper. Garnish with olives and onion rings.

# CLASSIC BREAKFAST
# CHEESE BLINTZES

Usually cheese blintzes are rolled into an oval shape, but I like to fold the pancake over the filling like an envelope so the result is a flat blintz. This makes them much easier to fry, and also the sour cream and preserves can't roll off the top of the blintzes.

2 pounds hoop, farmer, or
pot cheese

1 tablespoon sugar

½ teaspoon salt

2 eggs

Blintz batter (see page 180)

Unsalted butter or margarine

An assortment of preserves:
raspberry, lingonberry,
marmalade

Bowls of sour cream, yogurt,
and sugar

In a large bowl, mix together the hoop cheese, sugar, salt, and eggs until blended. Cover with plastic wrap and chill in the refrigerator until ready to assemble the blintzes.

In an 8-inch skillet or crepe pan, melt 1 tablespoon of butter over medium heat. When the butter begins to bubble, pour in about ⅛ cup of the batter to cover the bottom of the pan with a thin layer. Rotate the pan quickly to spread the batter as thin as possible. Cook on one side only for about 1 minute, or until the edges begin to brown. Turn onto dish towels and transfer to a platter. Repeat with the remaining batter and stack the blintzes with wax paper in between. Cover with plastic wrap and refrigerate until ready to fill.

Fill the brown side of each prepared pancake with the cheese mixture and fold, tucking ends in. Melt 2 to

3 tablespoons of butter in a large skillet. Cook the blintzes on both sides, 2 or 3 minutes on each side, or until lightly browned. Repeat with the remaining blintzes, adding more butter as needed. With a metal spatula, carefully transfer the blintzes to a serving platter. Serve with bowls of preserves, sour cream, yogurt, and sugar.

# SCANDINAVIAN MENU

## THREE-COURSE BRUNCH

FOR 12

▼▲▼▲▼▲▼▲▼▲▼▲▼▲▼▲▼▲▼▲▼▲▼▲▼

### Swedish Cold Fruit Soup

**OPEN-FACE SANDWICHES**

Sardine and Red Onion

Herring with Horseradish
Sauce

Gravlax with Mustard-Dill
Sauce

Beet and Onion Salad

Kerstin Marsh's Beet and
Herring Salad

Cucumber Salad with Dill

Cheese Platter

Pumpernickel Loaves

Limpa Bread

If anyone can take credit for inventing brunch, it's the Scandinavians. Those creators of the smorgasbord enjoy an array of fish, meats, cheeses, and salads, along with their favorite breads and strong coffee, in a meal that combines the best of breakfast and lunch.

This hearty all-year brunch can be served when friends and family gather on holidays, to watch a special event on television, to celebrate a birthday or anniversary, or for no particular reason at all. If you want to be remembered for the best brunch ever, serve the entire menu in three separate courses: soup, open-face sandwiches and salad buffet, then pancakes and other desserts.

The menu is amazingly simple to prepare—only the pancakes have to be served hot, so everything else can be made in advance and refrigerated, ready to present as a fabulous feast.

# SWEDISH COLD
# FRUIT SOUP

2 quarts freshly squeezed orange juice

2 pints fresh raspberries

2 pints fresh strawberries,
sliced

8 bananas, peeled and thinly
sliced

Mint leaves for garnish

Put the fresh orange juice in a large glass pitcher. Cover
and refrigerate.

Arrange the raspberries in the centers of shallow soup
bowls, surrounded by the strawberries; arrange slices of
banana around the berries. Garnish with fresh mint leaves.
Place the soup bowls on serving plates on the table and
carefully pour the cold orange juice over the fruit.

# OPEN-FACE SARDINE AND
# RED ONION SANDWICHES

12 thin slices Pumpernickel
Loaves (see page 327)

6 tablespoons unsalted butter, softened

12 very small Bibb lettuce
leaves

2 cans (4 ounces each) sardine
fillets, drained

1 small red onion, thinly
sliced

12 small parsley sprigs

12 paper-thin lemon slices,
halved

Place the bread slices on a work surface and spread them
with butter. Place a lettuce leaf along one edge of each
slice of bread, like a decorative fringe. Arrange the sar-
dines on each slice. Top each with an onion slice. Garnish with parsley and lemon slices.

# HERRING SANDWICHES WITH HORSERADISH SAUCE

12 thin slices Limpa Bread
(see page 328)

¼ pound unsalted butter,
softened

1 jar (16 ounces) herring in
wine sauce, drained and
thinly sliced

6 red radishes, thinly sliced

6 green onions (scallions),
thinly sliced

1 small red onion, thinly
sliced

Horseradish Sauce (recipe follows)

12 tiny sprigs of dill

Spread the bread slices with butter and arrange a few slices of herring on top. Add the radishes, green onions, and red onion decoratively on top.

Fit a pastry bag with a star tip and fill it with the Horseradish Sauce. Pipe the sauce onto each sandwich. Transfer the sandwiches to individual plates or a large platter; garnish with sprigs of dill and serve the remaining sauce separately.

## HORSERADISH SAUCE

½ cup cream

1 cup mayonnaise

4 tablespoons grated fresh
horseradish or prepared
horseradish

In a bowl, beat the cream until soft peaks form. Fold in the mayonnaise and horseradish until blended.

# OPEN-FACE GRAVLAX SANDWICHES WITH MUSTARD-DILL SAUCE

These are best prepared just before serving, but the ingredients can be assembled a few hours before, wrapped tightly with plastic wrap, and refrigerated.

12 thin slices Pumpernickel
Loaves (see page 327)

6 tablespoons unsalted butter, softened (optional)

Place the bread slices on a work surface and spread them with butter. Arrange a tiny lettuce leaf on top, then add the Gravlax and cucumber slices decoratively on top.

Transfer the sandwiches to individual plates or a large

12 small Bibb lettuce leaves

12 thin slices Gravlax (recipe
    follows)

1 cucumber, thinly sliced

2 tablespoons minced chives

½ cup Mustard-Dill Sauce
    (recipe follows)

12 small cherry tomatoes

12 tiny dill sprigs

platter and garnish them with chives, Mustard-Dill Sauce, cherry tomatoes, and a sprig of dill.

# GRAVLAX
## MARINATED SALMON

This is a popular specialty served in California restaurants such as Scandia on the Sunset Strip in Los Angeles. It is well worth the time it takes to make. Salmon is a perfect appetizer or first course to accompany almost any menu. After I tire of serving it cold, I broil or sauté the leftover salmon and serve it hot as a main course with tiny boiled new potatoes.

This does take two or three days to marinate, so think ahead. It is a superb menu choice whenever salmon is good and fresh and the price is right.

1 salmon, 3½ pounds, scaled
    and boned to make 2 fillets

1 large bunch fresh dill

¼ cup kosher salt

¼ cup sugar

2 tablespoons white or black
    peppercorns, crushed

2 tablespoons aquavit

Mustard-Dill Sauce (recipe
    follows)

Place one of the salmon fillets skin side down in a shallow glass baking dish or casserole. Place the dill on top of the fillet. (If the dill is a hothouse variety and not very strong in flavor, coarsely chop it to release the flavor and sprinkle it over the fish instead.)

In a separate bowl, combine the salt, sugar, and peppercorns. Sprinkle this mixture over the dill with the aquavit. Top with the other half of the salmon, skin side up. Cover with plastic wrap and aluminum foil and then with a platter slightly larger than the salmon, but smaller than the baking dish. Cover the platter with cans of food or bricks to weight it down. Refrigerate for 2 or 3 days. Every 12 hours, unwrap the fish, lift off the top fillet, baste both fillets with the juices from the dish, reassemble, and turn the fillets over together. Then replace the wrappings, platter, and weights.

When ready to serve, remove the fish from its marinade, scrape away the dill and seasonings, and pat dry with paper towels. Place the separated halves, skin sides down, on a carving board and slice the salmon very thin at an almost horizontal angle, detaching each slice from the skin.

Serve with Mustard-Dill Sauce and garnish with lemon wedges, sprigs of fresh dill and toasted pumpernickel.

## MUSTARD-DILL SAUCE

This sauce can be prepared several days ahead, while the salmon is marinating. Cover with plastic wrap and refrigerate. It is especially good with the Gravlax, and also with fresh tuna, cold sliced chicken, turkey, corned beef, and pastrami. Try replacing the dill with basil leaves, cilantro, watercress, parsley, or sorrel.

3 tablespoons Dijon mustard
1 teaspoon powdered mustard
2 tablespoons sugar
1 tablespoon white vinegar
⅓ cup safflower or vegetable oil
3 tablespoons chopped (or snipped) fresh dill

In a small deep bowl, combine the Dijon mustard, powdered mustard, sugar, and vinegar and blend well. With a wire whisk, slowly beat in the oil until it forms a thick mayonnaise. Stir in the chopped dill. Cover with plastic wrap and refrigerate until ready to serve.

# BEET AND ONION SALAD

5 Pickled Beets, drained and sliced (recipe follows)
1 large red onion, peeled and thinly sliced
1 cucumber, peeled and thinly sliced
⅓ cup of olive oil
Juice of 1 lemon
Salt
Freshly ground black pepper
Lettuce leaves
2 hard-boiled eggs (see page 23) peeled and chopped
1 cup minced parsley

In a large salad bowl, toss together the beets, onion, and cucumber.

In a small bowl, combine the olive oil and lemon juice. Just before serving, pour the olive oil mixture over the beet mixture and toss. Season to taste with salt and pepper. Serve in a bowl or in individual servings on a bed of lettuce. Garnish with chopped egg and parsley.

## PICKLED BEETS

5 large fresh beets
1½ teaspoons mustard seeds
½ teaspoon whole allspice
½ teaspoon whole cloves
1 stick (2 inches long) cinnamon, or ½ teaspoon
  ground cinnamon
1 cup cider vinegar
½ teaspoon salt
1 cup sugar

Trim the beets, leaving 1 inch of the stem. Wash the beets, place them in a saucepan, and cover with cold water. Bring to a boil, cover, and simmer for 1 hour, or until the beets are tender. Reserve 1 cup of the cooking liquid. While the beets are still warm, slice off their stems and peel off and discard the outer skins. Transfer the beets to a large ovenproof bowl. Set aside.

Place the mustard seeds, allspice, cloves, and cinna-mon stick in a cheesecloth bag and tie securely. In a large saucepan, combine the vinegar, salt, reserved 1 cup beet liquid, sugar, and the spice bag. Bring to a boil and simmer for 5 minutes. Pour this mixture over the beets; cover and refrigerate. Chill overnight.

# KERSTIN MARSH'S BEET AND HERRING SALAD

From the first taste of this salad you will be hooked. The contrasting flavors of the herring, pickled beets, macaroni, and crisp apples are *so* delicious.

This recipe comes from the Swedish kitchen of our good friend Kerstin Marsh's mother. We have been enjoying it in Kerstin's home every year during the holidays for at least twenty years, and I finally got her to copy her cherished recipe from the original tattered and torn pages of her handwritten cookbook.

1 jar (8 ounces) herring in
  wine sauce, drained and
  diced
1½ to 2 cups chopped or
  thinly sliced pickled beets
  (see preceding recipe)
8 ounces macaroni, cooked
2 apples, peeled, cored, and
  diced
1 small red onion, thinly
  sliced
½ cup Classic Homemade
  Mayonnaise (recipe follows)
2 tablespoons white wine
  vinegar
Salt
Freshly ground black pepper
1 bay leaf, crumbled

In a large bowl, combine the herring, beets, macaroni, apples, and onion and toss to blend. Blend in the may-onnaise and vinegar. Season to taste with salt and pepper and mix well with the bay leaf. Cover with plastic wrap and chill.

## CLASSIC HOMEMADE MAYONNAISE

2 egg yolks
Juice of ½ lemon
2 teaspoons prepared mustard
¼ teaspoon salt
Freshly ground black pepper
1½ cups safflower or vegetable oil

In a food processor or blender, with the metal blade in place, blend the egg yolks, lemon juice, mustard, salt, and pepper. Continue processing and pouring the oil in a thin stream through the feeder tube, by tablespoons at first. Then pour in a steady stream until the mayonnaise thickens. This will hold for a few days, well covered, in the refrigerator.

## CUCUMBER SALAD WITH DILL

1 cup water
1 cup white vinegar
¼ teaspoon salt
1 cup sugar
2 large (hothouse variety) cucumbers, sliced paper-thin
1 tablespoon fresh minced dill, or 2 tablespoons dried dill
1 head of Bibb lettuce
1 bunch of watercress
Cherry tomatoes for garnish

In a large glass bowl, mix the water, vinegar, salt, and sugar until the sugar dissolves. Add the cucumbers and dill and toss. Cover with plastic wrap and chill in the refrigerator for at least 2 hours.

Drain and serve on lettuce leaves. Garnish with watercress and cherry tomatoes.

## PUMPERNICKEL LOAVES

There are many stories about how this bread got its name but here is the most popular one: It seems that Napoleon had a horse named Nicole, said to have been very fond of black bread. Napoleon frequently demanded "Pain pour Nicole," which non-French-speaking people corrupted to "Pumpernickel".

Pumpernickel is only one step away from basic rye bread, the extra step usually being the addition of cocoa and molasses, which always surprises my students. These ingredients transform it into a darker bread with a richer, more pungent flavor.

2 cups rye flour
¼ cup cocoa powder
2 packages active dry yeast
Pinch of sugar
1½ cups warm water (110 to 115°F)
½ cup molasses
1 tablespoon kosher salt
2 tablespoons caraway seeds
2 tablespoons golden raisins, plumped (see page 25)
1 tablespoon unsalted butter or margarine, melted
3¾ cups unbleached flour
Yellow cornmeal

In a bowl, combine the rye flour and the cocoa. Set it aside. Dissolve the yeast with a pinch of sugar in ½ cup of the warm water. Set aside until foamy.

In the bowl of an electric mixer, beat together the remaining 1 cup of water, the molasses, salt, caraway seeds, and raisins. Add the yeast mixture, butter, and rye flour mixture and blend well. Gradually add the unbleached flour, 1 cup at a time, blending with a beater after each addition, until the dough is soft and thick enough to work by hand, yielding about 2 cups of dough in all. Spread the dough on a floured board and knead it for 5 to 10 minutes, adding additional flour as necessary, until the dough is smooth and elastic. (It will be heavier than regular dough—this is a very dense bread.) Place the dough in an oiled bowl and oil its top. Cover it with a towel and let it rise in a warm place until doubled in size, 1½ to 2 hours.

Divide the dough into 4 equal pieces to make 4 individual loaves. Generously oil four 3½ × 7½-inch loaf pans and sprinkle with cornmeal. Form each piece of dough into a loaf to fit into the prepared pans, kneading out any air bubbles that might form. Cover the loaves with towels and let them rise in a warm place until doubled, about 1½ hours.

Preheat the oven to 375°F. Bake for 35 to 40 minutes, or until the loaves begin to shrink away from the sides of the pan and have a hollow sound when tapped on top with a finger. Remove from the pans immediately and cool on racks.

# LIMPA BREAD

The slightly sweet and spicy flavor of the anise in this Scandinavian bread is always a delightful taste surprise.

MAKES 4 LOAVES

1 package active dry yeast
2 tablespoons sugar
1 cup warm water (110 to 115°F)
1 cup lukewarm milk (105 to 110°F)
4 cups unbleached flour
¾ cup dark corn syrup
2 teaspoons aniseeds
1 teaspoon fennel seeds
5⅓ tablespoons unsalted butter or margarine, melted
1 tablespoon orange zest
2 teaspoons kosher salt
3 cups rye flour
Yellow cornmeal

In the bowl of an electric mixer, dissolve the yeast and the sugar in the water until foamy. Add the milk and 3 cups of the unbleached flour, beating well. Cover with a towel and let rise in a warm place for 1 hour, until doubled in size.

In a heavy saucepan, bring the corn syrup, aniseeds, and fennel seeds to a boil; cool.

Add the corn syrup mixture, butter, orange zest, and salt to the yeast mixture and blend well. Add the rye flour and enough of the remaining 1 cup unbleached flour until the dough is firm enough to work by hand. Spoon it out onto a floured board and knead for 5 to 10 minutes until smooth and elastic. Place the dough in an oiled bowl and oil the top. Cover with a towel and let rise in a warm place until doubled in size, about 1½ hours.

Punch down the dough and knead it again for 4 to 5 minutes, until smooth and elastic. Divide it into 4 equal pieces and shape into loaves. Oil four 7½ × 3¾-inch bread pans; sprinkle them on the bottom with cornmeal. Place the loaves in the prepared pans, cover with towels, and let rise again for 45 minutes, until doubled.

Preheat the oven to 375°F. Bake the breads for 35 minutes, or until tops are golden brown and the breads begins to shrink away from the pans. Remove from the pans immediately, loosening the sides with a metal spatula. Cool on racks.

# DANISH APPLE PANCAKES
## AEBLESKIVERS

In order to serve these special golf-ball-shaped pancakes, you must purchase a special aebleskiver pan, available at most good kitchen supply stores. It is well worth searching for, as you will definitely use it more than once.

2 eggs
1 tablespoon sugar
2 cups flour
½ teaspoon salt
1 teaspoon baking powder
½ teaspoon baking soda
1½ cups buttermilk
Unsalted butter for frying
2 apples, peeled and diced
Granulated or powdered
   sugar for garnish
Lingonberry and raspberry
   preserves

In the bowl of an electric mixer, beat the eggs and sugar. Combine the flour, salt, baking powder, and baking soda and add them to the egg mixture alternately with the buttermilk. Beat until the batter is smooth.

Heat the aebleskiver pan over medium heat and pour 1 teaspoon melted butter in each well (there are 7 wells in most pans). Spoon in the batter, filling the wells almost to the top. Cook until the bottoms of the pancakes begin to brown. Drop 1 teaspoon of diced apple into the center of each pancake. Carefully turn each pancake with a fork, metal skewer, or a knitting needle. Fry until golden brown (they will resemble large golf balls). Roll them in granulated sugar or sprinkle with powdered sugar. Serve with preserves.

# AUNT BETTY'S ORANGE COFFEE CAKE

¼ pound unsalted butter or
   margarine
1 cup sugar
2 eggs
Grated zest of 1 orange
⅓ cup orange juice
2 cups cake flour
1 teaspoon baking soda
1 teaspoon baking powder
½ teaspoon salt
1 cup sour cream
1 cup toasted, chopped walnuts or pecans (see
   page 24)
¼ cup ground walnuts or
   pecans
Orange Juice Syrup (recipe
   follows)

Preheat the oven to 350°F.

In the large bowl of an electric mixer, beat the butter and sugar until light and fluffy. Beat in the eggs, 1 at a time, until well blended. Add the zest and juice and blend well.

Combine the flour, baking soda, baking powder, and salt. Add to the butter mixture alternately with the sour cream until completely blended. Fold in the chopped walnuts.

Grease a 10-inch bundt or fluted tube pan. Sprinkle with the ground walnuts. Pour the batter into the prepared pan. Bake for 40 minutes, or until a toothpick inserted into the center of the cake comes out dry and the cake begins to shrink away from the sides of the pan.

Spoon the hot syrup over the cake as soon as you remove it from the oven.

## ORANGE JUICE SYRUP

¾ cup orange juice
2 tablespoons lemon juice
½ cup sugar

In a saucepan, combine the orange juice, lemon juice, and sugar. Bring to a boil, stirring until the sugar dissolves, and simmer for 5 minutes. Set aside.

# GINGERBREAD COOKIES
## PEPPARKAKOR

Kerstin Marsh's super-thin, subtly spiced cookies are another of her mother's specialties.

MAKES 8 DOZEN

¾ cup solid vegetable shortening
1 cup dark brown sugar
1 egg
¼ cup molasses
2½ cups flour
2 teaspoons baking soda
1 teaspoon cinnamon
1 teaspoon ginger
½ teaspoon cloves
¼ teaspoon salt

In the large bowl of an electric mixer, blend the shortening, brown sugar, egg, and molasses. Beat until smooth.

Combine the flour, baking soda, cinnamon, ginger, cloves, and salt. Add to the shortening mixture and beat until smooth. Knead into a ball and wrap in plastic wrap and foil. Refrigerate for at least 2 hours or overnight.

Preheat the oven to 375°F.

Pull off small pieces of dough and roll them out paper thin on a well-floured board. Cut with cookie cutters and use a metal spatula to transfer to a greased baking sheet. Bake for 5 to 10 minutes, until lightly browned. Remove each cookie from the baking sheet as it browns and place on a rack to cool.

# PART 3

# SPECIAL CELEBRATIONS

AMERICANA THANKSGIVING FEAST FOR 12

NEW YEAR'S EVE GALA FOR 12

FATHER'S DAY FEAST FOR 12

BRIDAL SHOWER SALAD BUFFET FOR 24

ISRAELI BAR MITZVAH BUFFET FOR 48

SOPHISTICATED SUMMER SUPPER FOR 10

PUMPKIN HARVEST DINNER FOR 8

TRADITIONAL SUNDAY BRUNCH FOR 12

# AMERICANA THANKSGIVING FEAST

FOR 12

Thanksgiving is a time when American Jewish families can enjoy the best of both their heritages—hearty American food and an occasion to give thanks for their blessings. So I like to plan a lot of old-fashioned farmhouse food for the holiday. Everyone enjoys a handsome bronzed turkey with lots of stuffing, an appealing array of relishes, and a lavish dessert buffet. We pour cider for the children and a robust red wine for the grown-ups, and catch up on all the news while enjoying our family feast.

The baking and much of the rest of the menu can be started days in advance to allow time to arrange some cheery Thanksgiving decorations. They can be as simple as autumn leaves in a vase, an assortment of pumpkins and squash, or a cornucopia of polished apples, grapes, and nuts.

Since this is a day off for almost everyone, have them pitch in setting the table, cutting and chopping ingredients, and so on. Dinner can begin early, which gives the younger family members a chance to share in the fun. And if there is room, it is always nice to invite friends who don't have families of their own—a warm-hearted Jewish tradition.

# BITE-SIZE BISCUITS WITH DEVILED CORNED BEEF

MAKES 30 1-INCH BISCUITS

2 cups flour

3 teaspoons baking powder

½ teaspoon salt

4 tablespoons vegetable shortening or unsalted margarine

⅔ cup water

Deviled Corned Beef (recipe follows)

Parsley or watercress for garnish

Preheat the oven to 450°F.

In a mixing bowl, sift together the flour, baking powder, and salt. Add the shortening and cut it into the flour until the mixture has the consistency of coarse meal. Add the water, mixing lightly with a fork until a ball forms that separates from the sides of the bowl. Turn out onto a lightly floured board. Knead gently for 30 seconds. Roll out or pat out the dough to a ½-inch thickness. Cut with a 1½-inch round cookie cutter.

Bake on an ungreased baking sheet for 10 minutes, or until golden brown. Slice biscuits and hollow out the centers with a small melon-ball cutter. Fill each biscuit with a heaping teaspoon of the Deviled Corned Beef and replace the top; place on a foil-lined baking sheet and bake for 5 to 10 minutes. Arrange the biscuits on a large platter and garnish the center with parsley or watercress.

## DEVILED CORNED BEEF

½ cup fresh corn kernels or thawed frozen corn

½ cup minced corned beef

½ cup minced celery

⅓ cup mayonnaise

2 tablespoons Dijon-style mustard

Pinch of cayenne

2 teaspoons fresh lemon juice

Salt

Freshly ground black pepper

In a bowl, stir together the corn, corned beef, celery, mayonnaise, mustard, cayenne, and lemon juice. Season to taste with salt and pepper. Place mixture in a nonstick skillet and toss well until heated through.

# PUMPKIN SOUP

3 tablespoons unsalted margarine

1 large onion, thinly sliced

In a heavy saucepan, heat the margarine and sauté the onion, leek, and garlic until tender. Add the apple and pumpkin slices and sauté for 3 minutes, or until tender.

1 leek, white part only,
  cleaned and thinly sliced
1 garlic clove, minced
1 tart apple, peeled and thinly
  sliced
4 cups peeled and thinly
  sliced pumpkin (if not available use banana or Hub-
  bard squash)
6 cups Chicken Stock (see
  page 390)
Pinch of nutmeg
Salt
Freshly ground black pepper
1 cup Toasted Pumpkin Seeds
  (see page 379)

Add the stock, bring to a boil, and simmer for 20 minutes.

With a slotted spoon, transfer the pumpkin and onion mixture to a processor. Process the mixture, slowly adding 1 cup of the broth, until puréed. Return the puréed mixture to the saucepan and simmer briskly for 10 minutes, or until the soup thickens. Season to taste with nutmeg, salt, and pepper. Ladle into heated soup bowls and sprinkle with toasted pumpkin seeds.

# SAVORY GRAIN, LEEK, AND NUT BREAD

Two kinds of nuts and chopped leeks add a chewy texture and unique flavor to this attractive loaf. Heat and serve it in thin slices, wrapped in a napkin to keep them warm.

2 packages active dry yeast
2 cups warm water (110 to
  115°F)
Pinch of sugar
¼ pound unsalted margarine,
  melted
1 tablespoon salt
½ cup whole wheat flour
½ cup rye flour
4 to 5 cups unbleached flour
4 tablespoons unsalted margarine
1 cup finely chopped leeks,
  white part only
½ cup toasted chopped
  walnuts (see page 24)
½ cup toasted chopped
  pecans
Yellow cornmeal

Dissolve the yeast in 1 cup of the warm water with a pinch of sugar. Set aside until foamy. In the bowl of an electric mixer, beat together the remaining 1 cup water, melted margarine, and salt. Blend in the yeast and the whole wheat and rye flours. Add the unbleached flour, 1 cup at a time, blending with a beater after each addition, until the dough comes together.

Transfer the dough to a floured board and knead it for 8 to 10 minutes, or until smooth and elastic. Place the dough in an oiled bowl and oil the top. Cover with a towel and let rise in a warm place until doubled in size, 1½ to 2 hours.

In a skillet, heat the 4 tablespoons margarine and sauté the leeks until soft. In a medium bowl, combine the leeks, the toasted walnuts and pecans, and 2 tablespoons of unbleached flour. Punch down the dough and knead in the leek mixture.

Divide the dough into 3 equal portions and form each into a loaf. Place the loaves on baking sheets, or in loaf pans, lightly greased and generously sprinkled with cornmeal. Cover with a towel and let rise in a warm place until doubled, 30 to 40 minutes.

Preheat the oven to 400°F. Bake the loaves for 30 to 40 minutes, until they sound hollow when tapped. Transfer to racks to cool.

# TURKEY IN A BAG WITH VEGETABLE STUFFING

1 turkey, 15 to 20 pounds
Vegetable Stuffing (recipe follows)
¼ cup safflower or vegetable oil
1 cup apricot preserves
Salt
Freshly ground black pepper

Clean the turkey and pat it dry with paper towels. Spoon the cooled stuffing into both cavities and close with a needle and thread or skewers. Rub the outside of the turkey with the oil and preserves and sprinkle with salt and pepper.

Preheat the oven to 325°F.

Grease the inside (seamless unprinted side) of a large brown paper bag, or use a large plastic baking bag. Place the turkey, neck first and breast down, inside the bag. For a paper bag, fold the open ends and seal it with paper clips or staples; if using a plastic baking bag, tie it with plastic ties supplied in the package. Place the turkey on a large rack over a roasting pan lined with heavy-duty foil. Bake for 3 hours or more, depending on the size of the turkey. (See suggested cooking times below.)

About 30 minutes before the turkey is done, make a slit in the bag under the turkey and let the liquid drain into a saucepan. When all the juices are poured off, remove the bag. Return the turkey to the oven to brown for the remaining cooking time. Remove the fat from the top and heat the juices. Remove the stuffing and transfer to a heated bowl. Carve the turkey and arrange the slices, legs, and wings on a large platter. Serve the juices in a gravy boat.

Suggested Cooking Time for Stuffed Turkeys:
10 to 12 pounds: 3½ to 4½ hours
14 to 16 pounds: 5 to 6 hours
18 to 20 pounds: 6 to 7½ hours

# VEGETABLE STUFFING

My mother was very proud of this very special stuffing and served it in chicken as well as turkey. She did not, however, cook the ingredients, but mixed everything together and placed it in the bird. I have found that cooking the stuffing first makes it cook more evenly and that the flavors blend better. I have also added raisins, which gives it a nice sweet taste. It is especially festive for Thanksgiving.

¼ cup safflower or vegetable oil
3 medium onions, finely chopped
3 garlic cloves, minced
4 celery stalks, finely chopped
1 bunch carrots, peeled and grated
1 parsnip, peeled and grated
2 large zucchini, grated
½ cup minced parsley
½ cup raisins, plumped and drained (see page 25)
8 to 10 mushrooms, chopped
2 to 3 tablespoons oatmeal
2 to 3 tablespoons flour
2 to 3 tablespoons dry bread crumbs
¼ cup dry red wine
Salt
Freshly ground black pepper

In a large heavy skillet, heat the oil and sauté the onions and garlic until transparent. Add the celery, carrots, parsnip, and zucchini; toss well. Sauté for 5 minutes, until the vegetables begin to soften. Add the parsley, raisins, and mushrooms and mix thoroughly. Simmer for 5 minutes. Blend in 1 tablespoon each of the oatmeal, flour, and bread crumbs. Add the wine and mix well. Add additional dry ingredients, a little at a time, until the stuffing is moist and soft yet firm in texture. Season to taste with salt and pepper.

# FRIED POTATO SKINS WITH SWEET POTATO PURÉE

These potato skins can be prepared a few hours ahead as long as they are fried very crisp and all the oil is drained off. If you like them crisper, place them on a foil-lined baking sheet and bake in a hot oven until crisp before serving.

Try them filled with applesauce for Hanukkah. They are perfect with brisket.

4 to 6 baking potatoes
Oil for deep frying
Sweet Potato Purée (recipe
    follows)

Preheat the oven to 375°F.

Scrub and dry the potatoes. Pierce the skins with the tines of a fork. Bake for 1 hour, or until soft to the touch. Remove from the oven. When the potatoes are cool enough to handle, cut them lengthwise in half. Then cut each half lengthwise in half again. Carefully spoon out the cooked potato, taking care not to tear the skins. Reserve the cooked potato for another recipe.

Heat the oil in a large heavy pot or a deep-fryer to 375°F on a deep-frying thermometer. Carefully drop the potato skins into the hot oil, 2 or 3 at time, and fry them for 15 seconds, or until they start to turn brown and crisp. Remove them from the oil with a slotted spoon and drain on paper towels. Just before serving, fill the shells with the Sweet Potato Purée.

## SWEET POTATO PURÉE

Thanksgiving would be disappointing without sweet potatoes. This is a delicious way to serve them, with or without the cranberry garnish.

6 small sweet potatoes (about
    4 pounds)
Salt
1 cup apple juice or water
4 tablespoons unsalted
    margarine
½ cup dark brown sugar
¼ teaspoon nutmeg
Cranberry Relish (see page
    339) for garnish

Cook the sweet potatoes in their jackets in lightly salted boiling water until tender. Drain, peel, and cut into small dice. Place in a greased, shallow baking dish.

Preheat the oven to 375°F.

In a saucepan, simmer the apple juice, margarine, and brown sugar, stirring frequently until the sugar has dissolved. Pour this mixture over the sweet potatoes. Sprinkle with nutmeg, cover with foil, and bake for 15 to 20 minutes. With a slotted spoon, transfer the diced sweet potatoes to a bowl. Mash and add enough of the apple juice mixture to moisten. Season to taste with salt. Just before serving, spoon into the potato skins, or use a pastry bag with a floret tip and pipe the purée into the potato skins. Garnish with Cranberry Relish.

# RED CABBAGE WITH APPLES

1 red cabbage (2½ pounds)

⅔ cup wine vinegar

2 tablespoons sugar

2 teaspoons salt

2 tablespoons unsalted margarine

2 apples, peeled, cored, and thinly sliced

1 small onion, chopped

1 whole onion, peeled and pierced with 2 cloves

1 bay leaf, crushed

5 cups boiling water

3 tablespoons dry red wine

3 tablespoons red currant jelly

Wash the cabbage under cold water and cut into quarters. Cut into ⅛-inch shreds. Drop into a large bowl and sprinkle with vinegar, sugar, and salt. Toss with a wooden spoon.

In a large (5-quart) saucepan, melt the margarine and sauté the apples and chopped onion for 5 minutes, or until the apples are lightly browned. Add the cabbage, whole onion, and bay leaf. Stir thoroughly and pour in the boiling water. Bring to a boil over high heat, stirring occasionally, and reduce the heat to a simmer. Cook, covered, for 1 hour, or until the cabbage is tender, stirring frequently with a wooden spoon. Remove the whole onion and bay leaf. Stir in the wine and currant jelly and season to taste with salt and pepper. Serve hot.

# CRANBERRY RELISH

MAKES ABOUT 6 CUPS

2⅓ cups firmly packed brown sugar

½ cup cider vinegar

¾ teaspoon curry powder

¼ teaspoon ground ginger

¼ teaspoon ground cloves

¼ teaspoon ground allspice

¼ teaspoon ground cinnamon

1¾ cups water

2 lemons, zest grated, pitted and sectioned

2 oranges, zest grated, pitted and sectioned

1 apple, peeled and coarsely chopped

½ cup golden raisins

6 cups (1½ pounds) cranberries, picked over

In a large heavy saucepan, combine the sugar, vinegar, curry powder, ginger, cloves, allspice, cinnamon, and 1½ cups of the water. Bring to a boil, stirring until the sugar dissolves.

Add the lemons, oranges, and apple and simmer for 10 minutes, stirring occasionally. Add the raisins and 3 cups of the cranberries; simmer for 30 to 40 minutes, until thickened.

Add the remaining 3 cups cranberries and remaining ¼ cup water; simmer for 15 minutes more. Transfer to a glass ovenproof bowl and cool to room temperature. Cover with plastic wrap and chill in the refrigerator.

# Onion and Pepper Relish

MAKES ABOUT 2 CUPS

Zest of 2 oranges, cut into thin julienne, juice reserved

1 pound pearl onions

2 tablespoons sugar

¼ cup red wine vinegar (or raspberry vinegar)

3 tablespoons olive oil

1 roasted red bell pepper (see page 278), thinly sliced

2 large tomatoes, peeled, seeded, and chopped

½ cup golden raisins

¼ cup currants (optional)

1 tablespoon tomato paste

⅛ tablespoon ground red pepper (cayenne)

Salt

1½ to 1¾ cups dry white wine

Blanch the orange zest in a saucepan of boiling water for 2 to 3 minutes; drain. Rinse under cold running water and drain well on paper towels.

With a small sharp knife, cut an X at the root end of each onion. Blanch the onions in a large saucepan of boiling water for 2 to 3 minutes; drain. Rinse under cold running water until cool enough to handle. Peel and trim the stem ends. Drain well on paper towels.

In a heavy saucepan over low heat, melt the sugar with a little water. When the sugar is light brown, about 5 minutes, remove from the heat. Carefully stir in the vinegar, mixing well.

Return to the heat, stir until the caramel is dissolved, and set aside.

Preheat the oven to 375°F.

In a large, heavy stainless steel skillet, heat 2 table-spoons of the oil over medium heat. Add the onions and sauté them, shaking the pan frequently, until the onions are deep brown, about 8 minutes. Add the roasted pepper, orange zest, reserved orange juice, tomatoes, raisins, currants, tomato paste, ground red pepper, salt to taste, and the vinegar mixture. Add enough wine to cover the ingredients and bring it slowly to a boil, stirring gently.

Transfer the mixture to a baking dish and bake, covered, for 1 hour. The liquid should be thick enough to coat the vegetables; if it is too thin, strain it into a small saucepan and boil it until reduced to a syrupy consistency. Place the vegetables and the reduced liquid in a bowl, cover, and chill. Sprinkle with the remaining 1 tablespoon olive oil before serving.

# Corn and Pepper Relish

MAKES ABOUT 8 CUPS

2 packages (16 ounces each) frozen corn kernels

In a large heavy saucepan, combine the corn, peppers, onion, carrots, sugar, mustard, celery seeds, and tur-

1 green bell pepper, seeded and chopped

1 red bell pepper, seeded and chopped

1 yellow bell pepper, seeded and chopped

1 medium onion, chopped

2 medium carrots, peeled and chopped

1½ cups sugar

1 teaspoon powdered mustard

½ teaspoon celery seeds

¼ teaspoon turmeric

1¼ cups cider vinegar

meric. Stir in the vinegar. Bring to a boil, stirring until the sugar is dissolved. Simmer the mixture until the vegetables are tender and the mixture is thick, about 20 minutes. Transfer to a bowl and cool. Cover with plastic wrap and chill in the refrigerator.

# KOSHER MINCEMEAT TART

Mincemeat is not forbidden in a kosher kitchen—if you leave out the meat. By eliminating the fatty beef and/or suet, you also cut down on fats and calories. So go ahead—bake a beautiful spicy mincemeat pie and enjoy it.

Prebaked Pastry for a 9-Inch Pie (recipe follows)

1½ cups seedless raisins

4 tart apples, peeled and cored

½ orange, unpeeled and cut into chunks

½ lemon, unpeeled and cut into chunks

½ cup cider vinegar

1½ cups dark brown sugar

½ teaspoon salt

½ teaspoon ground cinnamon

½ teaspoon ground nutmeg

½ teaspoon ground cloves

Prepare and bake the tart shell.

Coarsely chop the raisins, apples, orange, and lemon and put into a medium saucepan. Add the vinegar and heat to the boiling point. Reduce the heat and simmer for 10 minutes. Add the brown sugar, salt, cinnamon, nutmeg, and cloves. Mix well. Simmer for 15 minutes more. Cool. Fill the baked tart with the cooled mincemeat.

## PASTRY FOR A 9-INCH PIE

This recipe gives you two choices; you may either roll out the dough or simply pinch off pieces and press them into the tart pan. In this meat menu, use margarine for the dough; in dairy menus, you may substitute butter.

1 cup flour

1 tablespoon sugar

⅛ teaspoon salt

6 tablespoons unsalted margarine, cut into small pieces

1 egg yolk

1 teaspoon cold water

In a bowl of an electric mixer, blend the flour, sugar, and salt. Add the margarine and blend until the mixture resembles coarse meal. Beat the yolk and water together. Add to the flour mixture and blend until the pastry comes together. Wrap in plastic wrap and refrigerate for at least 15 minutes.

Preheat the oven to 375°F.

Roll out the dough on floured wax paper into a 12- to 14-inch round; or pat it into a tart pan with your hands, pulling pieces of dough from the ball and pressing them over the bottom and sides of the pan, using the heel of your hand.

Prick the bottom of the pastry shell with a fork and bake for 10 minutes.

# CHOCOLATE-RASPBERRY BROWNIES

MAKES ABOUT 16

¼ pound unsalted margarine, melted

½ cup sugar

2 eggs

1 teaspoon vanilla extract

½ cup raspberry preserves

2 ounces unsweetened chocolate, melted (see page 21)

¾ cup flour

½ teaspoon baking powder

¼ teaspoon salt

½ cup toasted, chopped pecans (see page 24)

Powdered sugar (optional)

Chocolate Glaze (recipe follows)

Toasted pecan halves (see page 24) for garnish

Preheat the oven to 350°F.

In the bowl of an electric mixer, blend the margarine and sugar. Beat in the eggs and vanilla. Add the preserves and melted chocolate and mix well. Combine the flour, baking powder, and salt and blend into the egg mixture until smooth. Fold in the chopped nuts.

Pour into a greased 8- or 9-inch square baking pan and bake for 30 minutes, or until a toothpick inserted in the center comes out clean. Cool.

Just before serving, sprinkle with powdered sugar or spread the Chocolate Glaze over the top and garnish with pecan halves.

# CHOCOLATE GLAZE

¼ cup powdered sugar
2 tablespoons unsalted
  margarine
2 tablespoons fruit-flavored
  brandy
1 teaspoon vanilla extract
2 ounces semisweet choco-
  late, grated

In a small saucepan, combine the powdered sugar, margarine, and brandy. Simmer over low heat for 3 minutes. Stir in the vanilla.

Place the grated chocolate in a bowl and pour the sugar mixture on top. Stir until the chocolate is melted and the mixture is smooth. Cool slightly.

# New Year's Eve Gala

FOR 12

New Year's Eve is a perfect time to entertain at home. It's much more fun to spend this long evening with people you care about than in a boisterous crowd.

A special holiday calls for glamorous food, so begin with Buckwheat Blinis and Caviar and a beautiful Leek Terrine, then proceed to eat your way through a variety of small well-planned courses. Fellow gourmets will be impressed with your homemade Chicken Sausages (easy to do with plastic wrap!), the sophisticated French salad, and an Italian dessert.

Horns, hats, confetti, and printed menus (See "How I Entertain") and bottles of sparkling Champagne, served all evening, will add to the party atmosphere.

By midnight, the first New Year's resolution will probably be "Let's do it again next year!"

## Buckwheat Blinis and Caviar

MAKES 36 BLINI

| | |
|---|---|
| 1 cup warm water (110 to 115°F) | In a small bowl, combine the water, sugar, and yeast. |
| 1 teaspoon sugar | In the bowl of an electric mixer, beat the egg yolks until thick. Add the yeast mixture, salt, margarine, and |

½ package yeast (½ table-
  spoon)
4 eggs, separated
½ teaspoon salt
3 tablespoons unsalted margarine, melted
1½ cups sifted buckwheat
  flour
Caviar

flour and beat until smooth. Cover with a towel and let rise in a warm place for 1 hour, or until doubled.

In another bowl, beat the egg whites until stiff and gently fold into the yeast mixture.

Preheat a lightly oiled pan or griddle until hot. Using 1 tablespoon of batter for each pancake, cook until golden brown on one side, then turn and cook until golden brown on the other side. Add more margarine for each batch. Serve with caviar or Gravlax.

# LEEK TERRINE WITH ORANGE MAYONNAISE

Leeks are one of the most interesting—and most neglected—vegetables. Don't be afraid to try them—their distinctive flavor is very appealing and their subtle green and white color adds eye appeal to this classic terrine.

2 quarts lightly flavored
  Chicken Stock (see page
  390)
16 leeks, cleaned and
  trimmed, roots and dark
  green parts discarded
1 tablespoon unflavored gelatin (1 envelope)
Salt
Freshly ground black pepper
1 large tomato, peeled (see
  page 26) and chopped
Orange Mayonnaise (see page
  372)

In a large saucepan, bring the stock to a boil. Add the leeks and simmer until tender, 20 to 30 minutes. Drain. Remove ½ cup of stock and soften gelatin in it.

Line a 3 × 7-inch loaf pan with plastic wrap and place the leeks lengthwise in layers, alternating white and green ends, and seasoning each layer to taste with salt and pepper. Spread a thin layer of gelatin over each layer. Turn the pans right side up again. Place heavy cans or other weights inside the top pan to press down on the leeks. Refrigerate for at least 6 hours.

Remove the weights and top pan. Carefully unmold the terrine onto a platter. Peel away the plastic wrap. Just before serving, cut the terrine into ½-inch slices with an electric knife or a *very* sharp knife. Garnish with chopped tomato and Orange Mayonnaise.

# CHICKEN SAUSAGES

8 whole chicken breasts, halved, skinned, and boned
Duxelles (recipe follows)
3 carrots, sliced into 16 long thin matchsticks
3 zucchini, sliced into 16 long thin matchsticks
Salt
Freshly ground black pepper
1 quart Chicken Stock (see page 390)
2 tablespoons safflower or vegetable oil
Bean Sauce (recipe follows)

Remove the long fillets attached by membranes to the chicken breasts; finely dice these fillets and mix with Duxelles.

Place each breast between two pieces of plastic wrap and pound with the flat side of a meat tenderizer or rolling pin until it is paper thin.

Remove the top piece of plastic wrap. Spread each prepared chicken breast evenly with 1 tablespoon of the Duxelles; place a carrot and zucchini matchstick on top. Sprinkle with salt and pepper to taste. Roll the breast into a sausage and wrap with the plastic wrap, allowing 3 inches overlapping. Twist the ends lightly together and tie securely to seal.

Poach the sausages in simmering chicken stock for 10 minutes on each side. Remove and unwrap, reserving the juices in a bowl for the Bean Sauce.

In a large skillet, heat the oil and brown the sausages on both sides. Spoon the Bean Sauce on heated plates and serve a scoop of the Venetian Potatoes on one side.

## DUXELLES
### MINCED MUSHROOMS

1 tablespoon unsalted margarine
2 medium shallots, minced
2 tablespoons finely chopped onion
1 pound mushrooms, finely chopped
Salt
Freshly ground black pepper

In a skillet, melt the margarine and sauté the shallots, onions, and mushrooms until lightly browned. Stir and continue cooking until the moisture has evaporated, about 5 minutes. Season to taste with salt and pepper. Cool.

## BEAN SAUCE

2 tablespoons olive oil
1 small onion, finely chopped
½ cup dry red wine
1 can (15 ounces) pinto beans
Reserved juices from poached sausages

In a skillet, heat the olive oil and sauté the onion until lightly browned. Add the red wine and cook over high heat to reduce. Stir in ⅓ cup of the beans and all of their liquid and the reserved juices from the sausages. With a fork, mash the beans into the liquid. Transfer the mixture to a processor or blender and purée. Return to the skillet

1 cup chicken stock that sausages were poached in
Salt
Freshly ground black pepper

and add the chicken stock and remaining ¾ cup of beans. Add salt and pepper to taste. Bring to a boil, cover, and keep warm.

# VENETIAN POTATOES

2 tablespoons unsalted margarine
2 tablespoons olive oil
6 medium potatoes, peeled and cut into ¼-inch dice
3 medium tomatoes, peeled (see page 26) and cut into ¼-inch dice
2 garlic cloves, minced
1 cup Chicken Stock (see page 390)
1 teaspoon dried thyme
1 bay leaf
12 medium mushrooms, cut into ¼-inch dice
Salt
Freshly ground black pepper

In a large heavy skillet, melt the margarine with the oil over medium heat. Add the potatoes and sauté for 5 minutes, stirring occasionally. Add the tomatoes, garlic, stock, thyme, and bay leaf. Simmer, covered, for 20 minutes, stirring occasionally. Add the mushrooms and simmer for 20 minutes more; then uncover and simmer for 10 minutes longer. Season to taste with salt and pepper.

# ROASTED GARLIC AND SHALLOT SALAD

The unusual part of this salad is the shallots and unpeeled garlic, which guests can squeeze to obtain the delicious self-contained filling.

2 whole heads of garlic, cloves separated but unpeeled
Olive oil
8 small shallots, unpeeled
6 Japanese eggplants, thinly sliced
6 cups mâche lettuce
3 heads of endive
Salt

Preheat the oven to 375°F.

Generously coat the unpeeled garlic cloves with olive oil; wrap them in foil and seal well. Coat the shallots with olive oil, wrap them in foil, and seal well. Place the foil packages on a baking sheet and bake for about 30 minutes, until the garlic and shallots are tender.

In a large skillet over medium heat, heat a thin layer of oil and brown the eggplant slices on both sides. Drain on paper towels.

Wash the mâche lettuce thoroughly and dry on paper towels. Wash the endive and slice lengthwise in thin strips. Toss the mâche and endive in a bowl. Just before serving, toss with olive oil and salt.

To assemble the salad, place ½ cup of the mâche mixture in the center of each serving plate. Place eggplant slices, garlic, and shallots on top and around the greens on each plate. Serve warm.

# BITTERSWEET CHOCOLATE AND CHAMPAGNE SHERBET

MAKES ABOUT 1 QUART

2 cups water
2 cups sugar
8 ounces bittersweet chocolate, melted (see page 21)
2 cups champagne

In a saucepan, bring the water to a boil and add the sugar. Pour into the bowl of an electric mixer. Pour in the chocolate in a thin stream, mixing well. Place over ice water and mix until cool.

Stir in the champagne. Pour into the canister of an ice cream maker and freeze according to manufacturer's directions. Or place in the freezer and freeze until firm, 3 to 6 hours, stirring occasionally with a fork to break up ice crystals. Continue stirring and freezing until the mixture is set.

Scoop the sherbet into chilled glass bowls or goblets.

# FILO WAFERS

MAKES ABOUT 4 DOZEN

¾ pound unsalted margarine, melted
1 cup sugar
1 cup finely ground almonds (4 ounces)
1 package (1 pound) filo sheets
Powdered sugar

Preheat the oven to 350°F.

Line several baking sheets with foil and brush with margarine. In a bowl, combine the sugar and almonds.

Stack the filo and cut it into 3-inch rounds with a cookie cutter, trimming loose ends with scissors. Place 1 filo round on the baking sheet; brush lightly with margarine and sprinkle it evenly with the sugar mixture. Top with a second and third round, covering each with margarine and sugar mixture. Place a fourth round on top; brush with margarine and sprinkle with powdered sugar. Repeat entire process until all the filo rounds are used. Bake for 10 minutes, or until golden brown. Cool on wire racks.

# FATHER'S DAY FEAST

FOR 12

Onion Zemmel

Barbecue-Baked Short Ribs

Grilled Veal Knackwurst

Steamed Corn in the Husks

Dad's Favorite Potato Salad

Assorted Mustards

Platter of Sliced Onions
and Tomatoes

Watermelon Wedges

Strawberry-Almond Tart

SUGGESTED BEVERAGES:

Beer, sodas, hearty red
wine, iced tea, lemonade

Here's a hearty menu that can be served indoors or out—as a brunch or early dinner—and it makes a perfect picnic, because it's portable and some of the food can be grilled at your favorite recreation spot.

Homemade knackwurst is at its best when grilled over hot coals. The corn, wrapped in protective husks, can be finished on the stove or wrapped in foil and cooked on the same barbecue grill. Fathers might enjoy joining in the preparation.

The succulent Barbecue-Baked Short Ribs, marinated in a spicy sauce, can be easily carried to a picnic site and reheated if necessary.

Added attractions are Potato Salad with homemade mayonnaise and a pizzalike Onion Zemmel. The desserts are simple—strawberry tart and watermelon wedges. Have lots of beverages for young and old—ranging from beer and red wine to sodas and lemonade. Serve the drinks in big mugs and the food on big buffet plates, with lots of paper napkins.

## ONION ZEMMEL
### FLAT ONION ROLLS

Throughout Eastern Europe, this delicious flat bread topped with onions, salt, and poppy seeds is a staple. Most countries have Onion Zemmel in some form: In Italy it is pizza topped with onions. The French serve pissaladière. Even the Chinese make pancakes that are filled with onions and baked or fried. Ours uses a basic challah dough.

On a cold evening, serve a platter of hot Onion Zemmel with a thick meat soup or stew.

MAKES 12 TO 24 FLAT ROLLS

1 basic challah recipe (see page 212)

2 eggs, beaten with 1 table-spoon water

2 cups coarsely chopped onions

Kosher salt

Poppy seeds

Prepare the challah dough. After it has risen for 1 hour or has doubled in size, punch it down.

Break off balls of the dough just large enough to hold in the palm of your hand. Roll out each ball into a circular disk ½ inch thick. Place each disk on a greased baking sheet, brush them with the egg mixture, and sprinkle generously with the onions, kosher salt, and poppy seeds. Let them rise, covered, for 1 hour at warm room temperature.

Preheat the oven to 350°F.

Pierce the center of the zemmel all over with a fork, leaving a rim unpierced. Bake for 20 to 30 minutes, or until the onions begin to brown and the crust is crisp and golden.

# BARBECUE-BAKED SHORT RIBS

2 garlic cloves, minced

3 cups dry red wine

½ cup olive oil

¼ cup red wine vinegar

1 teaspoon dried thyme

1 teaspoon salt

½ teaspoon freshly ground black pepper

6 pounds lean beef short ribs, fat and gristle removed

½ cup catsup

¼ cup brown sugar

1 tablespoon powdered mustard

1 tablespoon grated fresh ginger

1 cup (about 6) thinly sliced green onions (scallions)

In a large shallow baking dish, combine the garlic, 1 cup of the wine, olive oil, vinegar, thyme, salt, and pepper. Mix well. Add the ribs, turning to coat them. Marinate in the refrigerator for at least 6 hours. Turn the ribs every hour.

Preheat the oven to 450°F.

Transfer the ribs to a large roaster. Reserve the marinade and store in the refrigerator. Bake the ribs, uncovered, for 30 minutes, turning once. Pour off the fat.

To the reserved marinade, stir in the catsup, brown sugar, the remaining 2 cups of wine, mustard, ginger, and green onions.

Spoon this sauce over the ribs, coating them thoroughly. Reduce the heat to 350°F, cover the ribs, and bake for 2 to 3 hours, until the meat is tender. Serve with extra sauce on the side.

# GRILLED VEAL
# KNACKWURST

MAKES ABOUT 2 DOZEN

3 pounds ground veal
2 large onions, diced
3 garlic cloves, peeled
1½ teaspoons salt
½ teaspoon freshly ground
    black pepper
½ teaspoon ground red pep-
    per (cayenne)
½ teaspooon paprika
½ teaspoon allspice
¼ teaspoon powdered bay
    leaf
1 tablespoon fennel seeds

In a meat grinder, grind the veal, onions, and garlic into a large bowl. Add salt, pepper, red pepper, paprika, all-spice, bay leaf, and fennel. Mix well. Divide the mixture into equal balls, about ½ to 1 cup each. Knead each ball into a sausage shape.

Place a sheet of plastic wrap, about 14 inches long, on a counter. Working with one sausage at a time, place it in the center of the plastic wrap, leaving about 3 inches margin on both ends. Take the plastic wrap closest to you and cover the sausage neatly, rolling tightly into a long sausage shape. Pull tightly on both ends; twist like a candy wrap and tie into knots.

Drop the knackwurst into simmering water and poach for 10 to 15 mintues, turning halfway during the poach-ing. Remove the plastic wrap and sauté the sausages in a lightly oiled skillet until golden brown, or cook them on a grill.

# STEAMED CORN
# IN THE HUSKS

The sweetest corn is that which is picked, cooked, and eaten the same day, so select the freshest ears possible. Leaving the inner husk on makes the corn tender and juicy.

12 ears of corn in their husks
Unsalted margarine
Salt

Strip off the outer husks of the corn, leaving the thin in-ner husk. With a sharp knife, cut off the stalks close to the cob and the tip of the cob.

In a large heavy saucepan, bring 3 to 4 inches of lightly salted water to a boil and add the corn. With the water at a steady low boil, cook for 5 to 10 minutes. Remove and serve at once with margarine and salt. Or wrap in foil and finish heating on the barbecue grill for added flavor and a golden brown color.

# DAD'S FAVORITE POTATO SALAD

Potato salad can be included in so many menus, dairy as well as meat. The home-made mayonnaise adds a special flavor. I always prepare too much salad, cover it with plastic wrap, and serve it the next day.

12 to 14 medium red pota-
toes, cooked and diced

6 hard-boiled eggs (see page 23), quartered and sliced

1½ cups diced celery

1 green bell pepper, seeded and diced

1 red bell pepper, seeded and diced

1 yellow bell pepper, seeded and diced

2 cups Classic Homemade Mayonnaise (see page 326)

½ to 1 cup finely sliced green onions (scallions)

½ cup minced parsley

Salt

Freshly ground black pepper

Yellow and red bell pepper slices for garnish

In a large bowl, combine the potatoes, eggs, celery, and peppers. Add enough mayonnaise to moisten and toss gently. Add the green onions and parsley and season to taste with salt and pepper; toss gently again. Garnish with thin slices of red and yellow bell pepper rings.

# STRAWBERRY-ALMOND TART

¼ pound unsalted margarine

½ cup sugar

5 ounces almonds, finely chopped (1¼ cups)

2 eggs

¼ teaspoon almond extract

Prebaked Sweet Pastry Tart Shell (see page 205)

2 pints strawberries, stemmed

1 jar (8 ounces) currant jelly, melted

Powdered sugar

Preheat the oven to 350°F.

In the bowl of an electric mixer, cream the margarine and sugar until well blended. Add the almonds and mix well. One at a time, beat in the eggs, blending thoroughly. Mix in the almond extract. Pour into the pre-baked tart shell, smoothing the top with a spatula. Bake for 20 to 30 minutes, or until browned and set. Cool on rack.

Dip the top of each strawberry in the jelly and place, stem side down, in a circle on top of the almond filling. Sprinkle powdered sugar around the edge of the tart.

# Bridal Shower Salad Buffet

FOR 24

A bridal shower is one of the most joyous parties to give, and the occasion calls for light, delicious, festive foods. This menu offers four of my personal favorite chicken salad recipes. (For a smaller shower, you could serve just two or three.)

Each salad has a totally different flavor and texture, yet surprisingly they're all based on a simple poached chicken recipe. Give the bride-to-be all the recipes, printed on pretty file cards, along with a file card holder. And why not share them with the guests, too? To help the bride with her recipe collection, you might want to include blank recipe cards with the invitations; suggest that each guest bring her own favorite recipe. If several of your friends are giving the shower with you, each can prepare a salad.

The beautiful golden Double Ring Bridal Cake symbolizes two joined wedding rings and serves as both centerpiece and dessert.

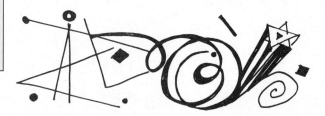

## Fruited Challah Twists

MAKES 36 SMALL TWISTS

3½ cups unbleached flour
1 package active dry yeast
⅓ cup honey

In the bowl of an electric mixer, combine 2½ cups of the flour with the yeast, honey, and salt. Gradually add the water and continue beating 2 to 3 minutes. Add the

1 tablespoon salt

1⅓ cups warm water (110 to 115°F)

¼ pound unsalted margarine, melted

2 cups whole wheat flour

¼ cup raisins

¼ cup diced dried apples

¼ cup diced dried apricots

¼ cup diced prunes

margarine and mix well. Add enough of the remaining unbleached and whole wheat flours to make a soft dough.

Transfer the dough to a well-floured board, kneading in the raisins, apples, apricots, and prunes. Continue kneading for 5 minutes. Place in an oiled bowl and oil the top of the dough. Cover with a towel and let rise 1 to 1½ hours.

Preheat the oven to 375°F.

Punch down the dough and knead for 3 minutes, then return it to the bowl and let it rise for 20 minutes.

Pull off a golf-ball-size piece of dough. Roll into an 8- to 10-inch-long rope and twist into a knot. Repeat with the remaining dough. Place the twists on a well-oiled baking sheet and bake for 15 to 20 minutes, or until golden brown and a crust forms on top. Cool on a wire rack.

# POLLO FORTE
## POWERFUL CHICKEN

I discovered this totally different chicken salad recipe at a little restaurant in West Los Angeles, appropriately called Mangia, which means "eat."

I've adapted it for kosher cooks and added a few of my own touches. It's delicious hot or cold, and is very portable for picnics. We love to serve it in the deluxe box suppers that we bring to the Hollywood Bowl each summer.

This basic recipe serves eight and can be easily doubled or tripled for large gatherings such as this shower.

1 whole chicken, about 4 pounds, poached (recipe follows)

2 tablespoons drained capers

½ cup olive oil

1½ tablespoons flour

3 red bell peppers, roasted (see page 278)

2 garlic cloves, minced

Salt

Freshly ground black pepper

3 tablespoons wine vinegar

Prepare the poached chicken. Remove the chicken and let cool, reserving the poaching liquid. Remove the skin from the chicken and lift the meat from the bones. Cut the meat into strips and place on a serving platter. Sprinkle with capers and cover.

Bring 1½ cups of the reserved poaching liquid to a boil. Heat the oil in a heavy saucepan. Add the flour and stir until golden. Continue stirring, adding boiling poaching liquid all at once. Stir 2 or 3 minutes. Add 1 of the red peppers and garlic. Simmer for 10 minutes, remove from heat, and blend well.

Return the sauce to the stove. Add salt and pepper to taste. Simmer for 10 to 15 minutes. Remove from the heat. Add the wine vinegar and mix well. Pour over the chicken. Slice the remaining 2 red peppers in thin strips and use as garnish. Cool. Cover and refrigerate for at least 4 hours.

## POACHED CHICKEN

Here is a simple way to prepare chicken breasts to be used in salads; they will always be tender and moist. A whole chicken may be cooked this way also, adjusting time to the size of the chicken.

1 large onion, diced
4 celery ribs, thickly sliced
4 carrots, peeled and thickly sliced
1 small parsnip, peeled and thickly sliced
4 parsley sprigs
1 bay leaf
12 whole peppercorns
6 to 8 cups Chicken Stock (see page 390)
Salt
8 chicken breasts, skinned and boned

In a large saucepan, combine the onion, celery, carrots, parsnip, parsley, bay leaf, peppercorns, and stock. Bring to a boil over high heat, reduce the heat, and simmer for 20 minutes. Season to taste with salt. Add the chicken breasts and poach them for 15 minutes. Transfer the poached chicken breasts to a shallow bowl and cover with chicken broth until ready to use.

## ORIENTAL CHICKEN SALAD

MAKES 8 SERVINGS

3 whole chicken breasts
1 teaspoon salt
3 tablespoons soy sauce
3 tablespoons sherry
2 ounces rice sticks (Mai Fun), or 10 wontons
3 cups vegetable oil for deep-frying
1 head lettuce, finely shredded

Preheat the oven to 375°F.

Rub the chicken with the salt, soy sauce, and sherry and bake for 30 minutes. Cool. Discard the skin and bones and tear the chicken into long thin pieces. Set aside.

Deep-fry the rice sticks in hot oil, a few at a time, until they puff. Drain on paper towels. Set aside. Or slice the wontons into ¼-inch strips and deep-fry in hot oil, a few at a time, until golden brown. Drain on paper towels. Set aside.

Just before serving, arrange the lettuce in a large bowl

4 green onions (scallions),
thinly sliced

½ cup toasted sliced almonds
(see page 24)

¼ cup preserved ginger

Soy Sauce Dressing (recipe
follows)

3 tablespoons toasted sesame
seeds

with the green onions, chicken, almonds, ginger, and rice sticks (or fried wonton strips) in layers; pour the dressing over the salad and toss well. Sprinkle with sesame seeds and serve immediately.

## SOY SAUCE DRESSING

6 tablespoons red wine
vinegar

¾ cup soy sauce

6 tablespoons sesame oil

6 tablespoons sugar

6 teaspoons hoisin sauce

4 green onions (scallions),
shredded

In a mixing bowl, blend the red wine vinegar, soy sauce, sesame oil, sugar, and hoisin sauce. Mix in the green onions. Chill in the refrigerator for at least 1 hour.

# CURRIED CHICKEN SALAD WITH ROASTED PEANUTS

MAKES 6 TO 8 SERVINGS

3 whole chicken breasts
(about 3 pounds), split and
poached (see preceding
recipe)

1 large cucumber, peeled and
diced

½ cup golden raisins

1 cup roasted peanuts (see
page 24)

1 cup mayonnaise

2 tablespoons medium-hot
curry powder

Salt

Freshly ground black pepper
or Tabasco sauce

Watercress for garnish

Transfer the poached chicken with a slotted spoon to a work area. Remove and discard the skin and bones and cut the meat into strips. Place the chicken in a large mixing bowl and toss with the cucumber, raisins, and peanuts.

In a small bowl, combine the mayonnaise, curry powder, and salt and pepper to taste. Mix well. Pour the dressing over the chicken mixture and mix gently until well coated.

Spoon the salad onto watercress-garnished plates.

# CHICKEN-PASTA SALAD

MAKES 6 TO 8 SERVINGS

2 cups fresh broccoli florets
¾ cup green pasta, cooked
(see page 290)
1 whole poached chicken
breast (see page 356),
skinned, boned, and cut
into bite-size pieces
3 tablespoons minced parsley
1 small red onion, thinly
sliced (optional)
1 small zucchini, diced
1 large roasted red bell pepper (see page 278), thinly
sliced
2 tablespoons red wine
vinegar
6 tablespoons olive oil
2 garlic cloves, minced
Salt
Freshly ground black pepper
4 to 5 fresh basil leaves

Drop the broccoli florets into boiling water and cook 3 to 4 minutes, or until tender. Drain, cool, and set aside.

In a large salad bowl, combine the pasta, chicken, parsley, onion, zucchini, and red bell pepper. Combine the vinegar, olive oil, and garlic and pour over the pasta mixture. Toss and season to taste with salt and pepper.

Top the pasta salad with the broccoli florets and basil leaves and toss lightly again.

# DOUBLE RING BRIDAL CAKE

This light, rich cake with its golden icing and garnish of gold sprinkles and "diamonds" is a sensational conversation piece for a bridal shower. Another plus is that without the icing, it keeps beautifully in the refrigerator for three to four days and may be iced the day of the shower.

MAKES 1 RING CAKE

¼ pound plus 2⅔ tablespoons
unsalted margarine
½ teaspoon ground mace
1½ cups sugar
6 egg whites
¾ cup liquid nondairy
creamer

Preheat the oven to 350°F.

In the bowl of an electric mixer, beat the margarine with the mace. Gradually add 1 cup of the sugar, beating until smooth. Beat in 3 of the egg whites and the remaining ½ cup sugar. Add the remaining 3 egg whites, 1 at a time, beating well. Combine the nondairy creamer and orange juice. Combine the flour, salt, and baking pow-

¼ cup orange juice
2½ cups sifted flour
½ teaspoon salt
3 teaspoons baking powder
Vegetable oil spray
Powdered Sugar Frosting (recipe follows)
Gold sprinkles and rock candy crystals for garnish

der. A little at a time, stir in the flour mixture alternately with the liquids. Beat the batter for 30 seconds. Coat a 2-quart dessert ring mold with vegetable oil spray and sprinkle lightly with flour. Turn the cake batter into the mold.

Bake for 50 minutes, or until a toothpick inserted into the center comes out dry.

Prepare another cake the same way. When both cakes are cool, using the mold as a guide arrange it on top of one cake and cut out two sections. Remove the mold and slide the second cake in its place. Fill in any spaces with the cut pieces to form a figure eight. Frost and garnish with gold sprinkles and some rock candy crystals for ''diamonds,'' to create two golden wedding rings.

## POWDERED SUGAR FROSTING

1 pound (3½ cups) powdered sugar, sifted
½ teaspoon cream of tartar
3 egg whites, unbeaten
½ teaspoon vanilla extract
1 tablespoon orange juice

In the bowl of an electric mixer, combine the powdered sugar, cream of tartar, egg whites, vanilla, and orange juice. Beat at low speed until the sugar is dissolved, then beat at high speed until the mixture is light and fluffy. Keep covered with a damp towel until ready to use.

# ISRAELI BAR MITZVAH BUFFET

FOR 48

## ▼▲▼▲▼▲▼▲▼▲▼▲▼▲▼▲▼▲▼▲▼

Pita Bread

Pita Garlic Toast

Eggplant with Tahini

Hummus

Taramosalata

Dolmas

Falafel

Tabbouleh

Teropeta

Olives, sliced tomatoes,
sliced red onions, and
sliced cucumbers

Baklava

Bourma

Chocolate-Covered Halvah

Bowls of fresh fruit

Bowls of raisins and nuts

SUGGESTED BEVERAGES:

Israeli champagne and dry
white wine

A Bar Mitzvah or Bat Mitzvah, celebrating a child's coming of age, is certainly occasion for rejoicing—but not if it causes trauma to the family finances. A religious rite should not be an extravaganza, so why not think twice before planning an elaborate celebration in a big hotel or club, or hiring expensive and impersonal caterers who serve the same menu for every party.

Our buffet was inspired by a recent trip to Israel, where we collected some intriguing recipes that are filled with the exotic spices of the Middle East. Thinking ahead to a Bar Mitzvah we were planning, an Israeli menu seemed just right. It would take us back to our roots.

This type of Israeli food is easy to make at home, but it can be augmented by ordering from one of the small Israeli restaurants that are cropping up all over these days. Most of them are happy to do catering or provide "take-outs."

Serve this menu indoors or out, depending on the season and the amount of room you have. Most of the food can be prepared at least partially in advance. The salads are the kind that will keep well in the refrigerator for a day or two and even improve in flavor during that time.

The Teropeta can be frozen, defrosted, and baked just before serving time. The cookie doughs were made in advance and frozen in batter form, then baked the day before the Bar Mitzvah.

The desserts should be served on a separate sweet table, along with baskets of fresh fruit and bowls of nuts and raisins.

All the recipes in this menu serve 12, so they can easily be adapted to serve 24, 36, and 48.

# PITA BREAD

When visiting the old market place in Jerusalem, I observed how this delicious bread was baked in cavernous wood-fired ovens. The rounds of dough are flattened by hand, then literally tossed against the inside walls of the ovens, where they puff up as they bake.

When cut in two, the center becomes a pocket that you can stuff with a variety of fillings—Falafel, ground meats, thick stews, salads, and soft cheese. You can also cut them into triangles and serve for dipping with Hummus. Or split the two sides of the pocket, then cut them in half, spread them with garlic-herb butter, and crisp them in the oven, for a perfect accompaniment to salads or soups.

MAKES 12 TO 14

2 packages active dry yeast
Pinch of sugar
2½ cups warm water (110 to 115°F)
3 tablespoons olive oil
1½ teaspoons salt
6 cups unbleached flour

Dissolve the yeast with the sugar in ½ cup of the water. Let stand in a warm place a few mintues, until foamy.

In the bowl of an electric mixer, stir together the remaining 2 cups of water, the olive oil, and salt. Add the yeast mixture and then the flour, 1 cup at a time, beating until the dough comes together. Turn the dough out onto a floured board and knead until shiny and elastic, 5 to 10 minutes. Place it in a lightly oiled bowl, and oil the top of the dough. Cover the bowl with a towel and let the dough rise in a warm place until doubled, 1½ to 2 hours. Punch down the dough and knead it until smooth and springy to the touch, about 5 minutes. Roll the dough into a sausage shape. Cut it into 15 equal pieces and knead each piece into a ball.

Roll out each ball on a floured board to a diameter of 6 to 6½ inches and a thickness of about ¼ inch. Place the pitas on individual pieces of foil or parchment paper, cover with towels, and let them stand for 1 hour.

Preheat the oven to 500°F. Bake the pitas on foil on the lowest shelf or the bottom of the oven about 5 minutes, just until they start to brown and puff like balloons. Remove immediately and serve hot.

# PITA GARLIC TOAST

¼ pound unsalted butter or
  margarine
1½ teaspoons lemon juice
2 garlic cloves, minced
1 tablespoon minced parsley
2 teaspoons fresh minced
  chives (optional)
Salt
Freshly ground black pepper
6 Pita Breads (see page 361),
  split

In a processor, blend together butter, lemon juice, garlic, parsley, and chives. Add salt and pepper to taste. (If not using the spread immediately, mold it into a cube, cover with plastic wrap, and refrigerate or freeze; let it come back to room temperature before continuing with the recipe.)

Preheat the oven to 400°F. Spread the inside surfaces of the pita halves with the butter. Cut each piece into halves or quarters. Arrange the pitas in one layer on a foil-lined baking sheet. Bake until lightly browned and crisp, about 5 minutes. Transfer to a serving plate and serve immediately.

# EGGPLANT WITH TAHINI

Eggplant is a versatile vegetable and is much neglected in this country. Beautiful dark purple eggplants are used throughout Israel and other eastern countries. White eggplants can be found in specialty produce markets. The delicate yet pungent flavor is enhanced with garlic, olive oil, and salt.

MAKES 2½ TO 3 CUPS

1 large eggplant
1 medium onion, finely
  chopped, juice squeezed
  out and discarded
1 cup finely chopped parsley
½ cup tahini (sesame seed
  paste)
2 to 3 tablespoons lemon
  juice
2 garlic cloves, finely chopped
2 teaspoons water
Salt
Dash of cayenne pepper
Parsley sprigs for garnish

Preheat the oven to 400°F.

Cut the eggplant in half lengthwise and place it cut side down on a baking sheet lined with foil. Bake it until its skin is charred and the inside is tender, about 20 minutes. Let the eggplant cool; peel it and chop fine. Place it in a mixing bowl; add the onion and parsley and blend well.

In a separate bowl, stir together the tahini, 2 tablespoons of the lemon juice, garlic, and water until well blended. Stir the tahini mixture into the eggplant mixture. Add salt to taste and cayenne pepper. Stir in more lemon juice to taste. Garnish with parsley.

# HUMMUS

Hummus is a simple, wonderfully flavorful dip or spread made from garbanzos (chick-peas) and tahini (sesame seed paste). Its texture is velvety, rich, and firm enough to scoop up with wedges of pita bread or crisp vegetables. The taste is robust, nutlike, garlicky, and so satisfying that you won't be able to stop eating it.

1 can (15 ounces) garbanzos, with liquid
1 cup tahini (sesame seed paste)
½ cup lemon juice
⅓ cup olive oil
4 garlic cloves, peeled
1 teaspoon ground cumin
6 fresh parsley sprigs, stemmed
1 to 2 teaspoons salt

Place the garbanzos in a processor or blender and process until coarsely puréed.

Add the tahini, lemon juice, olive oil, garlic, and cumin and process until smoothly puréed. Blend in the parsley leaves and 1 teaspooon of salt. Add additional salt to taste. Serve with hot Pita Bread and sliced vegetables such as carrots, zucchini, mushrooms, and jicama.

# TARAMOSALATA
## CARP ROE SPREAD

Carp roe is an economical substitute for caviar and makes an unusual and delicious appetizer. Don't use your blender to prepare this spread, because the tiny eggs are too delicate.

MAKES ABOUT 1½ CUPS

6 slices white bread, crusts trimmed
1 cup cold water
½ cup tarama (carp roe), rinsed well in cold water to remove the salt
¼ cup lemon juice
½ medium onion, grated
1 cup olive oil

Soak the bread in the water for 5 minutes. Drain and squeeze it dry. In a mixing bowl, mash the bread until smooth. With a fork, beat in the tarama, 1 teaspooon at a time, mixing continuously. Beat in the lemon juice and grated onion, beating until it forms a smooth paste. Add the olive oil in a thin stream, beating until the Taramosalata is thick. Cover with plastic wrap and refrigerate until ready to serve. Serve with Pita Bread.

# DOLMAS

## STUFFED GRAPE LEAVES

These grape leaves can be made days ahead (but hide them if you do so they don't get eaten). First, prepare the rice filling and store in the refrigerator—at least a day in advance. Then stuff, roll, and steam the grape leaves and store in advance. Be sure to buy the grape leaves in lemon juice and not in brine, because the brine is hard to wash off and the grape leaves will taste salty.

Grape leaves cause a lot of heated discussion as to who has the best recipe. I think this honor goes to an Armenian friend who generously shared his delightful version, which includes tangy dried apricots, an unbelievable amount of onions, olive oil, and lemon juice. I had to refine his recipe slightly, because the measurements were very vague—"a lot of this, a big bunch of that . . ."

Sometimes just one unusual addition to a recipe can earn you a reputation as a famous cook and host or hostess. In this case, the ingredient is the dried apricots. They're not really sweet, but their tart-sweet flavor blends perfectly with the lemon, pungent grape leaves, and aromatic spices.

MAKES ABOUT 60

1 cup olive oil

4 large onions, finely chopped

1 cup water

1 cup long-grain white rice

¼ cup chopped parsley

¼ cup chopped mint leaves

1 teaspoon ground allspice

1 teaspoon salt

½ teaspoon freshly ground black pepper

2 packages (6 ounces each) dried apricot halves

1 jar (16 ounces) grape leaves, rinsed

Juice of 3 lemons

In a large heavy skillet, heat the olive oil over medium heat. Add the onions and sauté, stirring frequently, until soft but not yet browned, about 10 mintues. Add ½ cup water, the rice, parsley, mint, allspice, salt, and pepper. Stir well, cover, and continue cooking on low heat for about 15 mintues, stirring every 5 minutes to prevent sticking. The rice will be undercooked. Cool to room temperature. Dice 3 ounces of dried apricot halves (½ of 1 package) and add them to the cooled rice.

Place 5 or 6 grape leaves on the bottom of a large pot. Place the remaining apricot halves on top of the grape leaves to cover. Set aside.

Snip off the stems of the remaining leaves and place on a work surface, vein sides up. Place a heaping tablespoon of the rice mixture in the center of each grape leaf. Roll the stem end over the filling, fold in the sides, and roll up the leaf to enclose the rice completely.

Place the stuffed leaves, seam sides down, in neatly packed layers on top of the apricots in the pot. Sprinkle with the remaining ½ cup water and the lemon juice. Place a heavy ovenproof dish inside the pot on top of the grape leaves. Cover and simmer for 20 to 30 minutes, until the grape leaves are tender. Serve them hot, if you like. Or carefully transfer them to a bowl, cover with plastic wrap, and chill in the refrigerator. Serve on a large platter surrounded by the cooked apricots.

# FALAFEL
## CRUSHED WHEAT AND GARBANZO FRITTERS

Serve these crisp fritters as an appetizer with toothpicks for easy handling and for dipping in a bowl of Hummus. Or serve them stuffed into Pita Bread, to make a traditional Israeli sandwich.

On one of my trips to Israel, I found an inexpensive little gadget that shapes and scoops up Falafel mixture, to drop into hot oil. Many of the Middle Eastern restaurants in the United States use them. If you or a friend are headed for Israel, be sure to look for one of these scoops in a cookware shop.

½ cup bulgur
1½ cups Pita Bread or white bread torn into chunks
2 cups canned garbanzo beans, drained
½ cup lemon juice
3 garlic cloves, peeled
2 tablespoons chopped cilantro
2 tablespoons chopped parsley
1 teaspoon crushed dried red pepper
1 teaspoon ground cumin
1 teaspoon salt
¼ teaspoon freshly ground black pepper
Vegetable oil for deep-frying

Soak the bulgur in enough cold water to cover for 15 minutes. Drain and set aside. Soak the bread in enough cold water to cover until soft and moist, about 5 minutes. Drain the bread, squeeze it dry, and set aside.

In a processor or blender, put the garbanzos, lemon juice, garlic, cilantro, parsley, red pepper, cumin, salt, and pepper. Process until smoothly puréed. Add the bulgur and bread and pulse until thoroughly combined. Moisten your hands with cold water. Shape the mixture into 1-inch balls. Fill a large heavy skillet with 3 inches of oil and heat to 375°F on a deep-frying thermometer. Fry the Falafel in several batches, without overcrowding, until golden brown, 1 to 2 minutes per batch. With a slotted spoon, transfer to paper towels to drain. Serve hot.

# TABBOULEH
## CRACKED WHEAT SALAD

The following recipe is for Tabbouleh at its most traditional. If you want to improvise, add a peeled and sliced cucumber, or a chopped green or red bell pepper. Chopped cilantro may be substituted for the mint.

1 cup bulgur
½ cup minced green onions (scallions)
1 cup finely chopped parsley
½ cup finely chopped fresh mint
4 medium tomatoes, peeled and coarsely chopped
⅓ cup lemon juice
Salt
Freshly ground black pepper
⅓ cup olive oil
2 heads of romaine lettuce, small center leaves only
1 lemon, thinly sliced for garnish

Soak the bulgur in enough cold water to cover for 10 to 20 minutes, until tender. Drain it well and squeeze it as dry as possible by hand or in a kitchen towel or a double layer of cheesecloth.

Place the bulgur in a large bowl. Add the green onions, parsley, mint, and tomatoes and toss well. Stir in the lemon juice, salt, and pepper. Let the mixture stand for about 30 minutes, to allow the flavors to blend. Stir in the oil.

Pile the mixture on a large platter and surround it with the romaine leaves to use for scooping. Garnish with lemon slices.

# TEROPETA
## CHEESE TRIANGLES

This is the very best filling I have ever tasted for these crisp pastries. The combination of cheeses, green onions, fresh dill, eggs, and baking powder all add up to a wonderful puffy texture and exciting flavor. One bite always leads to many more.

¾ pound Swiss cheese, grated
¾ pound Monterey Jack cheese, grated
½ cup minced green onions (scallions)
½ cup minced parsley
2 tablespoons fresh minced dill, or 1 teaspoon dried
6 eggs

In a large bowl, combine the cheeses with the green onions, parsley, and dill. One at a time, beat in the eggs. Then stir in the baking powder.

With scissors, cut the filo sheets crosswise into strips 2 inches wide. Work with 1 sheet of filo at a time, keeping the remaining filo covered at all times with wax paper and a damp towel. Work with each strip on top of a large sheet of wax paper placed on top of a damp kitchen towel. Brush each strip with melted butter. Place 1 teaspoon of the cheese mixture at one end of the strip and

1 teaspoon baking powder
1 package (1 pound) filo
  sheets
1 pound unsalted butter, clarified (see page 368)
½ cup sesame seeds

fold it over in a triangle along its length to make a neat triangular package. Place each triangle as it is finished on a baking sheet lined with buttered foil.

Preheat the oven to 375°F.

Brush the tops of the triangles with clarified butter and sprinkle with sesame seeds. (The Teropeta can be frozen at this point, if you like. Place them in the freezer uncovered, until the butter hardens, then cover with foil, seal, and freeze. Defrost before baking them.) Bake the Teropeta for 15 minutes, or until golden brown. Serve immediately.

# BAKLAVA
## LAYERED PASTRY

The trick in making Baklava is to assemble sheets of filo in just the right way. Usually several sheets are stacked, topped with ground nuts, then covered with several more filo sheets. With the first bite, the pastry separates and most of the nuts are lost forever. My way alternates thin filo layers with thin layers of nuts, and it holds together beautifully. The taste of crisp filo pastry, nuts, and sugar syrup is unbelievably rich and delectable. The preparation time is worth the effort—and you may be inspired to try other exotic filo recipes.

1 pound unsalted butter, clarified (recipe follows)
½ cup safflower or vege-
  table oil
1 package (1 pound) filo
  sheets
4 cups very finely chopped
  walnuts (2 pounds un-
  shelled)
Sugar and Honey Syrup (recipe follows)

Brush the bottom and sides of a 13 × 9 × 2½-inch baking dish with the clarified butter mixed with the oil. Trim the filo sheets to 12 × 9 inches. Place 1 sheet of filo on the bottom of the dish. Brush its entire surface lightly with clarified butter. Lay the second sheet on top and butter it lightly. Sprinkle it evenly with about 3 tablespoons of the walnuts.

Repeat the procedure, using 2 sheets of buttered filo topped with 3 tablespoons of walnuts, until you've used all the nuts and all but 2 sheets of filo. Place the 2 remaining sheets on top, brushing each with butter.

Preheat the oven to 350°F.

With a small sharp knife, score the top of the Baklava lengthwise with parallel lines, 2 inches apart and ½ inch deep. Then score diagonally across them with parallel lines 2 inches apart to form diamond shapes. Bake in the middle of the oven for 30 minutes. Reduce the heat to

300°F and bake for 45 minutes longer, or until the top is crisp and golden brown. Remove the Baklava from the oven and pour the syrup evenly over it. Let it come to room temperature, then cut the Baklava along the scoring lines into individual pieces.

## CLARIFIED BUTTER

1 pound unsalted butter

Melt the butter over medium heat. Remove the pan from the heat and cool about 30 minutes. Skim off the foam. Slowly pour the clear liquid into a clean container, stopping before the whey (the milky white sediment) escapes. Discard the whey. Or if time permits, place the melted butter in the freezer for a few minutes until the butter hardens. The whey will remain liquid and can be poured off. The butter will shrink about 25 percent in volume, so be sure you have enough for your recipe.

## SUGAR AND HONEY SYRUP

1½ cups sugar
¾ cup water
1 tablespoon lemon juice
1 tablespoon honey

In a heavy saucepan, over moderate heat, stir together the sugar, water, and lemon juice until the sugar dissolves. Bring to a boil, without stirring, and continue boiling until the syrup reaches 220°F on a candy thermometer, about 5 minutes. Remove from the heat and stir in the honey.

# BOURMA
## ROLLED NUT PASTRY

This is a very festive and exotic dessert that looks complicated, but is really fun to prepare, perhaps with your children helping.

Pistachio nuts are traditional, but other nuts may be used. Bourma enhances the look of a dessert table, or can be served by itself with a scoop of ice cream for a super-special dessert.

1 package (1 pound) filo
  sheets

Working with 1 sheet of filo at a time, spread it on a large sheet of wax paper placed on top of a damp towel.

1 pound unsalted butter, clarified (see above)

1 pound pistachio nuts, walnuts, almonds, or pecans, chopped

½ cup sugar

Sugar and Honey Syrup (see page 368)

Brush with butter. Stir together the nuts and sugar and sprinkle 2 to 3 tablespoons evenly over surface of the filo sheet. Fold the long edge nearest you over the nuts to make a 2-inch border.

Place a long 1-inch diameter dowel along the length of the border, and then loosely roll up the filo around the dowel. Gently push the pastry inward along the dowel from each end, crinkling it evenly until it is about two thirds of its original length. (If you crinkle it too tightly, the Bourma will not bake evenly and will not be flaky.) Gently pull the dowel, carefully lift the filo roll, and place it, seam side down, on a buttered baking pan. Brush the top with butter. Repeat the procedure with the remaining filo.

Preheat the oven to 350°F. Bake the Bourmas until lightly golden, 25 to 30 minutes. Cut each Bourma into 2 or 3 pieces and pour 1 to 2 tablespoons of syrup over each piece.

# CHOCOLATE-COVERED HALVAH

Like many other exotic foods, halvah is easy to prepare once you know the secret, although many experts claim it cannot be made at home. This Israeli version has the added advantage of lots of wholesome and nutritious ingredients.

MAKES 36 HALVAH

½ cup tahini (sesame seed paste)

⅓ cup honey

½ cup unsweetened grated coconut

½ cup wheat germ

½ cup unsalted sunflower seeds

2 tablespoons cocoa powder

½ teaspoon cinnamon (optional)

1 pound semisweet chocolate, broken into small pieces

In a mixing bowl, stir together the tahini and honey. In a processor, put the coconut, wheat germ, and sunflower seeds; process until finely chopped. Stir in the cocoa and cinnamon and stir into the tahini mixture until well blended and firm. Shape the mixture by hand into 1-inch balls.

Melt the chocolate in a double boiler over gently simmering water. With your hands, dip each halvah ball in the chocolate and place it on wax paper. Refrigerate until the chocolate is set.

# SOPHISTICATED SUMMER SUPPER

FOR 10

It's a balmy summer evening and maybe there's a full moon. And you want to serve something really new and different. So how about a French inspiration for your main course—a blend of delicate fish fillets, really too exotic to call sausages—served with a gingery fresh tomato sauce, which the French call a coulis. This flavorful combination is garnished with tender florets of cauliflower and broccoli in a decorative border.

The salad is served with a citrus-flavored Orange Mayonnaise and warm, fresh-from-the-oven Braided Herb Loaves, which scent the summer air. The pièce de résistance is the dessert—an unforgettable combination of buttery pastry, caramel, and chocolate that has become our family favorite for birthdays and special occasions. It will be your family's too.

If you have a patio, terrace, or outdoor dining area, serve this menu al fresco, of course, with candles and a lovely light white wine.

# BRAIDED HERB LOAVES

MAKES 1 LARGE OR 3 SMALL LOAVES

1 package active dry yeast
Pinch of sugar
1½ cups warm water (110 to 115°F)
4 tablespoons unsalted margarine or butter, melted

Dissolve the yeast and the sugar in ½ cup of the warm water.

In the bowl of an electric mixer, combine the margarine, 2 of the eggs, the herbs, green onions, salt, saffron, and pepper. Blend in the remaining cup water. Add the yeast mixture and mix well.

3 eggs
2 tablespoons minced parsley
2 tablespoons minced dill
2 tablespoons minced basil
2 tablespoons minced green
  onions (scallions)
1 tablespoon kosher salt
Pinch of saffron
⅛ teaspoon freshly ground
  black pepper
5 to 6 cups flour
¼ cup yellow cornmeal
1 tablespoon celery seeds

Add the flour, 1 cup at a time, blending after each addition, until the dough is thick enough to work by hand. Spoon it out on a floured board and knead for 4 to 5 minutes, adding additional flour to make a smooth and elastic dough.

Place the dough in an oiled bowl and oil the top. Cover with a towel and let rise in a warm place until doubled in size, about 1 hour. Punch down the dough and shape into 1 large or 3 small loaves. Place in lightly oiled bread pans (one 5 × 7-inch or three 3 × 5-inch that have been generously sprinkled with cornmeal. Cover with a towel and let rise in a warm place until doubled, about 1 hour.

Preheat the oven to 375°F.

Brush the loaf or loaves with the remaining beaten egg and sprinkle with celery seeds. Bake for 30 to 40 minutes, or until golden brown. Loosen the sides with a metal spatula and transfer to racks to cool.

# GREEN BEAN SALAD WITH ORANGE MAYONNAISE

This salad is best made with the ultra-thin, fresh green beans the French call *haricots verts*.

1 pound thin green beans
Salt
Freshly ground black pepper
Olive oil
1 cup Orange Mayonnaise
  (recipe follows)
Long thin strip of orange zest
  and orange sections for
  garnish

In a steamer basket set over a large saucepan of simmering water, steam the green beans, covered, for 5 to 10 minutes, until tender but still crunchy. Or plunge them into boiling salted water and boil for 3 to 4 minutes. Drain well.

Toss the beans with salt and pepper to taste and a little olive oil. Place bunches of them on plates and top with fresh Orange Mayonnaise. Garnish with orange zest curls and surround with the orange sections.

# ORANGE MAYONNAISE

Mayonnaise is always easier to make if the ingredients are at warm room temperature. Warming the bowl before you start making the mayonnaise will help ensure good results. Use your processor to save time.

2 large egg yolks
1 tablespoon fresh orange juice
2 teaspoons fresh lemon juice
1 teaspoon Dijon mustard
¼ teaspoon salt
1½ cups safflower oil
2 tablespoons grated orange zest
Freshly ground black pepper

Rinse a medium mixing bowl with hot water and dry it well. In the warm bowl, beat together the egg yolks, orange juice, lemon juice, mustard, and salt. In a slow, thin stream, add ½ cup of the oil, beating constantly; as the mayonnaise begins to mount and thicken, gradually add the remaining oil and the zest. Season to taste with additional salt and pepper.

# FISH SAUSAGES WITH TOMATO-GINGER COULIS

1 pound halibut fillets
1 pound salmon steak fillets
1 medium zucchini, peeled and cut into ⅛-inch dice
6 tablespoons olive oil
1 pound thin ling cod fillets
Salt
Freshly ground black pepper
Tomato-Ginger Coulis (recipe follows)

Cut the halibut and salmon fillets into cubes, and then mince them. Place them in a small bowl with the zucchini and 3 tablespoons of the olive oil; toss and marinate for 10 minutes.

Cut the ling cod into thin slices, about 3 by 4 inches. Place each slice between two 12-inch square pieces of plastic wrap and pound with the flat side of a mallet, rolling pin, or heavy skillet, until paper thin. Remove the top piece of plastic wrap. Spoon 2 tablespoons of the fillet mixture lengthwise along the center of the prepared ling cod. Season to taste with salt and pepper. Roll up the fish (jelly-roll fashion) into a sausage shape. Wrap tightly with plastic wrap, twisting the ends and tying securely into a knot to seal.

Poach in simmering water for 5 minutes. Cool. Unwrap, reserving the juices in a bowl for the coulis.

Preheat the oven to 375°F.

In a large heavy skillet, heat the remaining 3 tablespoons oil and brown the sausages on both sides. Transfer to a foil-lined baking sheet and bake for 5 minutes. Spoon the coulis onto plates; place sausages on top, surrounded with the broccoli and cauliflower florets. Serve immediately.

### TOMATO-GINGER COULIS

3 large tomatoes, peeled and
    seeded (see page 26)
1 piece (1 inch) fresh ginger,
    peeled and diced
1 garlic clove, peeled
Reserved fish juices
¼ cup white wine or rice
    vinegar
½ cup olive oil
Salt
Freshly ground black pepper

In a processor or blender, process the tomatoes, ginger, garlic, fish juices, and vinegar. Add the oil in a thin stream and blend well. Season to taste with salt and pepper. Cover with plastic wrap and chill in the refrigerator.

# STEAMED BROCCOLI AND CAULIFLOWER FLORETS

So often the simplest preparation for vegetables is the best. Timing is the most important part here. For my taste, undercooking leaves the vegetables too tough and raw-tasting. Overcooking makes them lose all their flavor. A good test for doneness is to take out a floret, slice it, and taste it.

6 to 8 large stalks broccoli, cut
    into florets (stalks reserved
    for another recipe)
1 large head of cauliflower,
    cut into florets
Olive oil
Salt
Freshly ground black pepper

In a steamer basket set over a large saucepan of simmering water, steam the florets, covered, for 10 to 15 minutes, or until tender but still slightly crisp. Toss with olive oil and salt and pepper to taste. Serve hot or cold.

# CARAMEL-WALNUT TORTE EN CROUTE

"En croute" simply means in a crust or pastry. The first time I tasted this delicious dessert was in the South of France and the second time was in San Francisco at a class with James Beard at the Stanford Court Hotel.

It is so rich that a small slice is enough to satisfy the sweetest tooth. The chocolate topping is superb, and I use it for many other cakes. Add a garnish of walnut or pecan halves.

### RICH PASTRY CRUST

3½ cups flour

4 tablespoons sugar

¼ teaspoon salt

½ pound plus 2 tablespoons unsalted butter, cut into small pieces

2 egg yolks

6 tablespoons cold water

### FILLING

1½ cups sugar

½ cup water

3½ cups toasted, chopped walnuts (see page 24)

1 cup milk, warmed

¼ pound plus 4 tablespoons unsalted butter, cut into pieces

⅓ cup honey

### TO FINISH

Chocolate Glaze (see page 165)

Toasted walnut halves for garnish

For the crust: In the large bowl of a mixer, combine the flour, sugar, and salt. Blend in the butter until the texture of coarse oatmeal. Beat the egg yolks and water together. Add them to the flour mixture, beating until the dough comes together. Do not overbeat.

Transfer the dough to a floured board and knead it into a smooth ball. Wrap in wax paper and refrigerate for 20 to 30 minutes.

For the filling: In a large heavy saucepan over medium heat, bring the sugar and water to a boil. Stir until the sugar dissolves. Boil until the mixture turns a light caramel color. Remove from the heat and add the chopped walnuts, milk, and butter. Bring to a simmer, stirring constantly for 10 to 15 minutes, until the sauce thickens and turns golden brown. Stir in the honey. Cool to room temperature.

Meanwhile, on floured wax paper, roll two thirds of the dough into a 14-inch circle. Fit it into an 11-inch tart pan, with 2 inches overlapping the sides. Chill for 30 minutes. Roll out the remaining dough into an 11-inch circle and chill.

Preheat the oven to 425°F.

Pour the cooled filling into the prepared pastry. Place the remaining pastry circle on top. Brush the overlapping pastry with water; fold it up over the top pastry and press and pleat the edges to seal them. With a sharp knife, cut a small slit in the center of the pastry top. Bake on the lower rack of the oven for about 20 minutes, until golden brown. Invert onto a serving platter and cool.

Spread the Chocolate Glaze over the torte. Garnish with walnut halves.

# PUMPKIN HARVEST DINNER

FOR 8

Once in a while we like to surprise our dinner guests with something different—and maybe even a bit bizarre. The idea for this strange but delicious menu came about one crisp fall evening when we were planning a dinner party that would take place the day before Halloween. What could we serve that would be appropriate for this high-spirited occasion, but that would still be interesting to sophisticated, food-oriented friends?

The answer was easy. Looking through my files I came upon some wonderful recipes using pumpkin—including several from our trips to Italy, where they have a special way with that vegetable. Each recipe suggested a different course: some, to be honest, seemed a little contrived, but all together they made a delightful and interesting menu. Our friends loved the evening—from the miniature pumpkins that they were invited to decorate with felt-tip markers as soon as they were seated, to their favorites of all the recipes, the fried pumpkin sticks and the ravioli-like tortelli with a sweet-and-spicy pumpkin filling.

## FRIED PUMPKIN STICKS

This recipe was inspired by the fried zucchini sticks that I make so often as appetizers. The uncooked pumpkin is cut into sticks, coated with seasoned bread crumbs, and deep-fried in very hot oil, then sprinkled with freshly grated Parmesan cheese. Hubbard or banana squash make good substitutes when fresh pumpkin is not available.

2 pounds pumpkin
1 cup flour
2 eggs
1 cup bread crumbs or matzo
  meal
2 garlic cloves, peeled
Salt
Freshly ground black pepper
Vegetable oil for deep-frying
1 cup freshly ground Parmesan cheese

Peel the pumpkin and cut into sticks ½ inch wide and thick by 2½ inches long. Put the flour into a small brown sandwich bag. In a bowl, beat the eggs. Place the bread crumbs in a processor; turn the machine on, drop in the garlic, and process until finely chopped. Add salt and pepper to taste.

Shake the pumpkin sticks, a small handful at a time, in the bag of flour to coat them evenly. Transfer them to a strainer and shake gently to remove excess flour. Then dip each stick in the beaten egg and roll it in the bread crumbs. Place on a baking sheet lined with paper towels until ready to fry.

In a large heavy pot, a wok, or a deep-fryer, heat the oil to 375°F on a deep-frying thermometer. Fry the breaded pumpkin sticks in several batches—without overcrowding—for 2 to 3 minutes, or until evenly crisp and browned. Drain on paper towels, then transfer to a serving platter and sprinkle with Parmesan cheese. Serve at once.

# TORTELLI DI ZUCCA
## PUMPKIN-FILLED PASTA

This is a very special pasta with an usual spicy-sweet pumpkin filling. It originated in northern Italy, where it can be found in many country restaurants. We ate it for the first time many years ago at Ristorante Dal Pescatore, owned by our dear friends Antonio and Nadia Santini, in a little town named Canneto Sull' Oglio. They serve it with a simple butter sauce.

No two Italian families cut and shape stuffed pastas such as tortelli, ravioli, or cappelletti the same way. The directions here are for tortelli the way the Santini family has prepared it for four generations.

You can find jars of fruit preserved in mustard in most Italian delis or specialty markets. If not, substitute a fruit chutney.

MAKES ABOUT 78 TORTELLI

2 cups Pumpkin Purée (recipe
  follows)
⅔ cup crushed amaretti (imported Italian cookies)
½ cup bread crumbs

In a large bowl, combine the pumpkin pulp with the amaretti and bread crumbs and blend well. Add the eggs, fruit, 1 cup of the Parmesan cheese, nutmeg, and salt and blend well. Cover with plastic wrap and refrigerate until ready to use.

2 eggs
4 tablespoons fruit preserved
  in sweet mustard sauce or
  fruit chutney (optional)
1½ cups freshly grated Parmesan cheese
¼ teaspoon freshly grated
  nutmeg
Salt
Basic Pasta Dough (see page
  288)
¾ pound unsalted butter

Roll out the pasta to a medium thickness. Cut it into rectangles, 3 inches by 4 inches. Place a generous spoonful of pumpkin filling in the center of each rectangle; lift one corner and fold it on an angle over the filling, then continue folding to completely enclose the filling. With your index fingers, press down firmly on either side of the filling to seal it in, giving the tortelli a shape like a bowknot.

As they are finished, place the tortelli on lightly floured kitchen towels and let them dry for at least 15 minutes, until ready to cook and serve.

If you want to store them in the freezer, place the towel with tortelli on a baking sheet, then cover with another towel and place in the freezer. When the tortelli are frozen, peel them off the towels and place in a plastic bag; return to the freezer. When ready to cook, remove from the plastic bags and defrost on towels, ½ inch apart. (Do not let the tortelli touch each other or they will stick together.)

To cook the tortelli, drop them into lightly salted boiling water and boil until tender, 5 to 10 minutes. While the tortelli are cooking, melt the butter in a large skillet. Drain the tortelli well and gently transfer them into the hot melted butter, sprinkling them with the remaining ½ cup Parmesan cheese and tossing to coat thoroughly. Spoon onto heated plates.

## PUMPKIN PURÉE

1 pumpkin, steamed (recipe
  follows)

Whip the cooked pumpkin by hand, or purée in a processor or blender. This purée keeps for weeks in the freezer. Use for Tortelli di Zucca or as a vegetable.

As a vegetable: Beat in butter, cream, nutmeg, salt, and pepper to taste.

## STEAMED PUMPKIN

Pumpkins are better steamed than boiled—they turn out less watery, with more vivid color and flavor.

1 small pumpkin

Cut the pumpkin, unpeeled, into large chunks; scoop out the fiber and seeds. Discard the fiber and set the seeds aside. Place the chunks of pumpkin on a steamer tray over simmering water. Cover and steam for 15 to 20 minutes, or until the flesh is soft to a fork. When the chunks are cool enough to handle, cut the flesh from the thick rind. The pumpkin is now ready to use for any cooked pumpkin recipe. The seeds can be toasted (see page 379).

# PAN-GRILLED SEA BASS WITH PUMPKIN SAUCE

This very simple recipe uses one of my favorite methods of cooking fish. Lightly coat the fish with seasoned flour and grill it in a nonstick pan until crisp on the outside and tender and moist within.

1 cup flour
Salt
Freshly ground black pepper
8 sea bass fillets (6 to 8 ounces each)
4 tablespoons unsalted butter or olive oil
2 garlic cloves, minced
Pumpkin Sauce with Corn Kernels (recipe folows)
½ cup cooked corn kernels
16 whole chives

In a shallow bowl, combine the flour with salt and pepper to taste. Dip the sea bass in the seasoned flour and shake off the excess.

In a large, heavy nonstick skillet, heat the butter and garlic. Add the fish fillets and sauté them just until cooked through, about 5 minutes a side.

Ladle the sauce into the centers of heated serving plates. Place a piece of fish in the center of each plate. Garnish with the corn kernels. Crisscross 2 chives over each serving.

## PUMPKIN SAUCE WITH CORN KERNELS

1 cup Fish or Vegetable Stock (see page 392 or 391)
⅔ cup Pumpkin Purée (see page 377)
½ cup fresh corn kernels
Salt
Freshly ground black pepper

Place the stock in a small heavy saucepan and simmer until reduced by half. Add the Pumpkin Purée and kernels and simmer until thick, about 5 minutes. Season to taste with salt and pepper.

# BROILED GOAT CHEESE
# AND PERSIMMON SALAD

My favorite way to eat goat cheese is hot—broiled as it is here or gently warmed as a salad topping.

The first time I made this salad, I coated the cheese with bread crumbs. Later I tried seasoning the crumbs with garlic and basil. Now I like to use a ground almond coating.

Crisp Japanese persimmons are in season at the same time as pumpkins. At other times of year I substitute pears or papaya.

2 packages (8 ounces each) creamy goat cheese in log or loaf shapes, well-chilled
1 cup finely sliced almonds
1 garlic clove
3 fresh basil leaves
6 Japanese persimmons
6 tablespoons olive oil
2 tablespoons sherry wine vinegar or balsamic vinegar
Salt
Freshly ground black pepper
2 heads Boston lettuce, rinsed, dried, and torn into bite-size pieces
½ cup Toasted Pumpkin Seeds (recipe follows)

Cut the cheese crosswise into ½-inch-thick slices, to get at least 24 slices. In a processor or blender, blend the almonds, garlic, and basil. Spread them on a flat plate and lightly press both sides of each piece of cheese into the crumbs to coat. Place the cheese slices on a foil-lined baking sheet, cover, and refrigerate for at least 1 hour.

Peel the persimmons and cut them into ½-inch-thick slices.

Preheat the broiler.

Stir together the oil, vinegar, salt, and pepper. Toss 1 tablespoon of the dressing with the lettuce and mound the lettuce in the center of chilled plates. Arrange the persimmon slices in spoke patterns around the lettuce.

Place the baking sheet with the cheese slices under the broiler close to the heat. Broil until the top crumbs just begin to brown and the cheese is soft to the touch, about 5 minutes.

While the cheese is broiling, bring the remaining dressing to a boil in a small saucepan over medium heat. Place 2 slices of broiled cheese on each salad plate. As soon as the dressing comes to a boil, quickly spoon it over each salad. Sprinkle with Toasted Pumpkin Seeds. Serve immediately.

## TOASTED PUMPKIN SEEDS

Pumpkin Seeds
Vegetable oil
Salt

Preheat the oven to 375°F.

Separate the pumpkin seeds from the fibers. Wash and dry the seeds. Line a baking sheet with lightly oiled foil. Rub oil on your hands and rub over the seeds lightly to coat them. Spread the seeds on the prepared baking sheet and bake for 15 minutes, shaking the pan occasionally so the seeds cook evenly. Sprinkle them with salt, toss to mix well, then continue baking until crisp and golden brown, about 5 minutes more. Serve as a garnish on a salad, or in a bowl as a snack.

# PUMPKIN ICE CREAM

2 cups milk
1 cup sugar
8 egg yolks
1 cup Pumpkin Purée (see page 377)
½ teaspoon ground cinnamon
½ teaspoon ground nutmeg
½ teaspoon ground ginger
¼ teaspoon ground cloves
⅛ teaspoon ground mace
2 cups cream

In a large heavy pot, combine the milk and ½ cup of the sugar. Bring it to a boil over medium heat. Stir until the sugar is dissolved.

In the bowl of an electric mixer, beat the egg yolks, gradually adding the remaining ½ cup sugar, until light in color and thick.

Pour a little of the milk mixture into the egg mixture to warm it. Pour the egg yolk mixture through a sieve or strainer into the pot with the milk mixture and cook it over medium heat until thick and it coats the back of a spoon.

Add the Pumpkin Purée to the milk mixture. In a small bowl, combine the cinnamon, nutmeg, ginger, cloves, and mace and blend into the milk mixture. Cook over medium heat until thick enough to coat the back of a spoon.

Transfer the custard to a large ovenproof bowl, set in another bowl of ice cubes and water. Blend in the cream and mix well until cool, about 5 minutes. Cover and chill until cool enough to place in an ice cream freezer. Freeze according to manufacturer's directions, or place in a glass bowl and freeze, removing the bowl and scraping and stirring the ice cream every hour until done.

# TRADITIONAL SUNDAY BRUNCH

FOR 12

Platters of Tomatoes, Olives, Red Onions, Pickles, Roasted Peppers (see page 278)

Cantaloupe Halves Filled with Port Wine

Broiled Grapefruit

Classic Water Bagels

Toasted Garlic Bagels

Bowls of Whipped Butter and Cream Cheese

Scrambled Eggs with Lox and Onions

Mini-Pecan Schnecken

Banana-Nut Loaves with Streusel Topping

Bran-Granola Muffins

Z and Z Yeast Coffee Cake

Freshly brewed coffee and tea

Pitcher of ice-cold milk

SUGGESTED BEVERAGE:

Champagne or white wine

This familiar menu, with a few additions, is directed to singles, newlyweds, new cooks, and experienced cooks alike. I hope it will inspire you to invite family and friends over on a Sunday or holiday—an easy, informal way to entertain.

I have included recipes for a choice of two fruit appetizers: broiled grapefruit halves, and cantaloupe with port wine, both of them easy but absolutely delicious. And then there's that traditional Sunday favorite—lox and eggs. You will also find some of my favorite yeast breads, quick breads, and coffee cakes, which can be made days ahead and stored in the freezer.

If the occasion is a birthday or anniversary, be sure to begin with a fruity champagne, or a light white wine.

Serve the brunch outdoors or in the dining room or the kitchen—whatever suits your mood and the occasion. Serve it buffet-style if you like, or pass platters at the table.

## CANTALOUPE HALVES FILLED WITH PORT WINE

To make it easier to serve these port-filled cantaloupe cups without spills, add the wine at the table. Guests will have a double taste treat when they eat a fragrant spoonful of cantaloupe bathed in port.

6 ripe cantaloupes
1 quart port or Concord grape
  wine
Fresh mint leaves

Using a sharp knife or a knife with a scalloped edge, cut each cantaloupe in half and remove the seeds. Place them, cut sides up, on a baking sheet. If the cantaloupe halves are not well balanced, slice a small piece off the bottom. Cover with plastic wrap and refrigerate.

Just before serving, place one cantaloupe half on each serving plate. At the table, carefully pour the wine into the centers. Garnish with mint leaves.

# BROILED GRAPEFRUIT

There are curved knives available for sectioning grapefruit, so be sure to use one or a sharp paring knife. If you don't, it will be almost impossible to spoon the sections from the grapefruit.

6 grapefruit, cut in half and
  sectioned
½ cup dark brown sugar
1 cup sweet white wine
Fresh berries for garnish

Place the grapefruit halves on a foil-lined baking dish. Generously sprinkle them with brown sugar and spoon the sweet wine on top just to overflowing.

Just before serving, heat the broiler and place the prepared grapefruit halves 3 inches from the heat. Broil just until they begin to brown lightly.

Carefully place on individual heated serving plates, garnish with fresh berries, and serve at once.

# CLASSIC WATER BAGELS

Bagels have always been available in cities where there was a large Jewish population. Today they are an American classic, and fresh hot bagels in many varieties can be found in small towns everywhere.

Of course, it's more fun to bake your own. When friends heard about my kosher cookbook, one of the first requests was, "Please have a good recipe for bagels." So here you are.

MAKES 8 LARGE OR 12 SMALL BAGELS

4 to 5 cups flour
1 package active dry yeast

In the bowl of an electric mixer, combine 1 cup of the flour, the yeast, and salt. Add the water and honey and

1 tablespoon kosher salt

1½ cups warm water (110 to 115°F)

2 tablespoons honey

1 egg white, lightly beaten

Kosher salt

3 tablespoons seeds (poppy, sesame, or caraway)

beat until smooth. Add the remaining flour, 1 cup at a time, to make a soft dough. Turn the dough out onto a generously floured board and continue working in the flour until the dough is stiff enough to knead. Knead until smooth and elastic, 5 to 10 minutes. Cover with a towel and let rise 15 minutes.

Divide the dough into 8 to 12 equal portions. Shape each portion into a flattened ball. With your forefinger, poke a hole in the center. Stretch and rotate the dough until the hole is 1½ to 2 inches wide. Place the bagels on a well-floured towel, cover with another towel, and let them rise for 20 minutes.

Preheat the oven to 375°F.

Fill a large shallow pan (a wok works well) with 3 inches of water. Bring the water to a boil, reduce the heat, and simmer. Add a few bagels at a time and simmer for 5 minutes. Remove the bagels from the pan with a slotted spoon and drain on a towel. Place the bagels on well-oiled baking sheets, brush with egg white, and sprinkle with kosher salt and seeds of your choice.

Bake for 30 minutes, until well browned. Transfer to racks to cool.

# TOASTED GARLIC BAGELS

Our family's favorite bagel treat is to slice the bagels in half, spread them with garlic butter, and then brown them under the broiler. When our children were growing up, these toasted garlic bagels were served either with salad or the main course or they were eaten as a snack. You will wonder why you didn't think of this sooner—it may replace Italian garlic bread at your home.

MAKES 16 BAGEL HALVES

¼ pound unsalted butter or margarine

3 or 4 garlic cloves

3 tablespoons minced parsley

Salt

8 bagels, sliced in half

In a processor, process the butter and garlic until well blended. Pulse in the parsley. Season to taste with salt. With a rubber spatula, transfer the mixture to a bowl. Cover with plastic wrap and refrigerate until ready to use. (You can also shape the mixture into a cube, wrap in plastic wrap and foil, and then freeze it; defrost until spreadable before use.)

Preheat the broiler. Spread the butter on the bagel

halves, place them on a baking sheet, and broil until the butter mixture bubbles and begins to brown. Serve immediately.

# SCRAMBLED EGGS WITH LOX AND ONIONS

For a delicious variation, we omit the lox and just as the eggs are setting, add thinly sliced pieces of a soft cheese like Monterey Jack. It melts as the eggs set and is delicious.

12 eggs
Salt
Freshly ground black pepper
4 tablespoons unsalted butter
3 garlic cloves, minced
8 green onions (scallions), thinly sliced
8 slices lox (smoked salmon), cut into thin strips
¼ cup finely chopped chives or parsley

In a large mixing bowl, beat the eggs with salt and pepper to taste. Set them aside.

In a large skillet over medium heat, melt the butter. Add the garlic and green onions and sauté until soft, 3 to 4 minutes. Add the lox and sauté until light pink, 2 to 3 minutes, mixing the lox thoroughly with the onions.

Add the beaten egg mixture. Cook slowly over low heat. Let the eggs begin to set around the edges and start mixing them, beginning at the edges and into the center of the mixture, carefully mixing in the onions and lox. Continue cooking, stirring occasionally, until the eggs have the texture you prefer, about 5 minutes or longer (depending on how firm you like your eggs). Transfer to a heated bowl or spoon onto heated plates. Sprinkle with chives or parsley. Serve immediately.

# MINI-PECAN SCHNECKEN

This recipe began when we lived on a big California ranch and gave Sunday brunches almost every week. It does take a lot of time to prepare, but can be done in steps over one or two days. The schnecken keep well in the freezer, if wrapped properly, and taste freshly baked when reheated just before serving.

They can also be made into large pecan rolls, but I prefer making the mini size. So I invested in ten mini-muffin pans, which I also use for little muffins, rolls, and pastries.

1 package active dry yeast

⅓ cup sugar

¼ cup warm water (110 to 115°F)

½ pound unsalted butter or margarine, softened

1 teaspoon salt

3 eggs

1 cup sour cream

3½ cups flour

2 tablespoons safflower or vegetable oil

2 to 3 cups (144) toasted pecan halves (see page 24)

Brown Sugar Glaze (recipe follows)

½ pound unsalted butter or margarine, melted

Pecan Filling (recipe follows)

Dissolve the yeast with a pinch of sugar in the warm water. Let stand until foamy, 2 to 3 minutes.

In the large bowl of an electric mixer, cream the softened butter. Add the remaining sugar and beat until fluffy. Blend in the salt, eggs, sour cream, and the yeast mixture. Continue beating until the batter is smooth. Add the flour, 1 cup at a time, beating well after each addition. Brush the top of the dough with oil and cover with a towel. Refrigerate overnight. Remove the dough from the refrigerator and let it rise in a warm place for 2 hours.

Brush the muffin pans with oil and place 2 pecan halves, flat sides up, in each well. Pour 1 heaping teaspoon of the glaze over the pecans. Set aside.

Preheat the oven to 375°F.

Divide the dough into 6 parts and roll out each part on a lightly floured board into a rectangle 4 inches wide, 12 inches long, and ½ inch thick. Brush with melted butter and sprinkle generously with the Pecan Filling. Roll up the dough lengthwise, jelly-roll fashion, and place it seam side down. Cut it into 1-inch-thick slices. Place a slice inside each prepared muffin cup (cut side up). Cover and let rise in a warm place about 45 minutes.

Place a large sheet of foil on the bottom rack of the oven to catch any glaze that may flow over the sides of the pan. Bake the schnecken for about 12 minutes, until golden brown. Remove from the oven and turn out onto a platter immediately, lifting the muffin tin off slowly and allowing the glaze to flow down over the rolls.

For storing: Wrap the cooled rolls in foil and seal well. Place them in plastic bags, then freeze.

## BROWN SUGAR GLAZE

¼ pound plus 4 tablespoons unsalted butter or margarine

1½ cups dark brown sugar

¼ cup water

Combine the butter, sugar, and water in a saucepan and bring to a boil. Simmer for 3 to 4 minutes. Set aside.

## PECAN FILLING

1 cup yellow or dark brown
  raisins, plumped (see
  page 25)
1 cup sugar
2 teaspoons cinnamon
2 cups toasted pecans, coarsely
  chopped (see page 24)

In a bowl, combine the drained raisins, sugar, cinnamon, and pecans and mix well. Cover and set aside.

# BANANA-NUT LOAVES
# WITH STREUSEL TOPPING

This loaf has been a family treasure and standby ever since I can remember—for breakfast, lunch, or even dinner, and to take as a gift when visiting friends. When friends pop in unexpectedly, I will microwave a frozen banana loaf (it is impossible, once the loaf is reheated, to tell that it was ever frozen) and serve it with a glass of sweet wine or a cup of tea or coffee.

MAKES FOUR 3 × 7 × 2-INCH LOAVES

¾ cup finely ground walnuts
  or pecans (6 ounces)
2 cups sugar
2½ cups flour
2 teaspoons baking soda
1 teaspoon salt
½ pound unsalted butter,
  margarine, or shortening,
  cut into pieces
2 cups toasted chopped walnuts or pecans (see
  page 24)
2 cups (about 5 large) mashed
  bananas
4 eggs
½ cup milk
Streusel Topping (recipe
  follows)

Preheat the oven to 350°F.

Grease four 3 × 7 × 2-inch loaf pans; sprinkle them with ground nuts and set them aside.

In the bowl of an electric mixer, blend the sugar, flour, baking soda, and salt. Add the butter and blend until crumbly. With a rubber spatula, add the chopped walnuts and mix well.

In a medium bowl, beat the bananas, eggs, and milk together. Pour the banana mixture into the flour mixture all at once. Stir gently just until all the dry ingredients are moistened; do not overstir. Spoon the batter into the prepared loaf pans. Sprinkle each loaf with 2 tablespoons of the Streusel Topping. Bake for 45 minutes, or until a toothpick inserted into the center comes out clean and the loaves begin to come away from the sides of the pans.

## STREUSEL TOPPING

MAKES ABOUT 1 CUP

½ cup brown sugar
¼ cup flour
½ teaspoon cinnamon
4 tablespoons unsalted butter,
   margarine, or shortening
½ cup chopped walnuts or
   pecans

In a large mixing bowl, stir together the brown sugar, flour, cinnamon, and butter just until crumbly; do not overmix. Stir in the chopped walnuts. Cover and set aside.


# BRAN-GRANOLA MUFFINS

These delicious muffins are mixed the day before and baked just before serving. Eaten freshly baked, the flavors are intense; nothing can compare. The batter can be kept in the refrigerator for one week, ready for you to bake as many muffins as you wish just before serving.

MAKES ABOUT 36

1 cup 100% bran cereal
1 cup boiling water
½ cup vegetable oil
1¼ cups brown sugar, packed
¾ cup honey
2 eggs
2 cups buttermilk
2½ cups whole wheat flour
2½ teaspoons baking soda
1 teaspoon salt
2 cups granola
½ cup raisins, plumped and
   drained (see page 25)
½ cup drained pineapple
   tidbits

In a bowl, stir together the bran and water. Cover and let stand 5 to 10 minutes, or until the water is completely absorbed.

In the bowl of an electric mixer, combine the oil, sugar, and ¼ cup of the honey and mix well. Add the eggs and beat until smooth. Add the buttermilk and blend thoroughly. Mix the bran mixture into the oil mixture.

Combine the flour, baking soda, salt, and granola. Blend it into the bran mixture. Fold in the raisins and pineapple. Cover and refrigerate for several hours or overnight.

Preheat the oven to 400°F.

Spoon the batter into oiled or muffin cup-lined muffin tins, filling them one half to two thirds full. Bake for 20 to 30 minutes, until well browned and a toothpick inserted into the center of the muffins comes out clean.

Heat the remaining ½ cup honey in a small saucepan. Let it sit about 4 minutes, or until slightly thickened, and brush on top of the warm muffins. Serve warm with butter, honey, or preserves.

# Z AND Z YEAST COFFEE CAKES

This coffee cake is named after my husband's business, because a friend delivered it to his office. He persuaded the donor to share her grandmother's recipe, knowing that I would want to include it in my book. It has a very special light and buttery texture.

The dough is prepared the night before, covered, and refrigerated. I always roll it out first thing in the morning and bake it so we have hot coffee cake for breakfast. The kitchen smells heavenly.

MAKES 2 COFFEE CAKES

2 packages active dry yeast
½ cup warm milk (110 to 115°F)
¼ pound unsalted butter
¼ pound unsalted margarine
1 cup plus 2 tablespoons sugar
3 eggs, separated
½ teaspoon vanilla extract
2½ cups flour
¼ teaspoon salt
1 cup chopped walnuts or pecans
1 cup raisins, plumped and drained (see page 25)
1 tablespoon cinnamon
Powdered sugar

Dissolve the yeast in the warm milk. In the large bowl of an electric mixer, cream the butter and margarine with 2 tablespoons of the sugar. Beat in the egg yolks and vanilla. Add the yeast mixture alternately with the flour and salt. Place the dough in an oiled bowl and oil the top of the dough; cover and refrigerate for several hours or overnight.

Preheat the oven to 350°F.

Divide the dough into 2 parts. Roll out each part on floured wax paper into a 16 × 20-inch rectangle.

Beat the egg whites until stiff but not dry peaks form. Blend in the remaining 1 cup sugar. Spread half this meringue over each rectangle. Sprinkle with the walnuts, raisins, and cinnamon, leaving a 1-inch margin around the edges. Starting from the long side, roll up each rectangle, jelly-roll fashion. Form the roll into a ring, joining the ends and pinching them together. Place each ring in a 10-inch pie plate. Brush the tops with milk. Bake for about 30 minutes, until lightly browned. Just before serving, sprinkle with powdered sugar. Serve hot.

# STOCKS FOR
# SOUPS AND
# SAUCES

**M**any of these stocks will convince guests that they took a long time to prepare. But with a little organization, you can make them at your leisure and store them in the freezer in ice cube trays to be transferred later to plastic bags. Then they'll be ready to defrost and use when a recipe calls for them.

The Lamb Stock is one that Grégoire Sein prepared for a special dinner in my kitchen. He dropped in the day before the big event, filled a large roasting pot with bones, etc., and said, "Watch this for eight hours, adding wine if needed, and I will see you tomorrow morning." We followed his instructions, strained the stock, and got the most deep, rich sauce you can imagine. All you really need is the ambition, the bones and vegetables, a large pot, and an oven. This stock is not only wonderful with lamb recipes, but makes a delicious soup with vegetables and barley, rice, or pasta added. When reduced, it may also be used as a glaze.

The stock made with duck bones, by Michel Richard, follows exactly the same procedure and theory. When reduced, the duck stock may be used as a sauce on the plate, under sliced or roasted duck, or try tossing it with noodles.

As for the Fish Stock, I have been preparing it this way for years, and all it needs is a large pot, fish bones, and vegetables.

# CHICKEN STOCK

MAKES ABOUT 6 CUPS

4 pounds chicken necks and giblets

1 large onion, stuck with 2 cloves

1 whole head of garlic, un-peeled and sliced in half

2 leeks, halved lengthwise, washed well, and thickly sliced

3 carrots, peeled and sliced

2 celery ribs, sliced

4 parsley sprigs

2 fresh thyme sprigs, or ½ teaspoon dried

1 bay leaf

10 whole peppercorns

Salt

In a large pot, combine the chicken parts and 3 quarts (12 cups) cold water. Bring to a boil and skim off the froth. Add the onion, garlic, leeks, carrots, and celery. Place the parsley, thyme, bay leaf, and peppercorns in a cheesecloth bag tied with twine or in a mesh herb container and add to the pot. Bring to a boil and simmer for 2 hours, skimming the froth. Add salt to taste. Simmer for 2 hours more, adding boiling water if necessary to keep the ingredients barely covered.

Strain the stock through a fine sieve into a bowl, pressing on the solids, and let it cool. Chill and spoon off the fat that hardens on the top. Refrigerate or freeze.

# VEAL STOCK

Veal is one of the more delicately flavored meats, and so the stock also has a delicate flavor. It is one of my favorites. Use some neck bones, if possible, as they add a lot of flavor.

MAKES 3 TO 4 CUPS

10 pounds veal bones (or veal and chicken), cut into 2-inch pieces

2 onions, cut into chunks

2 whole heads of garlic, un-peeled and cut in half

4 carrots, peeled and thickly sliced

4 celery stalks with leaves, thickly sliced

3 leeks, cleaned and thickly sliced

Preheat the oven to 425°F.

Place the bones in a large roasting or broiling pan. Bake for 1 hour, turning occasionally, until well browned. Transfer the bones to a stockpot. Discard the excess fat from the roasting pan. Add the onions, garlic, carrots, celery, leeks, tomatoes, and mushroom stems. Bake for 10 minutes and transfer to the stockpot.

Deglaze the roasting pan on top of the stove with the wine, scraping up the brown bits on the bottom of the pan. Add this liquid to the stockpot. Place the bay leaf, peppercorns, thyme, and parsley on top of the onion mixture. Pour in enough cold water to cover completely.

2 tomatoes, quartered
10 mushroom stems
1 cup dry white wine
1 bay leaf
30 whole black peppercorns
1½ teaspoons dried thyme
10 fresh parsley sprigs
Salt

Bring to a boil, skim the fat as it accumulates, and reduce the heat to a very low simmer. Do not allow it to boil as this will produce a cloudy stock. Simmer for 12 to 14 hours, adding water when necessary to keep the bones completely covered.

Strain carefully into a clean pot, return to the heat, and simmer, skimming as necessary. Reduce to desired thickness. Season to taste with salt.

# VEGETABLE STOCK

This Vegetable Stock is perfect to have on hand, especially for a kosher kitchen. You will find use for it in cheese dishes, to enhance and add additional flavor to sauces that call for cream, in soups, etc. Divide it into small portions, as small as ice cubes, and it will keep for two to three weeks in the freezer.

MAKES 2 TO 3 CUPS

2 tablespoons safflower or vegetable oil
2 large onions, peeled and sliced
6 garlic cloves, unpeeled and crushed
4 celery stalks, sliced with tops
2 large carrots, peeled and sliced
2 large leeks, well rinsed and sliced, including 2 inches of tops
1 cup white wine
2 large tomatoes, diced
1 tablespoon black peppercorns
6 fresh parsley sprigs
2 large thyme sprigs
2 large rosemary sprigs
2 bay leaves
1 tablespoon white wine vinegar
Salt

In a large stainless steel or enamel pot or roasting pan, heat the oil and sauté the onions, garlic, celery, carrots, and leeks for 5 to 10 minutes. Do not brown. Add the wine and tomatoes and simmer for 2 to 3 minutes. Cover with water and add the peppercorns, parsley, thyme, rosemary, and bay leaves. Bring to a boil and reduce the heat; add the vinegar and simmer for 30 to 40 minutes. Do not stir.

Strain the stock and return it to the top of the stove. Simmer for 15 to 20 minutes to reduce and thicken. Season to taste with salt. Store the stock in small bowls, jars, or ice cube trays, covered, in the refrigerator or freezer.

# FISH STOCK

MAKES 2 TO 3 CUPS

4 pounds fish heads, bones, and skin

2 onions, thinly sliced

1 large leek, white part only, cleaned and thinly sliced

3 carrots, peeled and thinly sliced

2 celery ribs, with tops, sliced

2 bay leaves, crushed

8 fresh parsley sprigs

1 teaspoon fennel seeds

1 cup dry white wine

Salt

Freshly ground black pepper

In a large heavy pot, place the fish parts, onions, leek, carrots, celery, bay leaves, parsley, fennel seeds, wine, and water to cover completely. Bring to a boil over high heat, reduce heat, add salt and pepper to taste, and simmer for 30 minutes, uncovered, allowing the liquid to reduce to 2 to 3 cups.

Strain through a fine-mesh sieve or cheesecloth. Cover and refrigerate or freeze.

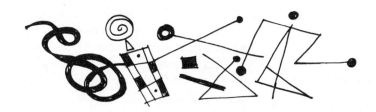

# A GLOSSARY OF JEWISH FOOD TERMS

**AFIKOMEN:** Means dessert. At the beginning of the Passover ceremony, the center matzo from the Seder plate is broken into two unequal parts and the larger part placed in a napkin in a safe place. This is secretly taken by a young member in the family and hidden—to be found, paid for, and eaten before the saying of the blessings-after-a-meal.

**BAGEL:** A ring-shaped bread roll, made from a yeast dough, which is first boiled, then glazed with an egg wash and baked in the oven. Water or egg bagels are most common, but onion, rye, pumpernickel, cinnamon-raisin, and cheese bagels, among others, are also available.

**BLINTZ:** A thin pancake, Russian in origin but similar to a French crepe, stuffed with various fillings and often topped with sour cream or preserves.

**BORSCHT:** A Russian-style soup that can be served cold or hot; made from various combinations of beets, spinach, sorrel, cabbage, and sometimes meat. Often served with sour cream, boiled potatoes, or chopped cucumbers.

**CHALLAH:** A yeast egg bread traditionally braided into fancy shapes for the Sabbath and holidays.

**CHOLENT:** A traditional meat and vegetable stew, assembled before sundown on Friday and then left to cook slowly overnight, to be eaten on the Sabbath, since orthodox laws forbid any work on the Sabbath.

**CHRAIN:** The Yiddish word for ground horseradish, from the Russian "khren." Beet juice is often added for color.

**CHREMSEL:** A Passover fritter made with matzo meal and glazed with honey.

**COMPOTE:** A French term that seems to have been adopted by Jewish cooks. It refers to a combination of dried and/or fresh fruits, sweetened and cooked.

**DERMA:** Beef casings, often stuffed with a seasonal filling and roasted. Also known as kishke.

**EINGEMACHTS:** Traditional Passover preserve of German origin, usually made from beets, spices, and nuts. Can also be made with carrots.

**FALAFEL:** A deep-fried chick-pea croquette, served as an hors d'oeuvre or stuffed into the pocket of pita bread along with lettuce and tahini or hummus. Middle Eastern in origin.

**FARFEL:** Noodle dough that has been grated or chopped into fine pieces. Farfel is used as a garnish for soup or meat dishes. When made with matzo, it is called matzo farfel.

**FLANKEN:** Flanken steak, a versatile kosher cut of beef.

**FLEISHIG:** Prepared with meat or meat products.

**GEFILTE FISH:** Gefilte is German for "stuffed." This refers to a mixture of ground fish, matzo meal, eggs, and vegetables shaped into balls and poached in a broth.

**GRIBENES:** Chicken cracklings, made from the skin, cut up and fried in rendered chicken fat (schmaltz) until crisp, then drained and sprinkled with salt.

**HAMANTASCHEN:** Triangular pastries, shaped to resemble the three-cornered hat of the villain Haman in the Purim story. They are filled with poppy seeds, fruit preserves, prunes, or other mixtures.

**HAROSETH:** A mixture of chopped fruits, nuts, and spices moistened with wine. Eaten during the Seder meal as part of the celebration of Passover.

**HELZEL:** Stuffed chicken neck. The skin of the chicken neck is filled with a vegetable-and-bread mixture, then baked.

**HOLISHKES:** Sweet and sour cabbage leaves stuffed with meat and rice.

**HUMMUS:** A Middle Eastern dip made from chick-peas and sesame seed paste.

**KARPAS:** Any nonbitter root vegetable—such as sweet onions or potatoes—served at the Passover Seder, sliced and dipped in salt water.

**KASHA:** Buckwheat groats, a grain served as an accompaniment for meat; also served in soups, salads, or as a breakfast cereal.

**KISHKE:** See Derma.

**KNAIDLACH:** Or matzo balls—matzo meal dumplings served in chicken soup or potted meat dishes.

**KNISHES:** Stuffed dumplings filled with potatoes, meat, cheese, or rice, then fried, boiled, or baked.

**KREPLACH:** Pockets of a pastalike dough, stuffed with meat or cheese, and then boiled in broth or fried. Similar to ravioli.

**KUGEL:** Potatoes or noodles combined with an egg mixture and baked in the oven like a pudding. Served as an accompaniment to an entrée or—when sweetened with raisins, sugar, and apples—as dessert.

**LATKES:** Small pancakes of potatoes, noodles, vegetables, or fruits. During Hanukkah, potato latkes are a traditional food, fried in oil.

**LEKACH:** Dark honey cake. Traditionally served during Rosh Hashanah or Yom Kippur.

**LEKVAR:** A prune preserve used for filling hamantaschen or other pastries.

**LOCKSHEN:** Egg noodles, traditionally served in soup or made into kugel.

**LOX:** Smoked salmon. A favorite with bagels and cream cheese or sautéed in hot dishes, such as omelets. Sometimes comes packed in oil.

**MAMALIGA:** Cornmeal cooked into a cereal or porridge, served with hoop cheese, sour cream, and sugar. Rumanian in origin.

**MANDELBROT:** Twice-baked crisp almond cookies. German in origin.

**MANDLEN:** A baked dough mixture cut into tiny squares and served in soup.

**MATZO:** Unleavened bread traditionally served during the eight days of Passover.

**MATZO BREI:** Matzo omelet.

**MATZO CAKE MEAL:** Matzo, ground extra-fine, for cakes and stuffings.

**MATZO MEAL:** Finely ground matzo, used as a substitute for flour during Passover.

**MILCHIG:** Made of milk or dairy products.

**MOHN:** A poppy seed mixture used for filling hamantaschen and other pastries.

**PAREVE:** "Neutral" food that contains no meat or dairy products; may be eaten with milchig or fleishig meals.

**PIROGEN:** Also called piroshki. Russian-style baked dumplings filled with meat, kasha, or liver mixture.

**PITA BREAD:** Middle Eastern flat round pocket bread.

**SCHAV:** Sorrel, used in cold soup or borscht, Russian in origin. Traditionally served in Israel during Shavuoth.

**SCHMALTZ:** Rendered chicken fat. Sometimes used instead of butter, margarine, or oil.

**STREUSEL:** Sweet crumb topping for coffee cakes and breads.

**STRUDEL:** A pastry made of very thin sheets of dough with various fillings, sweet or savory.

**SUFGANIYOT:** Deep-fried doughnuts, served during Hanukkah.

**TAHINI:** Sesame seed paste.

**TEIGLACH:** Dough confections, boiled in honey.

**TZIMMES:** A mixture of sweet potatoes, prunes, carrots, and assorted dried fruits, often sweetened and sometimes cooked with meat. German in origin.

**VARNISHKES:** Noodle dough rolled and shaped into bows, traditionally served with kasha.

# INDEX